T0350301

Supreme Court of India

Supreme Court of India

The Beginnings

George H. Gadbois, Jr

Edited and introduced by
Vikram Raghavan and Vasujith Ram

OXFORD

UNIVERSITY PRESS

OXFORD
UNIVERSITY PRESS

Oxford University Press is a department of the University of Oxford.
It furthers the University's objective of excellence in research, scholarship,
and education by publishing worldwide. Oxford is a registered trademark of
Oxford University Press in the UK and in certain other countries.

Published in India by
Oxford University Press
2/11 Ground Floor, Ansari Road, Daryaganj, New Delhi 110 002, India

© Oxford University Press 2017
Introduction © Vikram Raghavan and Vasujith Ram

First Edition published in 2017

ISBN-13: 978-0-19-947216-1
ISBN-10: 0-19-947216-5

Disclaimer: The introduction reflects the editors' personal views. It does not
represent the author's views or those of any institution or employer to
which the editors may be professionally associated.

Typeset in ITC Giovanni Std 9.5/13
by Tranistics Data Technologies, Kolkata 700091
Printed in India by Replika Press Pvt. Ltd

Contents

Author's Preface

In undertaking this study of the paramount judiciary in India, an effort has been made to become familiar with virtually all the primary and secondary source material available on the subject, in order that a very comprehensive book might be written. Finding that much more material was available than could possibly be utilized in a single study, and discovering that much of the complexity and enigma of India is reflected in judicial decisions, the scope of this book had to be limited. The research reported in the opening two chapters on the Federal Court is probably sufficient to enable one to gain a general understanding of the limited role it played during its brief period of existence, for a substantial number of the relatively few decisions of the Federal Court are discussed. The Supreme Court, however, which replaced the Federal Court in 1950, and which is endowed with an extremely comprehensive jurisdiction, has handed down thousands of decisions over the past fifteen years bearing upon a bewildering variety of subjects. Of necessity, therefore, my treatment of the Supreme Court is limited in scope. Broadly speaking, the four chapters devoted to the Supreme Court seek to explore the role of the Supreme Court in the Indian political system. Considerable attention is devoted to the nature of the review powers exercised by the Supreme Court, to the expectations of the constitution-makers regarding the role of the Supreme Court, and to those decisions of the Supreme Court which have brought it into conflict with the Government.

I wish to express my deep gratitude to all those individuals and institutions who have been of assistance to me in the preparation of this book. My intellectual debts to Professors Ralph Braibanti and Richard Wheeler are especially great, for they aroused my interest in South Asia. In India I was assisted by, among others, former Chief Justice of India Bhuvaneshwar Prasad Sinha, and Dr. A. T. Markose, former Research Director of the Indian Law Institute. Mr. G. V. Mirchandani, Chief Librarian of the Library of Parliament, and Mr. Amreek Singh, Chief Librarian of the Supreme Court Library took a personal interest in my research, and were always helpful. The field research reported in the pages which follow was made possible through grants from the American Institute of Indian Studies, USA and the Duke University Commonwealth-Studies Center, USA. This financial support is gratefully acknowledged.

George H. Gadbois, Jr
April 1965

Introduction

On a mid-September morning in 1962, a scooter rickshaw drove up New Delhi's Hardinge Avenue. Lined with diplomatic residences, the road had been recently renamed Tilak Marg. At the intersection with Bhagwan Das Road, the three-wheeler turned right and halted to let out its passenger. A young, blond-haired American with tortoise-shell glasses emerged from the vehicle. In front of him was a majestic sandstone-dressed building with a colonnaded central verandah. Large pillars on the verandah supported a roof with protruding eaves. Above the roof rose an imposing dome with two companion canopies. The building's arms emerged on either side of the courtyard to symbolize the scales of justice.

The structure did not figure in the British architect Edwin Lutyens's plans for the capital city. But Lutyens and his associate, Herbert Baker, clearly influenced Ganesh Deolalikar under whose supervision the edifice was erected in the late 1950s. It had been only four years since President Rajendra Prasad had inaugurated the building to house the Supreme Court of India. The Court had, as Prasad put it, finally acquired a "habitat of its own."

On the pavement facing the building, the young American stood for a moment to take in the sight. And then he walked inside. A graduate student at Duke University, George H. Gadbois, Jr had been studying India for a few years. He had travelled to Delhi to do research for his doctoral dissertation in political science. After spending a year in the capital, Gadbois returned to the United States where he continued his work. He completed and submitted his dissertation in April 1965. Fifty-two years later, that dissertation is being edited and republished as this book.

I

Growing up in a hardscrabble Boston suburb, Gadbois worked his way through high school by delivering newspapers, shovelling snow, and caddying on golf courses. At seventeen, he enlisted in the United States Army. He was promptly sent to Taiwan from where his unit monitored Chinese aircraft movements on the mainland. After three years in the army, Gadbois wanted to become an officer. But he lacked a college degree. Determined to get one, he returned home in 1956 to enrol at Marietta College, a small liberal arts school in Ohio.

At Marietta, Gadbois took several classes with Robert Jones, a Harvard-trained agricultural historian. Jones had wide-ranging interests including European and African studies, and he left a formative impression on the young undergraduate. In college, Gadbois remained an active member of the army reserves. Gradually, however, his interest in a military career declined. He aspired to be a lawyer, but he lacked the funds to pursue that ambition. After considering careers in the Navy and the Central Intelligence Agency (CIA), he decided to try his hand at teaching.

Gadbois obtained a fellowship to attend Duke University and moved to Durham, North Carolina in 1959. His first preference was to focus on China because he had really enjoyed his time in Taiwan. But Duke had no subject expert who could guide him. And convinced that he was not very good at languages, Gadbois doubted whether he would ever become fluent in Mandarin. Thus, abandoning his initial attempt to study China, Gadbois turned instead to India.

In the early 1960s, Duke had no dedicated South Asia department although it had at least one Pakistan specialist on its faculty. There were, in addition, a few Indian scholars, notably A.K. Ramanujan, the poet and writer whom Gadbois befriended. Gadbois also signed up for Hindi lessons and read voraciously about subcontinental history, law, and politics. He made full use of the university's rapidly growing collection of books and journals from India.[1]

Under the terms of his fellowship, Gadbois was required to broadly focus on civil rights. So he chose to study India's Supreme Court. For his master's thesis, he concentrated on the Court's first decade following its opening in January 1950. Gadbois turned in his paper in November 1961.[2] Written in easy

---

[1] Like some other American universities, Duke was a beneficiary of Public Law 480. That law authorized the United States government to sell wheat to India on rupee terms. Under the Library of Congress's oversight, these rupees were used to acquire Indian books and journals for libraries across America. Maureen L. P. Patterson, "The South Asian P. L. 480 Library Program, 1962–1968," *The Journal of Asian Studies*, 28 (1969, 4), pp. 743–754.

[2] George H. Gadbois, Jr, *Fundamental Rights and Constitutional Remedies in the Indian Supreme Court* (M.A. thesis, Duke University, 1961).

and inviting prose, the master's thesis critically examined the Court's early record in fundamental rights cases.

Gadbois recalled that a bill of rights had been a core demand of India's national movement for many decades. Sentenced to lengthy prison terms under British rule, the movement's leaders knew first hand why rights mattered. After India attained independence, many of these leaders assumed high constitutional positions and adopted a Constitution that enshrined several fundamental rights. And yet, barely a decade later, their views had dramatically evolved. Many in Nehru's government, Gadbois lamented, believed that citizens who asserted their rights in court were impeding India's social and economic progress. And judges, who sought to uphold these rights, were being criticized vehemently.[3]

Dismayed by this criticism, Gadbois emphasized the judiciary's constitutionally ordained role in enforcing fundamental rights. But he also cautioned that one could not rely only on the courts for this purpose. Public opinion had to be rapidly mobilized to ensure the long-term survival of civil liberties in India. In our estimation, this yet-to-be-published monograph is among the best scholarly assessments of the Court's first years. And although it was largely written on Duke's campus, it offers rich and mature insights about a country that the young man had yet to visit.

II

After obtaining his master's degree, Gadbois stayed on at Duke for a PhD. He wanted to further study India's legal system and courts—a subject that had been largely neglected by Western scholars. Gadbois initially worked with Richard Wheeler who was teaching temporarily at Duke.[4] Ralph Braibanti, a professor of South Asian politics and administration, later became his principal faculty advisor and dissertation supervisor.

Again, the university's large India collection came in handy when Gadbois began his research. But he also needed to access other material for his ambitious dissertation topic: the history of the Supreme Court. Securing funding from

---

[3] See Granville Austin, *Working a Democratic Constitution* (Oxford University Press, 2000), p. 37.

[4] Wheeler's own dissertation was on the political evolution of Pakistan's constitution. Its detailed chapter on the Federal Court and the Pakistan Supreme Court may have influenced Gadbois's search for a suitable dissertation topic. See Richard S. Wheeler, *Government and Constitution-Making in Pakistan* (PhD dissertation, University of California, Berkeley, 1957).

the American Institute of Indian Studies, Gadbois landed in Bombay with his young family in early September 1962. Traveling to Delhi, they rented a modest home in Defence Colony from where Gadbois set out every morning by scooter rickshaw for Tilak Marg.

Unlike most other visitors to the Court, Gadbois was not there to watch its proceedings or meet lawyers. He worked largely in the quiet and well-stocked judges' library. He was formally accredited to the Indian Law Institute, which had been founded only a few years before.[5] The Institute's headquarters were still under construction, and it was temporarily housed within the Court's premises. Its faculty and researchers including Gadbois were able to use some Court facilities, notably the Judges Library.

The Institute's director was A. T. Markose, a jovial scholar who was adored by his students.[6] Markose helped Gadbois in so many ways that he earned the American's lifelong admiration and affection. One afternoon at Markose's urgings, Gadbois called on a senior judge in chambers. The judge was closely involved with the Institute's affairs, and Markose believed that Gadbois would profit from meeting him. To the young scholar's dismay, however, the judge showed very little interest in his research. Disheartened, Gadbois sought no more meetings with that judge or anyone else, and he remained largely library bound. This singular focus allowed Gadbois to become extraordinarily productive. Pleased with his early work, Markose commissioned Gadbois to write two articles for the Institute's journal. These articles later became the first and second chapters of the dissertation, and consequently, this book.[7]

Gadbois's research interests intersected with those of Granville Austin, an American studying modern Indian history at Oxford. Austin's dissertation focused on the making of India's constitution and included a detailed discussion on the judiciary. But neither man seemed aware of the other's work. Austin preceded Gadbois in Delhi by two years and he returned again shortly after Gadbois left the capital in 1963.

Austin and Gadbois's research methods also varied. As a historian, Austin specialized in uncovering private papers and unpublished documents. He

[5] See Rajeev Dhavan, "Legal Research in India: The Role of the Indian Law Institute," *Journal of the Indian Law Institute*, 27 (1985, 2), pp. 223–251.

[6] N.R. Madhava Menon, *Turning Point: The Story of a Law Teacher* (Universal, 2009), p. 21.

[7] "The Evolution of the Federal Court of India: An Historical Footnote," *Journal of the Indian Law Institute*, 5 (1963), pp. 19–45, and "The Federal Court of India: 1937–1950," *Journal of the Indian Law Institute*, 6 (1964), pp. 253–283. The first article was reprinted by the University of North Carolina Press as a separate monograph.

also interviewed many persons who were involved with the Constituent Assembly, which debated and adopted the Constitution. Gadbois, on the other hand, buried himself in thick law reports, parliamentary debates, and scholarly journals that he found in the Supreme Court's library. In Delhi, he appears to have only interviewed B. P. Sinha, who was then Chief Justice of India.

On his way back from India in August 1963, Gadbois stopped off in Honolulu. Visiting the University of Hawaii's campus, he was promptly hired to teach political science for a year. Gadbois later found an administrative job at the university's East-West Center. He worked at the Center's Institute for Advanced Projects under Edward Weidner, its vice chancellor. Inspired by John F. Kennedy's idealism, Gadbois also grew involved with the local U.S. Peace Corps. And it was in Honolulu that Gadbois completed and turned in his dissertation, which he titled *The Paramount Judiciary in India: 1937–1964*.

III

In 1966, Weidner was recruited by the University of Kentucky and arranged for Gadbois to accompany him to Lexington. With some reluctance, Gadbois left Hawaii and joined Kentucky's political science department as an assistant professor. Gadbois remained active with the Peace Corps even after he moved to Lexington. In a few months, he became the director of its local unit. The unit's volunteers helped small farmers in Karnataka's drought-prone Raichur district improve their crop yields. But advancing scientific agriculture was not among Gadbois's passions and he eventually returned to full-time teaching.

Gadbois continued to do research on the Indian judiciary after he moved to Kentucky. He focussed his attention on the Court's first thirty-six judges who were appointed between 1950 and 1967. As part of his study, he tracked down information on each judge's background: his religion, caste or community, educational and professional qualifications, and pre-appointment legal career. In 1969, Gadbois published his findings in a piece he called 'Indian Supreme Court Judges: A Portrait'.[8] In it, he declared that an archetypal Supreme Court justice was an upper caste, well-educated Hindu man in his late fifties with surprisingly little or no involvement in the nationalist movement.

Continuing his research, Gadbois noticed that chief justices and senior judges of certain high courts had been declining promotions to the Supreme

---

[8] "Indian Supreme Court Judges: A Portrait," *Law and Society Review*, 3 (November 1968–February 1969), pp. 317–336. Gadbois's analysis may have been inspired by John Schmidhauser's study on American judges. "The Justices of the Supreme Court: A Collective Portrait," *Midwest Journal of Political Science*, 3 (February 1959, 1), pp. 1–57.

Court.[9] Chief Justice M. C. Chagla of the Bombay High Court, for instance, turned down an offer to move to Delhi.[10] His counterpart at the Madras High Court, P. V. Rajammanar, also refused to accept an elevation. It took several years before any chief justice from either of those chartered high courts came to the Supreme Court.[11] These relatively unnoticed facts made Gadbois even more determined to investigate how Indian judges are selected.

Meanwhile, tensions were growing between the judiciary and the legislature over the government's authority to acquire property under eminent domain. The Court repeatedly held that the government must pay fair compensation when taking private property. Responding to adverse judgments, Parliament passed successive constitutional amendments to overturn them. The amendments expressly sought to bar judges from reviewing whether the government had paid fair compensation in property acquisitions.

The stage was set for *Golak Nath's Case*[12] in which the Supreme Court tried to halt further constitutional amendments. In a narrow verdict, Chief Justice Subba Rao joined five colleagues in declaring that Parliament could no longer amend any fundamental rights under the Constitution. Five other justices disagreed and filed dissenting opinions. The *Golak Nath* judgments led to considerable debate and academic criticism. The government's reaction was swift and furious. It immediately began to explore how the decision could be overturned.

Watching these developments unfold, Gadbois grew fascinated by the sharp differences among the justices on the *Golak Nath* bench. Why did six judges vote one way, he wondered, while five others took an entirely different approach? Moreover, *Golak Nath* wasn't the only case in which the Court was bitterly divided. In major cases throughout the 1960s, judges were openly disagreeing with one another. Gadbois believed that he could explain these developments using basic data analysis. To that end, he read and coded every reported Supreme Court decision for multiple variables: the

[9] George H. Gadbois, Jr, "Selection, Background Characteristics, and Voting Behavior of Indian Supreme Court Judges, 1950–1959," in Glendon Schubert and David J. Danelski (eds), *Comparative Judicial Behavior: Cross-Cultural Studies of Political Decision-Making in the East and West* (Oxford University Press, 1969).

[10] Abhinav Chandrachud, "My Dear Chagla," *Frontline* (February 7, 2014).

[11] Continuing where Gadbois left off, Abhinav Chandrachud reveals that at least ten chief justices (or senior puisne judges) declined Supreme Court promotions. "The Need to Have a Uniform Retirement Age for Judges," *Economic and Political Weekly*, XLVII (November 2012, 46), pp. 24–27.

[12] *I.C. Golaknath v. State of Punjab*, AIR 1967 SC 1643.

underlying subject matter, the parties involved, the judges on the bench, and the winners and losers.

In early 1970, Gadbois published some of his research in a short, but remarkably insightful, article in the *Economic and Political Weekly* ("EPW").[13] It focused primarily on cases involving civil-liberties or government regulations on private economic activities. A judge's voting pattern in these cases, Gadbois reasoned, could reveal his underlying ideological preferences. He used a simple two-row, two-column table to illustrate his point. Each box or quadrant in the table bore one of four captions: classical liberal; classical conservative; modern liberal; and modern conservative. Based on their ratings in individual cases, Gadbois assigned each judge to one or another quadrant that best reflected his ideological leanings.

No one had attempted anything like this before in India. Gadbois's research considerably intrigued Justice Hidayatullah and a few of his colleagues.[14] It was also mischievously used in an unsuccessful campaign to impeach Justice J.C. Shah. Yet, to Gadbois's disappointment, the piece was largely ignored by the Indian bar and legal scholars. Undaunted, Gadbois set himself up to do even more research on the judiciary.

Alongside his EPW article, Gadbois also published an ambitious empirical study on the Court.[15] The study surveyed litigation at the Court by focussing on some basic questions. Which of the Court's jurisdictional bases contributed the most number of cases to its docket? Where was the Court's work primarily coming from? How was the Court handling appeals? Who were its principal litigants? What subjects most occupied the judges' time? And how did individuals fare in litigation against the state?

Unsurprisingly, Gadbois found that the government was the largest litigant before the Court. He was surprised, however, to discover that it was losing at least forty percent of its cases. Businessmen were also responsible for bringing a large number of appeals to the Court for final resolution. Property and monetary disputes dominated the judges' workload. Gadbois also reported that a disproportionately large number of appeals came from the Punjab and Haryana High Court.[16]

---

[13] "Indian Judicial Behaviour," *Economic and Political Weekly*, V (January 1970, 3, 4 & 5), pp. 149–166.

[14] See M. Hidayatullah, *My Own Boswell* (Arnold-Heinemann, 1980), p. 198.

[15] "The Supreme Court of India: A Preliminary Report of an Empirical Study," *Journal of Constitutional and Parliamentary Studies*, 4 (January–March 1970, 33–54), p. 54.

[16] Several decades after Gadbois, Nicholas Robinson analyzed the geographic distribution of the Court's docket. He, too, found that a disproportionate number of appeals

Golak Nath was overruled in 1973 in *Kesavananda Bharati's Case*.[17] Again, the Court was closely divided. Seven judges declared that Parliament could not amend the Constitution's basic features. Six judges declined to accept any such limitation. Fascinated by the verdict, Gadbois wanted to return to Delhi to better understand what was happening at the Court. From his perch at Lexington, the professor had also been closely following political developments in the subcontinent. Incensed by the news from East Pakistan, he joined the Bangladesh movement in the United States and desperately campaigned to get the Nixon administration to change its South Asia policies. He caused a major furore when he angrily confronted the Pakistan ambassador about reported atrocities.[18]

Despite his activism, Gadbois was denied a visa in 1973 to spend a sabbatical year in India. Although he was hurt and frustrated by this action, he later reasoned that the Indian government suspected him to be a CIA agent as India-U.S. relations deteriorated in the early 1970s. Unable to travel to Delhi, Gadbois spent 1974 in Papua New Guinea researching that country's legislature.

Chief Justice Sikri retired immediately after *Kesavananda* was decided. Setting aside a long-held convention, the government made A. N. Ray his successor. In so doing, it superseded three justices who were Ray's seniors on the bench. Amidst the outrage over this action, Gadbois sought to empirically uncover the government's real motivation in selecting Ray.[19] Ray, Gadbois argued, had been a reliable vote for the government in major cases. As chief justice, Ray could play an outsized role in corralling his colleagues to rule more consistently in favour of the regime. He could certainly help advance the ruling Congress party's agenda for radical constitutional changes and sweeping economic and social reforms.[20]

By the late 1970s, Gadbois noticed a marked decline in non-unanimous judgments from the Court.[21] The number of cases decided by constitution

---

came from high courts, like Punjab and Haryana, which are close to Delhi. "A Quantitative Analysis of the Indian Supreme Court's Workload," *Journal of Empirical Legal Studies*, 10 (2013), pp. 570–601.

[17] *Kesavananda Bharati* v. *State of Kerala*, AIR 1973 SC 1461.

[18] "History of the Political Science Department at the University of Kentucky" (undated; University of Kentucky, Political Science Department website).

[19] "Supreme Court Decision Making," *Banaras Law Journal*, 10 (1984), pp. 1–49.

[20] "Judicial Appointments in India: The Perils of Non-Contextual Analysis," *Asian Thought and Society*, VII (July 1982, 20), pp. 124–143.

[21] "The Decline of Dissent on the Supreme Court: 1950–1981," in Ram Avtar Sharma (ed.), *Justice and Social Order in India* (Intellectual Publishing House, 1984), pp. 235–259.

benches of the Court with five or more justices fell considerably. Most of the Court's workload was being handled by division benches with only three or two judges. When assigned to smaller benches, Gadbois observed judges were less inclined to dissent from one another.

The consequent reduction in non-unanimous judgments made it difficult for Gadbois to continue empirically analysing the Court's overall trends. But he continued to produce high-quality research papers on topics such as the "participation" of Supreme Court judges.[22] Some of these papers, which were published in obscure and difficult-to-locate journals, continue to offer us important lessons about the judicial process in India.

IV

In 1983, Gadbois returned to Delhi for more research. By this time, he was interested in more than just pure empirical work. He was increasingly drawn to the craft of judicial biography. He wanted to learn more about the lives of individual justices and how they got to the bench. In so doing, Gadbois emulated his mentor, Braibanti, who late in his career, wrote a biography of Pakistan's Chief Justice Alvin Robert Cornelius.[23] Relying on a variety of sources, Gadbois located and contacted the Court's serving or retired judges. He sought to interview them about their life and work.

Impressed by Gadbois's previous scholarship, most judges agreed to meet him. Some had to be coaxed and cajoled to do so. But no one turned him down including the reclusive A. N. Ray whom Gadbois met in Kolkata. Gadbois typically asked for a forty-five-minute meeting. Most judges readily gave him more time. Many would invite him back for lunch or dinner. And he corresponded extensively with quite a few justices for several years thereafter.

Gadbois's most memorable session was with Vivian Bose in 1983. The nonagenarian judge's memory was fading. But he still managed to provide valuable information about the Court. He continued to correspond with the professor through self-typed letters whose lines went up and down like musical notes. Gadbois also spent many hours with Sikri. The two men bonded at the Delhi Golf Club, where they played golf and continued talking at the bar.

---

[22] "The 'Contribution to Law' Literature: Dealing with Inequalities of Tenure, Participation, and Opinion Writing of Supreme Court Judges," *Banaras Law Journal*, 16 (1980), pp. 111–121 and "Participation in Supreme Court Decision-Making: From Kania to Vaidialingam, 1950–1967," *Journal of the Indian Law Institute*, 24 (1981), pp. 1–23.

[23] *Chief Justice Cornelius of Pakistan: An Analysis of Letters and Speeches* (Oxford University Press, 1999).

Gadbois grew particularly close to V. R. Krishna Iyer. On one occasion, the judge asked the professor to meet him at the crack of dawn at Kerala House, a state guesthouse in New Delhi. Their conversation continued unabated even as Krishna Iyer bathed, ate breakfast, and got ready for the day. Gadbois also travelled across India to meet retired judges. He spent several days in Bombay, Calcutta, Madras, and Hyderabad interviewing former justices and visited K. S. Hegde in his village Nitte in Karnataka. By 1989, Gadbois had interviewed every sitting or retired judge who was still living. And for judges who had passed away, he contacted their spouses, children, or known confidants to learn more.

After he completed his research, Gadbois returned to Lexington to begin writing-up a manuscript. But he soon fell ill and had to retire prematurely from the university in 1992. Gadbois eventually recovered, but he lost his appetite for full-time scholarship. His interview notes and files were put away in the garage. He turned to playing golf and lecturing on cruise ships about American politics and history.[24] In 2004, Gadbois received an invitation to speak at a conference on judicial appointments at the London School of Economics. This invitation was just the spark he needed to revive his dormant book project. He quickly retrieved his files from the garage and resumed work as a single-finger typist.

Eight years and several drafts later, Oxford University Press published Gadbois's *Judges of the Supreme Court of India*.[25] The book contains biographical essays on the Court's first ninety-three judges. It discusses each justice's background, bar and bench career, life in retirement, and honours, distinctions, and publications. For most judges, Gadbois offered carefully researched or reasoned inferences about how they came to be nominated for appointments. Some reviewers were disappointed that the book ignored judges' voting patterns and ideological preferences. But Gadbois had been there and done that. He wanted to focus exclusively on his subjects' neglected lives.

The book sold briskly, and Gadbois received many approving letters and e-mails from readers. Invigorated by this long-overdue recognition, Gadbois began to rework several unpublished papers and incomplete drafts. He even prepared to return to India after an absence of nearly two decades. But his plans were rudely interrupted when he was diagnosed with a terminal illness in 2015. Gadbois calmly accepted his grim prognosis. He began

---

[24] Gadbois continued to do sporadic academic work after he retired from teaching. See "Mandal and Other Backward Classes: Affirmative Action in India in the 1990s," *Journal of Law and Social Challenges*, 1 (1997), pp. 71–84.

[25] See *Judges of the Supreme Court of India: 1950–1989* (Oxford University Press, 2012).

settling his affairs and giving away his treasured collection of Indian books and manuscripts.

Two years ago, while visiting Gadbois in Lexington one of us noticed two bound black volumes on his desk. They were his master's thesis and doctoral dissertation. Gadbois leafed through them with nostalgic pride. He had left them unpublished as he did not believe they had much scholarly worth. Upon reading both monographs, we felt otherwise. It took a great deal of effort to convince the professor that at least one of them, his dissertation, ought to finally become a book. He ultimately relented after three influential scholars certified that the dissertation remained fit for publication five decades after it had been written.

Before signing the book contract, Gadbois asked us to join him in editing the manuscript. His deteriorating health made it impossible for him to substantially revise the text in any manner. But he did make one important change. Discarding the dissertation's stilted title, he rechristened it: *Supreme Court of India: The Beginnings*.

V

Beginnings argues that it was Hari Singh Gour who first mooted the idea of a supreme court for India. A distinguished lawyer, poet, and parliamentarian, Gour was among the first generation of Indians elected to the central legislative assembly in 1920. Shortly after the legislature convened in 1921, Gour introduced a resolution proposing the creation of a "Court of Ultimate Appeal" for India. At the time, final appeals from Indian courts were decided by the Judicial Committee of the Privy Council in London. Gour's motivations for wanting an ultimate appellate court in India remain unclear. But it was a cause that he seems to have consistently championed for the rest of his life.[26]

Gour's proposal evoked mixed reactions from the central assembly's Indian stalwarts. Mohammed Ali Jinnah enthusiastically embraced the proposal while Motilal Nehru and Tej Bahadur Sapru opposed it. All three were distinguished lawyers who had practiced extensively before British Indian courts and had also dealt with the Privy Council. Eventually, Sapru, and later, the elder Nehru accepted Gour's proposal.

As Gadbois tells us, the initial resistance to Gour's proposal may have been due to the fact that, in the 1920s, the nationalist movement focused primarily on

---

[26] Hari Singh Gour, *The Future Constitution of India* (Nagpur University, 1930), p. 62, (describing the supreme court as a grand pillar on which a future Indian constitution would rest).

securing institutional and political reforms.[27] Changes to the judiciary were not a pressing concern for the movement's leaders. Many were convinced that final appeals from courts in India were best handled by a distant tribunal that was not susceptible to local politics, influence, and prejudices. Gadbois also suggests that the proposal was not enthusiastically welcomed because the Privy Council commanded widespread respect among Indian lawyers.[28]

The Privy Council's stellar reputation was tarnished in 1931 when it summarily dismissed Bhagat Singh's appeal against his death sentence.[29] The revolutionary was hanged within a few weeks of the Judicial Committee's decision. Curiously, in *Beginnings*, Gadbois does not discuss the impact of Bhagat Singh's hanging on the ongoing debate for an appellate court in India. He focuses, instead, on the Round Table Conferences, which took place in London in the early 1930s.

At the Round Table Conferences, Indian princely states agreed to form a federation with the existing provinces of British India. To provide a constitutional framework for the federation, the British Parliament enacted the Government of India Act 1935 (the "1935 Act"). Among other things, the 1935 Act established a Federal Court in Delhi to resolve constitutional controversies relating to the act itself or the federation to be created under it. The act also provided that the Federal Court could, if authorized by law, accept civil appeals from provincial high courts. The Federal Court did not fully satisfy Gour's demand for an "ultimate" appellate tribunal. Even so, Gour's desire for a national court within the subcontinent had been partially fulfilled.

As Gadbois points out in chapter 2, the Federal Court convened for the first time in early December 1937. As the Court lacked its own building, its inaugural sitting was held in the "beautiful and dignified" Chamber of Princes, a semicircular assembly room within what is now Parliament House. Donning grand robes, Chief Justice Maurice Gwyer attended the event with his two associate

---

[27] Gour believed that his proposal received only tepid support because the legal profession was very conservative and Gandhian beliefs about litigation's evils were rampant. See Rohit De, "A Peripatetic World Court: Cosmopolitan Courts, Nationalist Judges and the Indian Appeal to the Privy Council," *Law and History Review*, 32 (2014, 4), pp. 821–851, 845n85.

[28] Widespread respect for the colonial judiciary was no accident. Arudra Burra argues that the judiciary valued its independence and did not always support the colonial executive's imperial interests. "What Is 'Colonial' About Colonial Laws?," *American University International Law Review*, 31 (2), pp. 137–169.

[29] See A.G. Noorani, "Jinnah's Case for a Supreme Court," *Frontline*, 26 (October 10–23, 2009), p. 21.

judges and the chief justices of several provincial high courts.[30] Welcoming the judges, Advocate General Brojendra Mitter prophesied that the Federal Court would inherit the "precious heritage" of the high courts' independence and integrity.

Gwyer responded with a soaring speech that set lofty ambitions for his court. Among other things, he compared it to the supreme courts of Canada and the United States and the High Court of Australia. To the surprise of some who were present, Gwyer promised that the court would protect individuals from government tyranny.[31] He clearly foresaw a more expansive role for his court beyond its responsibility to interpret the 1935 Act.

Gadbois points out that, until independence, the Federal Court's Chief Justice was always an Englishman. His companion judges were a Hindu and a Muslim respectively. Similar communal conventions in judicial appointments were followed at some provincial high courts. For instance, during a part of its colonial history, two of the seven seats on the Bombay High Court were informally reserved for a Hindu and a non-Hindu Indian judge.[32] Consequently, it is unsurprising that, even today, caste and communal diversity are important considerations in selecting judges.[33]

Due to its limited jurisdiction, the Federal Court began with a whimper. It does not appear to have handed down any reported judgments during its first year. It gradually added cases to its docket but Gwyer and his colleagues still dealt with far fewer cases than their counterparts in provincial high courts. And in its early years, the Federal Court largely steered clear of any legal disputes with political dimensions. This changed, however, rather suddenly in April 1942, when the court dramatically overturned wartime detentions of thousands of political activists.

[30] Gwyer had been closely involved in drafting the 1935 Act. He is also regarded as one of the most influential vice chancellors of Delhi University.

[31] See "Proceedings at the Inaugural Sitting of the Federal Court," 1 F.C.R. 1 (1939).

[32] Abhinav Chandrachud, *An Independent, Colonial Judiciary: A History of the Bombay High Court during the British Raj, 1862–1947* (Oxford University Press, 2015), p. 95.

[33] Abhinav Chandrachud, *The Informal Constitution: Unwritten Criteria in Selecting Judges for the Supreme Court of India* (Oxford University Press, 2014), p. 254ff. Abhinav Chandrachud suggests that there simply was not a large enough pool of interested Federal Court nominees. Anticipating this problem, the 1935 Act had set mandatory retirement for Federal Court judges at sixty-five. They would be eligible to serve for at least five years longer than high court judges who retired at sixty. Even so, few provincial chief justices seemed interested in going to Delhi. As discussed earlier, this trend that would continue well into the Supreme Court's second decade.

Gadbois underscores the fact that a British chief justice joined his Indian colleagues in handing down this landmark ruling and similar judgments that followed it. These unprecedented decisions, he argues, demonstrated the Federal Court's impartiality and independence from the colonial executive. They inspired a high degree of public confidence in the fledgling institution and put the Viceroy's administration on notice that someone was watching.

As Rohit De recently points out, despite repeatedly ruling against the government in detention cases, the Federal Court largely acquiesced in the Viceroy's subsequent executive actions that effectively undermined the impact of its judgments. As a consequence, few, if any, political prisoners actually benefitted from the Federal Court's decisions invalidating their arrests.[34] Niharendu Dutt Mazumdar, who lent his name to the leading judgment on preventive detention, was himself rearrested within minutes after being set free. And the Privy Council eventually overruled most of the Federal Court's key anti-government rulings.[35]

The Privy Council remained the final appellate court for India for several months after independence. Its jurisdiction over Indian appeals only ended a few weeks before the Constitution came into force in January 1950. Gadbois attributes this longevity to the high regard that key members of the Constituent Assembly had for the Privy Council. This extended lifeline came in handy as the Privy Council faced the prospect of a substantial reduction in its docket. As De reveals, by the 1940s, Indian appeals constituted a substantial part of the Judicial Committee's business. The Committee's members desperately sought to preserve their role and influence as Indian independence dawned.[36]

Gadbois argues that the Privy Council helped bolster the Federal Court's early quest for legitimacy. The Judicial Committee's basic appellate jurisdiction was relatively unaffected by the Federal Court's creation in 1937. It continued to accept appeals from two broad categories of appellants. First, the Federal Court could permit parties to appeal a judgment to the Privy Council. Second, the Privy Council could directly accept an appeal from a Federal Court judgment by granting the appellant "special leave." During its tenure, the Federal Court permitted parties to go to the Privy Council in ten cases. In five of these cases, the Privy Council chose not to disturb the Federal Court's judgments. The Privy

---

[34] Rohit De, "The Federal Court and Civil Liberties in Late Colonial India," in Terrence Halliday, Lucien Karpik, and Malcolm Feeley (eds), *Fates of Political Liberalism in the British Post-Colony: The Politics of the Legal Complex* (Cambridge University Press, 2012), pp. 59–90.

[35] Rohit De, "A Peripatetic World Court: Cosmopolitan Courts, Nationalist Judges and the Indian Appeal to the Privy Council," *Law and History Review*, 32 (2014, 4), pp. 821–851, 847.

[36] De, "A Peripatetic World Court", p. 848.

Council granted "special leave" to appellants from the Federal Court in only four cases. It upheld the Federal Court's judgments in three of those cases.[37]

By all accounts, the Federal Court outperformed the low expectations set for it. It pioneered judicial review in the subcontinent by invalidating laws inconsistent with the 1935 Act. This made it easier for its successor, the Supreme Court, to inherit that counter-majoritarian power to set aside laws made by Parliament and the state legislatures. Furthermore, the Federal Court's decisions on key constitutional issues like preventive detention, the executive's ordinance-making power, and delegated legislation, greatly influenced its successor, which also had to grapple with several of the same issues.

In chapter 3, Gadbois examines the Constituent Assembly's role in fashioning an independent judiciary for India. Early on, the Assembly tasked an "ad hoc committee" to make recommendations on what the Constitution should say about the judiciary. This committee was chaired by S. Vardachariar, a Federal Court judge and included Brojendra Mitter and Alladi Krishaswami Ayyar, the eminent Madras lawyer. The ad hoc committee submitted a slew of recommendations, and the Assembly eventually accepted most of them.

In designing the Supreme Court, the Constitution's drafters in the Assembly drew upon the Federal Court's basic framework. But they greatly expanded that framework to give the Supreme Court sweeping constitutional powers and multiple jurisdictional bases under which it could hear cases. The Assembly included so much detail about the Court that no less than twenty-four articles of the Constitution dealt only with that subject. In so doing, the founders disregarded the ad hoc committee's plea that the Assembly only codify the Court's most essential features in the Constitution. Details, the committee had suggested, could be covered by a separate judiciary act to be subsequently enacted by Parliament. Gadbois wonders why the drafters ignored the committee's advice on this point. Austin, contemplating precisely the same question in his own dissertation, argues that the Assembly wanted to thwart any future attempts to subvert the judiciary.[38]

Gadbois tell us that the Assembly swiftly resolved to vest the Constitution's several fundamental rights with an independent institutional guardian. The Supreme Court was chosen to be that guardian. Breaking with British

---

[37] De arrives at a different conclusion. He argues that both the Privy Council and the high courts saw the Federal Court as a potential encroacher on their jurisdiction and privileges. Rohit De, "Constitutional Antecedents," in Sujit Choudhry, Pratap Bhanu Mehta, and Madhav Khosla (eds), *The Oxford Handbook of the Indian Constitution* (Oxford University Press, 2016), pp. 17–37.

[38] Granville Austin, *Indian Constitution: Cornerstone of a Nation* (Oxford University Press, 1966), p. 327 (citing Ambedkar's speech to the Constituent Assembly).

precedent and practice, the Assembly expressly gave the Court the counter-majoritarian power of judicial review. The Assembly also placed the Court on top of a vertically integrated national judiciary. There would be no division of judicial power between the Union and the states as is the case for executive and legislative power under the Constitution. And unlike the United States and other federal jurisdictions, the Assembly resolved that there would be no state courts in India.

The bulk of the Assembly's time, as Gadbois reports, was spent debating judicial appointments. He emphasizes that members were adamant that political considerations should play no role in selecting judges. Anticipating future litigation on this topic, he argues that the chief justice's concurrence for an appointment is not a constitutional requirement even while he acknowledges the importance of consultations.

Also in chapter 3, Gadbois discusses the early practice of judicial appointments. He criticizes the rigid insistence on the seniority principle in selecting chief justices of India.[39] He points out that seniority-based selections invariably lead to shorter terms for incumbent chief justices. This affects their ability to reform the Court's practices or transform its jurisprudence.[40] In later work, however, Gadbois conceded that the seniority principle helps prevent patronage-based appointments.[41]

In chapter 4, Gadbois examines the Court's multiple jurisdictional bases under the Constitution. He methodically explores each base, its anchoring constitutional provision, and the manner in which it has been interpreted in practice. He reveals that, as the Assembly was so consumed by the debate on judicial appointments, it had very little time to discuss what types of cases the Court ought to entertain. Writing when he did, Gadbois may have heard no drumbeats about impending "litigation explosion." Yet, he presciently warns that the Court was accepting too many cases under its "special leave" jurisdiction that it inherited from the Privy Council.

Gadbois's analysis of the Court's advisory jurisdiction is particularly insightful. Analysing the early advisory opinions, Gadbois singles out *Keshav Singh's Case*.[42] The matter arose from the Uttar Pradesh Assembly's threat to

---

[39] Seniority was not the norm for colonial judicial appointments. See Abhinav Chandrachud, "Supreme Court's Seniority Norm: Historical Origins," *Economic and Political Weekly*, XLVII (February 2012, 8), pp. 26–30.

[40] Abhinav Chandrachud's *Informal Constitution* discusses the informal norms associated with judicial appointments.

[41] George H. Gadbois, Jr, "Judicial Appointments in India: The Perils of Non-Contextual Analysis," *Asian Thought and Society*, VII (July 1982, 20), pp. 124–143.

[42] Special Reference No. 1 of 1964, 1965 AIR SC 745.

imprison two Allahabad High Court judges. The judges had granted bail to a local politician whom the state legislature had found to have breached its privileges. To prevent a full-blown constitutional crisis, the President asked the Supreme Court for an advisory opinion on the controversy. Responding to the presidential request, the Court ruled that the Uttar Pradesh legislature's privileges could not trump a citizen's fundamental rights, which the judiciary was sworn to uphold.

Gadbois largely agrees with this outcome. To him, the case reveals the existence of flashpoints in the Constitution, which borrows and blends provisions from very diverse constitutional and legal traditions.[43] In this instance, the Constitution conferred Parliament and the state legislatures with the same privileges as the United Kingdom's House of Commons. The exercise of these privileges can sometimes result in direct conflict with the fundamental rights guaranteed by the Constitution.

In chapter 5, Gadbois takes us through the major constitutional questions that the Court grappled with in the 1950s and early 1960s. This chapter is somewhat of a sequel to his M.A. thesis on the Court's early fundamental rights judgments. Although Gadbois reprises some elements of that thesis, he is a lot more selective in *Beginnings* about the cases he discusses.

Appropriately, Gadbois begins with *A.K. Gopalan v. State of Madras*.[44] Gopalan, a communist leader, had been detained without being charged with a specific crime. He argued that his incarceration violated his personal liberty and freedom of movement. The Court dismissed his case reasoning dubiously that only a free citizen could exercise constitutionally protected freedoms. More importantly, it declared that it could not review whether Gopalan had been unfairly or unjustly detained. Taking somewhat of an originalist perspective, Gadbois reasons that *Gopalan* was correctly decided although he acknowledges that the decision had been roundly criticized by both Indian and foreign commentators.

After discussing *Gopalan*, Gadbois turns to the dominant constitutional issue that he encountered during his research: compensation in property acquisition cases. He carefully recounts the Assembly's debates about the right to property. A key question was whether the government owed owners market-value-based compensation when it acquired their property. Another American scholar,

---

[43] Gadbois returned to *Keshav Singh* in subsequent work. He argued that the controversy primarily arose because the Uttar Pradesh legislators threatened the Allahabad judges' belief in their own independence and impartiality. "Keshav Singh: Contemptuous Judges and Contumacious Legislators," in Theodore L. Becker (ed.), *Political Trials* (Bobbs-Merrill, 1971), pp. 34–48.

[44] AIR 1950 SC 27.

Herbert Merillat had argued that the Assembly was so divided on this question that it decided to leave the matter to the judiciary to resolve through downstream litigation.[45] In *Beginnings*, Gadbois vigorously disagrees with this interpretation of the relevant debates. The Assembly, he argues, did not require the payment of market value as compensation.

Gadbois then takes us through a series of cases in which the Court found that the government had not adequately compensated affected owners. To overcome these adverse decisions, Parliament repeatedly amended the Constitution to restrict the Court's ability to interfere in future property litigation. As he closes chapter 5, Gadbois introduces us to the Seventeenth Amendment. It was, at the time, Parliament's latest attempt to undo the Court's rulings on compensation. And property owners had already begun preparing to challenge that amendment. Their petitions eventually resulted in the landmark *Golak Nath* ruling whose consequences could not be foreseen when Gadbois submitted his dissertation.

Gadbois seems mildly annoyed, perhaps even amused, that Indian legal scholars were already boasting in the early 1960s that their court was the world's most powerful. Yes, he concedes, few other apex courts share their Indian counterpart's extraordinarily wide constitutional jurisdiction. But this jurisdictional breadth does not automatically mean that the Court wields the greatest judicial power on earth. Gadbois argues that the Court's powers were inherently restricted by the Assembly's decision to prescribe a low bar for constitutional amendments and to exclude a "due-process clause" from the Constitution.[46]

Gadbois recounts how Justice Felix Frankfurter, the American judge, warned B. N. Rau, who prepared an early draft of the Constitution with a due-process clause, that the clause had been recklessly used by conservatives on the U.S. Supreme Court to invalidate many progressive socio-economic laws. To ensure that the Indian judiciary did not emulate that example, at Rau's urging, the Assembly substituted the due-process clause for a watered-down provision borrowed from Japan. The resulting provision, Article 21 of the Constitution, enjoins the state from depriving any person of life or personal liberty without observing the "procedure established by law."

Writing in the early 1960s, Gadbois could not have predicted that, disregarding clear legislative history, the Court would adopt "due-process" reasoning to

[45] H.C.L. Merillat, "Compensation for the Taking of Property—A Historical Footnote to Bela Banerjee's Case," *Journal of the Indian Law Institute*, 1 (1959), pp. 384–92. A long-forgotten polymath, Merillat authored many articles and a book about land and the Indian constitution.

[46] The Fifth and Fourteenth Amendments to the United States Constitution declare that no person shall be deprived of "life, liberty, or property, without due process of law."

overturn laws and procedures that it found to be arbitrary or unfair.[47] It was also difficult for Gadbois to foresee the advent of public interest litigation in the early 1980s. Expanding the scope of its writ jurisdiction, the Court issued sweeping orders on subjects as diverse as water pollution, forests, blood banks, and medical college admissions. As a consequence, the Court's standing and public prestige rose dramatically. In subsequent writing, Gadbois readily acknowledged that the Court's influence had sharply increased since he first began studying the institution in the early 1960s. He went on to argue that the Court had acquired considerable political power through its decisions and rulings.[48]

In chapter 6, Gadbois discusses the inherent tension between the Court's power of judicial review and the development goals of a modern welfare state. This tension simmers as the Court completes its first decade during which it frequently invalidates land reform and property ceiling laws. Gadbois posits that the resulting constitutional amendments passed by Parliament to overcome the Court's decisions seriously diminished the institution's ability to meaningfully exercise judicial review. This conclusion leads Gadbois to investigate the philosophical underpinnings for disagreements between the courts and the legislature over property questions. He avers that these disagreements occur because the Constitution admonishes the judiciary to protect the fundamental rights even as it directs the state to carry out radical social and economic policies that inevitably interfere with those rights.

This tension between constitutional rights and welfare goals extends beyond the property context. A good example, according to Gadbois, is *Champakam Dorairajan's Case*.[49] Dorairajan challenged community-specific admission quotas in Madras medical colleges for violating her fundamental right to equality. The state government defended the quotas relying on the Constitution's express directive that the state promote the educational and economic interests of weaker sections.[50] The Court, however, was unpersuaded by this argument. It

---

[47] David G. Barnum, "Article 21 and Policy Making Role of Courts in India: An American Perspective," *Journal of the Indian Law Institute*, 30 (1988, 1), pp. 19–44.

[48] "The Indian Supreme Court as a Political Institution," in Rajeev Dhavan, R. Sudarshan, and Salman Khurshid (eds), *Judges and Judicial Power: Essays in Honour of Justice V.R. Krishna Iyer* (Sweet & Maxwell, 1985), pp. 251–267. Gadbois wrote the first draft of this paper before he read Upendra Baxi's magisterial work *The Indian Supreme Court and Politics* (Eastern Book, 1980). He later revised his paper taking into account Baxi's analysis.

[49] *State of Madras* v. *Champakam Dorairajan*, AIR 1951 SC 226.

[50] Gadbois returned to reservations in his later work. "Affirmative Action in India: The Judiciary and Social Change," *Law & Policy* (July 1986, 8), pp. 329–364 and "Mandal and the Other Backward Classes: Affirmative Action in India in the 1990s," *Journal of Law & Social Challenges* (Fall 1997, 1), pp. 71–84.

held that that directive could not be implemented by overriding the fundamental rights protected by the Constitution. Parliament disagreed with this verdict and passed the First Amendment to overturn it.

Gadbois goes on to explore in chapter 6 how judges reason in constitutional cases. He finds that the Court's early judges largely relied on black-letter and technical approaches to interpret the Constitution. In their quest to maintain "objectivity," they frequently overlooked important social and political dimensions in cases that came before them. This obsession with objectivity went so far that the Court, when *Beginnings* was first written, consistently declined to consult the relevant Assembly debates when interpreting a constitutional provision. To be sure, the Court would later reverse itself and accept the debates as a legitimate interpretative tool. Even so, *Beginnings* reminds us that judicial reasoning in constitutional litigation can swing like a pendulum.

The final chapter is a short and cogent summary of the book's principal arguments. Gadbois wrote this chapter rather hurriedly over a Spring weekend in 1965. He was overwhelmed by a heavy teaching load and substantial administrative responsibilities in Honolulu. But his dissertation supervisor, Braibanti, was breathing down his neck. In his rapidly written conclusion, Gadbois wagers that the Court was shifting towards a more liberal reading of the Constitution under P. B. Gajendragadkar, who had become the Chief Justice of India. A formidable judge, Gajendragadkar, strongly believed that the Constitution must be interpreted consistently with the changing needs of a modern welfare state.[51]

But Gajendragadkar's ascendancy obscured the fact that many of his colleagues were already preparing to battle Parliament over constitutional amendments. This was evident from Justice Hidayatullah's opinion in *Sajjan Singh* in which the judge wondered whether fundamental rights were "play things of a special majority."[52] *Sajjan Singh* was decided in late 1964. Like *Golak Nath*, it came too late for Gadbois to include in his dissertation.

VI

In *Beginnings*, Gadbois argues that an impartial and independent Indian judiciary is, to a large extent, a colonial legacy. Here Gadbois reflects not just his own views, but a widely held opinion at the bar and on the bench. After all, despite its republican foundations in the Constitution, the Supreme Court inherited

---

[51] See P.K. Tripathi, "Mr. Justice Gajendragadkar and Constitutional Interpretation," *Journal of the Indian Law Institute*, 8 (October–December 1966, 4), pp. 479–587.

[52] *Sajjan Singh* v. *State of Rajasthan*, AIR 1965 SC 845, 862.

many colonial forms, traditions, and conventions. Its first judges and lawyers had spent their careers at the Federal Court or in the provincial high courts of British India. Many had been involved with either the Privy Council or the Federal Court. They did not change their robes, advocacy styles, or argumentation strategies when the Supreme Court opened for business in 1950.

Throughout this book, Gadbois treats the Court as a composite institution. To be sure, he includes multiple references to individual justices' views and separate or dissenting opinions. Yet, he largely refrains from attributing judicial outcomes to particular justices' voting patterns, beliefs, or ideas. Gadbois concedes some of these points as *Beginnings* draws to a close. He readily acknowledges that the specific outcomes in individual cases could have been influenced judges' personal values. He is, however, unwilling to draw specific conclusions without adequate data, which he did not possess when he completed the manuscript in 1965.

In his concluding pages, Gadbois goes on to say that it is difficult to neatly label Indian justices as conservative or liberal. Indeed, it could be disrespectful and irreverent, he warns, even to raise such questions in India. It did not take very long, however, for Gadbois to reverse himself. In post-dissertation work, he pursued those very questions that he had earlier believed were off limits. Barely five years after *Beginnings* was completed, Gadbois was deeply immersed in studying judges' backgrounds and how they "behave" in major cases.[53]

Beginnings must be read bearing in mind the context in which it was written. As a historical treatise, the book's focus is largely on the Supreme Court and its predecessor, the Federal Court. It does not deal much with the high courts or the lower judiciary. A historical appraisal of the entire judicial system was much beyond the scope of Gadbois's doctoral dissertation. And although *Beginnings* covers only the Court's first fourteen years, its analysis and conclusions are, by no means, antiquarian or simplistic. To the contrary, by surveying the Court's antecedents and early foundations, the book helps us to better understand, evaluate, and critique the Court of today.

VII

With its focus on history and case law, *Beginnings* does not read like a book that a contemporary political scientist would write. We must remember, however,

---

[53] George H. Gadbois, Jr, "Selection, Background Characteristics, and Voting Behaviour of Indian Supreme Court Judges, 1950–1959," in Glendon Schubert and David J. Danelski (eds), *Comparative Judicial Behaviour: Cross-Cultural Studies of Political Decision-Making in the East and West* (Oxford University Press, 1969).

that Gadbois undertook his research as the discipline of political science was undergoing profound changes. Quantitative analysis was quickly becoming the preferred research methodology for a new generation of political scientists. To keep up with these changes, Gadbois had to "retool himself" in Hawaii even as he raced to complete his dissertation. It was too late for him to incorporate quantitative analysis in his doctorate work.

In much of his subsequent work, however, Gadbois relied extensively on statistical analysis and large data sets.[54] Indeed, few others have followed Gadbois in using data to systematically analyse Indian judicial outcomes.[55] But it is also important to emphasize that Gadbois pointedly refrained from crude empirical modelling. Rather, he evaluated cases and judgments with exactitude and precision and, in some instances, their historical context. As a student of comparative politics, he adopted a multidisciplinary approach to studying the Indian judiciary. He respected every discipline's integrity and varying methods even as he sought to identify points of equivalence among them.[56]

To some readers, *Beginnings*'s assessments may seem like period impressions. They reflect the temporal views of a young scholar ploughing a lonely furrow in the late 1960s. His voice and perspectives would evolve as he grew older, even as he would maintain the same accessible style and confidence on display in *Beginnings*. This book's footnotes and bibliography reveal Gadbois's persistence in searching for every primary and secondary source. He maintained the same zeal while working on his *Judges* book almost four decades later.

While researching his doctoral dissertation, Gadbois was unable to consult official correspondence or private papers of key personalities like Gwyer, Alladi, or Nehru. Some of these materials have now been published or are readily accessible in archives or libraries. Yet, even if Gadbois had the opportunity to revise his manuscript after consulting these new materials, it is unlikely that he

---

[54] See Upendra Baxi, "Who Bothers about the Supreme Court? The Problem of Impact of Judicial Decisions," *Journal of the Indian Law Institute*, 24 (1982, 4), pp. 848–862, 848 (citing Gadbois's pioneering quantitative work).

[55] See, e.g., Rajeev Dhavan, *The Supreme Court under Strain: The Challenge of Arrears* (N. M. Tripathi, 1978) and *The Supreme Court of India: A Socio-Legal Study of Its Juristic Techniques* (N. M. Tripathi, 1977); Robert Moog, "Indian Litigiousness and the Litigation Explosion: Challenging the Legend," *Asian Survey*, 33 (1993), pp. 1136–50; Varun Gauri, "Fundamental Rights and Public Interest Litigation in India: Overreaching or Underachieving?," *Indian Journal of Law & Economics*, 1 (2011, 1), pp. 71–93; and Aparna Chandra, William Hubbard, and Sital Kalantry, "The Unintended Consequences of Case-by-Case Rescue: An Empirical Study of Indian Supreme Court Cases from 2010 to 2014" (forthcoming 2017).

[56] We are grateful to Rajeev Dhavan for alerting us to this point.

would significantly revisit his basic assessments of the Court's history and its early years.

In addition to being a dedicated researcher, Gadbois was an exceptionally talented writer. His elegantly written dissertation remains crisp and accessible even after fifty-two years. The chapters that follow this introduction are largely verbatim reproductions of that dissertation with certain modifications. We have inserted a few additional footnotes to update information about the Court (e.g., the number of judges and their salaries). But we deliberatively chose to make few, if any, substantive edits to the text as a whole. We want readers to appreciate the original dissertation's beauty and simplicity without the ugly scaffolding of subsequent parentheses or editorial footnotes.

VIII

We must express our gratitude to many persons. At the top of our list is George himself. His oral histories gave us valuable insights into his life and work. He also gave us the honour and privilege to join him in this fascinating project. More importantly, he trusted us to see it through after he left us earlier this year. We thank the commissioning team at Oxford University Press, which readily agreed to our suggestion that this book be published. We are also grateful to the three eminent reviewers who strongly recommended its publication.

We received sound advice, detailed comments, and encouraging criticism from several people. They include Iqra Zainul Abedin, Upendra Baxi, Justice Ravindra Bhat, Abhinav Chandrachud, Justice Jasti Chelameswar, Arvind Datar, Rohit De, Rajeev Dhavan, Judy Papania Gadbois, Michael Gee, Ramachandra Guha, Sanjay Hegde, Mathew John, Alok Prasanna Kumar, Fali Nariman, Prashant Padmanabhan, N. L. Rajah, Raju Ramachandran, P. P. Rao, Nicholas Robinson, Howard Schaffer, Arghya Sengupta, Mitra Sharafi, M. P. Singh, B.N. Suchindran, Arun K. Thiruvengadam, V. Venkatesan, K. V. Viswanathan and Richard S. Wheeler. All or any errors, omissions, or mistakes remain entirely ours.

We acknowledge the research assistance we received from Chaitanya Deshpande and the editorial team at Oxford University Press. Finally, we are indebted to George's family, particularly his wife, Judy Papania Gadbois, for their support, assistance, and cooperation.

In his last phone call with us, George reminisced about that September day in 1962 when he first walked into the new Supreme Court building. Not every visitor to Tilak Marg had been impressed by the structure. Visiting a few years before George, the American architect Edward Durell Stone was appalled. He publicly criticized the Court and other post-Lutyens buildings as "cubistic structures" with no privacy.

Yet, to George, the edifice on Tilak Marg was not just another Lutyens-inspired building. It reminded him that his curiosity about the Court as a graduate student had evolved into a life-long scholarly obsession with an institution whose role and record he cared about deeply. "It was just a marvelous first impression," he declared as his voice gradually trailed away.

Vikram Raghavan
Vasujith Ram
May 2017

1 Evolution of the Federal Court of India

Before October 1, 1937, the inaugural date of the Federal Court of India, neither British India nor the Indian States had experienced the jurisdiction of an indigenous, all-India judicial tribunal. In the absence of such a court, disputes between the Centre and the Provinces, between the Centre and the States, and the Provinces and the States inter se, were decided by the Government of India, i.e., by the central executive, even when the latter was a party to a dispute. Furthermore, the High Courts and courts of like authority, being coordinate with and independent of one another, were subject to no common court of appeal. As a result, the statutes and codes which enjoyed application throughout British India and much of Princely India might conceivably have been given as many different interpretations as there were courts which applied them. The only corrective to such conflicting interpretations was the Judicial Committee of the Privy Council, an Imperial body sitting some six thousand miles from India. Although the Judicial Committee, which for decades heard more appeals from India than from any dominion or colony, was not to be lightly regarded as a unifying element in Indian law, it did not hear Indian appeals indiscriminately. Civil appeals, governed by the Code of Civil Procedure, 1908,[1] were restricted to suits in which at least 10,000 rupees were involved and, if the order or decree appealed from affirmed the decision of the court immediately below, the appeal also had to involve "some substantial question of law." Special leave to appeal in criminal cases was granted very rarely, for, the Judicial Committee emphasized in the case of *Arnold* v. *The King Emperor*,[2] "this Committee is not a

---

[1] Sections 109–112.
[2] (1914) Appeal Cases 644, 648.

Court of Criminal Appeal." Only when some clear departure from the require-ments of justice was alleged to have taken place, and "it is shown that, by a disregard of the forms of legal process, or by some violation of the principles of natural justice, or otherwise, substantial and grave injustice has been done,"[3] would the Judicial Committee interfere with the course of criminal justice.

Apart from these and other practical or administrative considerations, it was inevitable that there would be political or nationalistic demands for the estab-lishment of an indigenous, supreme judicial tribunal for, as Professor Keith once remarked, "it is idle to deny that the taking of appeals to the Privy Council is a mark of inferior status and partial servitude."[4] Proponents of such a court in India offered numerous justifications for its establishment, some of which were weighty and rational, others at best specious. It is the purpose of this chapter to trace the evolution of the Federal Court of India in terms of the arguments offered for and against the creation of an all-India judicial tribunal.

Published evidence indicates that an agitation aimed at the creation of an all-India court was initiated during the first term of the Central Legislative Assembly when Sir Hari Singh Gour introduced the following resolution to that effect on March 26, 1921:

> This Assembly recommends to the Governor-General in Council to be so pleased as to take early steps to establish a Court of Ultimate Appeal in India for the trial of Civil Appeals now determined by the Privy Council in England and as the court of final appeal against convictions for serious offences occasioning the failure of justice.[5]

Dr Gour argued that such a court should be established in India immediately because (i) "the Judicial Committee of the Privy Council is not a tribunal or a court, but merely an advisory body constituted and intended to advise the King in his capacity as the highest tribunal for his Dominions";[6] (ii) since Canada, Australia and South Africa had such a tribunal "there is no reason whatever why we should not have a Supreme Court of our own in this country";[7] (iii) the

---

[3] *In re Abraham Mallory Dillet* (1887) 12 Appeal Cases 459, 467. Under existing law applicable to India, there was no recourse as of right to the Privy Council in crimi-nal matters. What were loosely called "criminal appeals to the Privy Council" were instances in which the Privy Council, acting on behalf of the Crown, granted special leave to appeal.

[4] Arthur Berriedale Keith, *Responsible Government in the Dominions* (two volumes; second edition; London: Oxford University Press, 1927), II, 1102.

[5] *Legislative Assembly Debates*, I (1921), p. 1606.

[6] *Legislative Assembly Debates*, I (1921), p. 1606.

[7] *Legislative Assembly Debates*, I (1921), p. 1607.

expense of an appeal to the Privy Council is prohibitive;[8] (iv) the distance from India of the Privy Council resulted in unnecessary delay ("in many cases four to five years") in the final disposition of cases;[9] (v) the Judicial Committee was not equipped to decide cases involving the intricacies of Hindu and Muhammadan law;[10] and (vi) the Privy Council refused to hear criminal appeals unless there had been a gross failure of justice in the Indian court.[11]

Dr Gour, however, did not suggest that the creation of an Indian Supreme Court should preclude further appeals to the Privy Council. On the contrary, he preferred "to follow the examples of the two larger Colonies of Canada and Australia, giving the litigant the option of either appealing to the Supreme Court here or to the Judicial Committee of the Privy Council in England."[12] In short, the Supreme Court which Gour sought was one which would parallel the Judicial Committee in jurisdiction with the exception that the Indian Court would have a "real revisional jurisdiction in all criminal cases."[13]

Following Gour's explanations of his resolution, Dr Tej Bahadur Sapru, the then law member, suggested that debate on the resolution be postponed until such time as public opinion in India had been sounded as to the desirability of establishing such a court, a suggestion which Gour accepted.

Eighteen months later the matter of a Supreme Court was raised again by Dr Gour when he requested leave to introduce "a Bill to establish a Supreme Court for British India."[14] Dr. Sapru, however, raised the question of whether the Legislative Assembly had the power to establish a court which would be superior in jurisdiction to the High Courts, and concluded that it did not. After some discussion, the assembly president ruled that it was not the intention of the Imperial Parliament to confer such a power upon the Indian Legislature. The Legislature, therefore, had to be excluded from taking into consideration a bill, but was not prevented from discussing the desirability of a Supreme Court by way of resolution.[15]

Gour, accordingly, again introduced his resolution, urging that the establishment of a Supreme Court "is well justified by reason of the fact that now that India has got a written constitution, it should also have a Supreme Court to interpret it and uphold it."[16] In the floor debate which followed,

[8] *Legislative Assembly Debates*, I (1921), p. 1608.
[9] *Legislative Assembly Debates*, I (1921), p. 1608.
[10] *Legislative Assembly Debates*, I (1921), p. 1608.
[11] *Legislative Assembly Debates*, I (1921), p. 1609.
[12] *Legislative Assembly Debates*, I (1921), p. 1609.
[13] *Legislative Assembly Debates*, I (1921), p. 1610.
[14] *Legislative Assembly Debates*, III (1922), September 20, 1922, p. 712.
[15] *Legislative Assembly Debates*, III (1922), September 20, 1922, p. 715.
[16] *Legislative Assembly Debates*, III (1922), September 23, 1922, p. 828.

however, it was evident immediately that the Gour resolution was not popular among his colleagues. It was opposed for a variety of reasons. "It will not be practicable for us to get very great lawyers and jurists from England to come out and serve on the Bench of that Supreme Court."[17] Competent members of the Indian Bar would refuse appointment to the Supreme Court because "in this country unfortunately we measure everything by the salary and emoluments that go with an office."[18] "We are only at the earliest stages of responsible Government and ... no dominion in its earlier stages ever got a Supreme Court."[19] Another member of the Assembly asserted that "our Supreme Court is now situated in London and it will be robbing it of much of its dignity and prestige to remove it from the metropolis of the Empire and plant it in the uncongenial soil of this country torn with communal and religious differences."[20] Another argued, with some emotion, that "a Court such as Dr. Gour suggests will be a mere travesty on the Privy Council, lacking alike in dignity and in its glorious traditions and its calm and detached atmosphere, and in fact in all that we are hitherto accustomed to associate with that august institution."[21] A further objection was that the establishment of a Supreme Court would impair the independence of the High Courts because the judges of the High Courts would be aspiring to appointment to the Supreme Court, i.e., in their judgments they would seek to win the favor of the authorities who had the power of making appointments.[22] A final, but quite significant, criticism of the resolution was that of the Bench of the Calcutta High Court who,

> confining themselves to considerations bearing directly on the efficiency of the judicial system, and expressing no opinion which would depend on sentimental or political considerations, ... think it plain that the proposal must primarily be judged by its probable effect upon the decision of cases and upon the confidence felt in India as to the justice and soundness of such decisions. In the case of an Ultimate Court of Appeal everything depends on the reputation of the Court in the eyes of the legal profession, which is the condition of wider prestige. Viewing the matter in this light, the judges are unanimous that the proposed Court is undesirable because it would entail a distinct sacrifice of efficiency and the conditions of public confidence.[23]

[17] *Legislative Assembly Debates*, III (1922), September 23, 1922, p. 831.
[18] *Legislative Assembly Debates*, III (1922), September 23, 1922, p. 831.
[19] *Legislative Assembly Debates*, III (1922), September 23, 1922, p. 833.
[20] *Legislative Assembly Debates*, III (1922), September 23, 1922, p. 835.
[21] *Legislative Assembly Debates*, III (1922), September 23, 1922, p. 837.
[22] *Legislative Assembly Debates*, III (1922), September 23, 1922, p. 837.
[23] *Legislative Assembly Debates*, III (1922), September 23, 1922, p. 840.

At the conclusion of the discussion, the Gour resolution was defeated by a voice vote, marking the first of several defeats such a proposal was to receive.

There the matter of a Supreme Court for India rested until, in February of 1924, Sir Malcolm Hailey, the Home Member, made public the results of the Government's sampling of public opinion. According to Hailey, there was

> no identity of opinion between Local Governments, High Courts or legal authorities, whether Indian or European, in favour of the early institutions of a Supreme Court, while the question of its location also involves much difficulty. We consider also that the opinions clearly indicate that there will be great difficulty in any circumstances in securing a personnel for the Court which would be likely to give it a status and reputation equal to that of the Judicial Committee of the Privy Council. Further, our financial conditions render the institution of a Supreme Court impracticable at the present time.
>
> We have therefore decided that in the present circumstances ... serious consideration cannot be given to the proposal on its merits.[24]

The indefatigable Dr Gour, however, remained an inveterate advocate of an indigenous central court, and in 1925 he again introduced his "Resolution *Re* Establishment of a Supreme Court in India."[25] The arguments he offered the Assembly at this time were very similar to those he put forth in 1921 and 1922, with the exception that at this time he attached considerable importance to the charge that numerous matters of dispute between the Executive and the Legislature were being decided by the Executive alone, much to the dissatisfaction of the Legislature. He urged that an impartial tribunal offered the only satisfactory solution for the disposition of such justiciable matters as, e.g., the precise delimitation of provincial, transferred and reserved subjects, the extent of the Governor's veto power, the interpretation of various sections of the Government of India Act, and the scope of the Legislative Assembly's control over the military budget. Furthermore, Gour was considerably more forthright in questioning the competence of the Judicial Committee, and he alleged that "in recent years the decisions of their Lordships of the Privy Council have not commanded universal and unqualified confidence, ... particularly cases involving decisions on Hindu and Muhammadan Law."[26] He was still willing to allow, however, that "those who swear by the Privy Council might be left free to appeal to that body"[27] rather than to a local tribunal.

---

[24] *Legislative Assembly Debates*, IV (1924), February 5, 1924, p. 191.

[25] *Legislative Assembly Debates*, V (1925), February 17, 1925, p. 1160.

[26] *Legislative Assembly Debates*, V (1925), February 17, 1925, p. 1162.

[27] *Legislative Assembly Debates*, V (1925), February 17, 1925, p. 1164.

Discussion of this resolution followed much the same lines as that of three years earlier, with Gour's adversaries again far outnumbering his supporters. Furthermore, it was clear that the opposition included nearly all shades of political opinion represented in the Legislative Assembly. It was criticized by Muslim members who argued that the requisite judicial talent could not be secured in India, that it was "impossible in India for any Judge, whether Indian or English, to get that healthy and that free atmosphere which prevails in England,"[28] and that such a court would serve only to "increase the mania of litigation which is already sucking the life-blood of the people of this country."[29] The proposal was opposed by Colonel Sir Henry Stanyon, a European representative, because Supreme Courts had so far been created only in the self-governing Dominions, because the anticipated expenses such a court would entail would be prohibitive, because there was no physical location for such a court which would be equally accessible to all the Provinces, and because of the difficulty of finding and selecting personnel for the court who would command respect throughout India.[30]

The most eminent critic of the proposed Supreme Court, however, was Pandit Motilal Nehru, who observed that in

> a country where the executive and the judicial functions are combined, where a controversy has been raging for years past over the separation of these two functions without any results, a country where there are racial discriminations in the administration of criminal justice, is not the country to have a Supreme Court within its own borders. ... A distance of six or seven thousand miles between the highest court of appeal and the Government of India is in my opinion none too long.[31]

Furthermore, Nehru argued, since an appeal to an Indian Supreme Court would be a luxury enjoyed only by the wealthy, and since such a court would be maintained by taxation, "there is no reason whatever why this luxury should be enjoyed by the rich at the expense of the poor."[32] In short, concluded Nehru, "there is every reason at the present stage for us not to think of a Supreme Court in India. ... The time for it will be when we are a self-governing people and not a day before."[33]

---

[28] *Legislative Assembly Debates*, V (1925), February 17, 1925, pp. 1170–1171.

[29] *Legislative Assembly Debates*, V (1925), February 17, 1925, pp. 1169–1170.

[30] Stanyon's argument on this latter point was that there were no all-India lawyers available on either the High Court Benches or at the Bar, i.e., that Indian lawyers and jurists, although eminent and respected, possessed Provincial experience only. *Legislative Assembly Debates*, V (1925), February 17, 1925, pp. 1166–1167.

[31] *Legislative Assembly Debates*, V (1925), February 17, 1925, p. 1171.

[32] *Legislative Assembly Debates*, V (1925), February 17, 1925, p. 1171.

[33] *Legislative Assembly Debates*, V (1925), February 17, 1925, p. 1172.

Mohammad Ali Jinnah, on the other hand, "strongly support[ed]" the Gour resolution, and observed: "I have no hesitation in saying that the Privy Council have on several occasions absolutely murdered Hindu law, and slaughtered Muhammadan law."[34] The support of Jinnah and a few others, however, was considerably less than Gour needed, for his resolution suffered defeat by the embarrassingly decisive margin of fifty-six to fifteen.[35] So apart from the likelihood of a Supreme Court being created had the resolution won the approval of the Legislative Assembly—an Act of Parliament, of course, would have been necessary—the fate of the Gour resolution indicated that the overwhelming majority of India's legislators did not want a Supreme Court even if offered one.

Not all action taken with a view toward the establishment of an Indian Supreme Court occurred in the Legislative Assembly. Indeed, the most elaborate early sketch of a Supreme Court was set forth in the so-called "Commonwealth of India Bill," prepared largely by Mrs. Annie Besant, which was pressed unsuccessfully upon the House of Commons in 1925 and again in 1927. Therein it was provided that all High Court decisions hitherto appealable to the Privy Council would be appealable after the passage of the Bill to an Indian Supreme Court, and "the judgment of the Supreme Court shall be final and conclusive and shall not be reviewed or capable of being reviewed by any other court, tribunal or authority whatsoever."[36] But, "if satisfied that for any special reason the certificate should be granted," the Bill provided that the Supreme Court might certify a case as one fit for appeal to the Judicial Committee.[37]

In the year 1926 the Gour resolution received support from a significant quarter when M. K. Gandhi observed that "it has been a painful surprise to me to observe opposition to Sir Hari Singh's very mild and very innocent proposal, but we have lost all confidence in ourselves."[38] Gandhi added: "I have some little experience of the Privy Council cases, and it is my firm belief that the Members of the Privy Council are not free from political bias and on highly intricate matters of custom, in spite of all their labours, they often make egregious blunders."[39]

---

[34] *Legislative Assembly Debates*, V (1925), February 17, 1925, pp. 1175–1176. Jinnah also pointed out the incongruity of Nehru and Stanyon joining forces in opposition to the Gour resolution, which precipitated a heated exchange between Jinnah and Nehru.

[35] *Legislative Assembly Debates*, V (1925), February 17, 1925, p. 1180.

[36] *Parliamentary Papers*, I (1927), Bill 21, Section 57.

[37] *Parliamentary Papers*, I (1927), Bill 21, Section 58.

[38] *Hindustan Times*, August 7, 1926. Quoted in the *Legislative Assembly Debates*, III (1927), March 25, 1927, p. 2805.

[39] *Hindustan Times*, August 7, 1926. Quoted in the *Legislative Assembly Debates*, III (1927), March 25, 1927, p. 2805.

Another illustrious ally of Gour at this time was the distinguished liberal, Sir Tej Bahadur Sapru, who, writing in 1926, urged the immediate establishment of such a court in view of some recent unsatisfactory Privy Council decisions relating to Hindu personal law, "and also because it is felt that a country marching toward Responsible Government should have a Supreme Court of appeal of its own."[40] But while Sapru argued that India's relations with the Privy Council were not altogether satisfactory, he advocated only restriction, not elimination, of the right of appeal to the Privy Council.[41] Furthermore, Sapru's proposals, like Gour's made earlier, made no provision for appeals from State courts to the envisaged Supreme Court. In fact, it seems that the Supreme Court sought by Sapru would not be concerned with appeals in constitutional or criminal matters, but would serve only as a court of civil appeal over the Provincial High Courts.

During the year 1927, while Sir Hari Singh Gour continued in vain to press his proposals for a central court upon his colleagues in the Legislative Assembly, for the first time a "Resolution *re* Establishment of a Supreme Court" was moved in the Council of State.[42] Introduced by Sir Sankaran Nair, a former High Court Judge, the Resolution was worded as follows:

> This Council recommends to the Governor-General in Council to take early steps to secure that a Supreme Court is established in India with power
>
> (a)   to interpret and uphold the constitution;
> (b)   to act as a court of final criminal appeal against all sentences of death;
> (c)   to act as a revising court in specified serious cases;
> (d)   to hear civil appeals now heard by His Majesty's Privy Council; and
> (e)   generally to carry out the work at present entrusted to His Majesty's Privy Council
>
> provided that such court shall not affect His Majesty's prerogative safeguarded in the constitutions of Canada, Australia and South Africa.

In attempting to justify the need of a Supreme Court in India, Nair pointed to the heavy expense involved in an appeal to the Privy Council, and to the resultant advantage enjoyed by a wealthy litigant over a poor litigant. Nair also expressed his dissatisfaction with the then existing system of criminal justice, under which the accused, if acquitted by the Sessions Judge and jury after a

---

[40] Sir Tej Bahadur Sapru, *The Indian Constitution* (Madras: The National Secretary's Office, 1926), p. 145. Earlier, it will be recalled, Sapru, in his capacity as Law Member of the Governor-General's Council, was less enthusiastic about a Supreme Court.

[41] Sir Tej Bahadur Sapru, *The Indian Constitution* (Madras: The National Secretary's Office, 1926), p. 150.

[42] *Council of State Debates*, II (1927), August 31, 1927, p. 885.

full trial, might be sentenced to death by the High Court in the event that the Government's appeal was successful. However, against this conviction there was no recourse, for the High Court was the final court of appeal in view of the fact that the Privy Council usually refused to hear appeals in criminal cases.[43]

While elaborating on his proposals, Nair noted that he did not advocate a complete cessation of appeals to the Judicial Committee, but would offer the litigant the option of carrying his appeal either to the Privy Council or to the local appellate court. Since this amounted to little more than a mere duplication of the existing machinery for disposing of appeals, many members of the Council of State opposed the resolution for this reason alone. In general, Nair was simply unable to put forth weighty and practical reasons as to why it was imperative that India have its own Supreme Court. He and his supporters found it difficult to counter the argument that an aggrieved party would "get better justice, more unbiased and impartial justice in the Privy Council than from a Supreme Court constituted in India with local Judges imbibing local ideas and prejudices, local bias, local influences and otherwise."[44] Doubtless, many of the members agreed with S. R. Das, who noted that "from a political point of view we are all anxious to have a Supreme Court,"[45] but from a practical standpoint the difficulties far outweigh the advantages. Nair's resolution was defeated by a vote of twenty-five to fifteen.

A significant development in the evolution of an all-India tribunal occurred in 1928 when, at the celebrated All Parties Conference, provision for a Supreme Court which would take over the appellate work of the Privy Council found a place in the *Nehru Report*.[46] Such a court would have, in addition, an extensive original jurisdiction, and its judgments in all cases "shall be final and conclusive and shall not be reviewed, or be capable of being reviewed by any other court, tribunal or authority whatsoever."[47] But the Supreme Court might, at its option, certify a case as one fit for appeal to the Privy Council.[48]

---

[43] *Council of State Debates*, II (1927), August 31, 1927, p. 886.

[44] *Council of State Debates*, II (1927), August 31, 1927, p. 897.

[45] *Council of State Debates*, II (1927), August 31, 1927, p. 907.

[46] *Report of the Committee Appointed by the Conference to Determine the Principles of the Constitution for India* (Allahabad: All India Congress Committee, 1928), Articles 46–52. Motilal Nehru, the Chairman of the Committee, was instructed to frame a constitution providing for the establishment of *full* responsible government, which may explain why Nehru opposed a Supreme Court in 1925 but approved of it here.

[47] *Report of the Committee Appointed by the Conference to Determine the Principles of the Constitution for India* (Allahabad: All India Congress Committee, 1928), Article 51.

[48] *Report of the Committee Appointed by the Conference to Determine the Principles of the Constitution for India* (Allahabad: All India Congress Committee, 1928), Article 52.

In the following year the demand for an Indian Supreme Court was recorded for the first time in a Command Paper. This was the *Report of the Indian Central Committee, 1928–29,*[49] paragraph 138 of which related to the creation of an Indian Supreme Court:

> In the three great federations of English-speaking peoples—the United States of America, the Dominion of Canada, and the Commonwealth of Australia—a Supreme Court forms an integral part of the constitution, and although the Indian Commonwealth which we hope to see established will be formed by a system of devolution of power from the Centre, and not by the federation of independent states or provinces, the arguments in favor of establishing a Supreme Court for India are, in our opinion, not less cogent than in the cases referred to. A great deal of the appellate work of the Privy Council would devolve upon the Supreme Court in India, to the great advantage of litigants both in time and money. The Supreme Court would decide disputes between one province and another, or between provinces and the Centre, and might be entrusted with authority to give rulings on interpretation of the constitution. The Canadian or Australian model provides precedents for regulating the relationship of the Supreme Court and the Privy Council in London.
>
> We are convinced of the necessity for the establishment of a Supreme Court in India as an integral part of the constitution, and we recommend that a Supreme Court be so established.

The *Report of the Indian Statutory Commission,*[50] however, took no notice of any expression of Indian opinion relative to a Supreme Court.

With the convening of the First Session of the Indian Round Table Conference in London in November 1930, an unexpected announcement was made which marked a turning point in the evolution of an all-India judicial tribunal. It was announced by representatives of the Indian States that the States were prepared to federate with British India, provided the proposed federation was independent of British control. Thereafter, while there remained serious differences of opinion as to whether India needed a supreme civil and criminal appellate court, all parties involved agreed with Lord Sankey, the Lord Chancellor, who

---

[49] Great Britain, *Parliamentary Papers,* X (1929–1930), Cmd. 3451. The function of the Indian Central Committee, appointed by the Governor-General after the storm of indignation and protest which followed the announcement of the appointment of the all-British Simon [Indian Statutory] Commission, was to sit in "Joint Free Conference" with the Statutory Commission for the purpose of scrutinizing and elucidating, "from the Indian side, on free and equal terms," the memoranda and evidence presented to the Statutory Commission (*Report,* pp. 7, 83).

[50] *Parliamentary Papers,* XII (1929–1930), Cmd. 3568, 3569, 3572.

told the delegates to the Conference that in a federal system of government, "a Federal Court is an essential element."[51]

At the Second Session of the Conference, held the following year, the Federal Structure Committee submitted its Third Report, a section of which related to the creation of a Federal Court:

> The necessity for the establishment of a Federal Court was common ground among all members of the Committee, and such differences of opinion as manifested themselves were concerned, for the most part, with matters of detail rather than of principle. It was recognised by all that a Federal Court was required both to interpret the constitution and to safeguard it, to prevent encroachment by one federal organ upon the sphere of another, and to guarantee the integrity of the compact between the various federating Units out of which the Federation itself has sprung.[52]

Its necessity admitted, the Committee then turned to the question of jurisdiction, and it was "generally agreed that this jurisdiction must be both original and appellate."[53] It ought to have "an exclusive original jurisdiction in the case of disputes arising between the Federation and a State or Province, or between two States, two Provinces, or a State and a Province."[54] Such jurisdiction would embrace

> disputes of every kind between the Federation and a Province or between two Provinces, and not only disputes of a strictly constitutional nature; but that in the case of disputes between the Federal Government and a State, between a State and a Province, or between two States, the dispute must necessarily be one arising in the federal sphere, that is to say, one in which a question of the interpretation of the constitution (using that expression in its broadest sense) is involved, since otherwise the jurisdiction would extend beyond the limits of the Treaties of cession which the States will have made with the Crown before entering the Federation.[55]

It is evident from this quotation that the States, although willing to join an all-India federation, were quite unwilling to part with any more of their sovereignty

---

[51] Great Britain, *Indian Round Table Conference* (First Session) *Proceedings*, XII (1931), Cmd. 3778, p. 417.

[52] *Third Report of the Federal Structure Committee*, submitted to the Second Session of the Indian Round Table Conference, Cmd. 3997 (1932), paragraph 52, p. 27.

[53] *Third Report of the Federal Structure Committee*, submitted to the Second Session of the Indian Round Table Conference, Cmd. 3997 (1932), paragraph 53.

[54] *Third Report of the Federal Structure Committee*, submitted to the Second Session of the Indian Round Table Conference, Cmd. 3997 (1932), paragraph 53.

[55] *Third Report of the Federal Structure Committee*, submitted to the Second Session of the Indian Round Table Conference, Cmd. 3997 (1932), paragraph 53.

than was absolutely necessary in the interests of the federation. Seeking to retain the fullest freedom in their own affairs, the States would agree to submit only to a minimal amount of Federal Court jurisdiction. In short, the most perplexing problem to be faced by the various groups who attempted to determine the nature and jurisdiction of a Federal Court was the reluctance of the States to invest the proposed court with authority to settle disputes to which they would be parties.

In this report, the Federal Structure Committee agreed also that an appeal should not lie from the Federal Court to the Privy Council, except by leave of the Federal Court itself, though the right of any person to petition the Crown for special leave to appeal, and the right of the Crown to grant such a leave, was to be preserved. Again, however, the refusal of the Rulers to subordinate themselves to any institution, whether it be Federal or Imperial, was manifest when the Committee felt constrained to

> emphasize here, in order to prevent any misunderstanding, that any right of appeal from State Courts to the Federal Court and thence to the Privy Council in constitutional matters will be founded upon the consent of the Princes themselves. ... There can be no question of any assumption by Parliament or by the Crown of a right to subject the States to an appellate jurisdiction otherwise than with their full consent and approval.[56]

The final paragraphs of the section of the report dealing with the central judicature related to the more controversial matter of "the creation of a Supreme Court for British India to which an appeal should lie from all Provincial High Courts in substitution for a direct appeal to the Privy Council."[57] This, of course, is the same proposal as that made by Gour and others between 1921 and 1930, years before a Federal Court was envisaged. According to the report, "a strong opinion" was expressed that such a court should be established, and since the creation of such a Court was "in the natural course of evolution," the Committee adopted the suggestion "in principle."[58]

But again the Committee divided along Provincial and State lines. The British Indian delegates insisted that the Federal Court should be invested with this appellate jurisdiction, their proposal being that the Federal Court would sit in

---

[56] *Third Report of the Federal Structure Committee*, submitted to the Second Session of the Indian Round Table Conference, Cmd. 3997 (1932), paragraph 59, p. 29.

[57] *Third Report of the Federal Structure Committee*, submitted to the Second Session of the Indian Round Table Conference, Cmd. 3997 (1932), paragraph 63, pp. 30–31.

[58] *Third Report of the Federal Structure Committee*, submitted to the Second Session of the Indian Round Table Conference, Cmd. 3997 (1932), paragraph 63, p. 31.

two divisions, one dealing with Federal matters and the other with appeals from the Provincial High Courts. The States' representatives, however,

> dissented from this view, and were of the opinion that there should be a separate Supreme Court for British India on the ground that the Federal Court would be an all-India Court, while the Supreme Court's jurisdiction would be confined to British India; the mass of work with which it would have to cope would obscure its true functions as a Federal Court, and to that extent detract from its position and dignity as a Federal organ.[59]

Not only was there no general agreement among the interests represented on the nature of a Supreme Court, but

> a question of very real difficulty upon which there is a divergence of view [was] whether the Constitution Act itself should at once establish a Supreme Court or whether power should be given to the Federal Legislature to establish it either as a separate institution, or by conferring general appellate jurisdiction on the Federal Court as and when it may think proper to do so.[60]

The majority of the Committee, however, was impressed with the need to proceed cautiously in this matter, and thus recommended that the Constitution Act prescribe the jurisdiction and functions of the Supreme Court, and empower the Federal Legislature to establish such a court at some later date, if it should think fit to do so. The Committee was hesitant because it felt that it should be left to the Federal Legislature to decide whether the additional expense of a civil appellate court should be incurred, and because, in the early days of the proposed federation, "it would be unwise to run the risk of either overburdening it prematurely with work, or of weakening its position by setting up in another sphere a Court which might be regarded as a rival."[61]

Finally, it was acknowledged in the report that "a proposal to invest the Supreme Court ... with jurisdiction to act as a Court of Criminal Appeal for the whole of British India also found a certain measure of support."[62] However, after expressing the fear that "even if a right of appeal to this Court only in the graver criminal cases were given, the work of the Court, and therefore the number

---

[59] *Third Report of the Federal Structure Committee*, submitted to the Second Session of the Indian Round Table Conference, Cmd. 3997 (1932), paragraph 63, p. 31.

[60] *Third Report of the Federal Structure Committee*, submitted to the Second Session of the Indian Round Table Conference, Cmd. 3997 (1932), paragraph 64, p. 31.

[61] *Third Report of the Federal Structure Committee*, submitted to the Second Session of the Indian Round Table Conference, Cmd. 3997 (1932), paragraph 64, p. 32.

[62] *Third Report of the Federal Structure Committee*, submitted to the Second Session of the Indian Round Table Conference, Cmd. 3997 (1932), paragraph 65, p. 32.

of Judges would be enormously increased,"[63] the Committee decided that the matter of criminal appeals should be left for the future Federal Legislature to ponder.

In the interim between the Second and Third Sessions of the Round Table Conference, the question of a Supreme Court in India was debated again in the Legislative Assembly.[64] Although the resolution introduced at this time was a verbatim copy of that introduced unsuccessfully by Nair in the Council of State nearly five years earlier, this "Resolution re Establishment of a Supreme Court in India," put before the Assembly by B. R. Puri, was carried by a vote of thirty-four to seventeen. Although many reasons might be offered for this change in the attitude of the Assembly toward a Supreme Court, three stand out as significant: (i) general change in the political climate; (ii) dissatisfaction with the recommendations of the Federal Structure Committee, and (iii) increased concern over the alleged injustices of the existing system of criminal appeals. Indeed, the situation with regard to criminal cases, discussed earlier,[65] was considered to be so grossly unjust as alone to justify the creation of an Indian Supreme Court.

The final session of the Round Table Conference met during November and December of 1932. In that a Federal Court had been agreed upon at the previous meetings, "the only question that remained was whether there should be a Supreme Court as well."[66] Sir Tej Bahadur Sapru and a majority of his British Indian colleagues made it clear that they wanted both a Federal Court and a Supreme Court, but not two separate courts, for "in the interests both of economy and efficiency there must be only one Court which might sit in two divisions for the decision of Federal issues and of appeals from High Courts in India respectively."[67] Sapru suggested also that a purely Federal Court of three or four judges would not be likely to carry much weight while a larger court of nine-to-twelve judges would command confidence and attract talent.

Sir Zafrulla Khan, another distinguished British Indian delegate, agreed with Sapru that there should be ultimately a Supreme Court, but argued that as a Supreme Court was not an essential part of the new constitution, all that was necessary was to set forth the details of its nature in the Constitution Act, leaving

[63] *Third Report of the Federal Structure Committee,* submitted to the Second Session of the Indian Round Table Conference, Cmd. 3997 (1932), paragraph 65, p. 32.

[64] *Legislative Assembly Debates,* I (1932), February 10, 1932, pp. 571–606.

[65] *Council of State Debates,* II (1927), August 31, 1927, p. 886.

[66] *Indian Round Table Conference* (Third Session) *Proceedings,* (1933), Cmd. 4238, p. 71.

[67] *Indian Round Table Conference* (Third Session) *Proceedings,* (1933), Cmd. 4238, p. 71.

the Federal Legislature to decide the actual date of its establishment.[68] He agreed with Sapru that the right of appeal to the Privy Council should remain, that there should be some limitation on the number of appeals generally, and that the Supreme Court should have a certain criminal jurisdiction, e.g., in cases of capital punishment.

The British Indian contingent, however, was not by any means unanimous in urging the establishment of a Supreme Court, be it separate or joined to the Federal Court. Sir Nripendra Sircar was "definitely opposed"[69] to the idea. He argued that since any right of appeal to an Indian Supreme Court even in the limited criminal field of capital cases would be largely availed of, "some 20 or 25 judges would be necessary to deal with the work", with the result that the cost would be prohibitive. Sircar argued also that it would not be desirable to whittle away at the jurisdiction of the Privy Council, for that body, "sitting as the last impartial tribunal in an atmosphere remote from local colour and prejudice, has done much for British-Indian jurisprudence during the last 150 years, and its services should not be lightly set aside."[70]

The "general view of the States delegation"[71] was expressed by Sir Akbar Hydari, who maintained that it was essential that the Federal Court should be a separate and distinct entity, for

> a Federal Court was a constitutional necessity; a Supreme Court was not a matter of immediate importance, and, in any case, was the concern of British India alone. To visualise two divisions of the same Court, one Federal and one Supreme, was to confuse the issue. A Federal Court was a Federal essential and would be required to be manned by judges of outstanding integrity, with a knowledge of constitutional law, customarily associated with all-India interests and free from local prejudices. The question of a Supreme Court on the other hand was merely a question of supplementing the judicial system of British India.[72]

The States had, in fact, long been aware of the utility of an all-India judicial tribunal, but their interest was in a tribunal which would adjudicate inter-State disputes and prevent the invasion by the Central Government of the domain of State sovereignty. In the absence of such a tribunal under the existing semi-federal system, all questions of this nature were decided unilaterally by the Government of India by virtue of its claim of paramountcy. Further, since much of what was regarded by the States as an encroachment on their rights was done

---

[68] *Indian Round Table Conference* (Third Session) *Proceedings*, (1933), Cmd. 4238, p. 72.

[69] *Indian Round Table Conference* (Third Session) *Proceedings*, (1933), Cmd. 4238, p. 72.

[70] *Indian Round Table Conference* (Third Session) *Proceedings*, (1933), Cmd. 4238, p. 72.

[71] *Indian Round Table Conference* (Third Session) *Proceedings*, (1933), Cmd. 4238, p. 73.

[72] *Indian Round Table Conference* (Third Session) *Proceedings*, (1933), Cmd. 4238, p. 73.

in the name of paramountcy, the States had sought in the past the establishment of a central court which would have the authority to declare *ultra vires* and illegal any executive or legislative measure which violated the clauses of a treaty.[73] Accordingly, the creation of a purely Federal Court was in the interests of the Rulers. But having no interest in a Supreme Court for civil and criminal appellate purposes, the States were adamant in insisting that the Federal Court and the Supreme Court be considered separately.

At this final session of the Round Table Conference it was decided, in view of the absence of consensus on the matter of a Supreme Court, that it "would be of no advantage to appoint a Committee of the Conference to consider the question further."[74] The matter of a supreme civil and criminal appellate court was left hanging, to be taken up again at some later date by some other body.

In sum, the three sessions of the Indian Round Table Conference resulted in widespread agreement among the parties involved that a Federal Court was imperative to interpret the new constitution and to serve as the forum for the decision of disputes between the Federation and its constituent units. On the other hand, the Conference reports indicate seemingly irreconcilable differences of opinion over the question of a supreme appellate tribunal for British India. The States, who had no intention of using such a court, quite understandably opposed its establishment, especially as a division bench of the Federal Court. British Indian delegates, although in general championing an indigenous appellate court, were divided not only over whether it should be constituted separately or as a bench of the Federal Court, but also over whether it should be established immediately by the Constitution Act itself, or merely provided for in the form of a provision in the Act enabling the Federal Legislature to establish it later at its discretion. It was this absence of clear-cut and decisive proposals among the proponents of the court which forestalled a firm Conference recommendation with regard to a Supreme Court for India.

Although there was little agreement among the Indian interests involved concerning the several aspects of the Supreme Court proposal, the position of the British Government at this juncture seems to have been clear. They were not opposed, on principle, to the establishment of such a court and a reduction of Indian appeals to the Judicial Committee, and were prepared to provide for its establishment in the Constitution Act. However, they did object to its immediate establishment, for they could not be convinced of its

---

[73] K. N. Haksar and K. M. Panikkar, *Federal India* (London: Martin Hopkinson Ltd., 1930), pp. 20, 36, 125, 129.

[74] *Indian Round Table Conference* (Third Session) *Proceedings*, (1933), Cmd. 4238, p. 73.

urgency.[75] The position of the British Government was that if India actually required and desired such a court, the future Federal Legislature could create it at a later date by passing the required legislation. "There could be no effective reply to this contention, as the champions of the plan had built up an imposing edifice by claiming that there was an insistent demand by the Indian people for such a body."[76]

The Round Table Conference was followed by the publication of the *Proposals for Indian Constitutional Reform*,[77] i.e., the famous White Paper, in 1933. Containing the recommendations of His Majesty's Government concerning Indian constitutional advance, the White Paper treated at some length the matters of a Federal and Supreme Court. In general, however, the proposals set forth therein parallel the recommendations of the Federal Structure Committee. The one significant departure was the White Paper's recommendation that if and when the future Federal Legislature saw fit to establish a Supreme Court in India, such a court should be entirely separate and be distinct from the Federal Court.[78] Furthermore, if such a court was created,

> a direct appeal from a High Court to His Majesty in Council in either a civil or a criminal case will be barred. An appeal from the Supreme Court to His Majesty in Council will be allowed in civil cases only by leave of the Supreme Court or by special leave. In criminal cases no appeal will be allowed to His Majesty in Council, whether by special leave or otherwise.[79]

It is quite clear that the British Government was prepared to restrict drastically, if not eliminate entirely, Indian appeals to the Judicial Committee. All that prevented such action was the lack of unanimity of opinion among Indians that such action was in their own interests.

Immediately following the presentation of the White Paper, the Joint Committee on Indian Constitutional Reform was appointed[80] and charged with the task of considering the future government in India with particular reference

[75] Sir Shafa'at Ahmad Kahn, *The Indian Federation* (London: Macmillan and Co., Limited, 1937), p. 234. Sir Shafa'at was a delegate at each of the three sessions of the Round Table Conference.

[76] Sir Shafa'at Ahmad Kahn, *The Indian Federation* (London: Macmillan and Co., Limited, 1937), p. 234.

[77] *Parliamentary Papers*, XX (1932–33), Cmd. 4268.

[78] *Parliamentary Papers*, XX (1932–33), Cmd. 4268, paragraphs 163–167.

[79] *Parliamentary Papers*, XX (1932–33), Cmd. 4268, paragraph 167.

[80] This Committee was composed of thirty two members (sixteen from each House), with the Marquis of Linlithgow serving as chairman. Seven delegates from the Indian States, twenty from continental British India, and twelve from Burma were invited to attend the deliberations.

to the White Paper proposals. During the meetings of this Committee all aspects of the Federal Court–Supreme Court questions were discussed in greater detail than at any earlier date.

Discussion was initiated on October 19, 1933, when Sir Samuel Hoare, the Secretary of State for India, circulated a note in which he suggested two significant modifications in the White Paper proposals. Firstly, he expressed the opinion that paragraph 156 of the White Paper, which advised that the appellate jurisdiction of the Federal Court be limited to cases relating to the interpretation of the Constitution Act or of any rights or obligations arising thereunder, did not go far enough, for "no provision is therefore made for securing uniformity of interpretation in the several Provinces and States of Federal laws extending throughout the whole area of the Federation."[81] With a view toward securing such uniformity, Hoare proposed that the Joint Committee consider the propriety of extending the appellate jurisdiction of the Federal Court so as to include cases involving the interpretation of federal laws.

Secondly, Hoare reopened the controversy over whether the Supreme Court should be entirely distinct from, or constituted as a division of the Federal Court by taking issue with the White Paper proposal of a separate Supreme Court. According to Hoare, the establishment of two courts, "neither subordinate to the other, but each exercising a jurisdiction which, however carefully defined, must almost inevitably from time to time overlap that of the other, is likely to lead to grave difficulties. ... Undignified conflicts may ensue, which will detract from the prestige and reputation of both."[82] Hoare suggested, therefore, that the Joint Committee consider a provision which would enable the Legislature to extend the jurisdiction of the Federal Court "rather than to establish a new and (in a sense) competing Supreme Court."[83]

Hoare then made some remarks in which he betrayed his underestimation of the intensity of the Indian States' objections to the idea of associating, however remotely, whether then or at some future date, a Supreme Court of Appeal for British India with the Federal Court:

[T]he suggestion for the creation of a Supreme Court separate from the Federal Court was, I think, due in part to the influence of an idea which had taken shape before the question of Federation or of a Federal Court became an immediate issue

[81] Joint Committee on Indian Constitutional Reform: *Minutes of Evidence*, Vol. II-B, *Parliamentary Papers*, VII (1932–1933), p. 1240.

[82] Joint Committee on Indian Constitutional Reform: *Minutes of Evidence*, Vol. II-B, *Parliamentary Papers*, VII (1932–1933), p. 1241.

[83] Joint Committee on Indian Constitutional Reform: *Minutes of Evidence*, Vol. II-B, *Parliamentary Papers*, VII (1932–1933), p. 1241.

and in part to the assumption that it would be impossible to combine the functions of both in one organisation in a manner which would be acceptable to the States. Objections of the latter kind would, I suggest, be largely discounted if, as I assume, provision were made that the Federal Court, when endowed with the functions of a Court of Civil Appeal for British India, should be organised in two divisions, one of which would act as a Federal Court proper and the other as a Court of Civil Appeal.[84]

Although not oblivious to States' fear that to confer upon the Federal Court a jurisdiction extending beyond strictly constitutional issues would tend to push into the background its chief function as the interpreter of the constitution, Hoare expressed

> doubt whether these fears are well-founded, if the right of appeal to the Federal Court, on other than constitutional or Federal matters, were, in addition to limitations based on suit value, to be strictly limited … to cases where some important point of law is involved or where a divergence of opinion among Provincial or State Courts renders a judgment of the highest tribunal desirable.[85]

However, after advancing the division bench argument with regard to the Supreme Court—Federal Court controversy, the Secretary of State for India then announced that acceptance of this modification of the White Paper proposals would preclude the possibility of empowering the Federal Court to entertain criminal appeals, "for the possession of such powers would involve so large an accretion of business not germane to the functions of a Federal Court as to obscure and overweight its primary purpose, and to necessitate an expansion of personnel which might seriously affect its quality, and thus the prestige of the Court as a whole."[86] If, therefore, Indian opinion desired that there should be an appeal from High Court decisions in criminal cases, Hoare believed that "the Court so erected would have to be entirely separated from the Federal Court and subordinate to the latter."[87]

Although Hoare's memorandum precipitated a lengthy discussion of the structure of the central judicature, there was little evidence of any compromise among the dissident interest groups. The States' representatives continued to

[84] Joint Committee on Indian Constitutional Reform: *Minutes of Evidence*, Vol. II-B, *Parliamentary Papers*, VII (1932–1933), p. 1241.

[85] Joint Committee on Indian Constitutional Reform: *Minutes of Evidence*, Vol. II-B, *Parliamentary Papers*, VII (1932–1933), p. 1241, pp. 1241–42.

[86] Joint Committee on Indian Constitutional Reform: *Minutes of Evidence*, Vol. II-B, *Parliamentary Papers*, VII (1932–1933), p. 1241.

[87] Joint Committee on Indian Constitutional Reform: *Minutes of Evidence*, Vol. II-B, *Parliamentary Papers*, VII (1932–1933), p. 1241.

oppose the whole notion of a court of appeal for British India,[88] and, if any change in their attitude became evident during the discussions, it was in the direction of an even greater fear of a central court derogating from the sovereignty of the Princes. For example, directing his remarks to Hoare's proposal that the Federal Court be empowered to hear appeals from State and Provincial High Court decisions which related to the interpretation of federal laws, Sir Akbar Hydari informed the Committee that Hyderabad State

> appreciates the desirability of uniformity in the interpretation of Federal laws and would be prepared to consider favourably any proposal limited to this particular extension in the jurisdiction of the Federal Court ..., provided it were carried out in such a way as to secure that the intervention of the Federal Court was limited to the giving of an opinion on the construction of Federal statutes, the decision of cases being retained by the State Courts.[89]

The States, it seems, were willing to sound out the Federal Court's opinion on the interpretation of federal legislation, but insisted on reserving to themselves the option of accepting or rejecting the decision of the Federal Court. The Princes sought a central court which, in the important area of the interpretation of federal law, would function as hardly more than an advisory board.

Finally, close scrutiny of the *Minutes of Evidence and Records of the Joint Committee* discloses that the British Indian representatives added little to what they had said previously about the structure and jurisdiction of the central judiciary. Nothing significant was said with reference to Hoare's suggestion of a combined Federal—Supreme Court, and comment on his proposal that State and Provincial High Court decisions bearing upon the interpretation of federal law be brought under the appellate jurisdiction of the Federal Court was limited largely to arguments that Hoare should have included matters pertaining to the Concurrent, as well as Federal List.[90]

---

[88] See, e.g., Sir Akbar Hydari's comments in Joint Committee on Indian Constitutional Reform: *Minutes of Evidence*, Vol. II-B, *Parliamentary Papers*, VII (1932–1933), p. 1290, and Memorandum No. 21 submitted by Sir Maqbool Mahmood, K. M. Panikkar and Dr. P. K. Sen on behalf of the Chamber of Princes, *Minutes of Evidence*, Vol. II-A, *Parliamentary Papers*. VI (1932–1933), p. 278.

[89] Joint Committee on Indian Constitutional Reform: *Records*, Vol. III, *Parliamentary Papers*, IX (1932–1933), p. 171.

[90] Hoare, however, reasoned that matters in the concurrent field "are not really Federal; they are really Provincial. They are placed in the concurrent field merely to secure uniformity of legislation." *Minutes of Evidence*, Vol. II-B, p. 1246. Since the States were not to be involved in the concurrent field, Hoare thought it wise to restrict the appellate jurisdiction of the Federal Court to matters in which the Provinces and States would be jointly concerned. *Minutes of Evidence*, Vol. II-B, p. 1254.

The deliberations of the Joint Committee culminated in the publishing in November, 1934, of the *Report of the Joint Committee on Indian Constitutional Reform.*[91] The *Report* indicates general acceptance by the Committee of the White Paper scheme, as modified by Sir Samuel Hoare's memorandum. That is, the Joint Committee recommended that if the Federal Legislature decided to establish a court of appeal for British India, "this would most conveniently be effected by an extension of the jurisdiction of the Federal Court."[92] It was also recommended to Parliament that the appellate jurisdiction of the Federal Court be extended to include the interpretation by State and Provincial High Courts of federal laws for, in the opinion of the Joint Committee, "it is essential that there should be some authoritative tribunal in India which can secure a uniform interpretation of federal laws throughout the whole of the Federation."[93] However, after taking note of the concern of the Princes over further derogations from their sovereignty, the Joint Committee felt compelled to emphasize that

> the appellate jurisdiction of the Federal Court, so far as regards an Indian State, arises from the voluntary act of the Ruler himself, viz., his accession to the Federation; the jurisdiction is in no sense imposed on him *ab extra*. This being so, and since it is proposed that all appeals to the Federal Court should be in the form of a Special Case to be stated by the Court appealed from, we think the position of the States would be appropriately safeguarded if it were provided that the granting of leave to appeal by the Federal Court were in the form of Letters of Request, directed to the Ruler of the State to be transmitted by him to the Court concerned.[94]

Although this recommendation represents something less than what the States wanted,[95] it does indicate extraordinary deference to the Princes and demonstrates to what limits the Joint Committee was willing to go to arrive at a Federal Court which would be at least palatable from the States' point of view.

Only concerning one matter did the Joint Committee *Report* depart significantly from both the White Paper and the Hoare memorandum, this being the question of criminal appeals. Whereas the White Paper in paragraph 166

---

[91] *Parliamentary Papers*, VI (1933–1934). Paragraphs 322–330 pertain to the structure of the central judiciary.

[92] *Parliamentary Papers*, VI (1933–1934), paragraph 329.

[93] *Parliamentary Papers*, VI (1933–1934), paragraph 325.

[94] *Parliamentary Papers*, VI (1933–1934), paragraph 325.

[95] The Rulers argued that refusal by a State Court to grant leave to appeal to the Federal Court should be treated as final. *Parliamentary Papers*, VI (1933–1934), paragraph 325.

recommended a carefully defined right of appeal to the Supreme Court in criminal cases, and Hoare suggested that the Federal Legislature be empowered to erect an entirely separate Court of Criminal Appeal, the Joint Committee rejected both suggestions. This decision was reached after the Joint Committee concluded that under the prevailing system, "the rights of a condemned man seem to be very fully safeguarded, and we think that no good purpose would be served by adding yet another Court to which appeals can be brought."[96]

The final stage in the evolution of an all-India court was the drafting of, debate in Parliament on, and the passage of the Government of India Act, 1935. Except for one major amendment and certain other changes of not very considerable importance, the provisions in the 1935 Act relative to the central judicature reflect acceptance by Parliament of the White Paper proposals, as modified by the Joint Parliamentary Committee.

The Act provided for a Federal Court with original and appellate jurisdiction, but the nature and scope of this jurisdiction was made to depend upon whether the parties to a justiciable dispute were Provinces or States.[97] The Court was granted a relatively broad jurisdiction, both original and appellate, over disputes involving the Provinces, and over the Provincial High Courts. But with regard to the Federated States and the State High Courts, the reach of the Federal Court was restricted by the reluctance of the Rulers to invest it with the authority necessary to settle disputes to which they would be parties. By way of illustration, the Federal Court was obliged to follow the extraordinary procedure of sending out "letters of request" to the Rulers of the States asking for the execution of its orders,[98] thus treating the State Courts, which were supposed to be subordinate to it, as though they were foreign courts belonging to an entirely different sovereignty.

Further, it was provided that from any decision of the Federal Court given in the exercise of its original jurisdiction, and from decisions relating to the constitutional rights of the Federation and its constituent units, or of the units inter se, an appeal existed without leave, and in any other case with leave of the Federal Court or of His Majesty in Council, to the Judicial Committee in London.[99]

Conspicuously absent in the 1935 Act was any provision for appeal to the Federal Court in all cases affecting the interpretation of federal laws. Hence, the interpretation of federal law was left to the High Courts of British India and

---

[96] *Parliamentary Papers*, VI (1933–1934), paragraph 330.
[97] Government of India Act, 1935 [25&26 Geo. 5], Sections 204, 205, 207.
[98] Government of India Act, 1935 [25&26 Geo. 5], Section 211.
[99] Government of India Act, 1935 [25&26 Geo. 5], Section 208.

the States, thus providing no remedy for the bewildering variety of interpretations which Hoare and others feared might ensue. However, the Act did seek to
bring about some degree of uniformity by providing that the law declared by
the Federal Court and by any judgment of the Privy Council concerning matters
with respect to which the Federal Legislature had power to make laws, should be
followed by all courts in British India and in the States.[100]

In accordance with the recommendations of the Joint Parliamentary
Committee, the Federal Legislature was empowered, but with the previous sanction of the Governor-General, to enlarge the appellate jurisdiction of the Federal
Court so as to embrace civil appeals from the High Courts of British India, and
to cut off direct appeals from the High Courts to the Privy Council with or without special leave.[101] In the event that the Federal Legislature would do this, the
Federal Court would then sit in two divisions, one dealing with Federal matters
and the other with civil appeals from the Provinces.[102]

It is clear that the Federal Court provided for in the Government of India Act,
1935 fell far short of the hopes of Sir Hari Singh Gour and others who had long
sought the creation of a central judicial tribunal. The Federal Court was neither
a court of criminal appeal, nor in any sense the forum for the final disposition of
Indian appeals. Not only were British Indian High Court decisions still appealable to the Privy Council, but, instead of in any way reducing the number of such
appeals, the 1935 Act actually extended the jurisdiction of the Privy Council by
providing that decisions handed down by the Federal Court in the exercise of its
original jurisdiction were subject to appeal to the Privy Council. The proponents
of a Supreme Court were able to secure only a provision investing the Federal
Legislature with power to transfer to the Federal Court the appellate functions
of the Judicial Committee at some future date.

Undoubtedly, the opposition of the States to the establishment of a Supreme
Court for British India was one factor which serves to explain, in part at least, the

---

[100] Government of India Act, 1935 [25&26 Geo. 5], Section 212.

[101] Winston Churchill, a critic of countless features of the 1935 Act, was especially
unhappy with this provision enabling the Legislature to oust the jurisdiction of the Privy
Council: "Of course, one does not want to have the Privy Council here oppressed by an
immense volume of litigation coining across the Indian Ocean and, after a long process
both of time and space, arriving to be decided here; but I happen to know that the right
of appeal to the Privy Council is deeply valued by our Indian fellow subjects. Till they
have been taught worse manners by their new masters they will, no doubt, greatly value
the power of appealing to what is the most august Court that has ever been in existence
in modern times so far as justice between man and man is concerned." *Parliamentary
Debates*, Vol. 300 (1934–1935), col. 150.

[102] Government of India Act, 1935, Section 214.

failure of the 1935 Act to create immediately such a court and to reduce appeals to the Judicial Committee. However, it must be noted that while the matter of a Supreme Court inevitably became entangled with the debate over the nature and jurisdiction of a Federal Court, the introduction of the idea of a Federal Court at the First Session of the Round Table Conference in 1930 had really no bearing on the pros and cons of the Supreme Court proposal other than raising the question of whether the Federal Court and Supreme Court should be one or two institutions. In other words, the case for and against a Supreme Court of appeal for British India continued to depend upon the same merits or demerits as existed without regard to the question of federation. A Supreme Court had nothing to do with the federal scheme, and involved only the question of whether it was expedient and desirable to eliminate or restrict appeals to the Privy Council.

Not only would it be incorrect to blame the States' intransigence for the failure of the 1935 Act to provide for an all-India judicial tribunal with a broad, not purely federal jurisdiction, but in view of the apparent willingness of the British Government in the early 1930s to affect a reduction in Indian appeals to the Privy Council by transferring such appeals to an indigenous appellate court, it would be erroneous to argue that the colonial power denied this measure of judicial independence to India.

On the basis of the evidence adduced here, one is compelled to conclude that greater strides in the direction of judicial autonomy were not affected by the Government of India Act of 1935 largely because the demand for change or reform in the higher judicial structure was not accorded a prominent place on the agenda of Indian nationalist demands. That greater significance was attached to other more primary institutional and political reforms explains in part this attitude of the nationalist leaders. But it seems that equally as important a factor was the high regard in which the Privy Council was held by Indian leaders of this period. This does not imply, of course, that every Privy Council decision affecting Indian interests was lauded in India as entirely sound and just, but it does indicate that the Judicial Committee of the Privy Council earned a reputation for integrity and impartiality which put it in a category apart from other colonial institutions. Indeed, the argument most difficult to counter by those who from 1921 to 1935 sought the establishment of an indigenous appellate court was that the Judicial Committee had over the years established an enviable record as India's ultimate court of appeal, and that it was in India's interests, for the time being at least, to maintain its ties with the Privy Council.

2 The Federal Court of India
1937–1950

It is the purpose of this chapter to survey the history of the Federal Court[1] from October 1, 1937—the date of its formal inauguration—until January 26, 1950, when the Federal Court was replaced by the present Supreme Court of India. Special attention will be accorded to the Federal Court's jurisdiction and, though it would be impossible to examine within the confines of one chapter every decision rendered by the Federal Court, an effort will be made to discuss those decisions which can be regarded as representative of the types of cases which reached the Federal Court, as well as those which are especially noteworthy because of their public or political importance. Examined also will be the nature of the relationship which prevailed until 1949 between India's highest judicial tribunal and the Judicial Committee of the Privy Council. Other matters receiving attention here include a summary of the efforts of those Indian legislators and publicists who sought an enlargement of the jurisdiction of the Federal Court, the response of the Imperial Government to those efforts, and, finally, the impact of national independence on the Federal Court.

Although the federation of the Native States and the Provinces of British India envisaged by the Government of India Act of 1935 was not yet a reality—and was destined never to materialize—the Federal Court was inaugurated on October 1, 1937, on which date the Viceroy administered the oath of allegiance to the Court's first three judges: Chief Justice Sir Maurice Gwyer, and puisne

---

[1] Designated officially as the "Federal Court" until August 15, 1947, and as the "Federal Court of India" thereafter, until replaced by the Supreme Court of India on January 26, 1950.

judges Sir Shah Muhammad Sulaiman and Mukund Ramrao Jayakar. Gwyer was an Englishman who had no previous experience in India but had been involved in various stages of the preparation of the 1935 Act; Sulaiman was a Muslim who had earned distinction as Chief Justice of the Allahabad High Court, and Jayakar was a Hindu and a successful Bombay advocate. During the ten years in which the British were responsible for appointing judges of the Federal Court, the Chief Justice was always English and the puisne judges at all times a Muslim and a Hindu.[2]

Judges were appointed by the Crown from among those who had been (i) for at least five years a High Court judge, or (ii) a barrister or advocate of ten years' standing, or (iii) a pleader in a High Court of ten years' standing.[3] In order to qualify for the Chief Justiceship, however, one must have had fifteen instead of ten years' qualification, and had to be a barrister, advocate or pleader, or have been one when first appointed a judge.[4] It is evident that this latter provision was designed to exclude members of the judicial branch of the Indian Civil Service from the pinnacle of judicial rank.[5] Judges held office until age sixty-five, and could be removed only on the ground of misbehavior or of mental or bodily infirmity, and, at that, only after the Privy Council on reference by

[2] Gwyer retired in 1943 and was replaced by Sir William Patrick Spens. Sulaiman died in 1941 and was replaced by Sir Muhammad Zafrulla Khan. When the latter resigned in June 1947 he was succeeded by Sir Saiyid Fazl Ali. In 1939 Jayakar left the Federal Court to accept an appointment to the Judicial Committee of the Privy Council, and was replaced on the Federal Court by Srinivasa Varadachariar. The latter retired in 1946 and was succeeded by Sir Harilal J. Kania. Two days before independence Chief Justice Spens resigned, and the then senior-most puisne judge, Kania, became the first Indian to hold India's highest judicial office. (It should be noted, however, that Varadachariar served very briefly as acting Chief Justice in 1943 between the date of Gwyer's retirement and the arrival in India of Spens.) When Kania became Chief Justice, Patanjali Sastri was appointed a puisne judge. For brief periods during absences of permanent judges, Sir John Beaumont, Sir Torick Ameer Ali, and Francis George Rowland served as acting judges.

Although provision was made in the 1935 Act for the appointment of as many as six puisne judges, the strength of the Court from 1937 to 1947 was three judges, inclusive of the Chief Justice. It was raised to five in 1948 with the appointment of Mehr Chand Mahajan and Bijan Kumar Mukerjea, and to six in 1950 when Sudhi Ranjan Das was elevated to the Federal Court from his post as Chief Justice of the East Punjab High Court.

[3] Government of India Act, 1935, Section 200(3)(a)(b)(c).

[4] Government of India Act, 1935, Section 200(3)(i)(ii).

[5] Arthur Berriedale Keith, *A Constitutional History of India: 1600–1935* (second edition; Allahabad: Central Book Depot, 1961), p. 420, and Naresh Chandra Roy, *The Constitutional System of India* (Calcutta: Calcutta University Press, 1937), pp. 330–331.

the Crown had so recommended. Their salaries, allowances, leave, and pension provisions were determined by the Crown, and could not be varied after their appointment to their disadvantage.[6]

When compared with the highest judicial tribunals of other, even smaller, nations, India's Federal Court was hardly a busy one, for, during the course of its twelve and one-quarter year existence, it handed down only one hundred and thirty-five decisions and four advisory opinions.[7] Included in these totals are the applications for leave to appeal to the Privy Council from decisions of the Federal Court, which might more accurately be classified as other than "decisions." On the other hand, the Federal Court on several occasions disposed of more than one appeal in a single judgment, as, e.g., in *King Emperor* v. *Sibnath Banerjee*,[8] where nine separate appeals were heard and decided in one judgment. In any event, it is clear that the Federal Court handled very few cases each year. Indeed, it appears that the Court was in session on an average of less than thirty days per year.[9]

This paucity of judicial business is explained largely in view of the very limited powers conferred upon the Federal Court by the 1935 Act, as will be quite evident in the pages which follow. The Court was given an exclusive original jurisdiction in disputes between the Central Government and the constituent units, but the failure of the all-India federation to come into being meant that the full scope of this jurisdiction was never exercised. It had an advisory jurisdiction, but was called upon only four times for advisory opinions. Finally, the Court exercised a limited constitutional appellate jurisdiction. Also, though this latter jurisdiction accounted for over 90 per cent of the cases which were decided by the Federal Court, this jurisdiction could not be exercised unless a High Court certified that one of its decisions involved a substantial question of law as to the interpretation of the 1935 Act. In other words, the Federal Court had no authority to intervene, on its own initiative, with any activity of a lower court.

---

[6] Government of India Act, 1935, Section 201. Members of the Federal Court received substantial salaries: the Chief Justice received 7,000 rupees per month, and the puisne judges 5,500 rupees per month.

[7] This is the number of decisions and advisory opinions reported in the *Federal Court Reports* (hereafter F.C.R.). Federal Court decisions were privately reported in a number of journals, but the F.C.R. is the official source.

[8] (1944) F.C.R. 1.

[9] In 1946, e.g., the Federal Court was in session twenty-six days, during which time it heard fourteen cases and delivered eleven judgments. *Legislative Assembly Debates*, I (1947), February 10, 1947, p. 352.

It was, of course, the anticipated federation which was the *raison d'etre* for the Federal Court, for the framers of the 1935 Act recognized that such a court was essential in a federal system. Though the subcontinent-wide federation was not realized, a factor which accounts, in part at least, for the limited role played by the Federal Court,[10] it should be noted that the relationship of the Provinces of British India and the Centre after 1937 was of a federal nature, and, on a number of occasions the Federal Court, especially under its appellate jurisdiction, was confronted with cases which called for a delimitation of the respective jurisdictions and powers of the Centre and the Provinces. While one should be wary of exaggerating the importance of this aspect of the Court's work—this did mark the first time in the history of British India that an indigenous judicial tribunal exercised a jurisdiction of this nature.

Jurisdiction of the Federal Court

Original jurisdiction. In any dispute between the Central Government and a Province, or between two Provinces, which involved any question of law or fact on which the existence or extent of a legal right depended, the Federal Court exercised an exclusive original jurisdiction.[11] However, in the exercise of this jurisdiction the Court could pronounce only a "declaratory judgment," which meant that the Court lacked authority to give effect to a decision.[12] Furthermore, if the decision turned on an interpretation of the 1935 Act or of an Order of

[10] Even if the Federation had materialized, there is some doubt whether the workload of the Federal Court would have increased appreciably, for an appeal from a High Court in a Federated State was to have been "by way of special case to be stated for the opinion of the Federal Court by the High Court" (Government of India Act, 1935, Section 207(2)). Thus the initiative for an appeal was to have been taken by the High Court, and the Federal Court, after hearing the appeal, could have offered only its "opinion."

Moreover, in the event that the Federal Court was in need of assistance from the High Court of the Federated State, the Federal Court was to have caused "letters of request in that behalf to be sent to the Ruler of the State, and the Ruler shall cause such communication to be made to the High Court or to any judicial or civil authority as the circumstances may require" (Government of India Act, 1935, Section 211). There was nothing, however, which would have compelled a Ruler to comply with the matters mentioned in a "letter of request."

[11] Government of India Act, 1935, Section 204(1).

[12] Government of India Act, 1935, Section 204(2). Though the Federal Court could not enforce a decree, Section 210(1) provided that "[a]ll authorities, civil and judicial, throughout the Federation, shall act in aid of the Federal Court."

Council made thereunder, an appeal could be taken to the Privy Council as a matter of right.[13] Thus decisions rendered under this jurisdiction were not necessarily final pronouncements on the matter in dispute.

Three times the Federal Court was called upon to exercise this jurisdiction, twice to settle a dispute between a Province and the Centre, and once to hear the complaints against the Province of Bihar of a plaintiff who claimed to be the "Legal Ruler of Ramgarh State." In the first case,[14] the Government of the United Provinces sought a declaration from the Federal Court that the Cantonments Act of 1924, under which the Central Government had realized certain revenues, was *ultra vires* the Indian Legislature when passed. However, finding the impugned legislation *intra vires*, the suit was dismissed.

The second case, *The Governor-General in Council* v. *The Province of Madras*,[15] was unusual in that the major question submitted for a judicial determination— whether certain provisions of the Madras General Sales Tax Act of 1939 encroached upon the authority of the Central Legislature—had been decided by the Federal Court under its appellate jurisdiction a year earlier in favor of the Province of Madras.[16] From this earlier decision the Central Government had sought from the Federal Court leave to appeal to the Privy Council, but this had been denied.[17] Thus, in the present case, the Central Government, by instituting a suit under the Federal Court's original jurisdiction, was attempting not to persuade the Court to reverse its earlier decision, but in fact was attempting to circumvent the Federal Court, for from a decision under its original jurisdiction an appeal lay as of right to the Judicial Committee. The members of the Court were quite aware of the motives of the Central Government, and the suit was dismissed with one sentence: "We agree that substantially the same issue is raised in the present suit as in the appeal last year and we see no reason to modify the decision which we then gave."[18] The Centre then immediately exercised its right of appeal to the Privy Council, but the ruling of the Federal Court was affirmed by the Privy Council in *Governor-General in Council* v. *Province of Madras*.[19]

[13] Government of India Act, 1935, Section 208(a).

[14] *The United Provinces* v. *The Governor-General in Council*, (1939) F.C.R. 124.

[15] (1943) F.C.R. 1.

[16] *The Province of Madras* v. *Boddu Paidanna & Sons*, (1942) F.C.R. 90.

[17] *The Province of Madras* v. *Boddu Paidanna & Sons*, (1942) F.C.R. 90, 109. Appeals to the Privy Council are discussed as follows, pp. 75–83.

[18] *The Governor-General in Council* v. *The Province of Madras*, (1943) F.C.R. 1, 5.

[19] (1945) F.C.R. 179 P.C. As all Privy Council decisions on appeals from the Federal Court were reprinted in the Federal Court Reports, this form of citation will be used throughout this chapter whenever Privy Council decisions are discussed.

In *Ramgarh State* v. *The Province of Bihar*,[20] not only the first decision which concerned matters relating to India's independent status but also the first and only to involve a "State," the plaintiff, who identified himself as the "Legal Ruler of Ramgarh State" sought to obtain a declaration that Ramgarh was an "Acceding State," hoping thereby to end what he regarded as encroachments on his sovereignty by the Province of Bihar. The Federal Court, after noting that its original jurisdiction was limited to disputes involving the Dominion, the Provinces or the Acceding States,[21] proceeded to determine whether Ramgarh was in fact an "Acceding State." As the India (Provisional Constitution) Order of 1947 provided that an Indian State shall be deemed to have acceded to the Dominion "if the Governor-General has signified his acceptance of an Instrument of Accession executed by the Ruler thereof,"[22] and in view of the disclosure that the plaintiff had tried but failed to gain such recognition, the Court concluded that the plaintiff's willingness to sign an Instrument of Accession was insufficient to bring Ramgarh within the definition of an Acceding State. Accordingly, the Court declared that it had no jurisdiction to entertain the suit, which was dismissed without any consideration of the plaintiff's grievances.

There is no evidence that any of these three decisions handed down by the Federal Court under its original jurisdiction merit classification as either of great public importance or of long-term significance. The few notable decisions which the Federal Court had occasion to render came in exercise of its appellate jurisdiction.

Constitutional appellate jurisdiction. Not only the bulk of the work but also the most important decisions of the Federal Court were handed down under the authority of Section 205, which made provision for an appeal to the Federal Court "from any judgment, decree or final order of a High Court in British India, *if the High Court certifies* that the case involves a substantial question of law as to the interpretation of this Act or any Order in Council made thereunder. ..."[23] At one time it was thought that on a constitutional issue a litigant should have

[20] (1948) F.C.R. 79.

[21] Initially, the phraseology employed in Section 204 was "Federated States." But with the advent of independence, the 1935 Act, though it continued to be the framework of Indian government until 1950, was modified by the India (Provisional Constitution) Order, 1947. Many of the sections were reworded and new terminology was substituted for old. Hence, for "Federated States" was substituted "Acceding States," "His Majesty" was dropped in favor of "Governor-General."

[22] Government of India Act, 1935, as adapted by the India (Provisional Constitution) Order, 1947, Section 6.

[23] Government of India Act, 1935, as adapted by the India (Provisional Constitution) Order, 1947, Section 205(1). Emphasis supplied.

a right of appeal to the Federal Court, but this idea was dropped by the Joint Committee on Indian Constitutional Reform because of the fear that "in a country where litigation is so much in favour, this might result in an excessive number of unnecessary appeals."[24]

It was the "duty of every High Court in British India to consider in every case whether or not any such question is involved and of its own motion to give or withhold a certificate accordingly."[25] However, once the certificate was granted by the High Court, a litigant was able to appeal not only the constitutional issue, but also, with the permission of the Federal Court, any other issue involved. But after a decision of the Federal Court in the exercise of this appellate jurisdiction, a still dissatisfied party was then free to request the Federal Court for leave to appeal to the Privy Council or, if this failed, he could apply to the Privy Council for special leave.

In the very first decision of the Federal Court it was emphasized that this constitutional appellate jurisdiction could be exercised *only* if the High Court granted the requisite certificate.[26] In the absence of a certificate, the Federal Court was unable to interfere since it possessed no "inherent powers" which would give it a revisional jurisdiction over High Court decisions.[27] Later in 1939 the Court took the next logical step and ruled that under authority of Section 205 it possessed no inherent power to entertain an application for special leave to appeal from cases in which the High Court had refused to issue a certificate.[28] Furthermore, should the High Court refuse the certificate, the Federal Court had no authority to investigate the reasons for such refusal;[29] indeed, there was no obligation on the part of the High Court to offer the reasons which prompted this refusal.[30] Even when it was alleged that the refusal

---

[24] *Report of the Joint Committee on Indian Constitutional Reform*, vol. I, paragraph 325, *Parliamentary Papers*, VI (1933–1934).

[25] Government of India Act, 1935, Section 205(1).

[26] *Pashupati Bharti v. The Secretary of State for India in Council and Another*, (1939) F.C.R. 13.

[27] *Pashupati Bharti v. The Secretary of State for India in Council and Another*, (1939) F.C.R. 13, 15.

[28] *Lakhpat Ram v. Behari Lal Misir and Others*, (1939) F.C.R. 121, 122.

[29] *Kishori Lal v. Governor in Council, Punjab*, (1940) F.C.R. 12, 14.

[30] *K. L. Gauba v. The Hon'ble The Chief Justice and Judges of the High Court of Judicature at Lahore and Another*, (1941) F.C.R. 54, 56. The Privy Council, however, thought otherwise, for in a civil appeal from the Calcutta High Court it stated that since its jurisdiction was excluded (at least temporarily) if a High Court certified that a civil case involved a substantial question of constitutional law, the High Court, whether it grants or withholds the certificate, should record this determination not only for the information of the parties, but also to assist the appellate courts. *Errol MacKay and Others v. Oswald Forbes*, A.I.R. 1940 P.C. 16.

of a High Court to grant a certificate was "perverse, deliberate, illegal and oppressive," and that its refusal was a contempt of the Federal Court because the High Court had "deliberately deprived this [Federal] Court of a jurisdiction which Parliament has entrusted to it,"[31] the Federal Court merely acknowledged its complete inability to interfere.

Though the Court was powerless in the absence of a certificate, once the certificate was granted, "the case is at large and the appellant is not necessarily restricted in arguing his appeal to what may be called the constitutional issue."[32] Thus, although Section 205 provided that questions other than those relating to constitutional issues could be raised in the Federal Court only with the express permission of the Federal Court, in this very first decision the liberal view was taken that all findings of the lower court could be reopened and examined afresh as a matter of course, and without special consent from the Court in each case.[33] This did not mean, however, that the Federal Court regarded lightly High Court decisions, especially where the High Court had exercised discretion. As early as 1940 the Federal Court announced that it would not substitute its discretion for that of the High Court "unless it appears that the High Court did not apply its mind at all to the question, or acted capriciously or in disregard of any legal principle, or was influenced by some extraneous considerations wrong in law."[34]

Also, in 1940, the Court had occasion to point out that once jurisdiction to hear an appeal is vested in the Court by the grant of a certificate, no subsequent event could divest it of such jurisdiction: "A certificate is the key which unlocks the door into this Court, and a litigant who has once passed through that door cannot afterwards be ejected by the happening of events outside and beyond his control."[35] The constitutional issue in this case concerned a disputed section

[31] K. L. Gauba v. The Hon'ble The Chief Justice and Judges of the High Court of Judicature at Lahore and Another, (1941) F.C.R. 54, 55. In an obiter dictum, the Court noted that irrespective of its limited powers, it was not impressed by the appellant's argument: "The law of contempt of Court has at times been stretched very far in British India; but no one has ever contended that a Court could use its powers to punish for contempt for the purpose of extending its jurisdiction in other matters" (p. 56).

[32] Pashupati Bharti v. The Secretary of State for India in Council and Another, (1939) F.C.R. 13, 15.

[33] Three years later, however, the Court ruled that "the appellant is entitled with the leave of this Court to raise any point in his own defence" (Niharendu Dutt Majumdar v. The King Emperor, (1942) F.C.R. 38, 42).

[34] Jaigobind Singh and Others v. Lachmi Narain Ram and Others, (1940) F.C.R. 61, 64.

[35] Subhanand Chowdhary and Another v. Apurba Krishna Mitra and Another, (1940) F.C.R. 31, 35–36.

of an enactment by the Bihar Legislature. After the certificate had been granted, but before the Federal Court heard the appeal, the Act was repealed and then immediately re-enacted with retrospective effect. Since the new Act had received the assent of the Governor-General, the question whether the Provincial Act encroached upon the legislative competence of the Central Legislature was no longer justiciable.[36] Hence, the Advocate-General of India, who appeared on behalf of the respondents, argued that the disputed provision was no longer open to judicial challenge, for, since the later Act was retrospective in its effects, the certificate had become "infructuous" and the constitutional question of no more than "academic interest."[37] The unanimous Court, however, apparently feeling that the Act had been repealed and re-enacted for the purpose of eliminating its scrutiny, held that it could never "lightly adopt a construction which would have this result, that an appeal properly begun and continued in this court was suddenly, by the action of a Provincial Legislature, taken out of our jurisdiction and transferred to the jurisdiction of the Judicial Committee."[38]

Although the Federal Court came to have jurisdiction in a constitutional appeal only if the condition of a certificate was satisfied, on a number of occasions, especially in later years, the Court criticized certain High Courts for granting certificates in instances in which the Federal Court believed none should have been issued. In *J. K. Gas Plant Manufacturing Co., (Rampur) Ltd. and Others* v. *The King Emperor*,[39] the Federal Court emphasized that a certificate should not be issued unless the appeal was in fact from a "judgment, decree or final order," i.e., unless the decision of the High Court was a final determination of the rights of the parties:

> It is not enough merely that the case before the High Court should involve a substantial question of law as to the interpretation of the Constitution Act or any Order in Council made thereunder. Whilst this Court accepts the position that it is not for this Court to question certificates granted by High Courts or to permit

---

[36] Government of India Act, 1935, Section 107(2). Cf. *Shyamakant Lal* v. *Rambhajan Singh and Others*, (1939) F.C.R. 193, 197.

[37] *Subhanand Chowdhary and Another* v. *Apurba Krishna Mitra and Another*, (1940) F.C.R. 31, 33, 35.

[38] *Subhanand Chowdhary and Another* v. *Apurba Krishna Mitra and Another*, (1940) F.C.R. 31, 36. If the Court had accepted the Advocate General's argument, the case would have gone directly to the Privy Council because, without a constitutional issue, it would have been an ordinary civil appeal within the category of cases appealable to the Privy Council. Cf. *Surendra Prasad Narain Singh* v. *Sri Gajadhar Prasad Sahu Trust Estate and Others*, (1940) F.C.R. 39, 44–45.

[39] *J. K. Gas Plant Manufacturing Co., (Rampur) Ltd. and Others* v. *The King Emperor* (1947) F.C.R. 141.

an appeal to this Court against any refusal to grant a certificate, this Court does hold itself at liberty—it may indeed be the duty of this Court—to determine, if necessary, whether the appeal is really from a "judgment, decree or final order," so as to ensure that this Court has jurisdiction in the matter under the provisions of s. 205. A study of the provisions of sub-s.(2) of s. 205 seems to indicate important considerations why this Court should not be asked to deal with an appeal until the High Court has finally disposed of the case and the rights of the parties are fully determined.[40]

In this particular case, these were words of admonition, and the Court, although not fully convinced that any of the appeals involved here were from judgments, decrees or final orders, went ahead and heard the appeals. But in the very next case the Court arrived at the conclusion that the conditions of Section 205 had not been satisfied, and the appeal was dismissed.[41]

On the other hand, in a 1942 sedition appeal, although of the opinion that the "constitutional matter is of such minute dimensions as not to be readily discerned,"[42] the Court not only heard the appeal but ordered the acquittal of the appellant.

If these cases in which the Federal Court questioned the *bona fides* of a certificate indicate a degree of judicial self-restraint, other cases indicate that the Court was more inclined to adopt a quite liberal interpretation of its jurisdiction under Section 205. For example, in the 1944 case of *Rao Bahadur Kunwar Lal Singh* v. *The Central Provinces and Berar*,[43] the Court found nothing to prevent the hearing of an appeal from the judgment of a single judge of a High Court, even though, from a single judgment, a party could appeal as of right to a Divisional Bench of the High Court. The Court acknowledged that it was the practice of the Privy Council to refuse to entertain an appeal until the litigant had made use of his right of appeal to the Divisional Bench, but, since Section 205 did not impose this rule on the Federal Court, it held that all other conditions being satisfied, a certificate "not only may but should be granted" from the judgment of a single judge.[44]

Probably the best illustration, however, of how by a liberal interpretation of its powers the Court was able to extend its reach was the ruling in a 1939

---

[40] (1947) F.C.R. 178.

[41] *S. Kuppuswami Rao* v. *The King*, (1947) F.C.R. 180, 192. Cf. *Mohammad Amin Brothers Ltd. and Others* v. *Dominion of India and Others*, (1949–1950) F.C.R. 842, and *Rex* v. *Abdul Majid*, (1949) F.C.R. 29.

[42] *Niharendu Dutt Majumdar* v. *The King Emperor*, (1942) F.C.R. 38, 42.

[43] *Rao Bahadur Kunwar Lal Singh* v. *The Central Provinces and Berar* (1944) F.C.R. 284.

[44] *Rao Bahadur Kunwar Lal Singh* v. *The Central Provinces and Berar* (1944) F.C.R. 284, 291. Cf. *Sir Iqbal Ahmad* v. *Allahabad Bench of the Allahabad High Court*, (1949–1950) F.C.R. 813.

appeal that the words "judgment, decree or final order" did not limit its appellate jurisdiction to civil cases, for it could hear criminal appeals also.[45] The 1935 Act made no provision for the exercise of any criminal appellate jurisdiction by the Federal Court, and thus it was assumed that the High Courts would continue to be the final arbiters in criminal cases unless the Judicial Committee was willing to grant special leave to appeal. It must be stressed, however, that before a criminal appeal could reach the Federal Court, the High Court first had to issue the requisite certificate. In other words, a constitutional issue had to be involved. As a criminal case was only rarely compounded by a constitutional issue, the Federal Court was presented with few opportunities to pass upon criminal appeals, although, as will be seen presently, these few included some of the most important decisions ever rendered by the Federal Court. Finally, though it regarded criminal appeals as within its constitutional appellate jurisdiction, it once pointed out that normally "this Court was not a Court of criminal appeal."[46]

Now that the scope of the constitutional appellate jurisdiction has been defined, it may be noted that the most typical case decided by the Federal Court under this jurisdiction was one in which a Provincial or Central enactment was scrutinized in order to determine its constitutional validity. The majority of these cases concerned the vires of Provincial legislation, and turned on a judicial interpretation of the legislative powers set forth in the three lists: the Central legislative list, the Provincial legislative list, and the Concurrent legislative list.[47] In deciding such cases, the Court, early in its history, established principles which it applied throughout, the most important of which was that

> none of the items in the Lists is to be read in a narrow or restricted sense, and that each general word should be held to extend to all ancillary and subsidiary matters which can fairly and reasonably be said to be comprehended in it. We deprecate any attempt to enumerate in advance all the matters which are to be included under any of the more general descriptions; it will be sufficient and much wiser to determine each case as and when it comes before this Court.[48]

---

[45] *Hori Ram Singh* v. *The Crown*, (1939) F.C.R. 159.

[46] *Afzalur Rahman and Others* v. *The King Emperor*, A.I.R. 1943 F.C. 19, 24.

[47] Government of India Act, 1935, Section 100 and Schedule 7.

[48] *The United Provinces* v. *Mst. Atiqa Begum and Others*, (1940) F.C.R. 110, 134–135. An unusual feature of this appeal was that though the parties to this dispute in the High Court were a landlord and a tenant, it was the United Provinces Government which carried the case to the Federal Court. At the High Court level, the Provincial Government had requested that it be added as a party to the litigation. The High Court agreed that since the Government was interested in the outcome of the dispute, it could be admitted as a party. The Federal Court acquiesced after observing that "apparently the defendants were too poor to think of preferring an appeal to the Federal Court" (p. 144).

Furthermore, the mere fact that a Provincial enactment contained provisions bearing upon a subject reserved exclusively to the Central Legislative would not suffice to invalidate the Provincial enactment. The Federal Court applied the principle that if the essence or substance of the impugned enactment related to a matter within the competence of the Provincial Legislature, some trespass or overlap into the jurisdiction of the Central Legislature would not, *ipso facto*, result in a declaration that the legislation was unconstitutional:[49]

> To ascertain the class to which a particular enactment really belongs, we are to look at the primary matter dealt with by it, its subject matter and essential legislative feature. Once the true nature and character of a legislation determine its place in a particular list, the fact that it deals incidently with matters appertaining to other lists is immaterial.[50]

However, where there was a conflict between the provisions of a Provincial and Central enactment, each being in reference to a subject on which it was authorized to legislate, the "principle of repugnancy" was applied, and the provisions of the enactment of the Central Legislature prevailed.[51]

If the most usual case before the Federal Court was one relating to the validity of Central or Provincial legislation, the Federal Court decisions which were most controversial and of the greatest public importance concerned the validity of the sedition, preventive detention, and special criminal court ordinances and legislation promulgated or passed during World War II by the Governor-General and the Central Legislature. Indeed, it seems that all the important ordinances and enactments which owed their existence to the war in Europe and Asia or to the nationalist movement in the subcontinent were tested before the Federal Court under its constitutional appellate jurisdiction.

In the first such case to come before the Federal Court, through the infamous Defence of India Act, 1939,[52] was found to be a valid exercise of power by the

---

[49] A.L.S.P.P.L. *Subrahmanyan Chettiar* v. *Muttuswami Goundan, Advocate-General of Madras,* (1940) F.C.R. 188, and *Bank of Commerce Ltd.* v. *Amulya Krishna Basu Roy Chowdhury; Bank of Commerce Ltd.* v. *Brojo Mal Mitra,* (1944) F.C.R. 126.

[50] *Lakhi Narayan Das* v. *The Province of Bihar,* (1949) F.C.R. 693, 707.

[51] *Bank of Commerce, Ltd.* v. *Kunja Behari Kar and Upendra Chandra Kar,* (1944) F.C.R. 370.

[52] The Defence of India Act was preceded by a proclamation by the Governor-General that a grave emergency existed which threatened the security of India (September 3, 1939), which then enabled the Central Legislature (by virtue of Section 102 of the 1935 Act) to make laws for a Province with respect to any matter enumerated in the Provincial List. Though passed as a war measure, this Act was used primarily to keep the nationalist movement in check during the war.

Central Legislature, the appellant's sedition conviction was set aside after the Court decided that the speech which resulted in his conviction was not of the threatening or dangerous variety contemplated by the Act. The appellant, a member of the Bengal Legislature, had attacked verbally the Governor and the Provincial Ministry for their alleged misuse of the police forces during the Dhaka riots, and had charged the Governor and his ministers with inciting and encouraging communal disturbances. This resulted in the conviction of the appellant in a lower court and an affirmation of this conviction by the Calcutta High Court. The Federal Court, however, after a careful examination of the speech, ordered the acquittal of the appellant after concluding that the speech, although "a frothy and irresponsible performance ..., to describe it as an act of sedition is to do it too great honour."[53]

In the following year, in the celebrated case of *Keshav Talpade* v. *The King Emperor*,[54] probably the most commented upon decision ever handed down by the Federal Court, the notorious Rule 26 of the Defence of India Rules, which authorized detention without trial, was held to be *ultra vires* the rule-making powers conferred on the executive by the Defence of India Act. Rule 26 provided that the Provincial Government,

> if it is satisfied with respect to any particular person that with a view to preventing him from acting in any particular manner prejudicial to the defence of British India, the public safety, the maintenance of public order, His Majesty's relations with foreign powers or Indian States, the maintenance of peaceful conditions in tribal areas, or the efficient prosecution of the war it is necessary so to do, may make an order ... directing that he be detained.

Before declaring the invalidity of Rule 26, the Court removed any doubts others might have entertained that the Court was unaware of the implications of this decision when it observed that although

> we have ... to remember that the country is at war, and that in war as it is known today every Government in the world has found it necessary to arm itself with powers unknown and often unthought of in time of peace ..., we are not on that account relieved from the duty of seeing that the executive government does not seek to exercise powers in excess of those which the Legislature has thought fit to confer upon it, however drastic and far-reaching those powers may be and however great the emergency which they are designed to meet.[55]

[53] *Niharendu Dutt Majumdar* v. *The King Emperor*, (1942) F.C.R. 38, 51.
[54] (1943) F.C.R. 49.
[55] (1943) F.C.R. 49, 62.

The Court then concluded that Rule 26 was invalid because, whereas the Defence of India Act authorized preventive detention of persons *reasonably suspected* of certain wrongdoings, Rule 26 would enable the Central Government or any Provincial Government to detain a person about whom it need have no suspicions, reasonable or unreasonable, that he had acted, was acting, or was about to act in any prejudicial manner at all.[56] Finally, with these apologetic, if not also extraordinary words, the Court concluded its judgment:

> We recognise that our decision may be a cause of inconvenience and possibly of embarrassment, even though temporarily, to the executive authority. We regret that this should be so, especially in these difficult times; but we venture to express an earnest hope that greater care may be taken hereafter to secure that powers of this extraordinary kind which may affect, and indeed have affected, the liberty of so many of the King's subjects in India, may be defined with greater precision and exactitude, so as to reduce to as small a compass as possible the risk that persons may find themselves apprehended and detained without legal warrant.[57]

The immediate significance of this decision can be appreciated by the fact that at approximately the time this decision was rendered, "some 11,700 persons, including Mr. Gandhi and the members of the Congress Working Committee, were in detention" under authority of Rule 26.[58] However, the effect of this ruling was not the release of these 11,700 *detenus*, for the Court was correct in predicting that its decision would be of no more than a temporary inconvenience to the executive authorities. On April 28, 1943, a mere six days after this decision, the Governor-General promulgated an Ordinance,[59] the effect of which was to extend the rule-making power of the Central Government under the Defence of India Act so as to cover the terms of Rule 26. The Ordinance was phrased so as to make this change effective from the date of the Defence of India Act itself, and it was provided that

> no order heretofore made against any person under Rule 26 ... shall be deemed to be invalid or shall be called into question on the ground merely that the said rule purported to confer powers in excess of the powers that might at the time the said rule was made be lawfully conferred by a rule made or deemed to have been made under s. 2 of the Defence of India Act, 1939.

So the effect of the Ordinance was retroactive, and the many thousands of *detenus* were not released.

---

[56] *Keshav Talpade* v. *The King Emperor*, (1943) F.C.R. 68.
[57] *Keshav Talpade* v. *The King Emperor*, (1943) F.C.R. 68, 71.
[58] *Council of State Debates*, II (1943), August 2, 1943, p. 14.
[59] XIV of 1943.

However, in the six-day interim between the *Talpade* decision and the promulgation of the Ordinance, many *detenus* had filed applications for their release, and nine were successful in the Calcutta High Court. The Central Government appealed immediately to the Federal Court, and in the case of *King Emperor* v. *Sibnath Banerjee*[60] the Court, although finding the Ordinance valid, ordered the release of each *detenu* on the ground that before any detention order should be issued, the Provincial Government, i.e., the Governor acting with or without the advice of his ministers, should have applied its mind and become satisfied that detention was necessary in order to prevent the person proceeded against from acting in a manner prejudicial to the matters mentioned in Rule 26. In these cases before the Court the Provincial Government was unable to demonstrate to the satisfaction of the Federal Court that it had reviewed and confirmed in each case the recommendation of the police. The Court then ordered the release of those detained after observing that "it would be difficult to conceive of a more callous disregard of the provisions of the law and of the liberty of the subject."[61]

On June 4, 1943, only a few weeks after the *Sibnath Banerjee* decision, the Federal Court declared invalid the Special Criminal Courts Ordinance (II of 1942), under which, up to April 30, 1943, 23,710 persons had been convicted.[62] This Ordinance had empowered the Provincial Governments to constitute special criminal courts, specify the sentences which each of these courts might impose, prescribe certain rules of procedure to expedite the conduct of trials before these courts, and to that extent exclude from application the provisions of the Code of Criminal Procedure. Furthermore, convictions by such special courts were not to be reviewed by the regular courts, for the jurisdiction of the High Courts was expressly excluded by the terms of this Ordinance. Since the Federal Court could hear an appeal only from a High Court decision, this meant, of course, that the jurisdiction of the Federal Court was excluded also.

Before reaching the Federal Court, the validity of the Ordinance and the legality of sentences passed by special courts had been upheld by all the High Courts in British India with the exception of the Calcutta High Court. Thus it was on appeal by the Central Government from the Calcutta ruling that the Federal Court had an opportunity to pass upon the *vires* of this Ordinance. In finding the Ordinance invalid, the Federal Court based its decision on the view that so long as the Code of Criminal Procedure had not been repealed or, in the least, temporarily suspended from operation, a trial for any alleged crime could

---

[60] (1944) F.C.R. 1.

[61] *King Emperor* v. *Sibnath Banerjee* (1944) F.C.R. 37.

[62] *Council of State Debates*, II (1943), August 2, 1943, p. 19.

be held only by a court constituted under the Code and in accordance with the procedure prescribed therein. In addition, the Federal Court was of the opinion that only the Central Legislature, and not the Governor-General in exercise of his ordinance-making power, could invest a special court with jurisdiction to hold a criminal trial, and that only the Legislature could determine the classes of cases to be tried before such courts.[63]

It came as no surprise when, on the day after the *Benoari Lall* decision was handed down, the Governor-General responded by repealing the 1942 Ordinance, but then, by promulgating another one of the same name,[64] he rewrote most of its essential provisions in light of the Federal Court decision. Significantly, however, the new Ordinance made provision for an appeal from a decision of a Special Criminal Court to one of the regular courts. The new Ordinance also accorded retrospective validity to all sentences which had been passed under the earlier ordinance, and saved cases which were pending final disposition. In the ensuing weeks, a number of appeals reached the Federal Court in which the argument was presented that the new Ordinance did not, and in any event could not, give validity to sentences which had been passed under the earlier, now invalid, ordinance. The appellants argued further that their sentences should be treated as void, or set aside without any examination of the merits of their cases.

All these appeals were disposed of in the judgment in *Piare Dusadh and Others* v. *The King Emperor*.[65] In considering the argument that neither the Governor-General nor the Legislature had the authority to promulgate or enact a measure with such retrospective effect as to declare valid proceedings which had been found invalid earlier by the courts, the Federal Court compared the provisions of the 1935 Act with the due process clauses of the Fifth and Fourteenth Amendments to the Constitution of the United States, and concluded that the former offered much less protection to the individual than the latter. The Court ruled that personal freedom was not protected constitutionally in British India, but was only a principle of "private law" and, as such, was subject to legislative powers and policies.[66] Finding nothing in the 1935 Act to prevent retrospective legislation or ordinances, the Court upheld the validity of the Ordinance.[67]

[63] *The King Emperor* v. *Benoari Lall Sarma and Others*, (1943) F.C.R. 96, 140.

[64] XIX of 1943.

[65] (1944) F.C.R. 61.

[66] *Piare Dusadh and Others* v. *The King Emperor*, (1944) F.C.R. 104–105.

[67] *Piare Dusadh and Others* v. *The King Emperor*, (1944) F.C.R. 104–105, 109. Other Federal Court decisions which concerned convictions by special criminal courts include *R. Subbarayan and Others* v. *The King Emperor*, (1944) F.C.R. 161, *Devkishindas* v. *The King Emperor*, (1944) F.C.R. 165, and *Lieutenant Hector Thomas Huntley* v. *The King Emperor*, (1944) F.C.R. 262.

However, the Federal Court then proceeded to examine each case involved in this appeal, and, finding that certain procedural guarantees were not observed in each instance by the Special Criminal Courts, the Federal Court released some of the *detenus*, and ordered retrial, review or revision of others by the regular courts.

In 1944 the Federal Court again passed upon the validity of an ordinance arising out of the emergency—the Restriction and Detention Ordinance. This Ordinance authorized preventive detention for a number of reasons, one being for reasons connected with the "maintenance of public order." Since detention for this reason was, according to the 1935 Act, a matter on which only a Provincial Legislature could legislate, it was urged that the Ordinance invaded the legislative domains of the Provinces. The Court, however, decided otherwise, after noting that once a proclamation of emergency under Section 102 was made, the powers of the Central Legislature were so enlarged as to embrace Provincial subjects as well. Also the ordinance-making powers, according to the Court, must be regarded as similarly extended.[68]

In the following year, the same appellant again approached the Federal Court and argued that his detention by the Governor of Bihar for reasons connected with the "efficient prosecution of the war" was illegal, since neither the Central nor Provincial Governments had authority under the 1935 Act to issue detention orders for this reason. The Court, however, affirmed his detention order after ruling that the phraseology employed in the 1935 Act—"preventive detention for reasons of State connected with defence"—had essentially the same meaning as the impugned phraseology.[69] The Court then went on to say that though a *detenu* was entitled to challenge the *bona fides* of a detention order by alleging, e.g., that the order was a fraudulent exercise of power or that it was passed for ulterior ends unconnected with reasons such as the maintenance of public order, the burden of substantiating these allegations was on the *detenu* himself.[70] Then, for the first time, the Court explicitly admitted its inability to examine the sufficiency of the grounds for any detention order, although in earlier decisions it had relied upon certain English cases in which this rule was applied.[71]

---

[68] *Basanta Chandra Ghose* v. *The King Emperor*, (1944) F.C.R. 295, 306.

[69] *Basanta Chandra Ghose* v. *The King Emperor*, (1945) F.C.R. 81, 85–86, 295.

[70] But the fact that an order of detention was issued in anticipation of a High Court finding defects in an earlier order would not justify any inference of fraud or abuse of power (*Basanta Chandra Ghose* v. *The King Emperor*, (1945) F.C.R. 89).

[71] *Basanta Chandra Ghose* v. *The King Emperor*, (1945) F.C.R. 89. In this particular case, e.g., the Federal Court had cited *Liverside* v. *Anderson*, (1942) A.C. 206, and *Greene* v. *Secretary of State for Home Affairs*, (1942) A.C. 284.

Soon after the end of the Second World War, the Defence of India Act and related emergency legislation and ordinances were allowed to lapse. However, the end of one type of emergency was soon followed by the advent of another, for in the wake of independence and the partition of the subcontinent, there was communal violence and widespread criminal and otherwise disruptive activities. In an effort to cope with these and related problems, many of the Provinces of independent India passed or promulgated "public safety" or "public order" enactments and ordinances, all of which utilized the device of preventive detention. The validity of several of these measures was tested before the Federal Court.

When faced for the first time with a post-independence preventive detention measure the Court managed to evade the major issues by ruling that the High Court from which the appeal originated should not have certified the case as one fit for appeal to the Federal Court.[72] But then, in quick succession, the Federal Court declared invalid two enactments which authorized preventive detention. In the first of these cases, *Jatindra Nath Gupta* v. *The Province of Bihar*,[73] the Court declared unconstitutional the Bihar Maintenance of Public Order (Amendment) Act on the ground that the power granted to the Governor by the Bihar Legislature, which enabled him to extend and modify periodically the operation of the Act, amounted to an unconstitutional delegation of legislative power. Hence the extension of the Act by the Governor was *ultra vires* and the appellants in the eleven appeals disposed of in this judgment were ordered to be set at liberty.

A few days later, the Court declared invalid the United Provinces Prevention of Black-marketing (Temporary Powers) Act, 1947, which authorized detention without trial of any person who habitually indulged in black-marketing.[74] The Court wasted little time in condemning this legislation, for the 1935 Act, now being used as the Provisional Constitution, permitted the Provinces to employ the weapon of preventive detention only for "reasons connected with the maintenance of public order," and not for discouraging black-marketing. The following extract from its unanimous decision demonstrates, in language too clear to be misunderstood, the Federal Court's distaste for preventive detention.

> It is true that black-marketing in essential commodities may at times lead to a disturbance of public order, but so may, for example, the rash driving of an automobile or the sale of adulterated foodstuffs. Activities such as these are so remote in

[72] *Rex* v. *Abdul Majid*, (1949) F.C.R. 29.
[73] (1949) F.C.R. 29, 595.
[74] *Rex* v. *Basudev*, (1949) F.C.R. 657.

the chain of relation to the maintenance of public order that preventive detention on account of them cannot, in our opinion, fall within the purview of that entry. Preventive detention is a serious invasion of personal liberty, and the power to make laws with respect to it is, in the case of Provincial Legislatures, strictly limited by the condition that such detention must be for reasons connected with the maintenance of public order. The connection must, in our view, be real and proximate, not far-fetched or problematical.[75]

Another decision bearing upon a post-independence preventive detention measure was handed down in the case of *Lakhi Narayan Das* v. *The Province of Bihar*,[76] where at issue was the validity of the Bihar Maintenance of Public Order Ordinance of 1949. Immediately after the ruling in the *Jatindra* case that Bihar's public order legislation was unconstitutional, the Governor responded by promulgating this Ordinance under authority of Section 88 of the Provisional Constitution, which enabled a Governor to promulgate ordinances if the legislature was not in session and if he was "satisfied that circumstances exist which render it necessary for him to take immediate action." The main argument advanced by the appellants was that no circumstances existed as contemplated by the Provisional Constitution which could justify the Ordinance. The Federal Court, however, quickly replied that

this obviously is a matter which is not within the competence of courts to investigate. The language of the section shows clearly that it is the Governor and the Governor alone who has got to satisfy himself as to the existence of circumstances necessitating the promulgation of an Ordinance. The existence of such necessity is not a justiciable matter which the Courts could be called upon to determine by applying an objective test. ... On promulgating of an Ordinance, the Governor is not bound as a matter of law to expound reasons therefore, nor is he bound to prove affirmatively in a court of law that a state of emergency did actually exist.[77]

It is worth noting that during the course of this decision the Court sought to clarify once and for all its powers when preventive detention measures were impugned:

If a particular piece of legislation is entirely within the ambit of the Legislature's authority, there could be nothing arbitrary in it so far as a court of law is concerned. The Courts have nothing to do with the policy of the Legislature or the reasonableness of the legislation.[78]

---

[75] *Rex* v. *Basudev*, (1949) F.C.R. 661.
[76] (1949) F.C.R. 661, 693.
[77] *Lakhi Narayan Das* v. *The Province of* Bihar, (1949) F.C.R. 699–700.
[78] *Lakhi Narayan Das* v. *The Province of* Bihar, (1949) F.C.R. 699–700, 714.

The final decision of the Federal Court which concerned preventive detention was *Machindar Shivaji Mahar* v. *The King*.[79] Here the appellant questioned the validity of his detention under the Central Provinces and Berar Public Safety Act, 1948, which enabled the Provincial executive to detain a person:

> if satisfied that any person is acting or is likely to act in a manner prejudicial to the public safety, order or tranquillity, or is fomenting or inciting strikes with intent to cause or prolong unrest among any group or groups of employees. ...[80]

The appellant argued that the Provincial Government acted in excess of its constitutional powers when it excluded a judicial review of the sufficiency of the reasons for detention by stating merely that it was "satisfied" that the person detained was acting or was likely to act in a manner prejudicial to public safety. As there were, at this time, over ten thousand people under preventive detention in various parts of India, the Federal Court's ruling on this particular point was of no little importance:

> The responsibility for making a detention order rests on the provincial executive, as they alone are entrusted with the duty of maintaining public peace, and it would be a serious derogation from that responsibility if the court were to substitute its judgment for the satisfaction of the executive authority and, to that end, undertake an investigation of the sufficiency of the materials on which such satisfaction was grounded.[81]

The Court went on to state that in preventive detention appeals it could do no more than

> examine the grounds disclosed by the Government to see if they are relevant to the object which the legislation has in view, namely, the prevention of acts prejudicial to public safety and tranquillity, for "satisfaction" in this connection must be grounded on material which is of rationally probative value.[82]

The Court proceeded to examine the grounds communicated to the appellant, which were that he was working for the Communist Party of India, "which is spreading its doctrine of violence in different parts of the country, formenting industrial strikes, causing agrarian unrest, rendering life and property insecure,

---

[79] (1949–1950) F.C.R. 827. This case actually came to the Federal Court under the jurisdiction it inherited from the Privy Council as a result of the Abolition of Privy Council Jurisdiction Act, 1949. It is discussed here because it involves another preventive detention measure.

[80] Section 2(l)(a). Quoted in *Machindar Shivaji Mahar* v. *The King*, (1949–1950) F.C.R. 829.

[81] (1949–1950) F.C.R. 827, 829, 831.

[82] *Machindar Shivaji Mahar* v. *The King*, (1949–1950) F.C.R. 832.

and trying to seize power by violence," and that he was assisting a prominent member of the Party who had "gone underground." The grounds further stated that "from the secret information available to them, the Provincial Government are satisfied that you are likely to go underground and from there guide the various subversive activities of the Communist Party and thus act in a manner prejudicial to the public safety, order and tranquility.[83]

The appellant urged before the Court that in view of the fact that the Communist Party had not been banned in his Province, his alleged membership in the Party could not be regarded as a ground for preventive detention. In disagreeing with the appellant's reasoning, the Court made certain remarks which merit quotation in some length:

> While mere belief in or acceptance of any political ideology may not be a ground for detention under the Act, affiliation to a party which is alleged to be spreading its "doctrine of violence rendering life and property insecure and trying to seize power by violence" may, in certain circumstances, lead to an inference that the person concerned is *likely* to act in a manner prejudicial to the public safety, order or tranquility. The fact that the Party has not been outlawed *is* immaterial, that being a matter of expediency. The allegations regarding the subversive activities of the Party made on the grounds communicated to the appellant ... remain uncontradicted, the appellant having only stated the he was not a member of that Party and did not work for it and that he had always been a "constitutional trade unionist." It must therefore be taken, for the purpose of this case, that the said allegations are well-founded. If so, membership in that Party cannot be ruled out of consideration as material on which no satisfaction could rationally be grounded.[84]

In holding that the Provincial executive had good reason for detaining the appellant in the interests of "public safety, order or tranquillity," the Court managed to evade the major constitutional issue of whether the Province had any authority to detain a person who was or was likely to be "formenting or inciting strikes with intent to cause or prolong unrest among any group or groups of employees." Since Provincial Legislatures, according to the Provisional Constitution, could provide for preventive detention only for reasons connected with public order, one might have expected the Court to determine the relationship between public order and industrial peace.

A final category of decisions rendered by the Federal Court under its appellate jurisdiction which deserve some mention are those which may be classified as of social or economic importance, i.e., cases in which legislation designed

[83] *Machindar Shivaji Mahar* v. *The King*, (1949–1950) F.C.R. 3.

[84] *Machindar Shivaji Mahar* v. *The King*, (1949–1950) F.C.R. 3, 833.

to remove certain social and economic ills underwent judicial scrutiny. Much such legislation was enacted by the Provincial Legislature, especially in the eight Provinces in which the Congress Party had a majority, in the period between July 1937 and November 1939.[85] The dominating social issue at this time was the agrarian problem, and many enactments were passed in an effort to alleviate many problems faced by the agricultural-tenant, especially indebtedness.

This legislation was impugned frequently in the courts by the various vested interests, but in the large majority of cases the Federal Court could find nothing unconstitutional about these enactments. Thus in *Shyamakant Lal* v. *Rambhajan Singh and Others*,[86] the Bihar Money-lenders Act of 1938 was upheld.[87] In the following year, the Court upheld the validity of the Madras Agriculturists Relief Act of 1938, the aim of which was to enable agriculturist-debtors to have their debts reduced.[88] The Bihar Agricultural Income-tax Act of 1938 was declared a valid exercise of Provincial legislative power in *Hulas Narain Singh and Others* v. *The Province of Bihar*.[89] In 1942, the Punjab Alienation of Land Act of 1900 (as amended in 1938) was declared *intra vires* the Constitution Act, although portions of it were found to be discriminatory and were severed from the body of the Act.[90] And the Bihar Tenancy Act of 1934 was declared to be within the competence of the Bihar Legislature, even though it affected the rights of those who benefited from the Permanent Settlement.[91]

One of the most significant of these cases was that of *Thakur Jagannath Baksh Singh* v. *United Provinces*,[92] in which the United Provinces Tenancy Act of 1939

---

[85] During this period the Congress followed a dual policy—"to carry on the struggle for independence and at the same time to carry through the legislatures constructive measures of reform." Jawaharlal Nehru, *The Discovery of India* (Bombay: Asia Publishing House, 1961 edition), p. 390. These ministries resigned in 1939 after the Governor-General, without consulting the nationalist leaders, declared that India had joined the war on the side of the Allies.

[86] (1939) F.C.R. 193.

[87] By 1940 the Federal Court was quite familiar with the Bihar Moneylenders Acts of 1938 and 1939 for, of fourteen decisions reported in the F.C.R. of that year, no less than eleven concerned this Bihar legislation.

[88] *A.L.S.P.P.L. Subrahmanyan Chettiar* v. *Muttuswami Goundan, Advocate-General of Madras*, (1940) F.C.R. 188.

[89] (1942) F.C.R. 1.

[90] *Punjab Province* v. *Daulat Singh and Others*, (1942) F.C.R. 67.

[91] *Hulas Narain Singh and Others* v. *Deen Mohammad Mian and Others*, A.I.R. 1943 F.C. 9.

[92] A.I.R. 1943 F.C. 9, 29.

was upheld. The essence of this Act was the restriction of rights claimed by the taluqdars, and a corresponding increase of the rights of the tenant. Here the Federal Court observed that

> we hope that no responsible Legislature or Government would ever treat as of no account solemn pledges given by their predecessors; but the re-adjustment of rights and duties is an inevitable process, and one of the functions of the Legislature in a modern State is to effect that readjustment, where circumstances have made it necessary, with justice to all concerned. It is, however, not for this Court to pronounce upon the wisdom or the justice, in the broader sense, of legislative Acts; it can only say whether they were validly enacted. ...[93]

In other words, the Court's powers were such that once the subject matter of the legislation was found to be within the competence of the Provincial Legislature, the legislation was normally upheld, for the Federal Court lacked authority to raise or consider other questions.

A final decision which may be mentioned is that of *Mukunda Murari Chakravarti and Others* v. *Pabitramoy Ghosh and Others*.[94] Here the Bengal Non-Agricultural Tenancy (Temporary Provisions) Act of 1940, which provided certain safeguards to tenants who suffered eviction on account of nonpayment of rent, was upheld by the Federal Court.

Although most of the legislation designed to remedy social and economic ills was directed at the agrarian problem and the plight of the tenant, other measures were enacted during this period which aimed at mitigating other problems. There was, e.g., the Bihar Excise (Amendment) Act of 1940, which made provision for total prohibition. In *Bhola Prasad* v. *The King Emperor*,[95] this prohibition policy passed the judicial test after the Federal Court ruled that "a power to legislate 'with respect to intoxicating liquors'[96] could not well be expressed in wider terms, and would ... undoubtedly include the power to prohibit intoxicating liquors throughout the Province. ..."[97] Some years later, the Madras Temple Entry Authorisation and Indemnity Act of 1939, the aim of which was "the removal of the disabilities imposed by custom and usage on certain classes of Hindus in respect of their entry into and offering worship in Hindu temples," was upheld by the Federal Court.[98]

---

[93] *Thakur Jagannath Baksh Singh* v. *United Provinces* A.I.R. 1943 F.C. 35.

[94] (1944) F.C.R. 351.

[95] (1942) F.C.R. 17.

[96] Government of India Act, 1935, Seventh Schedule, List II, Entry 31.

[97] *Bhola Prasad* v. *The King Emperor*, (1942) F.C.R. 17, 25.

[98] *Manikkasundara Bhattar and Others* v. *R. S. Nayudu and Others*, (1946) F.C.R. 67, 68.

In concluding this discussion of the Federal Court's constitutional appellate jurisdiction, two observations are pertinent. Firstly, although this jurisdiction was limited by Section 205 of the 1935 Act to cases involving "a substantial question of law as to the interpretation of this Act or any Order in Council made thereunder," it is obvious that many appeals reached the Federal Court in which the constitutional issue was so obscure and remote as to cause one to conclude that the raising of a "constitutional issue" in a High Court was often a tactic employed by a clever counsel who wanted his case heard by another forum. As a result, a number of "constitutional appeals" were hardly such, for often a constitutional issue was raised only in order to secure an appeal to the Federal Court. Furthermore, in some of the cases which reached the Federal Court under Section 205, counsel for the appellant did not even raise in the Federal Court the constitutional issue which was the very basis of the appeal from the High Court decision, and instead argued other points of law and fact.[99] Implicitly, the Federal Court approved of this tactic and, in a very real sense, encouraged it from the very outset by ruling in 1939 that once a case reaches the Federal Court via the High Court certificate, "the case is at large and the appellant is not necessarily restricted in arguing his appeal to what may be called the constitutional issue."[100]

As a result, the Federal Court decided civil and criminal appeals in which the raising of the constitutional issue served only to blur the line which delimited the boundaries of the respective jurisdictions of the Federal Court and Privy Council. In other words, there were cases in which the Federal Court virtually exercised jurisdiction allotted to the Privy Council, i.e., appeals were decided by the Indian tribunal which, except for an obscure constitutional issue, otherwise would have gone from the High Court to the Privy Council.

The second matter is the manifest absence of finality attaching to those Federal Court decisions in which emergency legislation and ordinances were declared invalid, for these decisions were followed almost momentarily by ordinances designed to restore their validity. However, it is essential to observe that though these decisions thwarted the executive only temporarily, in no instance did the executive ignore or disregard a decision of the Federal Court. On the contrary, each decision was accepted as binding upon the executive, and the judicially-determined defects in these measures were "corrected" or "rectified" by subsequent ordinances. It is true that the revision of these ordinances and enactments made them only somewhat less arbitrary than they were

---

[99] See, e.g., *Sudhir Kumar Dutt* v. *The King,* (1948) F.C.R. 86.
[100] *Pashupati Bharti* v. *The Secretary of State for India in Council and Another,* (1939) F.C.R. 13, 15.

prior to judicial scrutiny, but the Court's powers were so limited that it had no authority to decide, e.g., that preventive detention in itself was an arbitrary and unconstitutional invasion of individual liberty. Probably at no other period in the British *raj* was the executive as strong or as unresponsive to public opinion as it was during World War II when it had to protect itself against both sedition and nationalist agitation.

But the role of the Federal Court during this critical period in modern Indian history, though clearly limited, should not be underestimated. Though the Court could not, e.g., secure the release for very long of a person undergoing preventive detention, its decisions did cause the alien rulers to be less oblivious of the rule of law and, accordingly, less arbitrary than they otherwise would have been. No government, alien or indigenous, relishes frequent court rulings which state that its measures are arbitrary and unconstitutional.

Advisory jurisdiction. Under the authority of Section 213 of the 1935 Act, the Governor-General was empowered, at his discretion, to refer to the Federal Court for its opinion questions of law of public importance on which it was expedient that the opinion of the Court be obtained. Such opinions were to be delivered in open court, thereby encouraging the care and deliberation which derives from public scrutiny, and avoiding the impression that the Federal Court gave private or secret advice to the Governor-General.[101] Although the terms of the Constitution Act—"the court may ... report to the Governor-General"—imposed no obligation on the Federal Court to accede to every request for its opinion, Chief Justice Spens once remarked that "we should always be unwilling to decline to accept a Reference, except for good reason."[102] Four times the Court was called upon to give its opinion, and in each instance it consented, but not without expressing, on occasion, some misgivings about both the expediency and utility of this consultative role.

The first concerned the constitutional validity of a Provincial sales-tax enactment, the implementation of which, though the legislative process had been completed, was delayed pending the Court's opinion.[103] The Court advised that a sales tax was within the ambit of Provincial legislative competence, but apparently the Central Government never publicly accepted or rejected the Court's opinion. This resulted in questions being raised in the Central Legislature in

---

[101] C. L. Anand, *The Government of India Act, 1935* (second edition; Lahore: The University Book Agency, 1944), p. 401.

[102] *In re the Allocation of Lands and Buildings in a Chief Commissioner's Province*, (1943) F.C.R. 20, 22.

[103] *In re the Central Provinces and Berar Sales of Motor Spirit and Lubricants Taxation Act*, 1938, (1939) F.C.R. 18.

1939 and 1940, for the Provincial Governments were uncertain about whether they could levy a sales tax.[104] Eventually, however, several Provinces went ahead and implemented such measures and, in the case of *The Province of Madras* v. *Boddu Paidanna & Sons*,[105] the sales-tax as a means of raising Provincial revenue was sanctioned by the Federal Court in an appeal under Section 205. Recalling its earlier advisory opinion, the unanimous Court stated at this time that "the Opinions expressed were advisory Opinions only, but we do not think that we ought to regard them as any less binding upon us on that account."[106]

This opinion is significant in that it concerned the first matter of any importance to come before the Federal Court, and because the Chief Justice announced that when interpreting the 1935 Act the Court would apply canons of interpretation and construction which were well established, would interpret the Act in a "broad and liberal spirit," and would not express any opinion on the expediency of a particular piece of legislation, nor would it be concerned with the motives behind any legislation.[107]

In the second advisory opinion, the Court, after defining the boundaries of Provincial and Central legislative competence, advised that certain enactments of the Central Legislature on the subject of the property rights of Hindu women were constitutional.[108] Of more interest, however, than the nature of this opinion is the fact that four years later, in a concrete case, the Federal Court denied the *stare decisis* effect of an advisory opinion, and reviewed completely the rationale of this opinion:

> Any opinion of this Court given upon a reference under s. 213 can properly be reconsidered at any time by this Court in any litigation coming before it and should be so reconsidered on the proper request of any party, however much respect for the learned Judges responsible for an opinion and a desire to secure continuity and certainty in the pronouncements of this Court may make a member of this Court hesitate to differ.[109]

It was in the 1943 opinion of *In re Allocation of Lands and Buildings Situate in a Chief Commissioner's Province*[110] that the Court expressed "some doubt

---

[104] *Legislative Assembly Debates*, II (1939), February 22, 1939, p. 1299.

[105] (1942) F.C.R. 90.

[106] *The Province of Madras* v. *Boddu Paidanna & Sons* (1942) F.C.R. 100.

[107] *In re the Central Provinces and Berar Sales of Motor Spirit and Lubricants Taxation Act, 1938*, (1939) F.C.R. 18, 36–37.

[108] *In re the Hindu Women's Rights to Property Act, 1937, and the Hindu Women's Rights to Property (Amendment) Act, 1938*, (1941) F.C.R. 12.

[109] *Rm. Ar. Ar. Rm. Ar. Ar. Umayal Achi* v. *Lakshmi Achi and Others*, (1944) F.C.R. 1, 36.

[110] (1943) F.C.R. 20.

whether any useful purpose would be served by the giving of an opinion under s. 213 of the Act."[111] Here the Court's opinion was invited with regard to a difference of opinion between the Central Government and the Punjab Government over the ownership of certain lands. The Court was hesitant to give any opinion because it felt that questions of title between the Centre and a Province might better be adjudicated under the Court's original jurisdiction, and because Section 172(5) of the 1935 Act seemed to contemplate the reference of such land ownership disputes to the Judicial Committee.[112] However, after learning that the Privy Council had been approached already in this matter and had suggested that the Federal Court first offer its opinion, the Federal Court did render an opinion.

The last time the Court was asked to provide an opinion was in 1944, when the Governor-General referred to the Court the question of the *vires* of a piece of legislation which the Central Legislature was contemplating passing.[113] There was considerable controversy both inside and outside of the Court over the propriety of the Court giving an opinion, for while at issue was the competence of the Central Legislature to impose an estate tax, the Legislature had not yet drafted a bill. In the absence of this, the Court was asked to consider a hypothetical "bill" upon which the interested parties had agreed. Probably the most noteworthy feature of this opinion was the brilliant dissent by Justice Zafrullah Khan who, after carefully reviewing the arguments pro and con relative to advisory opinions, declined to express any opinion about the "bill" because he felt the Court had not been provided with materials sufficient to enable it to arrive at a satisfactory determination of the questions raised.[114] Chief Justice Spens, however, who delivered the majority opinion, was unwilling either to defend or criticize the practice of consultative opinions, and noted only that "when Parliament has thought fit to enact s. 213 of the Constitution Act it is not in our judgment for the Court to insist on the inexpediency (according to a certain

---

[111] *In re Allocation of Lands and Buildings Situate in a Chief Commissioner's Province*, (1943) F.C.R. 22.

[112] "172(5). Any question which may arise within the five years next following the commencement of Part III of this Act as to the purposes for which any lands or buildings are by virtue of this section vested in His Majesty may be determined by His Majesty in Council."

[113] *In re the Power of the Federal Legislature to provide for the Levy of an Estate Duty in Respect of Property other than Agricultural Land, Passing Upon the Death of Any Person*, (1944) F.C.R. 317.

[114] *In re the Power of the Federal Legislature to provide for the Levy of an Estate Duty in Respect of Property other than Agricultural Land, Passing Upon the Death of Any Person*, (1944) F.C.R. 317, 332–349.

school of thought) of the advisory jurisdiction."[115] Spens and Varadachariar, therefore, proceeded to offer an opinion, the essence of which was that the Central Legislature lacked authority to impose an estate tax.

Although the Federal Court never evinced any enthusiasm for this advisory jurisdiction, it apparently delivered an opinion each time it was approached by the Governor-General, and each opinion apparently was well received. That is, in each instance the parties concerned accepted the opinion as binding, though there was no constitutional obligation which compelled the Governor-General to heed an advisory opinion. However, as noted, the Governor-General never announced his acceptance of the opinion in the sales-tax reference, which may indicate that he was less than completely satisfied with the nature of that opinion. Furthermore, after the Court's opinion with reference to the estate duty, the British Parliament amended the 1935 Act so as to enable the Centre to impose an estate duty.[116] But this indicates not a disregard of the Court's opinion, but an acceptance of it, followed by action aimed at conferring authority to levy an estate tax on the Legislature, a power which the 1935 Act, until amended, did not provide according to the Court's opinion.

One writer who has examined carefully the practice of advisory opinions in India arrived at the conclusion that of these four Federal Court opinions, only the first generated much public interest, and that probably because it was the first important matter to come before the Court.[117] The other three excited little interest, probably because when these were handed down, the war and the struggle for independence obscured other issues. Yet neither the absence of interest nor the fact that advisory opinions were not sought after 1944 can be taken as an indication of disapproval or disappointment with the Federal Court's experience with them, for the framers of free India's Constitution conferred a similar consultative jurisdiction on the successor to the Federal Court.

Federal Court and Privy Council

In any assessment of the role of the Federal Court, at least as important as the scope of the jurisdiction of the Federal Court and the nature of its

---

[115] *In re the Power of the Federal Legislature to provide for the Levy of an Estate Duty in Respect of Property other than Agricultural Land, Passing Upon the Death of Any Person,* (1944) F.C.R. 320.

[116] William D. Popkin, "Advisory Opinions in India," *Journal of the Indian Law Institute,* IV (1962), p. 404.

[117] Popkin, "Advisory Opinions in India," p. 419.

decisions and opinions is the relationship between India's supreme tribunal and the Privy Council from 1937 to 1949. This association was regulated by Section 208 of the 1935 Act, which provided for a right of appeal to the Privy Council from judgments of the Federal Court in the exercise of its original jurisdiction if such decisions involved an interpretation of the Constitution Act or of any Order in Council made thereunder. Of more importance (in view of the fact, noted here, that only one of the three decisions of the Federal Court in exercise of its original jurisdiction was taken to the Privy Council and there quickly affirmed),[118] an appeal could be taken to the Judicial Committee from a decision of the Federal Court in any other case, if the latter granted leave, or if the former granted special leave to appeal.[119] Thus it is obvious that a realistic assessment of the role of the Federal Court must include some discussion of the nature of these links with London and the Privy Council. Especially relevant are answers to the following queries: (i) when and why did the Federal Court, on its own accord, grant leave to appeal?; (ii) when and why did the Privy Council grant special leave?; and (iii) how did the Privy Council treat the decisions of the Federal Court which it reviewed?

The Federal Court was first approached for leave to appeal to the Privy Council in *Hori Ram Singh* v. *The Crown*,[120] and leave was denied simply because "no special circumstances had been made out" to justify a review of the Federal Court's decision. Two years later, leave to appeal was denied again in *A.L.S.P.P.L. Subrahamanyan Chettiar* v. *Muttuswami Goundan*,[121] in which case the Federal Court announced that it would not be disposed to grant leave to appeal "save in cases of real importance, cases which are likely to effect a large number of interests hereafter or cases in which difficult questions of law are involved."[122] Here the Court also refused to formulate "in advance any code of rules which it will take for its guidance in granting or withholding leave to appeal to the Judicial Committee, and will deal with each case on its merits as it comes before it."[123]

For several years, other requests were handled similarly, and appeals from Federal Court decisions to the Judicial Committee were discouraged as a matter of judicial policy. Thus from a decision in which a unanimous Federal

[118] *Governor-General in Council* v. *Province of Madras*, (1945) F.C.R. 179 P.C.
[119] Government of India Act, 1935, Section 208(b).
[120] (1939) F.C.R. 159, 192.
[121] (1941) F.C.R. 4.
[122] *A.L.S.P.P.L. Subrahamanyan Chettiar* v. *Muttuswami Goundan*, (1941) F.C.R. 5.
[123] *A.L.S.P.P.L. Subrahamanyan Chettiar* v. *Muttuswami Goundan*, (1941) F.C.R. 5.

Court had reversed a judgment of the Full Bench of the Allahabad High Court, leave to appeal was denied because the Federal Court was "unable to hold that there is room for such serious doubt on the point as to justify it in holding that there is a substantial question on which leave to appeal to His Majesty in Council is to be granted."[124] Similarly, in 1942, the Court refused the request of the Government of the North-West Frontier Province after pointing out that

> we think that the Government should be content with the legal position as established by the Judgment of the Court and should not seek to prolong the litigation. The case might be different if any fundamental principle of far-reaching importance had been involved in our decision, or if great administrative inconvenience was likely to arise from it; but that is not so, and the fact that the Government think that our decision was wrong is not itself a reason for granting leave to appeal.[125]

The most complete statement of the policy of the Federal Court with regard to appeals to the Privy Council was enunciated in a 1942 judgment in which several requests for leave to appeal were denied.[126] The Court again refused to establish rules by which its discretion in granting or refusing leave to appeal would be governed, and emphasized that

> we shall continue to treat each case on its own merits, but we repeat what we have said before, that we will not entertain an application for leave to appeal on the ground only that the applicant is of opinion that our decision was wrong, and still less for the purpose of enabling him, in the phrase used by counsel in one of the cases, to "try his luck" before yet one more tribunal. On general grounds of public policy litigation in the form of appeals to several Courts should be restricted rather than extended. ...[127]
>
> We are not disposed to encourage Indian litigants to seek for determination of constitutional questions elsewhere than in their own Supreme Court. We do not and indeed we cannot lay down a rule that we will never grant leave to appeal, for that would be to alter the provisions of the Act and to usurp legislative functions, but we shall grant it sparingly and only in exceptional cases.[128]

[124] *mst. Atiqa Begum and Others* v. *The United Provinces and Others*, (1941) F.C.R. 7, 9.

[125] *The North-West Frontier Province* v. *Suraj Narain Anand,* (1942) F.C.R. 66–67.

[126] *Megh Raj and Another* v. *Allah Rakhia and Others; Punjab Provinces* v. *Daulat Singh and Others; Hulas Narain Singh and Others* v. *The Province of Bihar; Messrs. Boddu Paidanna & Sons* v. *The Province of Madras,* (1942) F.C.R. 109.

[127] *Messrs. Boddu Paidanna & Sons* v. *The Province of Madras,* (1942) F.C.R. 110.

[128] *Messrs. Boddu Paidanna & Sons* v. *The Province of Madras,* (1942) F.C.R. 110, 112.

Of greater significance than its statement of policy with regard to appeals was the Court's conception of its role in the Indian polity, as set forth by Chief Justice Gwyer:

> [T]his Court is the first court sitting on Indian soil whose jurisdiction, limited though it may be at present, extends to the whole of British India. Its establishment marked a new stage in India's constitutional evolution; and the evolution of Indian political thought, of which we cannot pretend to be unaware, ever since we last heard an application for leave to appeal, has served only to increase and emphasize the significance of its authority. *It is not subordinate to any other Court;* and it is plain that this conception of its status was present in the minds of those who framed the present constitution when they gave to the Court itself the right to say whether it would permit any cases which came before it on appeal to be reviewed elsewhere. The ancient prerogative right of His Majesty to grant special leave to appeal, though it has not been made statutory by s. 208(b), does not affect this aspect of the matter.[129]

It was not until 1944 that the Federal Court saw fit to grant leave to appeal to the Privy Council. It did so then from its decisions in three cases because involved in these cases was "not only a question as to the interpretation of the Constitution Act, but broader questions which bear on a controversy which has long been agitated in the courts of India,"[130] and because the cases involved "substantial questions of law."[131] In the same year, however, in the case of *Hulas Narain Singh* v. *Deen Mohammad Mian and Others,*[132] the applicant, a Bihar zamindar, was denied leave to appeal because the points of law in question were "by no means substantial," even though the Federal Court agreed that "the question raised in the legislation is one affecting a large number of people, both zamindars and *ryots,* in the Province of Bihar."[133]

Thereafter, although the Federal Court claimed to follow its announced policy of discouraging litigants from seeking a determination of constitutional

---

[129] *Messrs. Boddu Paidanna & Sons* v. *The Province of Madras,* (1942) F.C.R. 111. Emphasis supplied.

[130] *Thakur Jagannath Baksh Singh* v. *The United Provinces,* (1944) F.C.R. 51, 56. Here the major question raised was the nature and extent of the rights guaranteed to *taluqdars* by the Oudh Settlement, and the extent of the immunity secured thereby from legislative interference with their rights.

[131] *Bechan Chero* v. *The King Emperor and Jubba Mullah and Ramphal Dhanuk* v. *The King Emperor,* (1944) F.C.R. 178. The decision actually appealed from here was the *Piare Dusadh* ruling in which the revised Special Criminal Courts Ordinance was upheld.

[132] *Hulas Narain Singh* v. *Deen Mohammad Mian and Others,* A.I.R. 1944 F.C. 24.

[133] *Hulas Narain Singh* v. *Deen Mohammad Mian and Others,* A.I.R. 1944 F.C. 24, 25.

questions elsewhere than in the Federal Court, there are indications that the Court became more liberal in granting leave. This is especially true with regard to its decisions in the important war emergency cases, for, with the exception of the *Keshav Talpade* judgment,[134] all of these reached the Privy Council with the express permission of the Federal Court.

Before considering how such appeals were handled by the Privy Council, it is important to observe that except for a few instances in the late 1940s, the Privy Council, when petitioned for a grant of special leave to appeal after the Federal Court had refused such leave, accepted the ruling of the latter and also denied special leave. The result was that the Federal Court decisions handed down under its constitutional appellate jurisdiction were regarded as final by the Privy Council, unless the Federal Court of its own accord granted leave to appeal to the Privy Council. This created the anomalous situation whereby important questions of constitutional law were decided by the Federal Court and were not reviewed by the Privy Council, but, at the same time, the Federal Court was statutorily incompetent to hear ordinary civil appeals because, as will be seen presently, the British Government chose to deny the Federal Court any civil appellate jurisdiction from 1937 to 1947.

Thus, when the Privy Council was faced for the first time with a special leave request, the application was dismissed quickly with the observation that "[t]heir Lordships ought not to forget the fact that the matter has been before the Federal Court and that an appeal from the Federal Court should not lightly be admitted by the Board, and should only be admitted if it arises in a really substantial case."[135] By application of this principle, the Privy Council for several years denied all applications for special leave. In fact, it was not until 1947 that the Privy Council handed down a decision in a case which had come before it by virtue of a grant of special leave.[136] Altogether, the Privy Council granted special leave only four times, and in these decisions it three times affirmed the decision of the Federal Court.[137] Only in the case of

---

[134] The Central Government had requested leave to appeal from this Federal Court decision, and the Federal Court hinted that it was willing to grant leave save for the fact that suddenly Talpade was released by the Government on its own initiative. With Talpade free, the Court said there was no longer any pending matter for which leave to appeal could be granted. *King Emperor* v. *Keshav Talpade*, (1944) F.C.R. 59, 60.

[135] *Hori Ram Singh* v. *The King Emperor*, (1940) F.C.R. 15 P.C., 16.

[136] *Megh Raj and Another* v. *Allah Rakhia and Others*, (1947) F.C.R. 77 P.C.

[137] *Megh Raj and Another* v. *Allah Rakhia and Others*, (1947) F.C.R. 77 P.C.; *High Commissioner for India and High Commissioner for Pakistan* v. *I. M. Lall.* (1948) F.C.R. 44 P.C, and *North-West Frontier Province* v. *Suraj Narain Anand*, (1943) F.C.R. 103 P.C.

Gill and Another v. *The King*[138] did the Privy Council come to a conclusion which differed from that of the Federal Court.

There remain for consideration only those cases in which the Federal Court granted leave to appeal to the Privy Council and, in effect, asked the Privy Council to make the final pronouncement. There were ten such cases—in five the decision of the Federal Court was affirmed;[139] in five it was reversed. Two of the five reversed related to Provincial legislation which had been found *ultra vires* the Constitution Act by the Federal Court. In the first of these, *Punjab Province* v. *Daulat Singh and Others*,[140] the Privy Council, on the basis of a different interpretation of the 1935 Act, upheld the validity of the impugned legislation. In the other, *Prafulla Kumar Mukherjee and Others* v. *Bank of Commerce, Limited, Khulna*,[141] the Privy Council delimited the respective jurisdictions of the Central and Provincial Legislatures more liberally than did the Federal Court, and was able thereby to accommodate the Provincial enactment.

The three most significant decisions of the Federal Court reversed by the Privy Council, each of which concerned individual rights, were the cases of *Benoari Lall, Keshav Talpade* and *Sibnath Banerjee* in which, respectively, the Federal Court had declared invalid the Special Criminal Courts Ordinance and Rule 26 of the Defence of India Rules, and had set at liberty a number of *detenus*. In *King-Emperor* v. *Benoari Lall Sarma*,[142] the Privy Council disagreed with both objections which the Indian Court had levelled against the Special Criminal Courts Ordinance. Whereas the Federal Court was of the view that the Ordinance had left so much discretion with the executive authorities as to amount to an unconstitutional delegation of legislative power, the Privy Council looked upon the arrangement of permitting the Provincial Governments to decide when the Ordinance should come into force as "merely an example of the not uncommon

---

[138] (1948) F.C.R. 19 P.C. The Federal Court decision appealed from was that of *H.H.B. Gill* v. *The King Emperor and Anil Lahiri* v. *The King Emperor*, (1946) F.C.R. 123, in which the Federal Court had affirmed the conviction of the petitioners on a criminal conspiracy charge. The Privy Council reversed this judgment on procedural grounds after finding that certain evidence used to obtain the conviction was not admissible.

[139] *Thakur Jagannath Baksh Singh* v. *The United Provinces*, (1946) F.C.R. 111 P.C.; *Bank of Commerce, Limited, Khulna* v. *Amulya Krishna Basu Roy Chowdhury and Others*, (1947) F.C.R. 54 P.C.; *Raleigh Investment Company, Limited* v. *Governor-General in Council*, (1947) F.C.R. 59 P.C.; *Wallace Brothers and Company, Limited* v. *Commissioner of Income Tax, Bombay City and Bombay Suburban District*, (1948) F.C.R. 1 P.C., and *Albert West Meads* v. *The King*, (1948) F.C.R. 67 P.C.

[140] (1946) F.C.R. 1 P.C.

[141] (1947) F.C.R. 28 P.C.

[142] (1945) F.C.R. 161 P.C.

legislative arrangement by which the local application of the provision of a statute is determined by the judgment of a local administrative body as to its necessity."[143] As to the Indian Court's finding that special courts could not hear criminal cases unless the Code of Criminal Procedure had been repealed or effectively excluded from operation, the Judicial Committee simply professed to be unable to find in the 1935 Act anything which would cause to be invalid a statute or ordinance which enabled the executive authorities to determine the type of court before which an accused might be tried. Whether it was a regular court or a special court was "a question of policy, not of law."[144]

The Federal Court decisions in the *Keshav Talpade* and *Sibnath Banerjee* cases were reversed by the Privy Council in a single judgment bearing the name *King-Emperor* v. *Sibnath Banerji*.[145] In reaching the conclusion that the ruling of the Federal Court in the *Keshav Talpade* case that Rule 26 was *ultra vires* because it went beyond the rule-making powers conferred on the Central Government by the Defence of India Act was incorrect, the members of the Privy Council said merely that they read the provisions of the Defence of India Act differently, for, in their view, Rule 26 was in conformity with the powers conferred upon the executive.[146] Similarly reversed was the Indian Court's judgment in the *Sibnath Banerjee* case. Whereas the Federal Court had interpreted Rule 26 to mean that each detention order must receive the personal approval of the Governor, the Privy Council construed Rule 26 differently, and as a result held that the issuing of detention orders was not a strictly personal function and did not require the personal scrutiny of the Provincial Governor.[147]

---

[143] *King-Emperor* v. *Benoari Lall Sarma* (1945) F.C.R. 172–173 P.C.

[144] *King-Emperor* v. *Benoari Lall Sarma* (1945) F.C.R. 172–173, 177 P.C. This particular decision of the Privy Council seems to have provoked more criticism in India than any other. M. V. Pylee, e.g., alleges that the Privy Council in this decision "was content to examine the entire question from an extremely legalistic, highly unrealistic and even political angle." *The Federal Court of India* (unpublished D.Litt. thesis, Patna University, 1955), p. 475. Further, M. C. Setalvad, writing in 1946, states that the "broad view of the majority of the Federal Court, based upon the peculiarity of conditions in India and the difference between the Constitution of this country and of Britain, was negatived by the Privy Council. One cannot help remarking that the Privy Council failed to approach the question from the point of view of Indian conditions, and the peculiar position of the Executive in India, and restricted themselves to a bare interpretation of the mere letter of the statute" (*War and Civil Liberties* (New Delhi: Indian Council of World Affairs, Oxford University Press, 1946), p. 46).

[145] (1945) F.C.R. 195 P.C.

[146] *King-Emperor* v. *Sibnath Banerji*, (1945) F.C.R. 214 P.C.

[147] *King-Emperor* v. *Sibnath Banerji*, (1945) F.C.R. 214, 222 P.C.

The fact that the Federal Court, of its own accord, sent up to the Judicial Committee for review ten of its decisions, as compared with only four instances in which the Privy Council granted special leave to appeal, indicates that the statutory subordination of the Federal Court to the Privy Council did not mean, in practice, that the latter treated the former as an inferior tribunal whose decisions required frequent scrutiny and revision. Indeed, by the single criterion of the number of occasions in which the Privy Council granted special leave, thereby intervening without invitation by the Federal Court, it is clear that the Privy Council was content to accept the vast majority of Federal Court rulings as sound and proper decisions. Thus, for all practical purposes, the Federal Court, within the limited sphere of its jurisdiction, was a supreme judicial tribunal, and its statutory subordination to the Privy Council was certainly not a crucial factor in an assessment of its role.

The Federal Court and Civil Appeals

The establishment of the Federal Court as an essentially constitutional appellate court did not curb the energies of those who, from 1921 to 1935, had sought the creation of an indigenous, supreme, civil appellate tribunal which would inherit the appellate jurisdiction then being exercised by the Judicial Committee over the High Courts of British India. After 1935, now that the principle of such a tribunal had been accepted by the British Parliament and embodied in Section 206 of the Government of India Act, 1935, the protagonists of a Supreme Court of India aimed at an early utilization of this section which provided that with the permission of the Governor-General, legislation could be introduced for the purposes of empowering the Federal Court with jurisdiction to hear civil appeals, and abolishing in whole or in part direct appeals from the High Courts to the Privy Council.

The first effort to accomplish these objectives after the advent of the 1935 Act was made in March of 1938, only five months after the Federal Court had begun to function and before it had heard a single case, and was in the form of a resolution introduced in the Council of State by Haji Syed Muhammad Husain:

> That this Council recommends to the Governor General in Council to take immediate steps to introduce measures to provide for civil appeals to the Federal Court from the judgments of High Courts in British India as provided by section 206(1) of the Government of India Act of 1935 and to establish at the earliest possible date a Supreme Court of Criminal Appeals in India.[148]

---

[148] "Resolution Re Establishment of a Supreme Court of Criminal Appeals," *Council of State Debates*, I (1938), March 10, 1938, p. 401. The Indian Legislature had no authority to

Husain, although he offered several of the customary justifications for a Supreme Court of Civil Appeals, was concerned primarily with the fact that no cases, up to that time, had been brought to the Federal Court. He considered it imperative "to provide work for the Federal Court," and urged that if the Government "want to get something out of the tremendous lot of money that they are spending on the Federal Court, [it] ought to take some measures to get the return and provide work for highly paid unemployment."[149]

The discussion which ensued, however, was marked not by a consideration of the merits of the resolution, but of its utility, for, although most of the powers conferred on the Federal Legislature by the 1935 Act could be exercised by the existing Indian Central Legislature, certain powers, including those found in Section 206, were being withheld from operation until either the Federation came into being, or until the British Parliament saw fit to bring them into operation. Although the precise reason or reasons why the Legislature was denied authority to enlarge the jurisdiction of the Federal Court were not made clear during the course of this debate in the Council of State, a Government spokesman did announce that the matter had been discussed in December 1936 and July 1937, and on these occasions "the main reason for continuing to exclude this section was the new Constitution had hardly started, and the Federal Court was then not actually in being."[150]

Thus, the constitutional situation was such that before the Indian Central Legislature could initiate legislation designed to confer a civil appellate jurisdiction on the Federal Court, two prerequisites had to be satisfied: (i) the Government of India would have to request the Secretary of State for India to seek an Order in Council for the purpose of bringing into operation Section 206, and (ii) the British Government would have to consent to this action. The matter was, at this stage, entirely in the hands of the Imperial Government, for until Section 206 was in operation, there was nothing the Indian Legislature could do.

Accordingly, Husain was informed by the President of the Council of State that though there was nothing to prevent an "academical discussion" of the resolution, even if passed it would be "absolutely unprofitable at this stage."[151]

---

invest the Federal Court with a criminal jurisdiction, and any criminal appellate tribunal would have had to have been completely separate from the Federal Court.

[149] "Resolution Re Establishment of a Supreme Court of Criminal Appeals," *Council of State Debates*, I (1938), March 10, 1938, p. 403.

[150] "Resolution Re Establishment of a Supreme Court of Criminal Appeals," *Council of State Debates*, I (1938), March 21, 1938, p. 403, 450.

[151] "Resolution Re Establishment of a Supreme Court of Criminal Appeals," *Council of State Debates*, I (1938), March 10, 1938, p. 403.

Husain admitted that he was aware of this situation even before he introduced his resolution, and confessed that the real object of the resolution was to discover the Government's general attitudes toward such a proposal. Then, on the basis of what he regarded as a favorable reaction by a spokesman of the Government, Husain withdrew his resolution before it was put to a vote.[152]

It soon became apparent, however, that Husain had misunderstood the Government's attitude toward bringing Section 206 into operation, for, a month later, the Home Member stated in answer to a question that the matter "has been considered but the view hitherto taken is that the section should not be applied during the transitional period, i.e., until Federation commenced or, at any rate, until further experience had been gained of the working of the Federal Court."[153] Throughout the remainder of 1938 and all of 1939 the Government took no action, and there is no evidence that the matter was discussed in the Indian Legislature during this period. But in February, 1940, owing to the unlikely factor of the war in Europe, the Government of India circulated a letter in which all Provincial Governments, High Courts and Bar Associations were invited to express their views on the question whether the time was ripe for an extension of the jurisdiction of the Federal Court. The Government took the initiative at this time because "a new situation has arisen owing to the outbreak of war since in war conditions appeals to the Privy Council inevitably present greater difficulty."[154]

In November of 1940 the Home Member was requested by a member of the Legislative Assembly to make available to the Assembly the nature of the responses to this letter. However, though admitting that all opinions had been collected and scrutinized, the Home Member refused to disclose the results to the Assembly because it was "not usual" to make public such

---

[152] "Resolution Re Establishment of a Supreme Court of Criminal Appeals," *Council of State Debates*, I (1938), March 21, 1938, pp. 449, 456. That is, he interpreted certain remarks by F. H. Puckle, who was in charge of the resolution on behalf of the Government, to mean that the Government would seek to activate Section 206.

[153] *Legislative Assembly Debates*, III (1938), April 7, 1938, p. 2720. This reply caused one member to suggest that until some cases came before the Federal Court, the Judges should be utilized temporarily as acting Provincial Governors or as members of committees on legislation. Serious consideration, however, was not given this proposal (*Legislative Assembly Debates*, III (1938), April 7, 1938, p. 2720).

[154] That such a letter had been sent was acknowledged in the Council of State on March 14, 1940. (*Council of State Debates*, I (1940), p. 255.) Although copies of the letter are no longer available, portions of it were quoted in the various law journals. This quotation was printed in the *Calcutta Weekly Notes*, XLIV (1939–1940), March 11, 1940, p. 62.

information.[155] On several occasions thereafter, the Home Member was asked whether the Government planned to take any further action, but the uniform reply was that the matter was still "under consideration" by the Government.[156]

Impatience with the Government's dilatory attitude caused P. N. Sapru to move in the Council of State on March 17, 1941 "[t]hat this Council recommends to the Governor General in Council to take such steps as may be necessary to enlarge the Appellate Jurisdiction of the Federal Court to the maximum extent permitted by section 206 of the Government of India Act, 1935."[157] Although bestowing praise upon the judges of the Privy Council and their decisions, Sapru argued that in view of the changed political conditions and the proximity of Dominion status, India must immediately have its own civil appellate court. Other justifications for the extension of the Court's jurisdiction offered by Sapru included the difficulties encountered in carrying an appeal to London because of the war conditions, and that the Federal Court as then constituted simply did not have enough work to do.[158]

In the debate which followed, the resolution received both support and criticism. The strongest, but probably least significant criticism came from one J. H. S. Richardson, whose constituency was the Bengal Chamber of Commerce. Richardson was particularly upset because the commercial interests, whom he said composed the largest single group of litigants before the High Courts and the Federal Court, had not been asked by the Government to express an opinion on the proposal to make the Federal Court a civil appellate court. He said he was certain that commercial interests would never support any proposal which would diminish or sever India's ties with the Privy Council.[159] Others opposed the resolution because no provision was made for criminal appeals;[160] and another said political independence must precede any expansion of the Federal Court's jurisdiction.[161] The debate ended inconclusively, however, when, after the Home Member announced that this matter had been referred by the Government of India to the Secretary of State for India, Sapru withdrew his

---

[155] *Legislative Assembly Debates*, IV (1940), November 11, 1940, p. 283.

[156] *Legislative Assembly Debates*, I (1941), February 13, 1941, p. 178; and *Council of State Debates*, I (1941), February 26, 1941, p. 92.

[157] "Resolution *re* Federal Court," *Council of State Debates*, I (1941), March 17, 1941, p. 366.

[158] "Resolution *re* Federal Court," *Council of State Debates*, I (1941), March 17, 1941, pp. 368–69.

[159] "Resolution *re* Federal Court," *Council of State Debates*, I (1941), March 17, 1941, p. 370.

[160] "Resolution *re* Federal Court," *Council of State Debates*, I (1941), March 17, 1941, p. 372.

[161] "Resolution *re* Federal Court," *Council of State Debates*, I (1941), March 17, 1941, p. 372.

resolution upon being assured that the transcript of this debate would be forwarded to the Secretary of State.[162]

Before considering further official announcements on the subject of the extension of the Federal Court's jurisdiction, it will be useful to consider briefly some unofficial reactions to the aforementioned resolutions and Government statements. Although the matter of extending the jurisdiction of the Federal Court was in no sense a leading political issue or a key plank in any political platform, which means there was no readily discernible "public opinion" on this issue, various law journals did comment, from time to time, on the matter of the Federal Court's jurisdiction and the efficacy of severing or retaining India's ties with the Privy Council.

A scrutiny of articles and editorial comment in the leading Indian law journals indicates that between the years 1938 and 1942 the preponderance of legal opinion looked with favor upon an extension of the jurisdiction of the Federal Court so as to embrace civil appeals from the High Courts in British India. Representative of such thinking were the views of the editor of the *Federal Law Journal*, a Delhi publication, who observed that the Government had acted wisely in not bringing Section 206 into operation in 1937, "but now [1940] the Federal Court has had time to settle down," and had established "a great reputation throughout the Empire."[163] His appraisal of the Privy Council, also, seems representative of the legal segment of Indian opinion:

> We are second to none in our admiration for the judgments of the Privy Council. In fact, reading the judgments of the Law-Lords of England has been our greatest delight in life, and we have never tired, during our career as editor for almost a quarter of a century, of impressing on India the excellence of their judgments. But this is no reason why we should leave the structure of the Indian Constitution incomplete. … So long as there is a Central Legislature passing laws which will have force throughout India there should be a Supreme Court to interpret them uniformly.[164]

Similarly, the editors of *Indian Cases*, a Lahore publication, came out strongly in favor of extending the Federal Court's jurisdiction, but on the condition that some provision be retained for appeals from such decisions to the Privy

---

[162] "Resolution *re* Federal Court," *Council of State Debates*, I (1941), March 17, 1941, pp. 373–76.

[163] "Enlargement of the Jurisdiction of the Federal Court," *Federal Law Journal*, III (1939–1940), p. 25.

[164] "Enlargement of the Jurisdiction of the Federal Court," *Federal Law Journal*, III (1939–1940), p. 27.

Council.[165] And the editor of *The Law Weekly*, published in Madras, was of the view that provided with "the right type of men of learning and experience constituting the final appellate tribunal in India, whether that tribunal is to be the Federal Court or some other, it will be as satisfactory and efficient as the Judicial Committee in England."[166]

Not all law journals, however, looked with favor on proposals to enlarge the appellate jurisdiction of the Federal Court. The editor of the *Calcutta Weekly Notes*, e.g., commenting on Husain's 1938 resolution in the Council of State, warned that

> those who strive for judicial autonomy before political autonomy has been attained, undoubtedly put the cart before the horse. We are therefore entirely opposed to the movement initiated in the Council of State for extending the appellate jurisdiction of the Federal Court. ... It must yet be admitted that it will be impossible to find in India judges of the eminence of the Lords of Appeal. ... It is also to be remembered that contact with English Law is the chief source from which Indian case-law derives whatever vigour or brilliance it is found occasionally to display and that those are best fitted to interpret and apply the English law who have been bred in it as in a living institution. To deprive Indian litigants of the high privilege of having their causes ultimately tried by an independent and supremely qualified tribunal, would be a great blunder; and to deprive Indian case-law of the services of the most brilliant exponents of British jurisprudence would be to take a disastrous step, however much might our political vanity be flattered by the reflection that in judicial matters we are self-dependent.[167]

Then, in 1940, the same publication printed an equally vehement attack on the Government's invitation to High Courts, Bar Associations and Provincial Governments to express their views on whether Section 206 should be brought into operation:

> So far as we are aware, there is not the slightest desire in any responsible quarter for the introduction of any measure which would curtail to any extent the inestimable privilege of an appeal to the Privy Council. ...
>
> We consider that the right of appeal to the Privy Council should be maintained in its entirety and the Privy Council should not even partially be replaced by the Federal Court for the following reasons. First, we would place the unparalleled quality of such judgments as emanate from the Lords of Appeal. We shall not

---

[165] "Enlargement of the Jurisdiction of the Federal Court," *Indian Cases*, CLXXXVII (1940), pp. 39–40.

[166] "Federal Court as Ultimate Court for Indian Appeals," *The Law Weekly*, III (1941), pp. 21–22.

[167] "The Federal Court," *Calcutta Weekly Notes*, XLII (March 28, 1938), pp. 73–74.

conceal our opinion that when Judges of so-called "Indian Experience" began to predominate in Boards hearing Indian appeals, there was a distinct decline in the quality of their pronouncements, but happily with an increasing association of the Lords of Appeal, the quality has, to a large extent, been recovered. ... To forego the privilege of having the Indian laws expounded by legal celebrities and judicial stylists of this order can only be suicidal. ... Divorced from contact with the Judicial Committee, Indian legal and judicial work is bound to stagnate and degenerate into the commonplace and the mechanical. It is only the living waters of the Privy Council judgments, vitalising in themselves and charged with an occasional inflow of English principles, which gives it such life as it at times betrays.[168]

Finally, as if enough had not been said already, the editor concluded with the extraordinary comment that "it is significant that the move for precipitating the operation of sec. 206 has come from the Indian Government, and people cannot be blamed if they think that the object is to cut off India from a tribunal of the type of the Judicial Committee while keeping political advance at a standstill."[169]

It is probably not surprising that the most adamant opposition to an extension of the Federal Court's jurisdiction came from Calcutta, for, being the principal headquarters of British capital in India, and populated by thousands of European businessmen, Calcutta was likely to be a bastion of conservatism.[170] Furthermore, as a representative of this commercial element pointed out in the Council of State in 1941,[171] the European commercial class was involved often in civil litigation, and many such cases were decided ultimately by the Privy Council. The alien commercial class was, quite expectedly, of the opinion that its position would be considered more sympathetically in London than in Indian courts. A final, but very significant, reason why thinking in Calcutta about weakening India's ties with the Privy Council was out of line with Indian

[168] "Federal Court, conversion of, into a Supreme Court," *Calcutta Weekly Notes*, XLIV (March 11, 1940), pp. 62–63.

[169] "Federal Court, conversion of, into a Supreme Court," *Calcutta Weekly Notes*, XLIV (March 11, 1940), p. 63. Cf. "Privy Council Appeals and the Federal Court," *Calcutta Weekly Notes*, XLIV (July 29, 1940), pp. 137–139; and "The Federal Court: a Problem," *Calcutta Weekly Notes*, XLIV (February 10, 1941), pp. 49–50.

[170] Although these views of the editor of the *Calcutta Weekly Notes* were extremely reactionary, there is evidence that the proposal to extend the jurisdiction of the Federal Court suffered criticism generally in Calcutta. See, e.g., remarks to this effect in B. Banerji, "Federal Court and Privy Council," *All India Reporter (Journal)*, XXVIII (1941), pp. 1–2, and in *Madras Weekly Notes*, October 25, 1943, p. xx.

[171] "Resolution *re* Federal Court,"*Council of State Debates*, I (1941), March 17, 1941, p. 366.

opinion elsewhere was the fact that most appeals (one source says 50 per cent[172]) from India to the Privy Council emanated from Calcutta, with the result that there was a sizable group of lawyers and others who had a vested interest in retaining India's links with the Privy Council.

Returning to the chronology of official pronouncements with regard to Section 206, all that can be said of the 1940–1943 period is that the Government of India chose not to divulge the results of its correspondence with the various Provincial Governments, High Courts and Bar Associations. When the intentions of the Government were sought in the Legislature during question periods, the uniform reply of the Government was that the matter was still "under consideration." On February 19, 1943, e.g., the Law Member (Sir Sultan Ahmed) replied in answer to a question that the matter of bringing into operation Section 206 was "under correspondence with the Secretary of State and I am not in a position to make any further statements at this stage." Asked how long this correspondence would last, the Law Member suggested that the legislator who asked this question should "go to the nearest astrologer."[173] By 1942 and early 1943 the matter received little attention in the Central Legislature, law journals or in the press.

However, with the arrival in India in the summer of 1943 of Sir Patrick Spens, who came from England to become Chief Justice of the Federal Court upon the retirement of Sir Maurice Gwyer, the issue in all its amplitude was raised again. This occurred because Spens, in his first public speech, told a Madras audience that "the whole matter of the extension of the jurisdiction of the Federal Court was being reconsidered both in India and in England in order that there should not be a breakdown in dealing with appeals to the Privy Council from India. The matter has been reopened because of enemy action in and around Great Britain."[174] Thus the war situation, which caused the Government of India to solicit opinion about Section 206 in 1940, again precipitated widespread discussion of this problem in 1943.

Spens informed his audience that the letter circulated by the Indian Government in 1940 had in fact resulted in proposals being put forward that the jurisdiction of the Federal Court be extended immediately, but "those proposals were discussed in England and they were turned down after discussion there on the ground that the Federal Court could not be regarded from the point of view of litigants, nor of the profession or anybody else, as an adequate substitute

172   "The Law Member of the Viceroy's Council in Madras," *Madras Weekly Notes*, 1944, v.

173   *Legislative Assembly Debates*, I (1943), February 19, 1943, p. 425.

174   "Enlargement of the Jurisdiction of the Federal Court," *Federal Law Journal*, VI (1943), 13–14. Spens' entire speech is reprinted here, pp. 8–20.

for the Judicial Committee of the Privy Council."[175] From this statement, three conclusions could be drawn about the 1940 letter: (i) the majority of those whose opinions were sought must have favored the application of Section 206; (ii) the Government of India did in fact recommend such action to the Secretary of State for India, and (iii) the British Government had decided to deny this measure of judicial autonomy to India.

Now, however, according to the new Chief Justice, who, incidentally, described himself "as the person who will be very largely responsible for doing whatever has to be done if any sort of change is made in the present situation,"[176] Parliament was preparing to amend the 1935 Act so as to give the Indian Legislature "absolute powers, sufficiently wide, to establish such Supreme Court on such terms and with such powers as the Central Legislature thinks fit."[177] But, during the course of his address, it became evident that something less than "absolute powers" were to be offered to the Indian Legislature, for Spens cautioned

> that if the proposals of 1939 and 1940 were repeated and pressed, that the Federal Court should immediately be turned into a Supreme Court of appeal and that all direct appeals to His Majesty in Council should be immediately excluded, those proposals would be opposed both in India and in England. They would be contentious measures which had no hope of being dealt with during the war period.[178]

The British Government was ready, however

> to take an immediate step forward on the basis of the Australian or Canadian system, that is to say, that the unsuccessful litigant in the High Court or other Courts from which an appeal now lies to the Judicial Committee would have his choice whether to appeal direct to London or to appeal direct to the new Supreme Court in India; but if he chose the latter, then that decision was to be completely final unless in the exercise of their discretion the Privy Council thought fit to grant special leave to appeal which it was quite clear would happen no more frequently than had happened in Australian and Canadian cases. With that in mind I was asked, when I got out to India, to moot it and find out what the profession and the public and everybody who were interested were likely to think of that as an immediate step forward. If I and others responsible

[175] "Enlargement of the Jurisdiction of the Federal Court," *Federal Law Journal*, VI (1943), p. 13.

[176] "Enlargement of the Jurisdiction of the Federal Court," *Federal Law Journal*, VI (1943), p. 15.

[177] "Enlargement of the Jurisdiction of the Federal Court," *Federal Law Journal*, VI (1943), p. 15.

[178] "Enlargement of the Jurisdiction of the Federal Court," *Federal Law Journal*, VI (1943), p. 14.

could report that there was a general measure of agreement inside the profession, among the trading and commercial classes and amongst any other party who came to be interested, then it would be possible for that alteration to be made and to be made as a non-contentious step forward and without any further delay.[179]

The key feature and, as was not long in becoming evident, the controversial feature of the proposals put forth by Spens was the condition that if the Federal Court was to become a civil appellate court, the Indian Legislature would not be permitted to sever completely India's links with the Privy Council, and the Indian litigant must be offered the option to choose the forum for his appeal. Spens commended these proposals to his audience because (i) they would mark the first step toward making the Federal Court the exclusive court of appeal, from which there would be no backtracking after the war; (ii) the prestige of the Privy Council would be available under this "optional scheme" to those who preferred it to an Indian tribunal, and (iii) the fact that all civil appeals would not suddenly descend upon the Federal Court would enable it to adjust to its new role in an orderly manner.[180]

The Indian reaction to the Spens proposal was both immediate and unfavorable. In fact, on the same platform as Spens that evening in Madras was T. V. Muthukrishna Iyer, the President of the Madras Advocates Association. On behalf of the Association, he minced a few words in informing Spens that

we would certainly welcome the extension of the appellate jurisdiction of the Federal Court, but if I may say so on one strict condition. Should there be a change, you should be prepared to go the whole hog so as to conform to the letter and spirit of Section 206. ... Every appealable case should necessarily find its way to the Federal Court and to the Federal Court alone. To be more explicit, my Lord, the Association is of opinion that it is undesirable to give the option to the litigant to chose the forum of his appeal. It is not in the best interests of the country and is calculated to retard the progressive growth of the Federal Court on healthy lines. In the opinion of this Association this proposal has not got even a single merit in itself ... Let there be no delusion on that matter in any quarter. This Association is definitely of opinion that the taking of such a step would mean that you are giving us a stone when we ask for bread.[181]

[179] "Enlargement of the Jurisdiction of the Federal Court," *Federal Law Journal*, VI (1943), pp. 14–15.

[180] "Enlargement of the Jurisdiction of the Federal Court," *Federal Law Journal*, VI (1943), pp. 16–17.

[181] "Enlargement of the Jurisdiction of the Federal Court," *Federal Law Journal*, VI (1943), pp. 11–12.

After leaving Madras, Spens visited most of the High Court centers for the purposes of introducing these proposals to various groups and ascertaining the reactions they provoked. One gains the impression, using the law journals as the measure, that Spens' proposals were greeted more frequently with criticism than support, although some measure of support there was. Critics of the optional scheme attacked the proposals for a variety of reasons. The editor of the *Madras Law Journal*, e.g., in a very carefully written essay, urged Indians to hold out for an exclusive right of appeal to the Federal Court because acceptance of the optional scheme would mean acceptance of the idea that the litigant, in choosing the forum, would be influenced either by nationalism or other political considerations, or by the prestige of the Judicial Committee. Accordingly, the editor asked, if more litigants elected to go to the Privy Council rather than to their own Federal Court, "will it not subsequently be urged as demonstrating a lack of enthusiasm for that Court in India itself?"[182] A similar approach was taken by the editor of the *Madras Weekly Notes*, who was quite correct in observing that the question "ultimately resolves itself into one of confidence in the Federal Court or the Privy Council of the litigant public and the Indian Bar."[183] It was his view that the Federal Court, at that time, did not enjoy as much confidence and prestige as the Judicial Committee, because the appointing authorities had not selected first-rate Chief Justices to preside over the Federal Court.[184]

Dr. Kailas Nath Katju, editor of *The Allahabad Law Journal*, stated that his investigations indicated that Spens' optional system "has not aroused enthusiasm anywhere, and those who have accepted it in principle have done so with reluctance and hesitation."[185] He was opposed to the optional scheme because it would lead to two types of justice—Federal Court justice and Privy Council justice—"with the implicit brand of inferiority invariably attaching to the former."[186] In a later issue of the *Journal*, Katju expressed the view that much of the anxiety caused by the proposed expansion of the Federal Court's jurisdiction "arose not so much out of the merits of the proposal, but was connected mainly with the possible personnel and the mode of appointment of Judges to that Court."[187] Katju said that though the Judicial Committee in London consisted of "the most experienced, learned and wise Judges in Great Britain," the two Englishmen who had served on the Federal Court were "imported lawyers of

---

[182] "Expansion of the Federal Court's Jurisdiction," *Madras Law Journal*, II (1943), p. 35.

[183] "The Law Member of the Viceroy's Council in Madras," *Madras Weekly Notes*, 1944, p. v.

[184] "The Law Member of the Viceroy's Council in Madras," p. v.

[185] "Federal Court and Its Expansion," *The Allahabad Law Journal*, XLII (1944), p. 31.

[186] "Federal Court and Its Expansion," p. 32.

[187] "Federal Court and Its Expansion—II," *The Allahabad Law Journal*, XLII (1944), p. 37.

much lesser calibre."[188] The reason for this, according to Katju, was that a judicial career in India had ceased to attract British lawyers of distinction because of the unhealthy climate, mandatory retirement at age sixty-five, high taxation, and the high cost of living. Thus he was led to conclude that "any scheme about the expansion of the Court must be accompanied by a definite assurance that Judges would be recruited in India and India alone."[189] But, Katju noted, an all-Indian Court would raise the problem of communal representation on the Bench, which impelled him to emphasize that though he conceded the desirability of recruiting Judges from all communities,

> we do not want second class brains on the Federal Court merely on the ground that one community or the other must be represented. ... The highest Court of Justice must not be treated as if it were a legislative chamber where every section of the community must be separately represented in order to voice its own sectional demands and grievances.[190]

Spens' proposal of a civil appellate jurisdiction shared concurrently between the Privy Council and the Federal Court was attacked with force by the editor of the *Calcutta Weekly Notes*, but for reasons different from those offered by others. It was his view that the Federal Court suffered from so many shortcomings that it could never be regarded as an adequate substitute for the Privy Council. Accordingly, he opposed any expansion of the Federal Court's jurisdiction on the ground that such action would weaken India's ties with the Privy Council.[191]

Of those who would accept Spens' proposals as satisfactory, only one writer was in any sense enthusiastic in his support. This writer (Gopal Behari) was impressed by Spens' argument that the concurrent or optional scheme would enable the Federal Court to adjust smoothly to its new role, and was of the view that "it would strike the golden mean between two extreme principles, the policy of total abolition of the Privy Council as a court of appeal, and the other which favours the continuation of the present state of affairs."[192] More typical

---

[188] "Federal Court and Its Expansion—II," p. 37.

[189] "Federal Court and Its Expansion—II," p. 38.

[190] "Federal Court and Its Expansion—II," p. 38.

[191] "The Federal Court: Proposed Extension of Jurisdiction of," *Calcutta Weekly Notes*, XLVIII (January 3, 1944), pp. 15–18, and "The Federal Court," (April 24, 1944), pp. 49–51. Cf. S. K. Achariar, "Extension of Jurisdiction of the Federal Court," *All India Reporter (Journal)*, XXXII (1945), p. 13. The latter opposed the optional scheme because the advantage enjoyed by the wealthy litigant in being financially able to carry an appeal to the Privy Council was retained.

[192] Gopal Behari, "Enlargement of the Federal Court's Jurisdiction," *The Allahabad Law Journal*, XLII (1944), p. 18.

of those who agreed with Spens was the Bar Council of Allahabad, whose members preferred that the jurisdiction of the Federal Court be exclusive, but would accept, as an initial step, the optional scheme.[193]

In the period during which Spens was seeking support for his proposals, questions pertaining to the enlargement of the Federal Court's jurisdiction continued to be raised in the Central Legislature and Council of State, but the Government maintained its silence.[194] The only comment other than that the matter was still "under correspondence with the Secretary of State" was made by the Law Member on November 10, 1944, when he stated that "the Chief Justice has authorised me to say that he is in fact in favor of the extension" of the jurisdiction of the Federal Court.[195] Soon after Spens completed his tour of the High Court centers, however, the matter was carried a step further when, on January 15, 1945, the Government of India published the text of a "resolution" on the subject.[196] Although no reference was made in this resolution to the fruits of Spens' salesmanship or to the nature of the responses provoked by the proposals he offered, the recommendations of the Indian Government were identical to those which Spens had advocated. That is, it was admitted that the proposal at first put forth by the Government of India was that Parliamentary legislation should be promoted for bringing into operation Section 206, so as to enable the Indian Legislature to confer a right of appeal to the Federal Court from decisions of High Courts in civil cases and, consequentially, to abolish direct appeals from such decisions to the Privy Council either with or without special leave. The Resolution continued with the statement that

> after exhaustive consideration, however, the Secretary of State has reached the conclusion, in which the Government of India concur, that the Indian Legislature ought not at this stage to be placed in a position enabling it to abolish direct appeals with special leave to the Privy Council from High Courts in cases outside the scope of section 205, or, in other words, that any Indian legislation under section 206 providing for an appeal to the Federal Court should

---

[193] "Chief Justice of India Meets Bar Council," *The Allahabad Law Journal*, XLII (1944), p. 18. Another who, though not enamored by the proposals, regarded them as a step in the right direction, was the editor of the *Federal Law Journal*, VI (1943), p. 9.

[194] *Council of State Debates*, III (1943), November 17, 1943, p. 17, and *Council of State Debates*, I (1944), February 21, 1944, p. 99.

[195] *Legislative Assembly Debates*, IV (1944), November 10, 1944, p. 553.

[196] "Resolution of the Government of India in the Legislative Department," No. F. 209/41-C&G (Judicial), dated January 15, 1945. *The Gazette of India*, January 20, 1945, p. 74.

not deprive a party of the option of seeking special leave to appeal to the Privy Council.[197]

Accordingly, it was proposed that Parliament should amend Section 206 so as to make it impossible for the Indian Legislature to abolish direct appeals in civil cases from High Courts to the Judicial Committee, followed by the issuing of the requisite Order in Council for the purpose of bringing into operation the amended Section 206.

In this Resolution the Government recommended also that only civil cases involving at least 15,000 rupees be appealable to the Federal Court without special leave, recommended that once the Federal Court was made a civil appellate court no more appeals from a single judge of a High Court should be permitted (i.e., all rights of appeal within the High Court should be exhausted before approaching the Federal Court), recommended that the Federal Court should be empowered to hear income tax appeals in the interest of securing uniformity in the judicial interpretation of income tax law, and recommended increasing the strength of the Federal Court to eight puisne judges.[198] The resolution concluded with the statement that "the Secretary of State has intimated that he will be prepared to promote Parliamentary legislation on the lines indicated in this statement if but not unless he is satisfied that the proposals would be acceptable to Indian opinion. Steps will therefore be taken to give utmost possible publicity to this statement."[199] Thus, again, the Government invited comments on the matter of an extension of the Federal Court's jurisdiction.

Although this Resolution would seem to indicate that some positive action with regard to Section 206 would soon be forthcoming, nearly two years passed before the matter was mentioned again in the Central Legislature. On October 31, 1946, the Law Member was asked what steps were being taken for the immediate enlargement of the power and jurisdiction of the Federal Court, and whether this matter would be discussed in the Legislature. His reply was that

no immediate action in this direction is contemplated. In view of the fact that the Constituent Assembly will be meeting soon to draft a constitution for India and must consider the question of a Supreme Court for India, it is not considered necessary to promote a discussion of this subject in the current Session.[200]

---

[197] "Resolution of the Government of India in the Legislative Department," No. F. 209/41-C&G (Judicial), dated January 15, 1945. *The Gazette of India*, January 20, 1945, p. 74.

[198] "Resolution of the Government of India in the Legislative Department," No. F. 209/41-C&G (Judicial), dated January 15, 1945. *The Gazette of India*, January 20, 1945, p. 74.

[199] "Resolution of the Government of India in the Legislative Department," No. F. 209/41-C&G (Judicial), dated January 15, 1945. *The Gazette of India*, January 20, 1945, p. 74.

[200] *Legislative Assembly Debates*, VII (1946), October 31, 1946, p. 304.

A few days later, however, referring to the proposals embodied in the Government's Resolution of January, 1945, the Law Member stated that "the large volume of opinion elicited by the publication of the proposals clearly established that there was no general support either for this proposal [optional scheme] in its original form or for the more far reaching proposal [that Privy Council appeals be abolished entirely]."[201] He reaffirmed that the present Government did not propose to reopen the matter.

The final comment on this question prior to the advent of national independence was made by Pandit Jawaharlal Nehru on February 10, 1947, and he said only that he contemplated "no immediate action" for extending the Federal Court's jurisdiction or doing away with Privy Council appeals.[202]

In sum, action with reference to Section 206 was abandoned owing to a combination of three factors: (i) by this time, public opinion, such as there was, was opposed to the optional scheme, and there seems to have been a general feeling that the civil appellate jurisdiction of the Federal Court should be exclusive;[203] (ii) the European war, which was the factor which precipitated the interest of the British in extending the jurisdiction of the Federal Court, had ended in 1945 and thus removed the *raison d'etre* of British interest in this matter; (iii) the nationalist movement was in its final stages, and it was all but absolutely certain that independence would soon be realized. Momentous changes and plans for far-reaching reforms obscured concern with such minor matters as the extension of the Federal Court's jurisdiction. Never a prominent plank in the platform of nationalist demands, this matter was of even less importance in the last two years preceding independence.

In the concluding remarks of the preceding chapter it was suggested that proposals put forth between 1921 and 1935 urging the creation of an Indian civil appellate tribunal failed in realization largely because Indian opinion was divided on the utility of a change in the relationship of Indian courts and the Privy Council. Yet, from 1937 to 1945, it was quite clearly the intransigence of

---

[201] *Legislative Assembly Debates*, VII (1946), November 6, 1946, p. 546.

[202] *Legislative Assembly Debates*, I (1947), February 10, 1947, p. 352. Nehru was then Leader of the House.

[203] An editorial in the *Federal Law Journal* is illustrative of this attitude: "Public opinion in India is strongly against an optional right of appeal to the Federal Court. The right of appeal to the Federal Court should be exclusive. ... There is a feeling that the British Government is being dictatorial in this matter and somewhat suspicious of Indian opinion. Whitehall's conclusions that the Federal Court cannot from the point of view of the litigants be regarded as an adequate substitute for the Privy Council is an incorrect assessment of public opinion" ("Government's Proposals for Expansion of the Federal Court's Jurisdiction," VII (1945), pp. 1–2).

the colonial rulers which provided the principal obstacle to any extension of the appellate jurisdiction of the Federal Court, for, by withholding the operation of Section 206, the Indian Legislature was without power to add to the Federal Court's limited jurisdiction. This does not mean that had Section 206 been in operation there was any real certainty that the Legislature would have conferred a civil appellate jurisdiction on the Federal Court. On the contrary, during this period Indian opinion was still divided on this issue, although less so than between 1921 and 1935. As late as 1945, in the significant *Constitutional Proposals of the Sapru Committee*, it was observed that

> there is no doubt that, when India has a self-contained Constitution of self-government, she cannot avoid having her own final court of appeal to deal with all civil appeals finally. The Committee is, however, divided in its views about the propriety of an immediate expansion of the Federal Court into a Supreme Court of appeal for the whole country and the opinion is strongly held by some members that such expansion should come only as a part of any free Constitution which India may obtain in the future and that the question cannot be settled independent of the constitutional status of India under the new Constitution. As the Committee's views are divided, we can express no positive opinion and we think that the Constitution-making Body, which will devise a complete scheme of the future Constitution of India, will be in a better position to deal with the question.[204]

The major reason offered by the British for denying the Indian Legislature the power to alter the relationship of India and the Privy Council was, as noted earlier, their view that the Federal Court could not be regarded as an adequate substitute for the Privy Council. There is little doubt that this reasoning, even if true, had the unfortunate effect of encouraging Indians to view the issue in nationalistic or political terms, whereas earlier such considerations were considerably less in evidence. It is difficult to ascertain how, by emphasizing the factor of the prestige of the Privy Council versus the Federal Court, the British contributed to the solution of this problem.

National Independence and After

As far as the Federal Court is concerned, the most obvious point which can be made about the realization of national independence on August 15, 1947, is that the Court was practically unaffected. The only visible changes were the

---

[204] *Constitutional Proposals of the Sapru Committee* (Bombay: Padma Publications, Ltd., 1945), paragraph 253. This report was compiled by Sir Tej Bahadur Sapru, M. R. Jayakar, Sir N. Gopalaswami Ayyangar, and Kunwar Sir Jagdish Prasad.

resignation of Chief Justice Spens two days before independence, and a geographical reduction in the jurisdiction of the Court to the extent of those areas of the subcontinent which became Pakistan. The powers and substantive jurisdiction of the Court were not changed in the least.

This remarkably smooth transition resulted in part from the issuance of the Federal Court Order, 1947,[205] and in part from the fact that India's new rulers elected to utilize the 1935 Act as the framework of government until a new constitution was drafted. The Federal Court Order, issued four days before independence, provided that (i) as from the date of independence, India would succeed to the Federal Court and, by implication, Pakistan would have to establish a new Federal Court of its own; (ii) the then judges of the Federal Court, "without making a fresh oath or observing any other formality," would continue in office; (iii) all proceedings pending in the Federal Court on August 15, 1947 would be disposed of by the Federal Court of India, unless the latter saw fit to transfer certain proceedings to the Federal Court of Pakistan; and (iv) orders made by the Federal Court on appeals brought before independence would be enforceable in India and Pakistan, and where such orders, either before or after August 15, had been confirmed, reversed or varied on appeal to the Privy Council, the decision of the Privy Council was to be enforced in India and Pakistan.

If the Federal Court Order contributed toward easing the impact of national independence on the Federal Court, the fact that the jurisdiction and powers of the Court were not altered was a result of the decision made by India's new rulers that the Government of India Act, 1935, after such amendments and modifications as were necessary in order to delete those portions which were regarded as subtractions from full responsible government, would be used as the Provisional Constitution until another was drafted.[206] It was thought that the new constitution would be completed and implemented by the end of 1948, but the drafting process took longer than anticipated, with the result that the Federal Court continued to derive its authority from the 1935 Act until January 26, 1950.

Not only the judiciary but also the executive and legislature continued to operate within the limits set forth in the amended 1935 Act. However, whereas the transfer of power heralded immediately an autonomous and completely sovereign Indian executive and legislature, the subordination of the Federal Court and the High Courts to the Judicial Committee in London continued

[205] Notification No. G.G.O. 3, published in the *Gazette of India, Extraordinary*, August 11, 1947.

[206] India (Provisional Constitution) Order, 1947. No. G.G.O. 14, dated August 14, 1947, *Gazette of India, Extraordinary*, p. 834.

to exist. That is, neither the Federal Court Order, the Indian Independence Act of 1947, nor the India (Provisional Constitution) Order of 1947 affected any change in the relationship of the Indian courts and the Privy Council. These ties with the Privy Council remained not as a condition of independence in the governing spheres imposed by the departing colonial power, but because the indigenous rulers elected to retain this association, if only as a temporary arrangement.

Though delayed, autonomy in the judicial sphere was destined to come eventually. The first significant step in this direction was marked by the enactment, in December of 1947, of the Federal Court (Enlargement of Jurisdiction) Act,[207] the aim of which was to enlarge the appellate jurisdiction of the Federal Court so as to embrace civil appeals from the High Courts, thus ending any further direct passage of appeals from the Indian High Courts to the Privy Council. The salient feature of this Act was the provision for an appeal to the Federal Court

(i)   without the special leave of the Federal Court, if an appeal could have been brought to His Majesty in Council without special leave under the provisions of the Code of Civil Procedure, 1908, or of any other law in force immediately before the appointed day [February 1, 1948], and

(ii)   with the special leave of the Federal Court in any other case. ...[208]

Thus the object of this Act was to bring an end to the system whereby appeals from High Court decisions in civil cases had by-passed the Federal Court and had gone directly to the Privy Council. Hereafter, all appealable civil cases would pass from the High Courts to the Federal Court. From any civil judgment of a High Court there could be no direct appeal to the Privy Council, and from any judgment of the Federal Court under this enlarged jurisdiction no direct appeal, i.e., no appeal as of right, would lie to the Privy Council. However, though the jurisdiction of the Privy Council was circumscribed to this extent, India's ties with the Privy Council were by no means severed by the Federal Court (Enlargement of Jurisdiction) Act. It was still possible, even after the passage of this enactment, for a civil appeal to be decided ultimately by the Privy Council, for there was nothing to prevent the Privy Council from granting special leave to appeal after a judgment of the Federal Court in a civil matter. Furthermore, the Privy Council retained also a criminal appellate jurisdiction (if it elected to grant special leave), and its position as an appellate court from decisions of the

---

[207] Act I of 1948. Cf. *Constituent Assembly of India (Legislative) Debates*, III (1947), December 11, 1947, pp. 1708–1727.

[208] Federal Court (Enlargement of Jurisdiction) Act, Act I of 1948, Section 3(a).

Federal Court under the latter's original and constitutional appellate jurisdiction was unaffected by this Act.

That the new government, at an early date, would sever the ties which bound the High Courts to the Privy Council was hardly surprising for, as we have seen, for many years prior to independence there was agitation in India for making an indigenous tribunal the final, or, in the least, an intermediate civil appellate court. But what is somewhat peculiar, given India's independent status, is the manner in which the Act was brought about, and the fact that the Act was a halfway measure in that the Judicial Committee remained India's ultimate appellate tribunal. While introducing the Federal Court (Enlargement of Jurisdiction) Bill in the Dominion Legislature, Dr. B. R. Ambedkar, the then Law Minister, admitted that the Bill was not designed to abolish all appeals to the Privy Council. Its purpose was only to enlarge the civil appellate jurisdiction of the Federal Court because, according to Ambedkar, the Dominion Legislature derived its powers from the 1935 Act, i.e., the Provisional Constitution of free India, and the only power to affect the jurisdiction of the Federal Court was that set forth in Section 206. In Ambedkar's words,

> ... anybody who reads section 206 will find that although the power to amend and enlarge the jurisdiction of the Federal Court is given to this Assembly, it is limited in certain particulars. It is limited to civil cases. Therefore no provision can be made for the abolition of direct appeals in criminal matters. Secondly, it refers to direct appeals, that is to say appeals from the High Court to the Privy Council. The reason why we are not able to abolish appeals from the Federal Court to the Privy Council is because of the existence of section 208 in the Government of India Act. ... What I wanted to tell the House was that if it was desirable to abolish all appeals to the Privy Council and to enlarge the jurisdiction of the Federal Court in as complete a manner as we want to do, for that purpose we would have been required to hold a session of the Constituent Assembly to pass a Bill, which it can do, notwithstanding any limitations in the Government of India Act, 1935, for the simple reason that the Constituent Assembly is a sovereign body and is not bound by the provisions of the Government of India Act, 1935. The position of this Legislature which is spoken of as the Dominion Legislature is very different. It is governed by the Government of India Act, 1935 and therefore it must conform in anything it wants to do. As I said, the only permissive section which we have in the Government of India Act is section 206 and we have taken the fullest liberty of this section to enlarge the jurisdiction of the Federal Court to the fullest extent possible. The deficiencies of the Bill I do not think need worry any members of the legislature for the simple reason that this Act will be in operation only for a very short time. As soon as our Constitution is framed and is passed by the Constituent Assembly, we shall then be in a position to make the amplest

provision for the jurisdiction of the Federal Court and to abolish appeals to the Privy Council.[209]

Ambedkar's attempts to distinguish between the legislative and constitution-making functions of the Constituent Assembly in an effort to explain procedurally, rather than justify politically, the postponement of judicial independence were not accepted without protest from those members of the Assembly who were becoming increasingly impatient about sovereignty in the judicial sphere. One member had this to say about the Law Minister's reasoning:

> The only distinction that I see between the two Houses is that this House sits in one room and the other House sits in another room, and while the other House has a President this House has a Speaker who are different persons. The members of both Houses are the same. ... I therefore fail to see how on account of these trivial and minute distinctions, which I do not consider to be relevant, the House loses the character of a sovereign body and cannot shape our law in any way it thinks fit. ... I hope this House will agree with me that this House is identical with the House from which it is sought to be artificially distinguished.[210]

The Law Minister, however, after admitting that the Bill did prolong India's judicial subordination to London, assured the Assembly that it was only a temporary measure and would be followed soon by complete judicial autonomy. The Assembly accepted Ambedkar's assurances and enacted the Bill in the form in which it was introduced.

The scope of the Act itself and the manner in which it was introduced might be explained as follows: (i) Judicial autonomy was delayed because a conclusion had not yet been reached on the future relationship of Indian courts and the Privy Council. In other words, by December 1947, it had not been decided whether India would sever all connections with the Judicial Committee or would follow the practice of Canada and Australia, Dominions which, as a matter of choice, retained some ties with the Privy Council. (ii) It had not yet been decided whether India would remain a Dominion in the Commonwealth or become a Republic with or without Commonwealth ties. When made, the nature of this decision would have a bearing on India's association with the Privy Council. (iii) The Privy Council was still held in high esteem by leading members of the Assembly and it may not have been possible to sever all ties at this juncture. In any event, the extension of the Federal Court's jurisdiction via

---

[209] *Constituent Assembly of India (Legislative) Debates*, III (1947), December 11, 1947, pp. 1710–11.

[210] *Constituent Assembly of India (Legislative) Debates*, III (1947), December 11, 1947, p. 1719.

Section 206 can be regarded as a compromise which served to satisfy, for the time being at least, both the supporters of limited ties with the Privy Council and those who desired complete autonomy in the judicial sphere.

Between 1948 and 1950, as a result of the civil appellate jurisdiction derived from the Enlargement Act, the Federal Court heard a greater number and a greater variety of appeals than in the years preceding 1947. Forty-five decisions were handed down in this two-year period, as compared with ninety decided between 1937 and 1947. Furthermore, no longer was it the typical case before the Court, as one concerning an interpretation of the Constitution Act; after 1948 the usual case before the Court was a civil appeal, for there was then a right of appeal to the Court in a civil case if the dispute involved at least 10,000 rupees or, if the order or decree appealed from affirmed the decision of the court immediately below, if involved also was "some substantial question of law."[211]

The final stage in the evolution of judicial autonomy came in late 1949, by which time the constitution-makers had decided that there would be no place for Indian appeals to the Privy Council once the new Constitution, then in its final stages of drafting, was inaugurated. By this time the nature of the judicial system under the new system of government had been agreed upon, and the Constituent Assembly in September passed the Abolition of Privy Council Jurisdiction Act[212] after much eulogizing of the Privy Council by leading members of the Constituent Assembly.[213] This Act, effective as from October 10, 1949, severed all connections which Indian courts had with the Judicial Committee. The Act repealed Section 208 of the 1935 Act, which had been the basis of the Privy Council's appellate jurisdiction over the Federal Court, transferred to the Federal Court from the Privy Council certain pending appeals, but left other appeals which had reached an advanced stage of decision to be disposed of by the Privy Council. The Privy Council disposed of the last appeal from India on December 15, 1949 in the case of N. S. Krishnaswami Ayyangar and Others v. Perimal Goundan (since deceased) and Others.[214]

Although, by virtue of the Abolition Act, the Federal Court inherited the jurisdiction of the Privy Council, the Act became effective only three and

---

[211] Code of Civil Procedure, 1908, Sections 109–112.

[212] Constituent Assembly Act No. V of 1949, published in the *Gazette of India, Extraordinary*, September 28, 1949.

[213] See, e.g., the remarks of K. M. Munshi, Pandit Thakur Das Bhargava, and Alladi Krishnaswami Ayyar. *Constituent Assembly Debates*, IX, September 17, 1949, pp. 1614–17.

[214] A.I.R. 1950 P.C. 105, and J. P. Eddy, "India and the Privy Council: The Last Appeal," *The Law Quarterly Review*, LXVI (1950), p. 214.

one-half months before the Federal Court was replaced by the Supreme Court
under the new Constitution, with the result that the Federal Court heard only
two appeals arising out of this jurisdiction. Both were criminal appeals, but
the first came up on the basis of a certificate granted by a High Court, whereas
in the second, the Federal Court, for the first time ever, granted special leave
to appeal. The first, *Machindar Shivaji Mahar* v. *The King*,[215] was discussed here
in connection with preventive detention and civil liberties.[216] The other was
that of *Kapildeo Singh* v. *The King*,[217] and its importance lies in the fact that it
was the first and only appeal by special leave admitted by the Federal Court
in the exercise of the criminal jurisdiction recently inherited from the Privy
Council, and because the Court, during the course of its ruling, emphasized
that "though this Court is no longer bound by Privy Council practice and
precedents, it sees no reason to depart from the principles which have been
laid down by it defining the limits within which interference with the course
of criminal justice dispensed in the subordinate courts is warranted. ..."[218]
Then, "to remove all misapprehension on the subject,"[219] the Court quoted
from ten Privy Council rulings on criminal appeals, the gist of which was
that an appellate court should be very reluctant to interfere in criminal cases,
and concluded with the observation that "following the principles laid down
in these cases, this Court will not interfere lightly in criminal cases. ..."[220]
Thus the Federal Court of India made it clear that though the era of the Privy
Council so far as India was concerned had ended, the principles enunciated by
the Privy Council were not *ipso facto* obsolete.

On January 26, 1950, soon after this decision was rendered, the Federal Court
was superceded by the new Supreme Court of India.

One who attempts to make an appraisal of the significance of the Federal
Court is very tempted to minimize its role. Not only was its jurisdiction very
limited at the outset, but the subcontinent-wide federation for which it was to
serve as the demarcator of spheres of authority failed to materialize, and then the
exigencies created by World War II resulted in a nearly complete centralization
of power in the hands of the Governor-General, which imposed further limitations on the Federal Court. Moreover, although its major function—indeed, its
chief reason for existence—was to serve as the interpreter of the Constitution

[215] (1949–1950) F.C.R. 827.
[216] See Chapter II, pp. 44–45.
[217] (1949–1950) F.C.R. 827, 834.
[218] *Kapildeo Singh* v. *The King*, (1949–1950) F.C.R. 839.
[219] *Kapildeo Singh* v. *The King*, (1949–1950) F.C.R. 839, 840.
[220] *Kapildeo Singh* v. *The King*, (1949–1950) F.C.R. 839, 842.

Act, it was not even the final interpreter, for appeals from its decisions could be taken to the Privy Council. In a number of respects, the Federal Court seemed hardly more than another step in the appellate ladder, interposed between the highly-regarded Judicial Committee of the Privy Council and the Provincial High Courts, which commanded more respect and public confidence than any other colonial institution in India.

Yet on the other hand, the Federal Court was the first federal institution to be established under the 1935 Act; it was India's first "constitutional court" in the sense that its primary function was the interpretation of the Constitution Act, and, as Sir Brojendra Mitter, the Advocate-General of India, remarked at the inaugural session of the Federal Court, "for the first time in the history of British India a tribunal has been set up in the country having jurisdiction over the Provinces. For the first time the rule of law has been extended to interprovincial disputes which hitherto had been subject to executive determination."[221]

Of the decisions handed down by the Federal Court, there seems to be little doubt that the most noteworthy were those concerning individual liberties and the efforts of the executive to restrict these liberties. Although the Court's jurisdiction was limited, although there was not a bill of rights which might have served as a standard for executive action, and with the executive in possession of vast powers with which to circumscribe individual liberties, the Federal Court, in seeking to prevent unreasonable inroads on the liberty of the individual, compiled a brilliant record. During this most critical period in modern Indian history, when the Provincial legislatures were rarely functioning, when many Provinces were ruled by the Central Government, and when press censorship was widespread, the courts were "the only forum to which the people could look for redress against the executive."[222] And in those cases in which the Federal Court passed upon the decrees, ordinances and legislation designed to thwart individual liberties, there is no evidence to indicate that the Court was ever anything less than resolute, impartial and independent. It exhibited no reluctance to declare unconstitutional an enactment or ordinance which it regarded as unreasonably restrictive of individual liberties. Indeed, one has to be reminded that, during the period in which the Federal, Court was boldly attempting to maintain a balance between individual freedom and the security of the State, the Federal Court itself was a part of the colonial administration.

[221] *Federal Law Journal*, I (1937–1938), p. 30.

[222] M. C. Setalvad, *War and Civil Liberties* (New Delhi: Indian Council of World Affairs, Oxford University Press, 1946), p. 57.

The Federal Court, in short, inspired a high degree of confidence in the mind of the public. As long as India maintained ties with the Privy Council the Federal Court was regarded by many as an intermediate appellate court, and therefore was denied the position of prominence it merited. Nonetheless, the Federal Court contributed significantly to India's constitutional development, and when it yielded to the Supreme Court of India on January 26, 1950, it passed to its successor a tradition of the highest standards of independence, integrity and impartiality.

3 The New Judicial Establishment

Although the present Supreme Court of India did not supercede the Federal Court until January 26, 1950, in the early months of 1947, even before the realization of national independence, the Constituent Assembly of India appointed a committee composed of five distinguished lawyers and ex-jurists,[1] and instructed this group to prepare a report containing their suggestions and recommendations regarding changes which should be made in the central judiciary after independence. The essence of this committee's brief report,[2] submitted on May 21, 1947, was that the jurisdiction and powers of the successor to the Federal Court should be much broader than the jurisdiction and powers then being exercised by the Federal Court. The committee recommended that the new court should have an exclusive original jurisdiction in disputes between the central government and a constituent unit and between the constituent units, jurisdiction to decide upon the constitutional validity of all legislative enactments, jurisdiction with respect to matters arising out of treaties, jurisdiction for the purpose of enforcing the Fundamental Rights which would be guaranteed by the Constitution, jurisdiction to give advisory opinions,[3] and a "general

---

[1] S. Varadachariar, Alladi Krishnaswami Ayyar, B. L. Mitter, K. M. Munshi, and B. N. Rao.

[2] *Report of Ad Hoc Committee on the Supreme Court*, No. CA/63/Cons./47, *Constituent Assembly Debates*, IV (1947), July 21, 1947, pp. 731–734.

[3] "There has been considerable difference of opinion among jurists and political thinkers as to the expediency of placing on the Supreme Court an obligation to advise the Head of State on difficult questions of law. ... Having given our best consideration to the arguments [*sic*] pros and cons, we feel that it will be on the whole better to continue this jurisdiction even under the new Constitution" (*Report of Ad Hoc Committee on the Supreme*

appellate jurisdiction similar to that now exercised by the Privy Council."[4] Furthermore, the Committee recommended that Parliament have power to confer upon the Supreme Court other powers and jurisdiction at any time after the Constitution became operative.[5]

In view of the extensive jurisdiction of the proposed court, the committee suggested that the court would require ten puisne or associate judges, in addition to the Chief Justice. After recommending that the qualifications for appointment to the Supreme Court should be very similar to those set forth in the 1935 Act for judges of the Federal Court, the committee demonstrated its great concern with the matter of judicial independence by devoting much attention to the mode of appointment of judges. Indeed, only with regard to this matter was the committee unable to offer a unanimous recommendation.

> We do not think that it will be expedient to leave the power of appointing judges of the Supreme Court to the unfettered discretion of the President of the Union. We recommend that either of the following methods may be adopted. One method is that the President should in consultation with the Chief Justice of the Supreme Court (so far as the appointment of puisne judges is concerned) nominate a person whom he considers fit to be appointed to the Supreme Court and the nomination should be confirmed by a majority of at least 7 out of a panel of 11 composed of some of the Chief Justices of the High Courts of the constituent units, some members of both the Houses of the Central Legislature, and some of the law officers of the Union. The other method is that the panel of 11 should recommend three names out of which the President, in consultation with the Chief Justice, may select a judge for the appointment. The same procedure should be followed for the appointment of the Chief Justice except, of course, that in this case there will be no consultation with the Chief Justice. To ensure that the panel will be both independent and command confidence the panel should not be an *ad hoc* body but must be one appointed for a term of years.[6]

Once submitted, this *Report* was turned over to the powerful Union Constitution Committee, which was under the chairmanship of Pandit Jawaharlal Nehru.

Court, No. CA/63/Cons./47, *Constituent Assembly Debates*, IV (1947), July 21, 1947, paragraph 11).

[4] *Report of Ad Hoc Committee on the Supreme Court*, No. CA/63/Cons./47, *Constituent Assembly Debates*, IV (1947), July 21, 1947, paragraph 9.

[5] *Report of Ad Hoc Committee on the Supreme Court*, No. CA/63/Cons./47, *Constituent Assembly Debates*, IV (1947), July 21, 1947, paragraph 7.

[6] *Report of Ad Hoc Committee on the Supreme Court*, No. CA/63/Cons./47, *Constituent Assembly Debates*, IV (1947), July 21, 1947, paragraph 14.

On July 21, 1947, this committee submitted to the President of the Constituent Assembly its *Report on the Principles of the Union Constitution,*[7] clause 18 of which made it clear that all recommendations of the Ad Hoc Committee had been accepted by the Nehru Committee with one exception—both modes of appointment of judges suggested for consideration by the Ad Hoc Committee were rejected. They were replaced by a recommendation that "a Judge of the Supreme Court shall be appointed by the President after consulting the Chief Justice and such other judges of the Supreme Court and such judges of the High Courts as may be necessary for the purpose."[8]

The next step was the discussion of the Nehru Committee's *Report* in the Constituent Assembly. However, comments by members of the Assembly relative to the Supreme Court were limited almost entirely to the matter of the mode of appointment of judges,[9] i.e., the *Ad Hoc Committee Report* itself was not discussed at all. Furthermore, even this brief discussion of matters pertaining to the new court served only to raise for consideration other alternative modes of appointment; there was little enthusiasm apparent concerning the mode of appointment recommended by the Nehru Committee.

In August of 1947, the constitution-making process moved into an important stage when the Constituent Assembly appointed the so-called "Drafting Committee," and selected Dr. B. R. Ambedkar as chairman.[10] The function of the Drafting Committee was

> to scrutinise the draft of the text of the Constitution of India prepared by the Constitutional Adviser giving effect to the decisions taken already in the Assembly and including all matters which are ancillary thereto or which have to be provided in such a Constitution, and to submit to the Assembly for consideration the text of the draft Constitution as revised by the Committee.[11]

At this point it is proposed to abandon this chronological discussion of various reports and of debates in the Constituent Assembly, and instead move directly to the provisions eventually embodied in the 1950 Constitution concerning

---

[7] No. CA/63/Cons./47, *Constituent Assembly Debates,* IV (1947), July 21, 1947, pp. 716–731.

[8] No. CA/63/Cons./47, *Constituent Assembly Debates,* IV (1947), July 21, 1947, p. 727.

[9] *Constituent Assembly Debates,* IV (1947), July 28, 1947, pp. 838–839 and July 29, 1947, pp. 889–908.

[10] The Drafting Committee's other members were N. Gopalaswami Ayyangar, Alladi Krishnaswami Ayyar, K. M. Munshi, Saiyid Mohammad Saadulla, N. Madhava Rau, and D. P. Khaitan.

[11] *Constituent Assembly Debates,* V (1947), August 29, 1947, p. 336.

the Supreme Court, reverting to the Assembly debates and the Draft Constitution only when necessary for the purpose of clarifying a particular article or clause.[12] However, one very important point must be made with regard to the Draft Constitution. Whereas the members of the Ad Hoc Committee concluded their *Report* with the recommendation that only the main outline of the powers, jurisdiction and nature of the Supreme Court be embodied in the proposed Constitution, and that detailed provisions be incorporated later in a "separate Judiciary Act to be passed by the Union Legislature,"[13] a view shared also by leading members of the Constituent Assembly in 1947,[14] the Draft Constitution, when it appeared in February 1948, contained twenty-one articles and numerous clauses and subclauses concerning all matters which might conceivably concern a Supreme Court. Why it was decided to abandon the idea of Constitutional brevity and a separate Judiciary Act is nowhere made clear. By the time the completed Constitution appeared in late 1949, even more detail had been added as a result of amendments and new articles inserted by the Constituent Assembly. In its final form, the Constitution contained twenty-four articles pertaining to the Supreme Court.[15]

Before embarking upon a discussion of the major constitutional provisions which concern the Supreme Court, it should be noted that the Supreme Court of India sits at the summit of a pyramidal, unified and integrated judicial system. Though the formal political structure of the Republic of India is primarily federal, its judicial organization is purely unitary. Both Union and State laws are interpreted and litigated in a single court system; there is no division of judicial business between the Union and the States. In short, unlike most federal constitutional structures which provide for a dual judiciary as well as a dual polity, independent India's constitution-makers provided for a single judicial structure. This was done, according to the

---

[12] This sudden departure from the chronological scheme is warranted because (i) the provisions in the Draft Constitution which related to the Supreme Court were amended and modified only slightly by both the Drafting Committee and the Constituent Assembly, and (ii) the papers of Sir B. N. Rao (the Constitutional Adviser) who, together with his staff, wrote the Draft Constitution, have not yet been published in their entirety, and one can only guess at this time why certain provisions concerning the Supreme Court were incorporated in the Constitution.

Recently, selected speeches, articles and papers of Sir B. N. Rao were edited by B. Shiva Rao and published under the title *India's Constitution in the Making* (second revised edition; Madras: Allied Publishers, 1963).

[13] *Report of Ad hoc Committee on the Supreme Court*, paragraph 16.

[14] See, e.g., *Constituent Assembly Debates*, IV (1947), July 29, 1947, pp. 900–901.

[15] Constitution of India, 1950, Part V, Chapter IV, Articles 124–147.

chairman of the Drafting Committee, in order "to eliminate all diversities in all remedial procedure."[16]

Immediately below the Supreme Court are the fifteen High Courts.[17] With the exception of the State of Nagaland,[18] each State in the Indian Union has a High Court of its own. Over these High Courts the Supreme Court exercises no direct administrative control, so in this sense the judiciary in India is not really centrally "supervised." But by exercise of its extensive review powers, the Supreme Court is in a position to scrutinize High Court decisions, and thus bring about a very high degree of uniformity in constitutional and statutory interpretation. Thus, though in 1955 Justice Bose stated that "this Court has general powers of judicial superintendence over all Courts in India ...,"[19] he was referring to the Supreme Court's appellate jurisdiction, and not to any formal power of superintendence. The High Courts, on the other hand, do exercise direct administrative control over the subordinate judiciary in each State.[20]

The unitary character of the judicial structure is reflected in several constitutional provisions which strengthen and reinforce the authority of the Supreme Court. Article 141, e.g., provides that "the law declared by the Supreme Court shall be binding on all courts within the territory of India." Under the Authority of Article 142, the Supreme Court "may pass such decree or make such order as is necessary for doing complete justice in any cause or matter pending before it, and any decree so passed or order so made shall be enforceable throughout the territory of India. ..." Also, Article 144 provides that "all authorities, civil and judicial, in the territory of India shall act in aid of the Supreme Court."

[16] *Constituent Assembly Debates*, VII (1948), November 4, 1948, p. 37. Article 247 of the Constitution, however, empowers Parliament to "... provide for the establishment of any additional courts for the better administration of laws made by Parliament or of any existing laws with respect to a matter enumerated in the Union List." Though the authority under this provision has been exercised so far only to establish administrative tribunals, it is possible that Parliament might establish a separate set of courts for the application and interpretation of Union laws.

[17] There are presently twenty-four High Courts in India-*Eds* (note by editors).

[18] For the time being, Nagaland, which became a State in December of 1963, is sharing the services of the High Court of neighboring Assam.

[19] *Nar Singh and Another* v. The *State of Uttar Pradesh*, (1955) I *Supreme Court Reports* 238, 241. Although reports of Supreme Court decisions are published by several private presses, the *Supreme Court Reports* (hereafter S.C.R.) is the official source.

[20] Article 227 of the Constitution provides: "Every High Court shall have superintendence over all courts and tribunals throughout the territories in relation to which it exercises jurisdiction." The extent of this superintendence is detailed in the clauses and subclauses of this article.

At present the Supreme Court is composed of a Chief Justice and thirteen puisne or associate judges.[21] Initially, provision was made for only seven puisne judges,[22] but, acting under the authority of Article 124, Parliament in 1956 increased the number to ten.[23] This increase in personnel was effected upon the recommendation of the Chief Justice, who earlier had asked for three additional judges in view of an increase in the work of the Court.[24] But from 1956 to 1960, although more cases were disposed of during each of these years, the number of cases in arrears continued to increase.[25] Accordingly, the Chief Justice suggested that an additional three judges be appointed in order to cope with the increasing arrears, and in order to dispose of cases with a minimum of delay.[26] Parliament responded quickly by passing the Supreme Court (Number of Judges) Amendment Act, 1960, which brought the number of puisne judges up to the present thirteen.

The fact that the personnel strength of the Supreme Court now stands at fourteen raises the question of whether there is a maximum number of judges which, if exceeded, might result in a group so unwieldy as to be inconsistent with effective action as a body. However, this question may not be of crucial importance in view of the fact that the Indian Supreme Court employs the "Division Bench" system. Unlike the Supreme Court of the United States, where all cases are decided by the full court (except when a judge disqualifies himself because of a personal interest in a particular case), the Supreme Court of India sits in four Benches, each of which functions simultaneously. Until 1960, there were only three Benches—Constitution, Civil and Criminal— comprised of five, three and three judges, respectively. However, after the personnel of the Court was increased to fourteen in 1960, Chief Justice Sinha created a fourth Bench, and also redesignated one of the existing Benches,

---

[21] The Supreme Court (Number of Judges) Amendment Act, 2008 increased the maximum number of judges of the Supreme Court to thirty, excluding the Chief Justice-*Eds.*

[22] The emergence of the Supreme Court in 1950 caused absolutely no change in judicial personnel—all five Federal Court puisne judges and Chief Justice Kania continued to serve on the highest Bench. The sixth puisne judge (N. C. Aiyar) was not appointed until September 23, 1950, and the seventh (Vivian Bose) until March 5, 1951.

[23] Supreme Court (Number of Judges) Act, 1956.

[24] *Lok Sabha Debates,* 2nd Series, 10th Session, XLIII (1960), April 27, 1960, col. 14145.

[25] According to statistics announced in Parliament, 2,272 cases were pending before the Supreme Court in 1957, while two years later the number pending had increased to 2598 (*Lok Sabha Debates,* 2nd Series, 10th Session, XLIII (1960), April 27, 1960, col. 14145).

[26] The Supreme Court attempts to dispose of criminal appeals within six months, and other appeals within a two-year period (*Lok Sabha Debates,* 2nd Series, 10th Session, XLIII (1960), April 27, 1960, col. 14146).

with the result that today there are five judges on the Constitution Bench, three on the Criminal Bench, three on the "Tax Bench" (although other civil matters are also considered by this Bench), and three which hear cases arising out of industrial or labor disputes.[27]

According to Chief Justice Sinha, the Bench assignments are made with a view toward best utilizing the experience and special qualifications of each member of the Court. Thus, e.g., those best equipped by training and temperament to hear criminal appeals are assigned to the Criminal Bench. In determining the number of Benches and their composition, the Chief Justice is restricted by only one constitutional provision: "The minimum number of Judges who are to sit for the purpose of deciding any case involving a substantial question of law as to the interpretation of this Constitution or for the purpose of hearing any reference under Article 143 shall be five ...,"[28] i.e., the Constitution Bench must be composed of at least five judges. Occasionally, however, when the Court is faced with a particularly important matter, the Chief Justice may increase the strength of the Constitution Bench, or, for that matter, any one of the other Benches.

The framers of the Indian Constitution were insistent not only that the judiciary be independent of the executive and legislature, but also that it be composed of the most competent people available; hence, the minimum qualifications for the appointment to the Supreme Court are set forth in the Constitution. In order to merit consideration, one must be a citizen of India and (i) have served for at least five years as a Judge of a High Court or of two or more such Courts in succession; (ii) have been for at least ten years an advocate of a High Court or of two or more such Courts in succession; or (iii) be, "in the opinion of the President, a distinguished jurist."[29] This last category, which did not appear in the Draft Constitution, was inserted by the Constituent Assembly in order "to open a wider field of choice for the President,"[30] and has the effect of making an academic lawyer with no judicial experience eligible for appointment to the nation's highest judicial tribunal.

All appointments to the Supreme Court are made by the President of India "after consultation with some of the Judges of the Supreme Court and of the High Courts in the States as the President may deem necessary for the purpose ..., provided that in the case of appointment of a Judge other than the Chief Justice, the Chief Justice of India shall always be consulted."[31] Though this particular

---

[27] Interview with Chief Justice B. P. Sinha, New Delhi, February 14, 1963.
[28] Constitution of India, Article 145.
[29] Constitution of India, Article 124(3)(c).
[30] *Constituent Assembly Debates*, VIII (1949), May 24, 1949, p. 241.
[31] Constitution of India, Article 124(2).

mode of appointment is nearly identical to that recommended in 1947 by the Nehru Committee, before it was finally accepted by the Constituent Assembly, this matter was the subject of more debate and greater attention than any other of the twenty-four articles concerning the Supreme Court. The aim of the framers was, quite clearly, to remove or guard against every possible danger of political considerations, political pressures or political patronage in the process of appointing judges. There was then in India the feeling, just as there is today, that the greater the role of the executive or legislature in the appointment process, the weaker and less independent will be the judiciary. Although documentation is hardly necessary, the following views quoted are very representative of Indian thinking: "It is always better that judges be appointed by judges rather than by party politicians. To allow the executive to appoint judges will only mean the destruction of judicial independence."[32] Another illustration of this attitude is the following, taken from a speech of Dr. Ambedkar:

> It seems to me, in the circumstances in which we live today, where the sense of responsibility has not grown to the same extent to which we find it in the United States, it would be dangerous to leave the appointments to be made by the President, without any kind of reservation or limitation, that is to say, merely on the advice of the executive of the day. Similarly, it seems to me that to make every appointment which the Executive wishes to make subject to the concurrence of the Legislature is also not a very suitable provision. Apart from its being cumbrous, it also involves the possibility of the appointment being influenced by political pressure and political considerations. The draft article, therefore, steers a middle course. It does not make the President the supreme and absolute authority in the matter of making appointments. It does not also import the influence of the Legislature. The provision in the article is that there should be consultation of persons who are *ex hypothesi*, well qualified to give proper advice in matters of this sort. …[33]

Although the Constitution vests the power of appointment in the President, the President of India is a Head of State, and not the Head of Government, with the result that the President acts not according to his own discretion, but in accordance with advice from the Council of Ministers, i.e., the Prime Minister and the Cabinet. Furthermore, it is important to note that whereas the Chief Justice must be *consulted* with regard to the appointment of puisne judges, his *concurrence* is not a constitutional requirement. An amendment was put forward in the Constituent Assembly to require the concurrence of the Chief Justice, but was not accepted.[34]

[32] P. Kodanda Rao, "Appointment of Judges in India," *Hindustan Standard*, April 16, 1962.

[33] *Constituent Assembly Debates*, VIII (1949), May 24, 1949, p. 258.

[34] *Constituent Assembly Debates*, VIII (1949), May 24, 1949, p. 261.

Since 1950, every appointment to the Supreme Court has been made from the ranks of the active or retired judges of the High Courts; neither members of the Bar nor "distinguished jurists" (in the constitutional sense) have been appointed.[35] According to the Law Commission, which reviewed carefully the selection process, members of the Bar have been excluded from appointment because of the "view of the appointment authorities that it will be somewhat hazardous to appoint to the Bench a person straight from the Bar without previous judicial experience."[36] The Government, however, while admitting that it "desires to appoint those who have much experience," claims to have offered Supreme Court judgeships to "at least two advocates," but both refused the appointment because they were unwilling to sacrifice a lucrative private practice for a less remunerative Supreme Court post.[37] No academic lawyer had been appointed because the Law Commission discovered, "we have not produced in our country academic lawyers and jurists of note who could, as in the United States, be honoured with seats on the Supreme Court Bench."[38]

Although the Law Commission was of the view that too much emphasis was being placed on previous judicial experience in the appointment of Supreme Court judges, there is much evidence of a more general approval of staffing the Court by "promotions" from the High Courts. By way of illustration, a former Chief Justice of India has been quoted as saying that

... the present method of selecting judges from the judges of the High Court, retired or about to retire has, by and large, worked satisfactorily so far. If the selection is properly made, this method is calculated to ensure some judicial experience and some capacity to form a sound and balanced judgment and to express it with clarity, the High Court being a good training as well as a testing ground for potential Supreme Court Judges. Selection from the Bar may not ensure these essential

[35] Members of the Bar were later appointed directly as judges of the Supreme Court. See George H. Gadbois Jr, *Judges of the Supreme Court of India: 1950–1989* (Oxford University Press 2012)-*Eds*.

[36] Law Commission of India, *Fourteenth Report: Reform of Judicial Administration*, two volumes. (New Delhi: Ministry of Law, 1958), I, 35. The Law Commission was appointed in 1955 and given the following terms of reference: "*firstly*, to review the system of judicial administration in all its aspects and suggest ways and means for improving it and making it speedy and less expensive; *secondly*, to examine the Central Acts of general application and importance, and recommend the line on which they should be amended, revised, consolidated or otherwise brought up to date."Of all the reports and recommendations which emerged from the deliberations and research by the Law Commission, there is no doubt that the *Fourteenth Report*, which related most directly to the judicial system, was the most controversial and drew the most comment.

[37] *Lok Sabha Debates*, 2nd Series, 10th Session, XLIII (1960), April 27, 1960, cols. 14150–51. See further, Law Commission's *Fourteenth Report*, I, 36.

[38] Law Commission's *Fourteenth Report*, I, 35.

qualities and qualifications. I have known several distinguished members of the Bar who would have made thoroughly bad judges.[39]

The Constitution fixes sixty-five as the mandatory retirement age for Supreme Court judges, and sixty for judges of the High Courts,[40] i.e., the same retirement ages as the 1935 Act established for Federal Court and High Court judges.[41] Considerable attention was given this matter of compulsory retirement by the Constituent Assembly, and the debates indicate that there were two major reasons why both mandatory retirement and the difference between the retirement ages of Supreme Court and High Court judges were decided upon. The former owes its existence to a widespread fear among the framers that unless a retirement age was fixed in the Constitution, judges might be inclined toward prolonging their periods of service on the Court beyond their years of usefulness.[42] In other words, many were of the view that once a judge of the Supreme Court reached age sixty-five, he might well no longer possess the mental alertness necessary for performing strenuous judicial duties. A concise but cogent expression of this attitude is found in "Memorandum from the Ministry of Home Affairs on the Provisions in the Draft Constitution Relating to the Judiciary,"[43] and, though the reference is to the High Court judges, it obviously applies equally to Supreme Court judges: "Experience has shown that most High Court Judges are well past the peak of their usefulness by the time they attain the age of 60. ..."[44]

Although the members of the Constituent Assembly were nearly unanimous[45] in sharing the view that a fixed retirement age was imperative, many recognized

[39] Quoted in Law Commission's *Fourteenth Report*. The Chief Justice is not identified.

[40] Articles 124 and 217.

[41] The retirement age for High Court judges was increased to sixty-two by the Constitution (Fifteenth Amendment) Act, 1963-*Eds.*

[42] *Constituent Assembly Debates*, VIII (1949), May 24, 1949, p. 236ff.

[43] *Comments on the Provisions Contained in the Draft Constitution of India* (New Delhi: Constituent Assembly of India, Government of India Press, 1943).

[44] *Comments on the Provisions Contained in the Draft Constitution of India*, p. 12.

[45] There were, however, other ages of mandatory retirement suggested and different reasons offered as to why there should be a fixed retirement age. One Assembly member, e.g., urged that Supreme Court judges should be compelled to retire at age sixty because "in our country, Sir, the ideal, the ancient ideal has been that every person in the fourth stage of his life must become a *Sanyasi* and must serve society in an honorary capacity. This is the standard which has been set before us by our ancient sages, and I think, Sir, we can reasonably expect of everybody, and more particularly of the learned ones like the Judges of the Supreme Court, to set a good example for everybody else, of service to the country in an honorary capacity after the age of sixty years" (*Constituent Assembly Debates*, VIII (1949), May 24, 1949, p. 237).

that a constitutional provision of this nature would result in certain disadvantages. The Chairman of the Drafting Committee, e.g., in the following words recognized that a fixed retirement age is not an entirely satisfactory solution:

> If you fix any age-limit, what you are practically doing is to drive away a man who notwithstanding the age we have prescribed ..., is hale and hearty, sound in mind and sound in body and capable for a certain number of years of rendering perfectly good service to the State. I entirely agree that sixty-five cannot always be regarded as the zero hour in a man's intellectual ability.[46]

Similarly, Prime Minister Nehru agreed that "when you need the best men, obviously age cannot be a criterion."[47] Nonetheless, he felt that sixty-five was a reasonable age at which Supreme Court judges should retire, for, though for members of Parliament or the Cabinet no age limit was prescribed, if the voters believed that a member of Parliament was too old to be useful, he would not be reelected. Nehru added that judges, on the other hand, are not subject to such periodic scrutiny; hence the need for a fixed retirement age.[48]

Although, at first glance, it appears somewhat incongruous that a judge of a High Court is constitutionally unfit to perform his duties upon reaching the age of sixty, while a judge of the Supreme Court may continue until age sixty-five, there is a quite rational explanation. The retirement age of High Court judges was set at sixty because it was anticipated that the most competent and experienced of these retired judges would be promoted to the Supreme Court,[49] an expectation which has been fulfilled time and time again since 1950.

Since 1950, the principle of mandatory retirement at age sixty-five has been the subject of both approval and criticism, and both have emanated from the highest quarters. For example, Chief Justice Patanjali Sastri, upon reaching retirement age in 1954, remarked that "it is a wise provision of our Constitution which says that a man becomes too old at sixty-five to be useful as a Judge. A Judge's work is very exacting."[50] On the other hand, a former Chief Justice of India, B. P. Sinha, holds firmly to the opposite view. In 1961, he asserted that the constitution-makers had "gone grievously wrong" in fixing a retirement age for judges because many judges who are compelled to retire "are not only willing

---

[46] *Constituent Assembly Debates*, VIII (1949), May 24, 1949, p. 259.

[47] *Constituent Assembly Debates*, VIII (1949), May 24, 1949, p. 247.

[48] *Constituent Assembly Debates*, VIII (1949), May 24, 1949, p. 247.

[49] See explanation of K. M. Munshi in *Constituent Assembly Debates*, VIII (1949), May 24, 1949, p. 670. Cf. *Lok Sabha* Debates, Part 2, 13th Session, VII (1956), August 20, 1956, col. 3827.

[50] *Supreme Court Journal*, XVII (1954), p. 5.

but are also able to discharge their onerous duties enthusiastically."[51] The Law Commission, however, though it considered recommending the raising of the age of retirement to seventy, hesitated to do so because

> the duties of a Judge of the Supreme Court are very onerous and the conditions as to the expectation of life and the age up to which persons can retain unimpaired their mental capacities are in our country very different from those obtaining in the United States of America and the United Kingdom. ... The raising of the age limit of retirement of the Supreme Court Judges beyond sixty-five will be an experiment fraught with hazards.[52]

Yet a far greater cause for concern than the effects of a mandatory retirement age per se, is the fact that the fixed retirement age *plus* the practice of appointing to the Supreme Court persons who have retired or are about to retire from the High Courts has meant that the personnel of the Court are constantly changing. Since 1950, no less than thirty judges, including seven Chief Justices, have served on the Supreme Court. Of the original six judges, by February 1956, only S. R. Das remained. The average tenure of the first dozen members of the Court was just under five years.

The Law Commission regarded this rapid turnover of personnel as an unhealthy situation:

> In our view, it is undesirable that a person who would have a short tenure of office should be chosen as a Judge of the Court. It is imperative in the interests of the stability of the judicial administration of the country that a Judge of the

---

[51] *The Hindustan Times* (Delhi), February 2, 1961. It should be pointed out that elsewhere in the Constitution (Article 128) there is a provision which authorizes the Chief Justice, with the consent of the President, to request a retired Supreme Court Judge to return to the Court for a specified period. Since 1950, this has been done six times with four retired judges (Saiyid Fazl Ali: October 15, 1951 to May 30, 1952; N. C. Aiyar: September 5, 1955 to October 31, 1955; December 1, 1955 to December 31, 1955, and from January 1, 1956 to May 11, 1956; Vivian Bose: September 9, 1957 to September 30, 1958; T. L. V. Aiyar: March 1, 1961 to April 30, 1961). It appears that retired judges are recalled usually to replace temporarily a permanent judge who is ill and unable to perform his duties.

In addition, "if at any time there should not be a quorum of the Judges of the Supreme Court ...," the Chief Justice, with the consent of the President, may request the attendance on the Supreme Court of a judge of a High Court who is qualified for appointment to the Supreme Court. He would be termed an "ad hoc Judge," and would remain on the Court only until his services are no longer required (Constitution of India, Article 127).

[52] Law Commission's *Fourteenth Report*, I, 38.

Supreme Court should be able to have a tenure of office of at least ten years. Too frequent a change of personnel has its disadvantages in a Court whose decisions lay down the law of the land and are binding on all the Courts in India. Certainty in the law and a continuity in the approach to some basic questions are fundamental requisites and these tend to be impaired if judicial personnel is subject to frequent changes.[53]

The remedy, according to the Law Commission, was to appoint younger High Court judges, who could look forward to at least a ten-year tenure on the Bench. In offering this recommendation, the Commission urged the appointing authorities to recognize that "prompt and unhesitating recognition should be given to merit and ability, regardless of considerations of seniority and experience. It must not be forgotten that youth carries freshness and vigor of mind which have their advantages as much as maturity and experience flowing from age."[54] Furthermore, the Commission suggested that distinguished members of the Bar might be more willing to accept a Supreme Court judgeship "if care is taken to invite them to the Bench at an age when they would have a fairly long tenure on the Bench."[55]

Whether the rapid turnover of judges has had the effect of keeping constitutional and statutory interpretation in a state of flux, as has been alleged by some writers,[56] is by no means readily apparent. Measured only by the few instances in which the Supreme Court has specifically overruled previous decisions, the turnover in personnel has not had that effect. There is little doubt, however, that frequent change in Court membership does create the possibility of a discontinuous approach to constitutional and statutory interpretation.

Before leaving this matter of short tenures, it should be noted that the appointing authorities apparently recognized a detrimental effect on the highest judiciary of short tenures several years before the publication of the Law Commission's *Fourteenth Report*, for those judges who have been appointed since 1955 can look forward to an average tenure of about eight years. Thus, the dangers of discontinuity in interpretation, if ever serious, are less a matter of concern today.

Probably more serious than the rapid turnover of puisne judges is the practice of the appointing authorities, observed in all instances but one since 1950, of promoting the senior-most puisne judge to the office of Chief Justice each

[53] Law Commission's *Fourteenth Report*, I, 37.

[54] Law Commission's *Fourteenth Report*, I, 37.

[55] Law Commission's *Fourteenth Report*, I, 37.

[56] K. V. Rao, *Parliamentary Democracy of India* (Calcutta: The World Press Private Ltd., 1961), p. 210.

time a vacancy has occurred.[57] As a result of this practice, the Supreme Court, in its first fifteen years, has been led by no less than seven Chief Justices, their average tenure being just over two years.[58]

In that the Chief Justice is the most important judicial officer in India, whose many responsibilities require the utmost of both judicial and administrative talent, it would seem that the appointing authorities would employ some criterion other than mere seniority. Indeed, when one is aware that the Chief Justice is responsible for the assignment of his colleagues to the several Benches, for the assignment of opinion writing (when the Chief Justice has voted with the majority), and is expected to play a key role in the process of selecting both Supreme Court and High Court judges, it would seem that the most able person available, regardless of whether he be the senior-most puisne Supreme Court judge, a High Court judge, an eminent advocate from the Bar, or a distinguished law professor, should receive the appointment. In short, the Chief Justice should be a competent administrator, a shrewd judge of men and personalities, and a towering personality himself. Under the present practice, where the pinnacle of judicial rank is reached on the sole basis of being "next in line," it is merely fortuitous if the Chief Justice happens to become a brilliant leader of the Court. At any rate, the criterion employed thus far has had the effect of each incumbent of the Chief Justiceship enjoying a tenure "too short to enable him to leave any powerful impression of his individuality or legal philosophy in regard to the work of the Court."[59] Thus there is little chance of any Chief Justice of India impressing the Court and nation with his leadership to the degree to which this was done by Marshall, Taney and other Chief Justices of the Supreme Court of the United States.

In its *Fourteenth Report*, the Law Commission was most emphatic in deploring the fact that India had utilized five Chief Justices during the first eight years, and urged that such an important office should not be regulated merely by the consideration of seniority on the Bench. The Commission recommended that

---

[57] The only exception was the appointment of P. B. Gajendragadkar as Chief Justice upon the retirement of B. P. Sinha on February 1, 1964. "Next in line" at this time was Justice Syed Jafer Imam. He, however, has been so ill in recent years that he has attended sessions of the Supreme Court only rarely. Thus, it appears that he was passed over because of the state of his health. Had he been appointed, he would have been India's first Muslim Chief Justice.

[58] In 1954, there were three different Chief Justices. Patanjali Sastri retired in January, was replaced by Mehr Chand Mahajan who reached retirement age in December, at which time Bijan Kumar Mukherjea became Chief Justice.

[59] "The Outgoing and Incoming Chief Justices of the Supreme Court," *Madras Law Journal*, II (1959), p. 33.

in choosing a Chief Justice, many criteria other than seniority should be considered, and recommended also that the tenure of the Chief Justice should be at least five to seven years because "on him rests the tone and tradition of the highest Court of the land. ..."[60]

Although the practice of seniority being the sole norm considered in the selection of a Chief Justice may, with much justification, be reproved, it does result in one "advantage" in a country where executive patronage and political considerations often are alleged to be important considerations in appointments, whether judicial, administrative or otherwise. The advantage, if it may be so termed, in considering only seniority when selecting a Chief Justice, is the fact that considerations of patronage or politics obviously do not enter into the promotion of the senior-most puisne judge to the Chief Justiceship, although, of course, these considerations may not have been absent earlier in the judge's initial appointment to a High Court and in his subsequent promotion to the Supreme Court.

Once appointed, a judge of the Supreme Court may be removed only on the ground of "proved misbehaviour or incapacity," and the President of India will issue the removal order only after "an address by each House of Parliament supported by a majority of the total membership of that House and by a majority of not less than two-thirds of the members of that House present and voting. ..."[61] To date there have been no instances of attempted or successful impeachment of a judge of the Supreme Court. In fact, the procedure for the presentation of an address and for the investigation and proof of the misbehavior or incapacity must be set forth in a Parliamentary enactment,[62] and such a law has not yet been enacted.[63] Furthermore, Parliament is prohibited from discussing the conduct of any judge in the discharge of his duties, except upon a motion seeking the judge's removal.[64] But this constitutional prohibition forbids only discussion with respect to the conduct of "any Judge," and does not immunize the Supreme Court or its decisions from critical discussion by the executive or legislature.

In addition to being immune from personal attacks by Parliament, the Supreme Court, "in order to maintain the dignity of the Court and to protect it from malicious and tendentious criticism,"[65] is empowered to punish for

---

[60] Law Commission's *Fourteenth Report*, I, 38–39.

[61] Constitution of India, Article 124(4). It may be observed that in an overwhelmingly one-party State, this provision may not offer much protection to a judge, for the Congress Party alone has the requisite majority.

[62] Constitution of India, Article 124(5).

[63] In 1968, Parliament passed the Judges (Inquiry) Act-*Eds.*

[64] Constitution of India, Article 121.

[65] M. V. Pylee, *Constitutional Government in India* (Bombay: Asia Publishing House, 1960), p. 427.

contempt of itself.[66] On several occasions the Supreme Court has invoked this power, the most notable case being that of *In Re the Editor, Printer and Publisher of "The Times of India."*[67] The editor of this widely-read daily newspaper had published a leading article entitled "A Disturbing Decision"[68] in which the Supreme Court was accused of arriving at a decision on the basis of "extraneous considerations." The Supreme Court ruled that although it "is never over-sensitive to public criticism," the article,

> when it proceeded to attribute improper motives to the judges it not only transgressed the limits of fair and *bona fide* criticism but had a clear tendency to affect the dignity and prestige of this Court. The article in question was thus a gross contempt of court. It is obvious that if an impression is created in the minds of the public that the judges in the highest court in the land act on extraneous considerations in deciding cases, the confidence of the whole community in the administration of justice is bound to be undermined and no greater mischief than that can possibly be imagined.[69]

This does not imply, of course, that decisions of the Supreme Court of India are immune from any constructive or thoughtful criticism, but it does mean that such criticism must be made in good faith and should not impute improper motives to those taking part in the administration of justice. The Judicial Committee of the Privy Council once had an occasion to remark that "justice is not a cloistered virtue; she must be allowed to suffer the scrutiny and respectful, though outspoken, comments of ordinary men."[70]

The Second Schedule of the Constitution sets the salary of the puisne Supreme Court judges at 4,000 rupees per month, and that of the Chief Justice at 5,000 rupees[71].[72] Prior to the advent of the 1950 Constitution, members of the Federal Court were paid higher salaries (5,500 rupees for

[66] Constitution of India, Article 129. This article provides also that the Supreme Court is a "court of record," i.e., "a court the records of which are admitted to be of evidentiary value and they are not to be questioned when they are produced before any court" (*Constituent Assembly Debates*, VIII (1949), May 27, 1949, p. 382).

[67] (1953) S.C.R. 215. Cf. *Brahma Prakash Sharma and Others* v. *The State of Uttar Pradesh*, (1953) S.C.R. 1169, and *In re Hira Lal Dixit and Two Others*, (1955) I S.C.R. 677.

[68] *Times of India*, October 30, 1952.

[69] (1953) S.C.R. 215, 217. However, "in view of the unconditional apology tendered by the respondents and the undertaking given by them to give wide publicity to their regret, we have decided to drop further proceedings and we accept the apology. ..." (p. 217).

[70] *Ambard* v. *Attorney-General for Trinidad and Tobago*, (1936) A.C. 335.

[71] The rate of exchange at the time of writing this was approximately 4.75 rupees to 1 dollar (U.S.).

[72] The Fifty-Fourth Amendment to the Constitution increased the salary of Supreme Court judges to 9,000 rupees per month. This was enhanced to 90,000 rupees per month

puisne judges and 7,000 rupees for the Chief Justice), but with the coining of independence there came also an interest in economy and in personal sacrifice, with the result that not only judges but also ministers and other government servants suffered decreases in salary.[73] However, to compensate somewhat for the lowered salaries, the Constitution does provide that each judge is entitled, rent-free, to the use of a furnished residence, and to certain other allowances and privileges.[74] Elsewhere in the Constitution it is provided that "neither the privileges nor the allowances of a Judge nor his rights in respect of leave of absence or pension shall be varied to his disadvantage after his appointment."[75]

The Law Commission looked carefully at the salary situation and, though noting that the salaries received by Indian judges compared unfavorably with those of their counterparts in the United States and United Kingdom, hesitated to recommend any increase because "we are at a most critical stage in our economic development. Our conditions demand that everyone should in the interests of the nation put forward his best effort for the lowest remuneration possible."[76]

A member of the Supreme Court, once he reaches retirement age, receives a pension, the amount of which is determined by rules set forth in the Government of India (Federal Court) Order, 1937, as amended periodically. Although the rules employed in computing pensions are somewhat complicated, for illustrative purposes one might make use of some hypothetical figures computed by the Law Commission. A Supreme Court puisne judge who retires after a total service of seven years, including service as a High Court judge, would receive a pension of approximately 844 rupees per month.[77] A judge who served for ten

---

by subsequent acts passed by Parliament for this purpose. Similarly, the salary of the Chief Justice was raised by the Constitution Amendment to 10,000 rupees month. This was raised to 1,00,000 rupees per month by acts of Parliament-*Eds*.

[73] However, the former Federal Court judges who transferred to the Supreme Court in 1950 continued to draw their former higher salaries until they retired (Constitution of India, Second Schedule, Part D, Section 9(1)).

[74] Constitution of India, Second Schedule, Part D, Section 9(2).

[75] Constitution of India, Article 125. There is one exception to this rule, for if the President, under authority of Article 360, declares that "a situation has arisen whereby the financial stability or credit of India ... is threatened, he may by a Proclamation make a declaration to that effect." He then is empowered to "issue directions for the reduction of salaries and allowances of all or any class of persons serving in connection with the affairs of the Union including the Judges of the Supreme Court and the High Courts." To date, no such "financial emergency" has been declared.

[76] Law Commission's *Fourteenth Report*, I, 43.

[77] Presently, the pension payable is provided under the Supreme Court Judges (Salaries and Conditions of Service) Act, 1958-*Eds*.

years, inclusive of service on a High Court, would be entitled to a pension of 1,278 rupees monthly.[78]

The Law Commission also published figures indicating the pension actually being received by certain unnamed judges who have retired from the Court:

> A Judge who retired as the Chief Justice of the Supreme Court after service as a Judge of a High Court and the Federal Court (with a total service of about 15 years) became entitled to a pension of Rs. 1,700 per mensem. Another Judge who retired after a total length of service of 10½ years became entitled to a pension of a little less than Rs. 1200. A third Judge of the Supreme Court who retired after a total service of 19 years which included five years as a Judge of the Supreme Court, became entitled to a pension of about Rs. 1,500 per mensem. The pension normally earned would, on the average, come to about a third of the salary.[79]

After considering briefly the pension scales of retired judges in other countries, the Law Commission concluded that the pension of an Indian Supreme Court judge was not only "meagre" in itself, but had at least two serious consequences:

> It deters eminent members of the Bar from accepting judgeships. The main inducement to a member of the Bar to sacrifice his large income and accept a judgeship is, apart from the high status and dignity of the office, the consideration that he would have more leisure and greater security in the matter of income even in his declining years. A Judge of the Supreme Court is not entitled after retirement to plead or act in any Court or before any authority within the territory of India. He has to depend during the declining years of his life on his savings and the pension to which he is entitled as a retired judge. The meagre pension has thus also the undesirable consequence of driving some of the judges who have retired to find some remunerative occupation which affects the dignity of the high judicial office they held.[80]

But the recommendations offered by the Law Commission to alleviate this situation are somewhat peculiar in what was recommended was not a higher minimum pension, but a higher maximum pension (at least 2,500 rupees monthly for a puisne judge and 3,000 rupees for the Chief Justice).[81] However, it must be added that the Commission, in making this recommendation, was assuming acceptance of its earlier recommendation that younger judges be

---

[78] Law Commission's *Fourteenth Report*, I, 43.
[79] Law Commission's *Fourteenth Report*, I, 43.
[80] Law Commission's *Fourteenth Report*, I, 44.
[81] Law Commission's *Fourteenth Report*, I, 2.

appointed, thereby assuring a longer tenure and, since pension is determined by length of tenure, a more substantial pension.

Though these recommendations of the Law Commission have not been formally accepted or implemented, a few months before this *Fourteenth Report* was made public, Parliament enacted the Supreme Court Judges (Conditions of Service) Act, 1958,[82] the main purpose of which was to liberalize pensions and to improve certain other conditions of service. The Act fixed a minimum pension at 7,500 rupees per year, in an effort to provide for a situation where a judge is appointed but reaches the retirement age quickly, and also set the maximum pension of puisne judges at 20,000 rupees per year, and that of the Chief Justice at 26,000 rupees. However, except for the minimum figure, the sole criterion employed to determine pensions continues to be the number of years a judge spends on the Bench. In short, this Act seems to improve the position of only the "short-termer," and does not enhance in any appreciable amount the pensions of those who have spent many years on the Bench.

Although it may seem that undue attention has been accorded to the matter of retirement pensions, this was done with a purpose, for there is a widely-held view in India that an inadequate pension is the chief reason why few Supreme Court judges who reach mandatory retirement age have gone into real retirement. Indeed, a number of retired judges have found post-retirement employment in a variety of official positions, which, according to some critics, creates an impression in the public mind that high judicial office is merely a stepping stone for post-retirement sinecures or other official posts.

This matter of post-retirement employment, and the consequential dangers to judicial independence (whether imagined or real), though provoked, no doubt, by a low pension, is compounded by a provision in the Constitution which denies a retired judge the right to "plead or act in any court or before any authority within the territory of India."[83] Evidence available indicates that the framers inserted this prohibition in the Constitution in order to remove any temptation of a judge to seek a lucrative, post-retirement legal position in, e.g., a private firm,[84] and to eliminate the danger of a retired judge assuming private law practice and being in a position to influence his former colleagues. However, the explanation of this provision is also partly historical, for prior to 1950 the practice was that when a member of the Bar was appointed a High Court judge, he gave an undertaking not to practice after retirement in the High

---

[82] Supreme Court Judges (Conditions of Service) Act, 1958. Cf. *Lok Sabha Debates* XX, XXI, (September 24 and 25, 1958), cols. 5250, 8465–8484, 8663–8729, and 8729–8756.

[83] Article 124(7).

[84] *Constituent Assembly Debates*, VIII (1949), May 24, 1949, pp. 239–244.

Court of which he was a judge and in the courts subordinate thereto, but he was left free to practice in any other court.[85]

But the present prohibition imposed on Supreme Court judges goes further, for it deprives one who might still possess both the ability and the desire to continue working after retirement in his chosen profession. According to former Judge P. B. Mukharji of the Calcutta High Court, this provision, "unknown to any other Constitution in the world," although "intended to maintain the dignity of this great office," has

> a very deleterious effect. All that was necessary for the maintenance of the dignity of that judicial office was to prohibit the Judge from practising before the Court of which he was the Judge. To prevent him from practising anywhere in India before any Court or Authority is an unjustified confiscation of a lifetime's qualifications. ...[86]

However, while a retired judge is prohibited from private law practice, there is no prohibition against a retired judge being appointed by the Government to any official post, and a number of ex-judges have found post-retirement employment in various official positions. The most criticized of these appointments was that of Saiyid Fazl Ali, who was appointed Governor of Orissa shortly after retirement from the Supreme Court Bench.[87]

More often than receiving purely political appointments, however, retired judges have been appointed by the Government to various investigatory or special enquiry commissions or tribunals. For example, N. C. Aiyar was appointed Chairman of the Delimitation Commission in 1953, T. L. Aiyar was appointed Chairman of the Law Commission in 1958, and Vivian Bose was appointed in 1959 to investigate and submit a report on the politically volatile "Mundhra deal."[88] Such employment of judicial talent in this specialized form is difficult

[85] "Memorandum Representing the Views of the Federal Court and of the Chief Justices Representing All the Provincial High Courts of the Union of India," *Comments on the Provisions Contained in the Draft Constitution of India* (New Delhi: Constituent Assembly of India, Government of India Press, 1948), p. 23.

[86] P. B. Mukharji, "The Aspirations of the Indian Constitution," *The All India Reporter*, XLII (1955), p. 106. Until 1956 the same prohibition applied to retired High Court judges, but as a result of the Constitution (Seventh Amendment) Act, 1956, Article 220 was amended so as to permit ex-High Court judges to practice in the Supreme Court or in any High Court other than the one on which they served as a judge.

[87] The Governor of a State is appointed by the President and holds office during the pleasure of the President (Constitution of India, Articles 155 and 156).

[88] Shortly after Bose submitted his report, in which he concluded that a deal made between one Mundhra, a private citizen, and the Life Insurance Corporation of India, a public corporation, was connected with the former's contribution to the Congress

to criticize, especially in India where the public approves of the practice of appointing a judge as chairman of a commission or for holding a judicial inquiry into controversial events. This particular use of judges, both active and retired, originated long before independence, and indicated then, as it does now, the confidence of the public and the Government in the ability and integrity of the higher judiciary.

The Law Commission, however, concluded that any utilization by the Government of retired judges was inimical to judicial independence, and recommended a constitutional amendment prohibiting such employment:

> The Government is a party in a large number of causes in the highest Court and the average citizen may well get the impression, that a judge who might look forward to being employed by the Government after his retirement, does not bring to bear on his work that detachment of outlook which is expected of a judge in cases in which Government is a party. We are clearly of the view that the practice has a tendency to affect the independence of the judges and should be discontinued.[89]

Although the doctrine of the separation of powers is not *as* much a feature of the Indian system of government as the American, it is obvious from the constitutional provisions discussed here that the framers were much concerned with the matter of judicial independence, and sought earnestly to insulate the judiciary in every conceivable way from either fear or favor from the governing branches. The provisions relating to the mode of appointment, tenure, salary and pension, removal, immunity from personal attacks by Parliament, and power to punish for contempt were all designed to ensure against derogation

---

Party treasury, the Prime Minister unleashed what has been termed an "unwarranted and undignified attack" on ex-Judge Bose. ("Mr. Nehru's Indefensible Remarks," *The Eastern Economist*, XXXII, June 19, 1959, p. 1117.) Incensed with the findings of the Bose Enquiry Board, Nehru told the press that anyone who could come to such a conclusion suffered from a "lack of intelligence …, even if he is a high judge." This was followed by a letter from the Bar Library Club of Calcutta addressed to the Prime Minister in which the Club expressed its disapproval of Nehru's remarks. Nehru promptly apologized, stating that "I realize I should not have made even a casual remark of this kind and am sorry for it" (*Calcutta Weekly Notes*, July 13, 1959, p. 110). Furthermore, according to the article in *The Eastern Economist* quoted from above, Chief Justice Das of the Supreme Court reportedly wrote a letter to the Union Government in which "he has strongly protested against Mr. Nehru's unkind remark against his former colleague … and threatened not to permit judges of the High Courts and Supreme Court to serve on tribunals and investigation committees if their findings are to be rejected light-heartedly and they are to be accused of 'lack of intelligence' and similar other failings."

[89] Law Commission's *Fourteenth Report*, I, 46.

from the independence of judicial administration. The framers aspired, in the words of Dr. Ambedkar, "that the independence of the Judiciary from the Executive should be made as clear and definite as we could make it by law."[90]

Yet such carefully designed provisions in a constitution are alone not sufficient to ensure the independence of any judiciary for, regardless of the mode of appointment, there is no way of eliminating entirely political and other considerations. Indeed, one need not be so naïve as to believe that members of any court are selected on the sole basis of their probable excellence as jurists. However, it does not necessarily follow that merely because a judge owes his appointment to a political party he in the course of his career on the bench will be partial to that political party. In England, e.g., where constitutional safeguards are absent, and where judges are appointed by the Lord Chancellor and Prime Minister, both of whom are active party politicians, the judiciary is nonetheless independent, owing to the appointment of able personnel and to a long tradition of an independent judiciary.[91] In the United States, although the Constitution contains certain provisions designed to ensure an independent judiciary, and though many argue that judges should be selected without regard to political considerations, the appointment of federal judges is patently part of the overall political process. From 1885 to 1955, over 90 per cent of all appointments to the federal judiciary have been filled by members—in many cases very active members—of the same party as the President who chose them.[92] President Theodore Roosevelt appointed seventy-two federal judges, of whom sixty-nine were Republicans two were Democrats and one an independent. When the second President Roosevelt assumed office in 1933, he found a federal court system composed of 90 per cent Republicans. By 1944, he had made one hundred and eight appointments, of whom one hundred and six were Democrats and two were independents.[93] So it is quite clear that Presidents of the United States have taken care to select men whom they hope will promote the same concepts of the public interest as they hold themselves, with the result that party politics is a major consideration in the selection process in the United States. Yet the higher courts in both England and the United States enjoy a wide reputation for bold independence, and it is seldom even alleged that judges of these courts bow to fear or favor from the governing branches.

[90] *Constituent Assembly Debates*, VIII (1949), May 27, 1949, p. 397.

[91] Cf. K. Umamaheswaram (Andhra High Court), "Role of the Judiciary under the Constitution," *The All India Reporter*, XLVII (1960), pp. 5–8.

[92] Jack W. Peltason, *Federal Courts in the Political Process* (Garden City: Doubleday & Company, 1955), pp. 31–32. Cf. Evan A., Evans, "Political Influences in the Selection of Federal Judges," *Wisconsin Law Review* (May, 1943), pp. 330–351.

[93] Peltason, *Federal Courts in the Political Process*, pp. 31–32.

In India, however, it is all but unanimously held that untold evils result automatically from any influence, however slight, of party politics in the selection and appointment of judges. An illustration of this view can be taken from the Law Commission's *Report*. After emphasizing that judges of the Supreme Court must be selected "with an eye solely to their efficiency and capacity," the Commission asked:

> Can we say that such a course has been followed? It is widely felt that communal and regional considerations have prevailed in making the selection of the Judges. The idea seems to have gained ground that the component States of India should have, as it were, representation on the Court. Though we call ourselves a secular State, ideas of communal representation, which were viciously planted in our body by the British, have not entirely lost their influence. What perhaps is still more to be regretted is the general impression, that now and again executive influence exerted from the highest quarters has been responsible for some appointments to the Bench. It is undoubtedly true, that the best talent among the Judges of the High Courts has not always found its way to the Supreme Court. This has prevented the Court from being looked upon by the subordinate Courts and the public generally with that respect and, indeed, reverence to which it is by its status entitled.[94]

These allegations, which, not surprisingly, provoked more controversy than any other of the Commission's findings or criticisms, were flatly and vociferously denied by the Government. According to the then Home Minister, the late Pandit G. B. Pant, "since 1950, 17 Judges have been appointed to the Supreme Court and every one of these Judges was nominated and recommended by the Chief Justice of India. ... To say that the Judges that have been recruited there have just been thrust on the Court by somebody else is against the facts and is absolutely incorrect."[95] These statements of Pandit Pant, incidentally, have been verified by none other than a Chief Justice of India, who said that the Chief Justice does in fact initiate the appointment procedure by suggesting a name.[96]

---

[94] Law Commission's *Fourteenth Report*, I, 34.

[95] *Lok Sabha Debates,* 2nd Series, 7th Session, XXVIII (1959), March 20, 1959, col. 7521.

[96] Interview with Chief Justice B. P. Sinha, New Delhi, February 14, 1963. It should be pointed out that Pandit Pant denied only executive influence in the selection of Supreme Court judges, and said nothing about the alleged communal and regional considerations. However, it is a fact that there has always been at least one Muslim on the Bench (at present there are three), but it must be made very clear that this is certainly not proof that communalism was a consideration in any of these appointments, and there is no evidence at all that the Muslims who have served on the Supreme Court are not at least as able and qualified as others.

The intense concern with the purity and independence of the judiciary in India is both overdone and, in a sense, unrealistic, because wherever judges are appointed, regardless of constitutional safeguards, some degree of partisan politics or some considerations other than, or, more accurately, in addition to, professional competence will enter into the selection process. Also, though it is true that "the decision as to *who* will make the decisions affects what decisions will be made,"[97] and true also that those who are responsible for making appointments will usually seek to select men who will promote the same concepts of the public interest as their own, these are matters which are not necessarily inimical to a strong, competent and independent judiciary. These considerations do prove, however, that those who do the appointing must exhibit a high degree of integrity and a strong sense of their responsibilities, for even if it is recognized that questions of political affiliation and social and economic philosophy enter the selection process, if there is a real disregard of other considerations such as professional competence, personal integrity, and a capacity to bring a detached and objective mind to bear on cases which come before the court, irreparable damage to the independence and prestige of the judiciary may be the result.

The best test of the independence of the Supreme Court of India lies in the nature of its decisions and in its willingness to exercise fearlessly its powers of judicial review of both legislation and executive action, just as the actual role of the Court depends largely upon the manner in which its decisions are regarded by the Government. These matters will be discussed in Chapters V and VI.

Although the Law Commission alleged also that regional considerations were a factor in selecting Supreme Court judges, it is not easy to substantiate this charge. Of the first twenty-seven judges who have served, or who are now serving, on the Supreme Court, the regional representation is as follows: Madras (6), Bombay (4), Calcutta (4), Patna (4), Allahabad (3), Nagpur (3), Punjab (2), and Orissa (1). About all these figures prove is that the High Courts of Madras, Bombay and Calcutta, which are the three oldest, most distinguished High Courts in India, and which for a century have produced the bulk of India's best lawyers and jurists, are over-represented in the geographical sense.

[97] Peltason, *Federal Courts in the Political Process*, p. 29.

4 Jurisdiction and Powers of the Supreme Court

I ndian writers are very fond of pointing out that the Supreme Court of India "has wider jurisdiction than any other superior court in any part of the world,"[1] that the jurisdiction of the Court is so wide that "it will appear to be the most potent judicial organ in the world today."[2] If one looks only at the formal jurisdiction of the Court as it is set forth in the Constitution, one would have to agree with these statements, for it would be quite evident that the Court is in fact endowed with an extremely broad jurisdiction, and that it serves as the final court of appeal not only on federal and constitutional matters, but also in civil, criminal and other matters. Certainly the jurisdiction of the Indian Supreme Court is far more extensive than that of the Supreme Court of the United States. But what Indian writers often neglect to note is that an extensive jurisdiction does not mean that the Court is necessarily "powerful." It will become quite evident, not in this chapter but in the next, that extensive though the jurisdiction of the Indian Supreme Court may be, it is not in possession of much "power," owing chiefly to the absence of a due process clause and to the ease with which the Parliament may vitiate its decisions by amendment of the Constitution. In succeeding chapters the real power and role of the Supreme Court vis-à-vis Parliament and the Cabinet will be discussed; in the present chapter the concern will be with examining the Court's formal jurisdiction.

Given the fact that the Supreme Court's jurisdiction is much more extensive than that of the Federal Court, one might have expected to find in the *Constituent*

---

[1] M. V. Pylee, *Constitutional Government in India* (Bombay: Asia Publishing House, 1960), p. 428.

[2] M. P. Jain, *Outlines of Indian Legal History* (Delhi: Delhi University Press, 1952), p. 393.

Assembly Debates some lengthy discussion of this aspect of the new Constitution. Yet there was little discussion in the Assembly about the enlargement of the jurisdiction; indeed, there was clearly a large amount of consensus that the successor to the Federal Court be endowed with original and appellate powers very wide in scope. There was, in fact, more debate over the mode of appointment of judges than over all the provisions of the Constitution concerning the Court's formal jurisdiction.[3]

The explanation for this absence of controversy lies primarily in the fact that courts in India have long enjoyed a vast amount of prestige and confidence among the public. The High Courts, some dating back nearly a century prior to independence, and the Federal Court, had established an enviable record of integrity and independence.[4] Thus, when it came to deciding upon the jurisdiction of independent India's supreme tribunal, endowing it with an extensive jurisdiction was seen by most as both wise and desirable.

The jurisdiction of the Supreme Court may be divided into three categories—original, appellate, and advisory.

Original Jurisdiction

The Indian Supreme Court exercises two types of original jurisdiction. The first relates to disputes involving the units of the Indian federation, and is not different from that exercised by the Supreme Court of the United States. The second, however, is both the most unique and most important jurisdiction of the Indian Supreme Court, for it enables a person subject to the laws of India to go directly to the Supreme Court if he believes that his fundamental rights have been infringed by the provisions of a law passed by the Union Parliament or a State Legislature, or by some action taken by the Union or a State executive.

Article 131 of the 1950 Constitution endows the Supreme Court with an exclusive original jurisdiction in "any dispute—(a) between the Government of India and one or more States; or (b) between the Government of India and any State or States on one side and one or more other States on the other; or

---

[3] Part V, Chapter IV of the Constitution, entitled "The Union Judiciary".

[4] Numerous writers have made such observations. See, e.g., Ralph Braibanti's "Public Bureaucracy and Judiciary in Pakistan," in Joseph LaPalombara (ed.), *Bureaucracy and Political Development* (Princeton: Princeton University Press, 1963). Professor Braibanti contrasts the judiciary as a "symbol of compassionate justice and independence" with the bureaucracy, "a symbol of alien rule" (pp. 409, 435).

(c) between two or more States ... [p]rovided that the said jurisdiction shall not extend to a dispute arising out of any treaty, agreement, covenant, engagement, *sanad* or other similar instrument which, having been entered into or executed before the commencement of this Constitution, continues in operation after such commencement, or which provides that the said jurisdiction shall not extend to such a dispute."

This proviso refers to the Instruments of Accession negotiated in 1947 and succeeding years between the Government of India and the Rulers of the several hundred Indian States. Until 1947 the British had exercised suzerainty over these States, but with the passage of the Indian Independence Act, suzerainty lapsed and these States became, if only temporarily, sovereign entities. Thereupon, the rulers of the States contiguous to India were persuaded or forced to join the Union of India. Since these Instruments of Accession were executed under the strain of the political situation of that time, were not identical in terms or conditions, and were of a patently political nature, the framers of the 1950 Constitution decided that disputes arising out of these agreements should not be justiciable. The framers probably acted wisely, for otherwise the courts might have been flooded with petitions challenging the validity of these agreements.[5]

Although the Constitution thus prohibits litigation involving these Instruments of Accession, the Supreme Court did hear one original suit which had been filed in the Federal Court only eleven days prior to the coming into force of the 1950 Constitution, and which, by virtue of Article 374(2),[6] was transferred to the Supreme Court. In this case[7] the Rulers of seven former Princely States sought enforcement of what they claimed were certain rights deriving from the Instruments of Accession they had signed in 1947. The Court, however, never considered the Rulers' arguments, for it held that its jurisdiction in this matter was clearly barred by both the proviso to Article 131 and by Article 363. Thus the Supreme Court was able to hold that Article 374(2) was controlled by Article 363. In one other decision—*Virendra Singh*

---

[5] Although this proviso affects only the Supreme Court, Article 363 makes it clear that no court in India is permitted to take cognizance of a dispute arising out of one of these agreements. However, as will be seen in this chapter, the President of India may consult the Supreme Court under its advisory jurisdiction in matters relating to these agreements.

[6] Article 374(2), one of the "Temporary, Transitional and Special" provisions, states, in part: "All suits, appeals and proceedings, civil or criminal, pending in the Federal Court at the commencement of this Constitution, shall stand removed to the Supreme Court, and the Supreme Court shall have jurisdiction to hear and determine the same. ..."

[7] *State of Seraikella and Others* v. *Union of India and Another*, (1951) S.C.R. 474.

and Others v. *The State of Uttar Pradesh*[8]—the proviso to Article 131 received brief mention, and here the Supreme Court stated that "it is undoubted that the accessions and the acceptance of them by the Dominion of India were acts of State into whose competency no municipal Court could enquire; nor can any Court in India, after the Constitution, accept jurisdiction to settle any dispute arising out of them because of Article 363 and the proviso to Article 131. ..."

Since 1950 only one suit has been instituted under Article 131,[9] but in this single case[10] the Supreme Court handed down a very significant decision pertaining to the nature of the Indian federation. At issue was the constitutional validity of the Coal-Bearing Areas (Acquisition and Development) Act of 1957, which authorized the Union Government to acquire compulsorily any land, whether belonging to an individual or a State, from which coal is obtainable. The purpose of the Act was to enable the Union Government to exploit all available coal resources in the interest of "a planned and rapid industrialization of the country."[11] When the Union Government sought to acquire some coal-bearing land owned by the State of West Bengal, this State objected on the grounds that it had itself a plan for the development of the coal-bearing areas, and that the Union Government had no power to acquire lands vested in a State.

In view of the importance of the questions raised, the Supreme Court invited other states to appear before the Court, and ultimately nine other states became involved in the litigation,[12] all of whom supported the position of the State of West Bengal. The main argument advanced by the States was that the Constitution having accepted the federal principle, the States shared the sovereignty of the nation with the Union, and, therefore, Parliament had no power to enact legislation for depriving the States of property vested in them as sovereign authorities.

By a majority of five to one, the Supreme Court rejected the arguments put forth by the various States, with the result that the first major legal battle in India over the question of States' rights was decided in favor of the Central Government. In deciding thusly, the Supreme Court pointed out that though there is nothing explicit in the Constitution authorizing the Union Government to acquire state-owned land by means of compulsion, given the nature of the Indian Constitution, this power must be regarded as implicit. The majority

---

[8] (1955) S.C.R. I 415.

[9] The *Seraikella* case was initiated under Section 204 of the Government of India Act, 1935, and the *Virendra* case reached the Court via a writ petition under Article 32.

[10] *State of West Bengal* v. *Union of India*, A.I.R. 1963 S.C. 1241.

[11] *State of West Bengal* v. *Union of India*, A.I.R. 1963 S.C. 1241, 1246.

[12] *State of West Bengal* v. *Union of India*, A.I.R. 1963 S.C. 1241, 1245.

spent considerable time discussing the "quasi-federal" character of the Union of India, and pointed out that Parliament's powers under Article 3 to alter the boundaries and name of a State and to create or destroy a State were conclusive proof of the Union's primacy. The majority's position is summed up well by Chief Justice Sinha's remark that to make "the States coordinate with and independent of the Union, is to envisage a Constitutional scheme which does not exist in law or in practice."[13]

Although this is not the place to go into a discussion of the nature of the Indian federation, it may be noted that this Supreme Court decision merely acknowledges the trend toward greater centralization which has been evident in India for many years. Political and economic factors have tended to increase the authority of the Central Government, and the issue of "States' rights" has never been an important one in independent India.[14]

The fact that "States' rights" is not a subject of significant debate in India is one reason why only one suit has been filed since 1950 under the Supreme Court's exclusive original jurisdiction, but this does not explain adequately the absence of other litigation between the Union and the States, or the States inter se. A more complete explanation is that when disputes have arisen, they have been settled extra-judicially, owing chiefly to the firm hold of the Congress Party over the Union and State Governments. In the words of Justice Basu, author of the invaluable, multi-volume *Commentary on the Constitution of India*, "whatever disputes may have arisen directly between the Union and the States must have been settled by negotiation and agreement. Even in matters arising between two States, the advice and intervention of the Union usually settle the differences."[15] The Supreme Court is, in short,

---

[13] *State of West Bengal v. Union of India*, A.I.R. 1963 S.C. 1241, 1255. Justice Subba Rao, in a minority judgment, held that the Indian Constitution accepted the federal principle, and that this meant that neither the Union nor the States could encroach upon the governmental functions of the other, unless the Constitution expressly provided for such interference. He found nothing in the Constitution which would permit the Union to absorb State property except by agreement of the State, and argued that the future stability of India, with its unity in diversity, depended upon strict adherence to the federal principle (p. 1278).

[14] Reaction to this decision from the press was uniformly favorable. See, e.g., the editorials in *The Times of India*, December 27, 1962, and in *The Statesman*, December 29, 1962.

[15] Durga Das Basu, *Commentary on the Constitution of India* (four volumes, fourth edition; Calcutta: S. C. Sarkar & Sons (Private) Ltd., 1963), III, 94. Similar views are expressed by N. A. Subramanian, "The Judiciary in India," *The Indian Year Book of International Affairs*, IV (1955), p. 278, and by K. Rangachari, "Relations between States and Centre," *The Statesman*, January 26, 1964.

not often directly involved in matters affecting the nature of the Indian federation.[16]

Whereas Article 131 is the least used jurisdiction of the Supreme Court, Article 32, which also confers upon the Court an original jurisdiction, has been the source of more Supreme Court decisions than any other article. Article 32(1) guarantees to all persons subject to the laws of India the right to move the Supreme Court for the enforcement of any of the fundamental rights, and clause (2) gives the Supreme Court the authority "to issue directions or orders or writs, including writs in the nature of habeas corpus, mandamus, prohibition, quo warranto and certiorari, whichever may be appropriate, for the enforcement of any of the rights conferred by this Part."

The most remarkable feature about this article is that anyone who believes that one of his constitutional rights has been infringed may apply *directly* to the Supreme Court for redress—he need not proceed from lower courts to the Supreme Court, as he has to do in cases not involving fundamental rights. Moreover, the availability of other remedies in other courts does not prevent an aggrieved person from petitioning the Supreme Court in the first instance. In one of the earliest decisions, *Romesh Thappar* v. *The State of Madras*,[17] the Advocate-General of Madras, appearing on behalf of the respondents, argued that since under Article 226 of the Constitution the High Court of Madras had a concurrent jurisdiction, the petitioner, "as a matter of orderly procedure,... should first resort to the High Court of Madras."[18] The Advocate-General then cited several American decisions in order to make the point that whatever judicial remedies remained open to an applicant in State or lower federal courts should be exhausted before resort is made to the Supreme Court. The Supreme Court of India rejected this argument, observing:

> We are of the opinion that neither the instances mentioned by the learned Advocate-General nor the American decisions referred to by him are really analogous to the remedy afforded by article 32 of the Indian Constitution. That article does not merely confer power on this Court, as article 226 does on the High Courts, to issue certain writs for the enforcement of the rights conferred by Part III or for any other purpose, as part of its general jurisdiction. ... Article 32 provides a "guaranteed" remedy for the enforcement of those rights, and this remedial right is itself made

---

[16] It should be noted that although only one dispute has reached the Supreme Court under Article 131, other disputes involving federal questions have been decided by the Court under other jurisdictions.

[17] (1950) S.C.R. 594.

[18] *Romesh Thappar* v. *The State of Madras*, (1950) S.C.R. 596. Article 226 confers a writ jurisdiction on the High Courts similar to that conferred on the Supreme Court by Article 32(2).

a fundamental right by being included in Part III. This Court is thus constituted the protector and guarantor of fundamental rights, and it cannot, consistently with the responsibility so laid upon it, refuse to entertain applications seeking protection against infringements of such rights. No similar provision is to be found in the Constitution of the United States and we do not consider that the American decisions are in point.[19]

Further, in 1959, in a notable decision,[20] the Supreme Court reviewed and reiterated the scope of its powers and jurisdiction under Article 32. In this case the following points were made: (i) "the mere existence of an adequate alternative legal remedy cannot per se be a good and sufficient ground for throwing out a petition under Art. 32, if the existence of a fundamental right and a breach, actual or threatened, of such right is alleged and is prima facie established on the petition...";[21] (ii) so broad are the powers conferred on the Supreme Court by Article 32 that the Court is not confined to the issuing of prerogative writs—the Court also has the discretion to frame its writs or orders to meet the exigencies created by various enactments;[22] and (iii) the Court would "fail in its duty as the custodian and protector of the fundamental rights if it were to decline to entertain a petition under Art. 32 simply because it involved the determination of disputed questions of fact."[23]

The Court acknowledged in this decision that

we are not unmindful of the fact that the view that this Court is bound to entertain a petition under Art. 32 and to decide the same on merits may encourage litigants to file many petitions under Art. 32 instead of proceeding by way of suit. But that consideration cannot, by itself, be a cogent reason for denying the fundamental right of a person to approach this Court for the enforcement of his fundamental right. ...[24]

---

[19] *Romesh Thappar v. The State of Madras,* (1950) S.C.R. 596–597.

[20] *Kavalappara Kottarathil Kochunni Moopil Nayar v. The State of Madras and Others,* (1959) S.C.R. Supp. II 316.

[21] *Kavalappara Kottarathil Kochunni Moopil Nayar v. The State of Madras and Others,* (1959) S.C.R. Supp. II 316, 326. Cf. *Rashid Ahmed v. Municipal Board, Kairana,* (1950) S.C.R. 566.

[22] *Kavalappara Kottarathil Kochunni Moopil Nayar v. The State of Madras and Others,* (1959) S.C.R. Supp. II 333–334. Cf. *Chiranjit Lal Chowdhuri v. The Union of India and Others,* (1950) S.C.R. 869.

[23] *Kavalappara Kottarathil Kochunni Moopil Nayar v. The State of Madras and Others,* (1959) S.C.R. Supp. II, p. 318. Cf. *Ramkrishna Dalmia v. Shri Justice S. R. Tendolkar,* (1959) S.C.R. 279.

[24] *Kavalappara Kottarathil Kochunni Moopil Nayar v. The State of Madras and Others,* (1959) S.C.R. Supp. II, pp. 318, 335–336.

But in two recent decisions the Supreme Court seems to have moved away from the liberal view that Article 32 was a guaranteed right available to any person who alleged infringement of his fundamental rights, and that the Court had the duty to entertain such a petition. In the case of *Daryao and Others v. The State of U.P. and Others*,[25] the Court ruled that if an aggrieved person, alleging a breach of his fundamental rights, filed a petition under Article 226 before one of the High Courts, and this petition was dismissed by the High Court, then this ruling would be res judicata and a similar petition under Article 32 would not be permitted. In other words, the Supreme Court said that if the High Court dismissed a writ petition on the ground that no fundamental right was involved, or, if involved, was not contravened, then a subsequent petition to the Supreme Court under Article 32 on the same facts would be barred by the principle of res judicata, i.e., decisions of courts of competent jurisdiction should be final.

A year later, in the case of *Smt. Ujjam Bai v. State of Uttar Pradesh*,[26] the Supreme Court further limited the scope of the remedy available under Article 32 when it ruled that a distinction must be made between an order of a quasi-judicial authority which, though rendered in pursuance of a law which is *intra vires*, is erroneous, and an order made under authority of a law which is *ultra vires*. In the former case, according to the Court, the order would be protected and no fundamental right could be invoked to challenge the order because it was made under the authority of a valid law. In the latter case the Supreme Court would accept the petition because the law itself was deemed to be *ultra vires* and thus authorized an unconstitutional interference with a fundamental right. The Court reasoned that where the authority had jurisdiction to decide rightly or wrongly, the decision, even if it was erroneous, could not be impeached on the ground of violation of fundamental rights. The proper remedy in such a situation would be for the aggrieved party to proceed by way of regular appeal, i.e., the aggrieved party should exhaust available statutory remedies and, if necessary, ultimately seek special leave to appeal from the Supreme Court under Article 136.[27]

There is some reason to believe that the Court reached this conclusion limiting the scope of Article 32 in order to stem the flow of petitions calling into question decisions of certain quasi-judicial bodies. Many such petitions

[25]   (1962) S.C.R. I 574.

[26]   (1963) S.C.R. I 778.

[27]   See discussion of Article 136, as follows, pp. 125–34. In reaching this conclusion, the Supreme Court overruled one of its earlier decisions which drew no such distinction between orders of quasi-judicial bodies. Overruled was *Kailash Nath v. State of U.P.*, A.I.R. 1957 S.C. 790.

had been filed before the Court in recent years, and the Court may well have decided that it would be more appropriate for aggrieved parties to make use of the other available avenues of appeal rather than to approach the Supreme Court directly under Article 32. It is still too early to determine the effect of this decision on the number of Article 32 petitions. In all likelihood, however, it will have the effect of substantially limiting the number of such petitions, for many of the cases which have been decided under Article 32 have involved orders or decisions of quasi-judicial authorities which were alleged to have been erroneous.

The sole object of Article 32 is the enforcement of the fundamental rights enumerated in Part III of the Constitution, and thus the judicial remedies provided by Article 32 may not be invoked unless there is alleged to be an infringement of a fundamental right.[28] It cannot be invoked merely to determine the constitutional validity of a legislative measure unless the legislation in question allegedly infringes the fundamental rights of the petitioner.[29] Moreover, one may seek redress via Article 32 only on the ground of alleged infringement of a fundamental right by "the State";[30] this remedy is not available to provide relief against acts of private persons.[31]

It would be difficult to exaggerate the importance of the jurisdiction and powers conferred upon the Supreme Court by Article 32. Referring to this article, Dr. Ambedkar once said: "If I was asked to name any particular article in this Constitution as the most important—an article without which this Constitution would be a nullity—I could not refer to any other article except this one. It is the very soul of the Constitution. ..."[32] The experience since 1950 has confirmed the estimate of Dr. Ambedkar, for more cases have reached the Supreme Court via Article 32 than via any other jurisdiction of the Court. Between 1950 and 1959, no less than 4,069 petitions were filed and 3,772 decided by the Supreme Court under Article 32.[33]

---

[28] *Rai Sahib Ram Jawaya Kapur and Others* v. *The State of Punjab,* (1955), S.C.R. II 225, 239.

[29] *Chiranjit Lal Chowdhuri* v. *The Union of India and Others,* (1950) S.C.R. 869.

[30] Article 12 defines "the State" as "the Government and Parliament of India and the Government and the Legislature of each of the States and all local or other authorities within the territory of India or under the control of the Government of India."

[31] *Shrimati Vidya Verma, Through Next Friend R. V. S. Mani* v. *Dr. Shiv Narain Verma,* (1955) S.C.R. II 983.

[32] *Constituent Assembly Debates,* VII (1948), December 9, 1948, p. 953.

[33] These figures, made available by the Supreme Court Registry, are cited in A. T. Markose, "The First Decade of the Indian Constitution," *Journal of the Indian Law Institute,* II (January–June, 1960), p. 160, xxv.

Of this large number of proceedings to enforce constitutional rights, the Law Commission said:

> The upsurge of national consciousness which led to Independence has to a great extent altered the psychology of the citizen. The change of his status from a subject in a dependency to a citizen of a democratic republic has reacted largely on the citizen's social, economic and political life. He is proudly conscious of the rights guaranteed to him by the Constitution; of his right to social and economic justice; and of his claim to equality of status and opportunity. In the context of his new freedom, the citizen displays a keenness in the assertion and protection of his new born rights which one would not have expected from him a decade ago. The attitude of the citizen has been encouraged by the changed aspect which the State has assumed. What formerly was a static machinery functioning largely for the purpose of the preservation of law and order, has now changed into a dynamic organization ordering the social and economic life of the citizen. The constant interference by the State with the everyday life of the citizen, however well intentioned and beneficial, comes into repeated conflict, real or apparent, with the guaranteed freedoms, and the citizen is naturally not content till he has the matter adjudicated upon by the courts. Thus, these recent changes in our constitutional, social and economic structure bring an increasing number of citizens to the courts.[34]

Of more significance to the student of Indian constitutional law than the gross totals of petitions filed under Article 32 is the fact that most of the important decisions rendered since 1950 have been "fundamental rights" cases arising out of Article 32. The Supreme Court, eager to ensure to the individual the maximum benefit from his newly-won liberties, has on several occasions under Article 32 handed down decisions in which major planks in the Congress Party platform have been declared unconstitutional. As will be seen in the next chapter, some of these decisions have provoked criticism of the judiciary from the Government, followed by, in some instances, amendments to the Constitution designed to overrule certain Supreme Court rulings.

Appellate Jurisdiction

Four articles in the 1950 Constitution are devoted to defining the Supreme Court's appellate jurisdiction. Article 132 defines its constitutional appellate jurisdiction; Article 133 relates to civil appeals, Article 134 to criminal appeals, and Article 136 confers upon the Supreme Court an extraordinarily extensive discretionary or special leave jurisdiction. Taken together, these provisions confer upon the Court an extremely comprehensive appellate jurisdiction, thus

---

[34] Law Commission's *Fourteenth Report*, I, 18–19.

enabling the Supreme Court to impose upon the State High Courts a uniform interpretation of the general law. The limits of this appellate jurisdiction have been defined not by constitutional provisions but by the judges themselves.

Constitutional appeals. Article 132 provides that an appeal shall lie to the Supreme Court from any judgment, decree or final order of a High Court, whether in a civil, criminal or other proceeding, if the High Court certifies that the case "involves a substantial question of law as to the interpretation of the Constitution."[35] If the High Court refuses to grant the certificate and the Supreme Court is satisfied that a substantial question of constitutional law is at issue, the Supreme Court is empowered to grant special leave to appeal.[36] Thus, whereas the Federal Court was powerless if a High Court refused to certify a case for appeal, the new Constitution does not so restrict the Supreme Court. According to the *Supreme Court Reports*, however, only once has the Supreme Court granted special leave in the face of a High Court refusal to grant the certificate.[37] On the other hand, the Supreme Court, as was true of its predecessor, does not consider itself bound by a certificate granted by a High Court, and will refuse to entertain an appeal if it is of the opinion that the High Court erred in granting it.[38] A final feature of this constitutional appellate jurisdiction is that once such a case reaches the Supreme Court, the appellant is not entitled to challenge the propriety of the decision appealed against on a ground other than that on which the certificate was granted, unless the Supreme Court expressly permits him to do so.[39]

The significance of this article lies in the fact that it makes the Supreme Court the final authority in all cases involving an interpretation of the Constitution. Regardless of whether the constitutional question arises in a civil, criminal or other proceeding, the Supreme Court is empowered to review the lower court decision. It was the intention of the framers of the Constitution that this provision would permit any case, even though otherwise unfit for Supreme Court

---

[35] In the case of *Election Commission, India* v. *Saka Venkata Subba Rao* (1953) S.C.R. 1144, 1149, the Court held that an appeal is permissible even from a judgment, decree or final order of a single judge of a High Court, provided the requisite certificate is granted. Thus, although Article 133, which applies to ordinary civil appeals in which no constitutional question is involved, prohibits the Supreme Court from hearing an appeal from a ruling by a single High Court judge, Article 132 contains no such restriction.

[36] Article 132(2).

[37] *Jammu and Kashmir and Others* v. *Thakur Ganga Singh and Another,* (1960) S.C.R. II 346.

[38] See, e.g., *Sardar Syedna Taher Saifuddin Saheb* v. *The State of Bombay,* (1958) S.C.R. 1007, 1012.

[39] Article 132(3). Cf. *Darshan Singh* v. *State of Punjab,* (1953) S.C.R. 319, 330.

scrutiny,[40] to be brought before the Supreme Court if questions of constitutional law were involved.[41]

The Supreme Court has been called upon fewer than a dozen times since 1950 to exercise its constitutional appellate jurisdiction, and none of these cases has been of special significance. This indicates not that the Supreme Court has seldom expounded on the meaning and intent of the Constitution, but that it has done so indirectly in the exercise of other of its powers, rather than directly under authority of Article 132.

Civil appeals. The Supreme Court's appellate jurisdiction in civil cases is set forth in Article 133, which provides for a *right* of appeal if the High Court certifies that the value of the subject matter in dispute is at least 20,000 rupees.[42] However, in instances where this pecuniary condition is met but where the judgment, decree or final order appealed from affirms the decision of the court immediately below, there is no right of appeal unless the High Court certifies that the case raises "some substantial question of law." Furthermore, irrespective of the pecuniary limitation or the fact of affirmance, an appeal would lie to the Supreme Court if the High Court, in its discretion, certifies that the case "is a fit one for appeal to the Supreme Court."[43]

It is evident that the Supreme Court is thus constituted as India's supreme civil appellate tribunal. Further, since 1950, literally thousands[44] of civil appeals have reached the Court via the provisions of Article 133.[45] Although it is not possible to determine precisely how all of these appeals came before the Supreme Court,[46] it is clear that a substantial portion of them reached the Court because

---

[40] In an ordinary civil case, i.e., one not involving a constitutional question, there is no right of appeal to the Supreme Court unless the value of the subject-matter of the dispute *is* at least 20,000 rupees. Under Article 132, this requirement is waived if a substantial question of law as to the interpretation of the Constitution is raised.

[41] *Constituent Assembly Debates*, VIII (1949), June 3, 1949, p. 595.

[42] As per the amended Article 133, an appeal shall lie only if the High Court certifies under Article 134A that the case involves a substantial question of law of general importance that needs to be decided by the Supreme Court-*Eds*.

[43] Article 133(1) (c).

[44] The Law Commission determined that 1852 civil appeals had reached the Supreme Court between January 26, 1950 and November 15, 1956, not including those civil appeals which reached the Supreme Court by special leave of the Supreme Court itself (Law Commission's *Fourteenth Report*, I, 59).

[45] Since, however, similar questions are sometimes raised in a number of separate appeals, it is not uncommon for several appeals to be decided by the Court in a single judgment.

[46] Impossible because the *Supreme Court Reports* often do not make clear whether the appeal was one of right (i.e., more than 20,000 rupees involved and the High Court ruling

the appellant had a right of appeal, i.e., more than 20,000 rupees was involved and the High Court decision had overruled the lower court decision. In such cases, it is the duty of the Supreme Court to hear the appeal; it has no discretion to stem the flow of these appeals. In the other category of civil appeals are those cases in which one of the fifteen High Courts certified the case as involving "some substantial question of law," or as one "fit for appeal to the Supreme Court." In these appeals, while the Supreme Court normally does not question the granting of the certificate by the High Court, it has ruled that "the mere grant of the certificate would not preclude this court from determining whether it was rightly granted and whether the conditions prerequisite to the grant are satisfied."[47] But, though the Supreme Court is not obligated to hear an appeal certified by a High Court, there have been very few instances in which the Supreme Court has refused to entertain an appeal after the High Court has granted a certificate, and there is little evidence in the law reports that the Supreme Court has sought by other means to stem the tide of civil appeals. On the contrary, for in construing Article 133 the Court has adopted the quite liberal view that once an appeal reaches the Supreme Court, the appellant is entitled to argue questions of both law and fact.[48] Ordinarily, however, the Supreme Court does not interfere with concurrent findings of fact of the courts below, nor does it review evidence a third time.[49] Yet, if the Court feels that there has been a miscarriage of justice, or that "very exceptional circumstances" are present, it is willing to re-examine concurrent findings of fact.[50] Moreover, of course, where the lower courts have reached opposite conclusions on a question of fact, the Supreme Court is quite willing to re-examine evidence.[51]

There would be little utility, for the purposes of this study, in examining at length the Supreme Court decisions rendered under Article 133, for few of the thousands of civil appeals decided ultimately by the Court are of any special constitutional importance. But worthy of note is the obvious fact that these civil appeals impose a heavy burden upon the Court. The docket of the Court

---

having reversed a lower court finding), or whether the High Court had certified the case as one fit for appeal to the Supreme Court.

[47] *Nar Singh and Another v. The State of Uttar Pradesh*, (1955) S.C.R. I 238, 241. Cf. *Hanskumar Kishanchand v. The Union of India.* (1959) S.C.R. 1177.

[48] *Keshavlal Lallubhai Patel and Others v. Lalbhai Trikumlal Mills Ltd.*, (1959) S.C R. 213, 216–17. Cf. *The Asiatic Steam Navigation Co., Ltd. v. Sub-Lt. Arabinda Chakravarti*, (1959) S.C.R. Supp. I 979.

[49] *Srinivas Ram Kumar v. Mahabir Prasad and Others*, (1951) S.C.R. 277, 281.

[50] *Trojan & Co., Ltd. v. Rm. N. N. Nagappa Chettiar.* (1953) S.C.R. 789, 800.

[51] *R. Muthamnal (Died) and Parameswari Thayammal v. Sri Subramaniaswami Devasthanan, Tiruchendur*, (1960) S.C.R. II 729, 732.

is literally glutted with these appeals and a large amount of time is expended in deciding these cases, some of which seem hardly of sufficient import to merit the scrutiny of the supreme tribunal of a nation of nearly half a billion people. Surprisingly, though, the literature indicates that Indians have few misgivings about this civil appellate jurisdiction. Even the Law Commission, which found much to criticize about the Supreme Court, was silent with regard to the Court's civil appellate jurisdiction. However, it would seem that in the not too distant future, Parliament will either have to raise the pecuniary requirement[52] or empower the Supreme Court with the discretion to accept or reject any civil appeal.[53]

On the other hand, the probability of any such action by Parliament may be very remote, for there is at present no evidence of any dissatisfaction with the Court's exercise of this jurisdiction since 1950. It may be appropriate to recall here that the first step taken after independence to enlarge the jurisdiction of the Federal Court was to confer a civil appellate jurisdiction on the Federal Court.[54] This had the effect of more than doubling the workload of the Federal Court between 1948 and 1950. The Constituent Assembly, whose membership included several of India's most eminent lawyers, was engaged during this period in the writing of India's new constitution. Though doubtless aware of the sudden rash of civil appeals, the framers conferred essentially the same jurisdiction upon the Supreme Court, the only major change being that the pecuniary requirement was raised from 10,000 to 20,000 rupees.

Criminal appeals. Whereas the Federal Court was without jurisdiction to hear criminal appeals, and the Privy Council had the prerogative but seldom the inclination to grant special leave to appeal from High Court decisions in criminal matters, the Supreme Court of India has been endowed with what would appear to be, from a reading of the Constitution, a *limited* criminal appellate jurisdiction. The Draft Constitution, which appeared in February of 1948, made no provision for a criminal jurisdiction; it was inserted by the Constituent Assembly in 1949 only after a small but influential segment of the Assembly successfully argued for its inclusion. In the absence of published reports of the deliberations of the Drafting Committee, it is impossible to state with certainty the reasons for the absence of such a provision. However, K. M. Munshi, a

---

[52] According to Article 133(1)(a), this may be effected by ordinary legislation; a constitutional amendment would not be necessary.

[53] Since Parliament is empowered only to add to and not diminish the jurisdiction of the Supreme Court by ordinary legislation, an amendment to the Constitution would be necessary.

[54] Federal Court (Enlargement of Jurisdiction) Act, 1948. See Chapter II, pp. 76–79.

member of both the Ad Hoc Committee on the Supreme Court and the Drafting Committee, told his colleagues in the Constituent Assembly in 1949 that he was opposed to the exercise of any criminal jurisdiction by the Supreme Court both because of the expense it would entail, and the physical impossibility of the Court dealing with a large number of such appeals. It was his view that "conceding a right of criminal appeal to the Supreme Court would mean not less than one hundred judges of the Supreme Court. Even if it is a question of death sentences [only], it would require a very large number."[55] In short, he was of the view that criminal appeals would be so numerous that the Supreme Court could not possibly exercise such a jurisdiction. In all likelihood, it was this fear that the Supreme Court would be swamped with appeals that explains the reluctance of the Drafting Committee to endow the Court with a criminal appellate jurisdiction.

Persuasive as this reasoning was to some, ultimately the more convincing argument was, that since the Draft Constitution had provided for a *right* of appeal to the Supreme Court in civil cases if 20,000 rupees were involved in the dispute, the Constitution should at least provide an appeal in instances where a High Court had reversed a lower court order of acquittal and sentenced a person to death. In other words, proponents of a criminal jurisdiction for the Supreme Court argued that life was at least as important as property.[56] This line of reasoning was not different from that offered in earlier decades by Nair, Gour and others, who pointed out that under the existing system of criminal justice, it was possible that one might be acquitted in a lower court, then sentenced to death by a High Court, and then be without not only a right of appeal to a higher court, but without any local forum to which to petition for special leave to appeal.[57] This reasoning, plus the argument that uniformity in the interpretation of criminal laws could be achieved only if the Supreme Court was endowed with a criminal appellate jurisdiction, led finally to the insertion into the Draft Constitution of what ultimately came to be Article 134.

Provided in this article is a *right* of appeal to the Supreme Court from any judgment, final order or sentence in a criminal proceeding of a High Court if the High Court on appeal reversed a lower court acquittal and handed down a death sentence,[58] or if the High Court withdrew for trial before itself any case from a subordinate court and, having found the accused guilty, sentenced

---

[55] *Constituent Assembly Debates*, VII (1949), June 3, 1949, p. 607.

[56] For the pros and cons of this argument, see *Constituent Assembly Debates*, VII (1949), June 3, 1949, pp. 595–615.

[57] See Chapter I, pp. 8–9.

[58] Article 134(1) (a).

him to death.[59] Moreover, even in non-capital cases, the High Court may, at its discretion, certify a criminal case as one meriting the scrutiny of the Supreme Court, and an appeal shall lie under such certification.[60] Finally, Article 134(2) provides that Parliament, by ordinary legislation, may enlarge (but not reduce) the scope of the Supreme Court's criminal appellate jurisdiction. Parliament has not yet exercised this authority[61] and, in view of the large number of criminal appeals now reaching the Supreme Court, it is hardly likely that Parliament would be inclined to do so.[62]

Article 134, then, indicates that the criminal appellate jurisdiction of the Supreme Court is confined primarily to cases where a High Court has imposed the death sentence. It is evident that these provisions were designed so as to limit the jurisdiction of the Supreme Court to only the most important criminal cases, leaving the High Courts to be the final courts of appeal in criminal cases generally. Yet, since 1950, upwards of fifteen hundred criminal cases have been decided by the Supreme Court, the majority of which are not "death-sentence" appeals. Moreover, most of these criminal appeals have come up to the Supreme Court not via the limited right of appeal provided by Article 134, but as a result of a grant of special leave to appeal by the Supreme Court itself under authority of Article 136, to be discussed in this chapter. So numerous have been the criminal appeals been that one of the Court's division benches is designated to hear only criminal appeals.

---

[59] Article 134(1)(b). It may be noted that there is no right of appeal in the situation in which a High Court enhances a lower court sentence by imposing the death penalty. The late Rajendra Prasad, then President of the Constituent Assembly, called attention to this apparent omission in the proposed article, but Dr. Ambedkar replied that the article "... recognizes conviction or acquittal as the basis for a right of appeal to the Supreme Court. It does not recognize the nature of sentence or the type of punishment as the basis. Further, in the case of enhancement of sentence, the punishment is not for the first time. The accused already stands convicted." *Constituent Assembly Debates* (1949), pp. 853–857.

[60] Article 134(1)(c).

[61] In 1970, Parliament passed the Supreme Court (Enlargement of Criminal Appellate Jurisdiction) Act-*Eds*.

[62] In the mid-1950s the Government of Madras urged the Law Commission to recommend that the limited right of appeal conferred by clauses (a) and (b) or Article 134(1) should be enlarged by Parliament so that all cases in which lower courts have sentenced a person to death should be heard ultimately by the Supreme Court. The Law Commission, however, noting that the Supreme Court is quite willing to exercise its special leave jurisdiction under Article 136 in cases where a miscarriage of justice was thought to have occurred, concluded that there was no need to enlarge the scope of Article 134 (Law Commission's *Fourteenth Report*, I, 51–52).

Over the years the Court has evolved or applied a number of principles and rules of interpretation which serve to define the scope of its criminal appellate jurisdiction.[63] Thus, e.g., as in civil appeals, the Supreme Court has ruled that in criminal appeals "when the court of first instance and the court of appeal arrive at concurrent findings of fact after believing the evidence of a witness, this court as the final court does not disturb such findings, save in most exceptional cases."[64] Since, however, a common feature of an appeal under Article 134(1) (a) and (b) is the absence of lower court concurrence on questions of fact, the Court has taken the position that "it has the power, and it is its duty, to hear appeals, as a Regular Court of Appeal, on facts involved in cases coming up to this Court on a certificate under Art. 134(1)(a) or (b)."[65] Thus the Supreme Court will concern itself with facts in appeals where lower courts have disagreed on findings of fact, and in capital cases in general.

But even in appeals in which the lower courts have agreed, i.e., appeals reaching the Supreme Court not as of right but by the granting of a certificate by a High Court, the Supreme Court has expressed a willingness, if not a duty, to re-examine evidence if "the evidence is such that no Tribunal could legitimately infer from it that the accused is guilty ...,[66] if the conclusions of the courts below "are vitiated by errors of law or that the conclusions reached by the courts below are so patently opposed to well established principles of judicial approach, that they can be characterized as wholly unjustified and even perverse,"[67] or if "the findings of fact were such as were shocking to our judicial conscience. ..."[68]

It has been noted that the Constitution provides a right of appeal in cases in which the requirements of subclauses (a) and (b) or Article 134(1) are met (i.e. the "death sentence" clauses). The Supreme Court can do nothing to increase or stem the flow of these appeals. However, relatively few criminal appeals have reached the Supreme Court as of right—most have come up either as a result of the grant of special leave to appeal by the High Court, or as a result of the Supreme Court itself exercising its own special leave jurisdiction (Article 136).

---

[63] Little distinction is made in this discussion between criminal appeals arising out of Article 134 and those in which the Supreme Court has decided under Article 136, for once the appeals reach the Court, the distinction between Articles 134 and 136 becomes blurred.

[64] *Hanumant* v. *The State of Madhya Pradesh and Raojibhai* v. *The State of Madhya Pradesh*, (1952) S.C.R. 1091, 1096. Cf. *Deep Chand* v. *The State of Rajasthan*, (1962) S.C.R. I 662, 669.

[65] *Khushal Rao* v. *The State of Bombay*, (1958) S.C.R. 552, 559. Cf. *Aher Raja Khima* v. *The State of Saurashtra*, (1955) S.C.R. II 1285, 1301.

[66] *Bhagwan Das* v. *The State of Rajasthan*, (1957) S.C.R. 854, 859.

[67] *Sarwan Singh* v. *The State of Punjab*, (1957) S.C.R. 953, 958.

[68] *Haripada Dey* v. *The State of West Bengal and Another*. (1956) S.C.R. 639, 641.

Over cases arising out of the discretionary certification of "fitness" by one of the High Courts, the Supreme Court has a measure of control, i.e., it has taken the position that it need not consider every such appeal merely because a High Court thought it warranted review by the Supreme Court. In this regard, the Supreme Court has insisted that the High Court make clear precisely why it decided to grant the certificate:

> The Supreme Court must be in a position to know first that the High Court has applied its mind to the matter and not acted mechanically, and, secondly, what the High Court's difficulty is and exactly what question of outstanding difficulty or importance the High Court feels the Supreme Court ought to settle. It is not enough to say "leave to appeal is given" and no more, because this is tantamount to saying that the High Court will usurp the functions of the Constitution-makers and allow the whole case to be opened up despite the fact that the Constitution has specifically limited the normal right of appeal to sub-articles (a) and (b) and has left (c) to meet extraordinary cases.[69]

Further, two years later, the Court added that under Article 134(1)(c)

> it is not a case of "granting leave" but of "certifying" that the case is a fit one for appeal to this Court. "Certifying" is a strong word and, therefore, it has been repeatedly pointed out that a High Court is in error in granting a certificate on a mere question of fact, and that the High Court is not justified in passing on an appeal for determination by this Court when there are no complexities of law involved in the case, requiring an authoritative interpretation by this Court.[70]

In these cases and others, the Supreme Court has indicated to the High Courts that it is unwilling to be converted into an ordinary court of criminal appeal, and on a number of occasions that Supreme Court has refused to review a case certified by a High Court as one fit for Supreme Court scrutiny.[71]

But this should not be taken to mean that the Supreme Court, as a matter of practice, discourages appeals in criminal cases for, as will be seen in this chapter in the discussion of Article 136, the Supreme Court, in exercising its own discretion, has permitted many hundreds of criminal cases to reach the Supreme Court. Though the Court has on occasion emphasized that it is not a court of criminal appeal, the reader of the *Supreme Court Reports* is left with the unmistakable impression that criminal appeals are a major feature of the docket. Indeed, the many criminal appeals decided since 1950 seem to confirm

---

[69] *Baladin and Others v. The State of Uttar Pradesh.* A.I.R. 1956 S.C. 181, 188.

[70] *Sidheswar Ganguly v. The State of West Bengal.* (1958) S.C.R. 749, 754.

[71] See, e.g., *Kalawati and Another v. The State of Himachal Pradesh,* (1953) S.C.R. 546, and *Haripada Dey v. The State of West Bengal and Another,* (1956) S.C.R. 639.

the predictions of Munshi and others who feared that much valuable Supreme Court time would be devoted to the handling of such appeals.

Special leave appeals. Of the constitutional provisions concerning the jurisdiction of the Supreme Court, only Article 32 rivals Article 136 in terms of extensiveness of jurisdiction conferred and constitutional importance. Employing the most permissive of phraseology, this article states that "[n]otwithstanding anything in this Chapter, the Supreme Court may, in its discretion, grant special leave to appeal from any judgment, decree, determination, sentence or order in any cause or matter passed or made by any court or tribunal in the territory of India." This is clearly an extraordinarily extensive discretionary jurisdiction, enabling the Court to bring before itself any lower court decision on any subject, the only exception being that no appeal lies to the Supreme Court from "any judgment, determination, sentence or order passed or made by any court or tribunal constituted by or under any law relating to the Armed Forces."[72] Subject to this one limitation, this omnibus jurisdiction extends to all cases and all matters, whether civil, criminal, constitutional or otherwise, regardless of the conditions which govern regular appeals. Thus Article 136 vests in the Supreme Court the special leave jurisdiction of the Privy Council,[73] for it enables the Court to interfere in any matter where the dictates of justice require it to do so.

Article 136 commences with the words "notwithstanding anything in this Chapter," which, as the Court pointed out in an early decision, "indicate that the intention of the Constitution was to disregard in extraordinary cases the limitations contained in the previous articles on this Court's power to entertain appeals."[74] Thus, whereas Articles 131–134 provide for appeals only from High Courts, by virtue of this provision an appeal is contemplated even in cases in which a tribunal or court subordinate to a High Court has done something which in the judgment of the Supreme Court requires immediate review. Moreover, whereas Articles 131–134 use the term "final order," Article 136 employs only "order" which means that the Supreme Court can grant special leave against even an interlocutory order.

One might anticipate that a provision such as this one, which not only confers upon the Court an extraordinary jurisdiction, but leaves it completely to the discretion of the Court to establish any limitations on such jurisdiction, would

---

[72] Article 136(2).

[73] The discretionary power conferred by Article 136 is actually more extensive than the prerogative power of the Judicial Committee for, whereas the prerogative of the Crown can be taken away or curtailed by Parliamentary legislation, the Supreme Court of India's jurisdiction under Article 136 cannot be affected by ordinary legislation.

[74] *The Bharat Bank Ltd., Delhi* v. *Employees of the Bharat Bank Ltd., Delhi,* (1950) S.C.R., 459, 471.

have been the subject of considerable discussion, if not heated debate, in the Constituent Assembly. But quite the contrary occurred—most of the members who commented at all expressed approval of this article, and it was adopted without any important debate.[75]

Although Article 136 provides the Supreme Court with a jurisdiction of the widest amplitude, the Court, on numerous occasions since 1950, has attempted to spell out, even if only in general terms, the circumstances which would justify the utilization of this discretionary power. Of necessity the Court has had to establish some general principles as to the exercise of this jurisdiction, but the Court's experience indicates that this has not been an easy task.

The first case to reach the Supreme Court by a grant of special leave was that of *Pritam Singh* v. *The State*,[76] and at this time the Court stated that this discretionary power must be

> exercised sparingly and in exceptional cases only, and as far as possible a more or less uniform standard should be adopted in granting special leave in the wide range of matters which can come up before it under this article. ... The only uniform standard which in our opinion can be laid down in the circumstances is that the Court should grant special leave to appeal only in those cases where special circumstances are shown to exist.[77]

Hardly less vague was the standard put forth a few weeks later in the *Bharat Bank* case by Justice Mahajan, who said that "exceptional and extraordinary powers of this character can only be justifiably used where there has been a grave miscarriage of justice or where the procedure adopted ... is such that it offends against all notions of legal procedure."[78]

This *Bharat Bank* decision ranks as one of the most important one ever handed down by the Supreme Court, for this was the first appeal from a "tribunal" other than a High Court, and this appeal marked the entrance of the Supreme Court into the field of labor-management disputes. The Court granted special leave to appeal to the Bharat Bank of Delhi, after the Bharat Bank expressed dissatisfaction with a decision of the Industrial Tribunal ordering the reinstatement of various employees who had participated in an allegedly illegal strike. The central government intervened in this case in an effort to persuade the Court that it had no jurisdiction to grant special leave to appeal against the determination of an Industrial Tribunal, because, according to Alladi Krishnaswami Aiyar, counsel for the Union of India, the Industrial Tribunal did not exercise the judicial powers of the State, its determination was not in the nature of a judgment, decree or

---

[75] *Constituent Assembly Debates*, VIII (1949), June 6, 1949, p. 636ff.

[76] (1950) S.C.R. 453.

[77] *Pritam Singh* v. *The State*, (1950) S.C.R. 458.

[78] (1950) S.C.R. 458, 459, 497.

order of a Court, and, therefore, the Court's jurisdiction under Article 136 was excluded. The Court majority, however, while agreeing that the term "tribunal" as employed in Article 136 does not mean the same thing as "court," held that the Industrial Tribunal possessed "all the trappings of a Court and performs functions which cannot but be regarded as judicial."[79] The Court went on to say that it could exercise review powers over all adjudicating bodies, provided they are constituted by the State and are invested with judicial as distinguished from purely administrative or executive functions.

But at the same time the Court said that though tribunal awards were subject to Supreme Court review, it would interfere only reluctantly and seldom, and that its role would be limited to policing the tribunal's jurisdiction and procedures:

> This Court is not to substitute its decisions for the determination of the tribunal when granting relief under article 136. When it chooses to interfere in the exercise of these extraordinary powers, it does so because the tribunal has either exceeded its jurisdiction or has approached the questions referred to it in a manner which is likely to result in injustice or has adopted a procedure which runs counter to the well-established rules of natural justice. In other words, if it has denied a hearing to a party or has refused to record his evidence or has acted in any other manner, in an arbitrary or despotic fashion. In such circumstances no question arises of this Court constituting itself into a tribunal and assuming powers of settling a dispute. All that the Court when it entertains an appeal would do is to quash the award and direct the tribunal to proceed within the powers conferred on it and approach the adjudication of the dispute according to principles of natural justice. The Court under article 136 would not constitute itself into a mere court of error. Extraordinary powers have to be exercised in rare and exceptional cases and on well-known principles.[80]

Notwithstanding such protestations against involvement, it is quite evident from the law reports that the Supreme Court since 1950 is frequently and deeply involved in industrial conflicts, and it would not be an exaggeration to say that the Supreme Court is hardly less than a regular court of appeal over labor tribunals. A mere digest of Supreme Court labor law decisions rendered from 1950 to 1958 fills a two hundred and fifty page volume.[81] In the single year of 1956, the Supreme Court granted no less than 257 special leave applications from labor tribunal decisions.[82] Moreover, as has been pointed out by Solomon E. Robinson, in only a small portion of these cases has the Court limited its role

[79] *The Bharat Bank Ltd., Delhi* v. *Employees of the Bharat Bank,* (1950) S.C.R. 463.

[80] *The Bharat Bank Ltd., Delhi* v. *Employees of The Bharat Bank* (1950) S.C.R. 463, 488–489.

[81] V. B. Kher, *Supreme Court Digest of Labour Law Cases* (Bombay: N. M. Tripathi Ltd., 1959).

[82] Law Commission's *Fourteenth Report*, I, 50, 58.

to questions of the tribunal's jurisdiction and procedures.[83] The Court has demonstrated a willingness to intervene and correct a tribunal if its award suggests that it has "approached the problem wrongly,"[84] "erroneously applied well-accepted principles of jurisprudence,"[85] "has not directed its mind to the real question,"[86] or merely "raises an important principle of industrial law requiring elucidation and final decision by this court."[87] These and many other cases led Robinson to conclude that the Supreme Court "had become the supreme rule-maker of the nation's industrial relations system ...,[88] the senior policy-making partner in labour relations."[89]

Appeals from awards of the Industrial Tribunals form only a part of the total number of tribunal appeals which have reached the Supreme Court. Having held in 1950 that tribunal findings are subject to review by special leave, the Court has since then exercised its review powers over all major tribunals functioning in India, including the Election Tribunals,[90] the Income-tax Appellate Tribunals,[91] the Labour Appellate Tribunal,[92] and the Railway Rates Tribunal.[93]

Another important case involving the scope of Article 136 was *Raj Krushna Bose* v. *Binod Kanungo and Others*,[94] in which the Supreme Court set aside an order of an Election Tribunal, even though the Representation of the People Act of 1951, under authority of which election tribunals are established, stated unequivocally that orders of an election tribunal shall be "final and

---

[83] "The Supreme Court and Section 33 of the Industrial Disputes Act, 1947-Part II," *Journal of Indian Law Institute*, III (April–June, 1961), pp. 181–182. Part I of this essay appeared in the January–March issue of this journal.

[84] *Mill Manager, Model Mills* v. *Dharam Das*, A.I.R. 1958 S.C. 311.

[85] *Clerks Depot and Cashiers of the Calcutta Tramway Co., Ltd.* v. *Calcutta Tramway Co.*, A.I.R. 1957 S.C. 78.

[86] *Rohtas Industries Ltd.* v. *Brijinandan Pandey and Others*, A.I.R. 1957 S.C. 1.

[87] *Bengal Chemical and Pharmaceutical Works Ltd.* v. *Their Employees*, A.I.R. 1959 S.C. 633.

[88] Robinson, in "The Supreme Court and Section 33 of the Industrial Disputes Act, 1947—Part II," pp. 183–184.

[89] Robinson, in "The Supreme Court and Section 33 of the Industrial Disputes Act, 1947—Part II," p. 202.

[90] *Raj Krushna Bose* v. *Binod Kanungo and Others*, (1954) S.C.R. 913; *Durga Shankar Mehta* v. *Thakur Raghuraj Singh and Others*, (1955) S.C.R. I 267.

[91] *Dhakeswari Cotton Mills Ltd.* v. *Commissioner of Income Tax, West Bengal*, (1955) S.C.R. I 941.

[92] *The Sree Meenakshi Mills, Ltd.* v. *Their Workmen*, (1958) S.C.R. 878.

[93] *Raigarh Jute Mills* v. *Eastern Railway*, A.I.R. 1958 S.C. 525.

[94] (1954) S.C.R. 913.

conclusive."[95] The Court simply pointed out that its discretionary jurisdiction under Article 136 embraced such tribunals, and that it would not permit its jurisdiction to be "taken away or whittled down by the legislature."[96] Thus the Court held that the Constitution is paramount, and provisions of any legislation are subject to the paramount law.

The most frequently cited statement by the Supreme Court relating to the scope of its special leave jurisdiction came in the famous case of *Dhakeswari Cotton Mills Ltd.* v. *Commissioner of Income Tax, West Bengal.*[97] By this time the Court, via Article 136, had become involved in a wide variety of litigation, and in this unanimous decision the Court devoted considerable time to spelling out both the scope of the jurisdiction and how it conceived of its role. Chief Justice Mahajan's remarks merit quotation at length.

> It is not possible to define with any precision the limitation on the exercise of the discretionary jurisdiction vested in this Court by the constitutional provision made in article 136. The limitations, whatever they are, are implicit in the nature and character of the power itself. It being an exceptional and overriding power, naturally it has to be exercised sparingly and with caution and only in special and extraordinary situations. Beyond that it is not possible to fetter the exercise of this power by any set formula or rule. All that can be said is that the Constitution having trusted the wisdom and good sense of the Judges of this Court in this matter, that itself is a sufficient safeguard and guarantee that the power will only be used to advance the cause of justice, and that its exercise will be governed by well-established principles which govern the exercise of overriding constitutional powers. It is, however, plain that when the Court reaches the conclusion that a person has been dealt with arbitrarily or that a Court or

---

[95] Act XLIII of 1951, Section 105.

[96] *Raj Krushna Bose* v. *Binod Kanungo and Others* (1954) S.C.R. 913, 918. In several later appeals efforts were made to persuade the Court that the legislature intended the decisions of these tribunals to be final on all matters, but in each case the Court reaffirmed that no ordinary legislation could limit the scope of Article 136. Cf. *Sangram Singh* v. *Election Tribunal. Kotah, Bhurey Lal Baya*, (1955) S.C.R. II 1, 7.

The Industrial Disputes Acts of 1947, in Section 17(2), stated similarly that awards of the Industrial Tribunal shall be "final and shall not be called into question by any court in any manner whatsoever." But the Supreme Court stated simply that "it is manifest that the provisions of the Act are subject to the paramount law as laid down in the Constitution. ... The provisions of the Act must be read subject to the over-riding provisions of the Constitution. ... Therefore, whatever finality may be claimed under the provisions of the Act ..., it must necessarily be subject to the result of the determination of the appeal by special leave" (*India General Navigation and Railway Co., Ltd.* v. *Their Workmen*, (1960) S.C.R. II 1, 10).

[97] *Dhakeswari Cotton Mills Ltd.* v. *Commissioner of Income Tax, West Bengal*, (1955) S.C.R. I 941.

tribunal within the territory of India has not given a fair deal to a litigant, then no technical hurdles of any kind like the finality of finding of facts or otherwise can stand in the way of the exercise of this power because the whole intent and purpose of this article is that it is the duty of this Court to see that injustice is not perpetuated or perpetrated by decisions of Courts and tribunals because certain laws have been made the decisions of these Courts or tribunals final and conclusive.[98]

There is no clearer statement than this of the scope of Article 136. The Court has gone no further in defining the circumstances which call for its interference by special leave. Understandably, the Court is unwilling to fetter its own jurisdiction by establishing criteria for the exercise of this power.

By the late 1950s the Supreme Court had become increasingly more involved with appeals from the various tribunals, and the Law Commission expressed concern over this situation. The Commission pointed out that the large number of labor tribunal appeals were "clogging the work" of the Court, and then observed that

the graver aspect, however, of the matter is that labour matters are being thrust upon a Court which has not the means or materials for adequately informing itself about the different aspects of the questions which arise in these appeals and therefore finds it difficult to do adequate justice. In many of these cases, the Supreme Court has not even the assistance of a properly written judgment such as it would have in appeals from the High Courts. Equally grave are the delays caused by these appeals in the disposal of industrial matters which essentially need speedy disposal.[99]

To remedy this situation the Commission recommended not any restriction of the Court's jurisdiction, but either the re-establishment of a Labour Appellate Tribunal,[100] or an amendment of the High Court's jurisdiction so as to enable

[98] *Dhakeswari Cotton Mills Ltd.* v. *Commissioner of Income Tax, West Bengal,* (1955) S.C.R. I 949.

[99] Law Commission's *Fourteenth Report,* I, 50–51.

[100] Parliament in 1950 had enacted the Industrial Disputes (Appellate Tribunal) Act, which provided for the creation of the Labour Appellate Tribunal. According to the Statement of Objects and Reasons, this Tribunal was created in order to bring about uniformity and coordination of decisions of the several labor tribunals which had taken divergent views on important questions. Statement of Objects and Reasons, *Gazette of India,* Part V, dated December 17, 1949, p. 447. After functioning for six years, the Labour Appellate Tribunal was abolished, the reason being, according to Parliament, that labor interests objected to the excessive delay and expense allegedly caused by it (Statement of Objects and Reasons of Amending Act XXXVI of 1956, quoted in Robinson, p. 183). While the Labour Appellate Tribunal functioned, many appeals terminated at that

appeals from the labor tribunals to be taken to the High Courts.[101] In order to affect this latter recommendation, a constitutional amendment would be necessary, for the jurisdiction of the High Courts is too narrow to afford relief from tribunal orders. Neither of these recommendations has been acted upon by Parliament.

Much could be said regarding the comments of the Law Commission, but space permits only a few brief remarks. That the Court may well have undertaken in these labor appeals a task exceeding its resources is a charge made by others as well.[102] Yet this question is not easily resolved, for Parliament has neither codified a substantive labor law, nor has it spoken with any precision on the compelling questions of national labor policy. Into this void the Supreme Court has stepped, and "the debate continues on whether the court's forum should remain open, should be streamlined, or should be supplemented by giving the High Courts larger review powers over labour tribunals."[103] Until this question is resolved, the Court continues to seek an equitable balance between the interests of management and labor, a delicate task in any free society, but especially in India where the Government seeks to bring about "social and economic justice" within the shortest period of time.

Most of the discussion thus far has concerned the exercise of the Supreme Court's special leave jurisdiction over the various administrative tribunals. While these tribunal appeals are a very important part of the Supreme Court's work under Article 136, the Court has hardly been less willing to grant special leave in criminal matters. A scrutiny of many of the criminal appeals which have come up under this discretionary jurisdiction would seem to indicate that the Supreme Court was following the pattern established by the Privy Council, i.e., that the Court would be most reluctant to interfere in criminal cases decided by

---

level. Following its abolition the number of special leave applications to the Supreme Court increased seven-fold. Robinson (Statement of Objects and Reasons of Amending Act XXXVI of 1956, quoted in Robinson, in "The Supreme Court and Section 33 of the Industrial Disputes Act, 1947—Part II," p. 183).

[101] Law Commission's *Fourteenth Report*, I, 51.

[102] The most perceptive and balanced assessment of the Supreme Court's role in industrial relations is Robinson's two part essay. See also Y. Kumar, "Supreme Court and Socialist Pattern," *Mainstream*, I, October 26, 1962, pp. 9–12. Kumar argues that the Supreme Court has been a conservative force in this area, reluctant to accept changing social concepts and conditions.

[103] Robinson, in "The Supreme Court and Section 33 of the Industrial Disputes Act, 1947—Part II," p. 198.

the High Courts. Indeed, in the very first criminal appeal to reach the Supreme Court, Justice Fazl Ali recalled that

> the Privy Council have tried to lay down from time to time certain principles for granting special leave in criminal cases. ... It is sufficient for our purpose to say that though we are not bound to follow them too rigidly since the reasons, constitutional and administrative, which sometimes weighed with the Privy Council, need not weigh with us, yet some of those principles are useful in furnishing in many cases a sound basis for invoking the discretion of this Court in granting special leave. Generally speaking, this Court will not grant special leave, unless it is shown that exceptional and grave injustice has been done and that the case in question presents features of sufficient gravity to warrant a review of the decision appealed against.[104]

In countless other criminal appeals the Court has stated similar views.[105] Yet the plethora of criminal appeals decided by the Supreme Court demonstrates clearly that expressions of restraint notwithstanding, it has in fact granted special leave in many hundreds of instances.

In this discussion of Article 134, it was seen that the intention of the framers of the Constitution was that the Supreme Court would not function as a general court of criminal appeal, i.e. that only the exceptional High Court decision would be appealed to the Supreme Court. Had their intention been otherwise, the Court's regular criminal jurisdiction would not have been as restricted as it is under Article 134. But what has actually happened since 1950 can best be illustrated by citing some figures compiled by the Law Commission. Between 1950 and 1956 a total of 794 criminal appeals reached the Supreme Court. Of this number, 248 came up by virtue of Article 134, and the remaining 548 were appeals in which the Supreme Court granted special leave under authority of Article 136.[106] In other words, more than two-thirds of the criminal appeals decided by the Supreme Court during this period reached the Court after it exercised its discretionary jurisdiction.

The Law Commission, although agreeing that the Supreme Court in exercising this discretionary jurisdiction had prevented some grave miscarriages of justice, concluded that the Court had been too liberal in granting special leave in criminal matters. In arriving at this conclusion, the Commission observed that the Supreme Court's extensive involvement in criminal cases "has considerably shaken the prestige of the High Courts as the highest courts

---

[104] *Pritam Singh* v. *The State*, (1950) S.C.R. 453, 458–459.

[105] See, e.g., *Hem Raj* v. *State of Ajmer*, (1954) S.C.R. 1133; *Haripada Dey* v. *The State of West Bengal and Another*, (1956) S.C.R. 639.

[106] Law Commission's *Fourteenth Report*, I, Table III, p. 60.

of criminal appeal in the States."[107] In this regard, the Commission quoted with approval the view expressed in testimony by an unnamed Chief Justice of a High Court that

> the finality which formerly used to attach to the decisions of High Courts has prac-tically disappeared, and this has to some extent unfavourably affected the prestige of the High Court Judiciary. Formerly, appeals to the Privy Council, especially in criminal matters, were so few that for all practical purposes the State High Court was the final Court of Justice, but the present tendency of the Supreme Court seems to be to convert itself into a revising Court of appeal and almost every case decided by the High Court is taken up to the Supreme Court. ... The prestige of the High Court has, therefore, been reduced to that of the Court of a District and Sessions Judge during the pre-Independence days.[108]

The Commission felt the need to conclude with the view that "in exercising this jurisdiction the Supreme Court has ... constantly to bear in mind that the Constitution has, except in cases provided for by Article 134, made the High Courts of the States the final courts of appeal in criminal matters. ..."[109] It must be noted, however, that the law reports in the years since the publication of the Law Commission's findings show no indication of any noticeable reduction in Supreme Court criminal appellate decisions. The Court continues to articulate its reluctance to interfere in criminal matters, as in 1961 when it reaffirmed its unwillingness to interfere "except in exceptional cases when the finding is such that it shocks the conscience of the court,"[110] but the reports show quite conclu-sively that the Court is still very much involved in criminal cases, and continues to look like a general court of criminal appeal.

The situation with regard to civil appeals is quite different from that of administrative tribunal and criminal appeals. Although the Supreme Court's discretionary jurisdiction permits it to grant special leave from High Court civil judgments even when the monetary test laid down in Article 133(1) is not satisfied, it is, relatively speaking, not often that the Supreme Court exercises this discretion. Usually, it is only when, in the judgment of the Supreme Court, substantial questions of law are involved that the Court will grant special leave to appeal after a High Court has rejected an application for a certificate under Article 133(1)(c).[111]

---

[107] Law Commission's *Fourteenth Report*, I, Table III, p. 49.

[108] Law Commission's *Fourteenth Report*, I, Table III, pp. 49–50.

[109] Law Commission's *Fourteenth Report*, I, Table III, p. 50.

[110] *Sanwat Singh and Others v. State of Rajasthan*, (1961) S.C.R. III 120, 135.

[111] See, e.g., *Karnani Properties Ltd. v. Augustin*, (1957) S.C.R. 20; *Santosh Kumar v. Bhai Mool Singh*, (1958) S.C.R. 1211.

This discussion of Article 136 may be concluded by observing that this jurisdiction permits the Supreme Court to sit in judgment over every court and tribunal in India. This is an extraordinarily extensive jurisdiction which enables the Supreme Court to impose a very high degree of uniformity in the interpretation of both Federal and State law in India. Any limitations on this jurisdiction must be imposed by the Court itself and, as is evident from this discussion, the Court has been most reluctant to tie its own hands by a restrictive interpretation of its own powers.

Advisory Jurisdiction

The Supreme Court, as was true of its predecessor, is vested with an advisory or consultative jurisdiction. Thus the President of India, "if at any time it appears ... that a question of law or fact has arisen, or is likely to arise, which is of such a nature and of such public importance that it is expedient to obtain the opinion of the Supreme Court upon it, ... may refer the question to that Court for consideration and the Court may, after such hearing as it thinks fit, report to the President its opinion thereon."[112] The use of the word "may" in this clause indicates that there is no obligation on the Court to report an opinion. Further, the debates in the Constituent Assembly prove quite conclusively that the choice of the term "may" was intentional, and that it was intended to be permissive.[113]

---

[112] Article 143(1). There is a second clause in Article 143 which authorizes the President to seek the Court's opinion in the event of a dispute arising out of any agreement to which a former Ruler of an Indian State was a party. Thus, though the courts in India possess no regular jurisdiction over such disputes (recall the proviso to Article 131, and see Article 363), the Supreme Court's opinion in such a dispute might be sought. The Court has not yet been so approached, but should such an occasion arise, the phraseology employed in this clause ("... the Supreme Court shall ... report to the President its opinion. ...") indicates that it would be obligatory for the Court to render an opinion. Apparently, the opinion is made compulsory in disputes involving a former Princely State in order to give the ex-Rulers some tangible assurance that they would not be completely without judicial relief.

[113] *Constituent Assembly Debates*, VIII (1949), p. 387. Yet one of India's most competent legal scholars, Professor T. K. Tope of Government Law College, Bombay, argues that the Supreme Court actually has no discretion to refuse to render an opinion. He cites the discussion in the House of Commons in connection with Section 213 of the Government of India Act, 1935. At one point in this discussion the Attorney-General of Great Britain pointed out that "in legislation, in certain circumstances 'may' and 'shall' are interchangeable expressions." Professor Tope concludes that since the present Article 143 is little more than a reproduction of Section 213, the same interpretation of "may" should apply.

However, though the Supreme Court has noted that it "may in a proper case and for good reasons decline to express any opinion on the questions submitted to it …,"[114] the Court has never declined a request of the President. On each of the five occasions on which the President has approached the Court, an opinion was rendered.

The first reference[115] came in 1951, when the President asked the Court to determine if certain pieces of legislation were *ultra vires* of the Constitution because of an unconstitutional delegation of legislative power. In 1949, the Federal Court, in the case of *Jatindra Nath* v. *Province of Bihar*,[116] had ruled that a key section of the Bihar Maintenance of Public Order Act, 1947, was *ultra vires* on the ground that the section conferred power on the Provincial Government to modify an Act of the Legislature, and thus amounted to an unconstitutional delegation of legislative power. This decision raised doubts about the validity of similar provisions in other legislation, prompting the Central Government to seek an opinion from the Supreme Court.

In an opinion which was neither clear nor concise,[117] the Court discussed at length all aspects of the matter of legislative delegations of power, the majority concluding that the legislation in question was constitutional, and that a legislature could delegate power to an agency or instrumentality of its choice so long as the delegating authority retains its own legislative power intact.[118] This

---

T. K. Tope, "Power of President of India to Consult the Supreme Court of India: How Far Is This Provision Desirable?" *Supreme Court Journal*, XIX (1956), p. 118.

[114] *In re the Kerala Education Bill, 1957*, (1959) S.C.R. 995, 1015. In this reference, Chief Justice Spens' remark in 1943 that "we should always be unwilling to decline to accept a reference, except for good reason" was cited with approval (p. 1016).

[115] *In re The Delhi Laws Act, 1912*, (1951) S.C.R. 747.

[116] (1949) F.C.R. 595. See Chapter II, p. 42.

[117] This opinion covers no less than 378 pages in the *Supreme Court Reports*. All seven justices delivered a separate opinion, leaving considerable doubt as to just what the Supreme Court intended to convey in its opinion. Indeed, in the following year, in the case of *Kathi Raning Rawat* v. *The State of Saurashtra*, (1952) S.C.R. 435, none other than the Chief Justice, who had himself contributed to the confusion by writing one of the separate opinions, observed that "while undoubtedly certain definite conclusions were reached by the majority of the Judges …, the reasoning in each case was different and it is difficult to say that any particular principle has been laid down by the majority which can be of assistance in the determination of other cases" (p. 444). The Law Commission undoubtedly had this opinion in mind when it urged the Court to provide "clear advisory opinions" (Law Commission's *Fourteenth Report*, I, 53).

[118] A large number of American and Commonwealth decisions were reviewed by the Court in the course of its opinion.

particular opinion, although of some importance, is probably the least significant of those rendered by the Supreme Court.

Far more important was the second opinion,[119] for in this instance the President's reference brought the Supreme Court into a politically volatile controversy. The Kerala Education Bill was passed by the Kerala Legislature in September 1957, some six months after the Communist government was established in power in Kerala. The ostensible object of the Bill was "the better organization and development of educational institutions in the State."[120] However, since the Bill contained provisions which, according to Anglo-Indians, Christians, and Muslims, violated their constitutional right to establish and administer their own primary and secondary schools,[121] the Governor[122] of Kerala withheld his assent and passed the Bill to the President of India for his consideration.[123] Then the President, because of the questionable constitutional validity of some of the Bill's provisions, asked the Court to express its views on a series of specific questions.

Although this Bill was sponsored by the Communist Party, this is nowhere mentioned in the ninety-page opinion of the Supreme Court, which indicates the absolute unwillingness of the Court to be drawn into any discussion of the general policy and underlying purpose of the Bill. In other words, the Court confined itself to the purely legal or constitutional issues raised in the reference. Indeed, so adamant was the Court in limiting its scrutiny to constitutional questions that, after observing that counsel for the Christian community had argued that the Bill

> represents a deliberate attempt on the part of the party now in power in Kerala to strike at the Christian Church and especially that of the Catholic persuasion, to eliminate religion, to expropriate the minority communities of the properties of their schools established for the purpose of conserving their distinct language, script and culture, and, in short, to eliminate all educational agencies other than the State so as to bring about a regimentation of education and by and through the educational institutions to propagate the tenets of their [Communist Party] political philosophy and indoctrinate the impressionable minds of the rising generation ...,

[119] *In re the Kerala Education Bill, 1957,* (1959) S.C.R. 995.

[120] From its preamble, quoted in *In re the Kerala Education Bill, 1957,* (1959) S.C.R. 995, 1023.

[121] Article 30 of the Constitution protects the right of minorities to establish and administer educational institutions of their choice.

[122] State Governors in India are appointed by the President and serve as representatives of the Central Government. The topmost political position at the State level is the Chief Minister.

[123] Constitution of India, Article 200.

the majority, somewhat curiously, commented that

> it is unfortunate that a certain amount of heat and passion was introduced in the discussion of what should be viewed as a purely legal and constitutional problem raised by the questions; but perhaps it is understandable in the context of the bitter agitation and excitement provoked by the said Bill in the minds of certain sections of people of the State. We desire, however, to emphasize that this Court is not concerned with the merit or otherwise of the policy of the Government which has sponsored this measure and all that we are called to do is to examine the constitutional questions referred to us and to pronounce our opinion on the validity or otherwise of those provisions of the Bill which may properly come within the purview of those questions.[124]

Approaching the questions raised by the President's reference in this light, the Court concluded by a majority of six to one that the Bill was in part constitutionally valid, but that some of its provisions violated the right of minorities to establish educational institutions of their choice.

This opinion was announced on May 22, 1958. In February of 1959 the Kerala Legislature amended the Education Bill in light of the Supreme Court's opinion, and the President then assented to it.[125]

It has been pointed out by one writer that this opinion probably has established a precedent of some federal significance. In later situations where a bill is reserved by a State Governor for the President's consideration, and where the President withholds his assent on the ground that the bill is of doubtful constitutional validity, this Kerala reference probably has established a precedent that he shall seek the Supreme Court's views and not merely arbitrarily withhold assent.[126] Moreover, when such a reference is made, and when the Court is unanimous or near-unanimous in upholding the validity of the bill, it is very unlikely that the President would withhold his assent any longer.

No less politically volatile and inflammatory were the questions put to the Court in the third reference, *In re The Berubari Union and Exchange of Enclaves*,[127] concerning an exchange of territories between Pakistan and India. Although the Radcliffe Award of August 12, 1947 and the Bagge Commission report of January 26, 1950 had sought to delineate precisely the boundary between India

---

[124] *In re the Kerala Education Bill, 1957*, (1959) S.C.R. 995, 1038.

[125] *Hindustan Times*, February 20 and 21, 1959. On July 31, 1959, the Central Government, on the ground that conditions of disorder were increasing in Kerala, issued a Proclamation of Emergency, thereby displacing the Communist Ministry.

[126] Lily Isabel Thomas, "Advisory Jurisdiction of the Supreme Court of India," *Journal of the Indian Law Institute*, V (October–December, 1963), pp. 491–492.

[127] (1960) S.C.R. III 250.

and Pakistan, certain disputes arose between the two countries subsequent to these awards. In an effort to remove these points of tension, the Prime Ministers of the two countries entered into an agreement, known as the Indo-Pakistan Agreement, on September 10, 1958. The terms of this Agreement provided for a division of the Berubari Union between India and Pakistan, and for an exchange of the Cooch-Behar Enclaves in Pakistan and Pakistan Enclaves in India. The areas to be transferred to Pakistan were in the State of West Bengal and, under-standably, emotions in West Bengal ran very high over the prospect of losing territory to Pakistan.

The Supreme Court became involved in this matter after disputes arose as to procedures involved in the implementation of the Agreement. The major question put to the Court by the President was whether the Agreement might be implemented by mere executive fiat, or whether Parliamentary legislation or an amendment to the Constitution was necessary.[128] Thus the Supreme Court was concerned with the purely technical question of how the Government might constitutionally cede territory, if the situation was, in fact, one of cession.

The Attorney-General of India argued before the Court that a cession of terri-tory to Pakistan was actually not involved, that the Agreement merely delineated a boundary which had already been fixed, and that the Agreement could be implemented by executive action alone. The Court, however, was unanimous in its conclusion that involved was a cession of a part of India's territory to Pakistan, and that the Agreement could be consummated only after an amend-ment of the Constitution.[129] Although the Court was thus agreeing with the contention of the State of West Bengal, the displeasure of certain elements in West Bengal over the loss of territory to Pakistan did not abate after this advi-sory opinion.[130] Indeed, the questions raised before the Court were really only ostensible ones, and it is quite clear that certain groups which were represented before the Court—the Jan Sangh,[131] e.g.—were concerned less with the proce-dural aspects of the Agreement than with any cession of territory to Pakistan,

---

[128] Just prior to the President's approach to the Supreme Court, the same question was raised in the Calcutta High Court in the case of *Nirmal Bose* v. *Union of India,* A.I.R. 1959 Cal. 506. This case was dismissed, however, because, in the view of the majority, the Central Government had not yet acted to implement the Agreement, and because the respondent–the Secretary of the Ministry of External Affairs–resided outside the jurisdiction of the Calcutta High Court, thereby preventing the Court from issuing any injunction.

[129] *In re The Berubari Union and Exchange of Enclaves* (1960) S.C.R, III 250, 295–296.

[130] See *Times of India,* November 26, and December 14, 1960.

[131] *In re The Berubari Union and Exchange of Enclaves* (1960) S.C.R. III 250, 259–261.

regardless of whether it be by executive fiat, legislation, or amendment of the Constitution.

Following the announcement of the Court's opinion on March 14, 1960, the Government drafted a Bill to amend the Constitution which, after receiving the required two-thirds approval of Parliament and the assent of the President, became effective on December 28, 1960.[132]

An important opinion affecting Union–State relations was announced in 1963 in the fourth reference under Article 143.[133] When the Union Government proposed to amend certain Acts of Parliament so as to enable the Central Government to levy customs and excise duties on goods produced or manufactured by a State Government, a number of State Governments objected, arguing that such action would be unconstitutional in view of Article 289, which provides that "the property and income of a State shall be exempt from Union taxation." In view of these objections, the President asked the Court to give its opinion on the true scope of Article 289, i.e., to render its opinion on the extent of the immunity from Union taxation provided by Article 289.

After hearing arguments presented by the Solicitor-General of India and by the Advocates-General or other counsel of twelve States of India, the Supreme Court, by a five to four majority, held that Article 289 provided an immunity to the States only from direct taxes on property and not from indirect customs and excise duties. The majority opinion was expressed by the then Chief Justice, B. P. Sinha, who regarded the distribution of taxation powers between the Union and State Governments as of little importance, in view of the fact that the Union Government used much of the revenue collected from the States for subsidizing various State activities. In his words, "the Union and the States together form one organic whole for the purposes of utilization of the resources of the territories of India as a whole."[134]

The four dissenting judges, after emphasizing that the Indian Constitution establishes a federal system, and after demonstrating no little knowledge of the doctrine of immunity of instrumentalities as it developed in the United States after *McCulloch v. Maryland*,[135] concluded that there was no need to

[132] The Constitution (Ninth Amendment) Act, 1960.

[133] This opinion, not yet reported in the Supreme Court Reports, bears the name *Reference by the President of India Under Article 143(1) of the Constitution* in *The Supreme Court Journal*, XXXI (July, 1964), p. 51.

[134] *Reference by the President of India Under Article 143(1) of the Constitution* in *The Supreme Court Journal*, XXXI (July, 1964), p. 60.

[135] Wheat. 316 (1819). Although these dissenting judges drew heavily upon the experiences of other countries, one of them did note that "it is necessary here to strike a note of warning. Each Constitution must be interpreted on its own terms and in its own

examine the niceties of the distinction between direct and indirect taxation, for no such distinction is made anywhere in the Constitution, and that Article 289 should be interpreted as exempting any State property from any Union tax.

In the fifth advisory opinion, the Supreme Court was confronted with some of the most important and spectacular[136] constitutional questions it has ever faced, under any of its various jurisdictions, in its fifteen-year history. The major questions which were raised either explicitly or implicitly in this reference were: (i) are the legislatures in India sovereign in the British sense?, (ii) or does India's written constitution mean that the constitution is supreme and that the legislatures must conform to the requirements of this constitution?, and (iii) is it the role of the Supreme Court to safeguard individual liberties and to serve as the ultimate interpreter of the constitution? In short, the major issue was that of judges versus politicians.[137]

The occasion for the reference was a sharp conflict between the Uttar Pradesh Legislative Assembly and the Allahabad High Court, which arose when the High Court ordered the release on bail of Keshav Singh, "a Socialist worker of Gorakhpur," whom the Assembly had committed to prison for contempt on a general warrant, i.e., one not stating the facts constituting contempt. Keshav Singh had published a pamphlet in which, according to the Assembly, he had libeled one of its members (he had charged that one member of the Assembly was a thief). The Assembly then passed a resolution that a reprimand be administered to him, but he refused to journey to Lucknow, the State capital. Thereupon, he was brought under the custody of the Marshal of the Assembly

---

setting of history, geography and social conditions of the country and nation for which the Constitution is made; a decision on a constitutional problem having an apparent similarity with a problem arising under a different Constitution may not be a sure guide as a solution of the problem. Basically, the problem must be solved on the terms of the Constitution under which it arises" ((1964) S.C.J. II, 51, 78–79).

[136] Certainly it was the most newsworthy item ever to involve the Supreme Court, for the opinion received headline coverage in all major English-language dailies on October 1, 1964, and continued coverage for the next several days. Moreover, it is the first Indian Supreme Court ruling to receive notice in the popular press in the United States. See "Constitutional Law: India Follows the U.S.," *Time*, October 23, 1964, p. 54, 56.

[137] This advisory opinion, having been announced only on September 30, 1964, is, of course, not yet reported in any law reporter or journal. The following account is based chiefly upon the coverage it received in *The Times of India*, October 1–4, 1964; *The Statesman*, October 1–3, 1964; *The Hindustan Times*, October 1–4, 1964; *The Hindu*, October 1–3, 1964; *The Hindu Weekly Review*, October 5, 1964, and *The Economist* (London), October 17, 1964.

in execution of a warrant issued by the Speaker, and he was made to appear before the Assembly on March 14, 1964. But he not only refused to give his name; he also turned his back to the Speaker and refused to answer all questions put to him. Indignant at such irreverence, the Assembly ordered that he be committed to jail for a week for contempt. Keshav Singh then petitioned the Lucknow Bench of the Allahabad High Court for a writ of habeas corpus, alleging deprivation of his personal liberty without any authority of law. After giving notice, which was ignored by the Assembly (no one appeared in court on behalf of the respondents), the Lucknow Bench on March 19th ordered the immediate release on bail of Keshav Singh. On March 21st, the irate Assembly ordered that he, his lawyer, and the two High Court judges, should be brought into custody and made to appear before the Assembly, on the ground that all of them had committed contempt of the Assembly. Warrants were issued on March 23rd, and on the same day the lawyer and the two judges moved petitions in the Allahabad High Court seeking to restrain the Speaker and others from implementing this order of the Assembly. These petitions were heard by the Full Bench (twenty-eight judges) of the High Court, and the ruling was in favor of Keshav Singh, his lawyer, and their colleagues of the Lucknow Bench. At this point, the Assembly withdrew the warrants of arrest against the two judges and lawyer, but still asked them to appear before its Committee of Privileges to explain themselves. Before the situation could become any worse, President Radhakrishnan on March 26th asked the Supreme Court for an advisory opinion, thereby bringing the Supreme Court into the midst of this extraordinary controversy. In doing so, the President formulated five questions for the Court's opinion:

(i)   Did the Lucknow Bench of the Uttar Pradesh High Court have the authority to entertain and deal with the petition of Keshav Singh, or was this a matter outside of the purview of a court in India? The unanimous Supreme Court answered that it was within the jurisdiction of the Lucknow Bench to get involved, and went so far as to point out that it was the duty of a High Court to entertain a habeas corpus petition if a question of individual liberty was raised, even in cases where a general warrant had been issued by a legislature directing the detention of a person for contempt.

(ii) Did Keshav Singh and his lawyer, by petitioning the Lucknow Bench for a writ of habeas corpus, and did the judges, by entertaining and dealing with the petition, commit contempt of the Assembly? A unanimous Supreme Court answered in the negative.

(iii) Did the Assembly possess the authority to order the lawyer and two judges to appear before it, or to call for their explanation for what it regarded as contempt of the Assembly? Six out of the seven Supreme Court justices participating in this opinion replied in the negative. Justice Sarkar

expressed the view that the legislature was competent to *request* an explanation, but he did not believe the legislature could *order* the lawyer and
judges to appear.

(iv)   Did the Full Bench of the High Court of Uttar Pradesh possess the authority
to entertain and deal with the petitions of the two judges and lawyer, and to
pass interim orders restraining the Speaker of the Legislative Assembly from
implementing the directions of the Assembly? The Supreme Court said yes,
unanimously.

(v)   Does a judge who entertains and deals with a petition challenging any
order or decision of a legislature which imposes any penalty for its contempt commit contempt himself, and, if so, is the legislature competent
to "take proceedings" against such a judge? Six members of the Court said
no; Justice Sarkar said the question is too general to lend itself to a single
answer.

The crux of this spectacular and, in part, ludicrous, altercation between the
judiciary and the legislature really centered on the question of whether the legislatures in India are omnipotent and in possession of powers sufficient to jail
critics for contempt with no judicial review whatever, or whether, since India
is governed by a written constitution with a bill of rights, conflicts between
legislative privilege and human rights must be resolved by the courts by an
interpretation of the Constitution. As is quite evident from the Supreme Court's
opinion, the Court has held that it is the Constitution which is supreme, and
that the Constitution "had entrusted to the judicature the task of construing the
provisions of the Constitution and of safeguarding the fundamental rights of
the citizens."[138]

As is pointed out by a reporter of *The Economist*, this controversy between
the courts and the legislature "hinged on a constitutional accident."[139] Article
194(3) of the Constitution of India provides that

the powers, privileges and immunities of a House of the Legislature of a State,
and of the members and the committees of a House of such Legislature, shall
be such as may from time to time be defined by the Legislature by law, and,
until so defined, shall be those of the House of Commons of the Parliament of the
United Kingdom, and of its members and committees, at the commencement of
the Constitution.[140]

[138] An extract from Chief Justice Gajendragadkar's majority opinion, quoted in *The*
Hindustan Times, October 1, 1964, p. 4, col. 5.

[139] "Judges versus Politicians," *The Economist,* October 17, 1964, p, 249.

[140] Emphasis supplied. Article 105(3) provides that the same applies to the Union
Parliament.

Though both the Union Parliament and State Legislatures have the power to make a law defining their own privileges, no legislature has ever passed one. If such a law was passed there is no doubt that it would be held invalid by the Supreme Court if it sanctioned infringements on fundamental rights, for Article 13, which provides the basis for judicial review in India, states unequivocably that "the State shall not make any law which takes away or abridges the rights conferred by this Part [Part III: Fundamental Rights] and any law made in contravention of this clause shall, to the extent of the contravention, be void." Chief Justice Gajendragadkar said just this in his majority opinion.[141] There is little doubt that the State Legislatures and the Union Parliament have refrained from passing a law defining their own powers, privileges and immunities precisely because they are aware that such a law would be declared invalid if it contravened any of the fundamental rights. But in the absence of such a law, the legislatures in India have assumed, and, indeed, argued before the Supreme Court in the present dispute, that they enjoy the same powers, privileges and immunities as enjoyed by the House of Commons, and that these are not only not subject to the fundamental rights set out in the Constitution, but also that no court in India is empowered to question, let alone restrict by interpretation of the Constitution, these privileges.[142]

The Supreme Court, however, was of the opinion that the Constitution is supreme in India, that the sovereignty of the legislatures is limited by the fact of a written Constitution, and that the supremacy of the Constitution is guaranteed by an independent judicial body acting as the exclusive interpreter of the Constitution. This being established, the Court proceeded to interpret Article 194(3) in light of the total constitutional system, in order to arrive at what it termed a "harmonious construction" of the Constitution. In doing so, it adduced much evidence which pointed toward the conclusion that legislative privilege could not be understood as being so extensive as to abrogate individual rights. For example, the Court noted that Article 32 confers an absolute, unqualified right upon any citizen to move the Supreme Court if he believed any of his fundamental rights to be infringed by the legislature or executive. The Court said the framers simply could not have intended that this guaranteed right should be subject to any power or privilege vesting in any legislature in India.

---

[141] See summary of the majority opinion in *The Hindustan Times*, October 1, 1964, pp. 1, 4–5. In an earlier decision in the case of *Pandit M.S.M.* Sharma v. *Shri Sri Krishna Sinha and Others*, (1959) S.C.R. Supp. I 806, 858, the then Chief Justice, S. R. Das, made the same observation.

[142] The Lucknow Assembly underlined these points by refusing even to send a representative to state its opinion before the Lucknow Bench on March 19th. *The Hindustan Times*, October 1, 1964, p. 4, cols. 3–4.

This opinion caused an uproar both in Uttar Pradesh and in New Delhi. An article on the front page of the October 1st issue of *The Hindustan Times* entitled "State in throes of crisis" states that some legislators in Lucknow immediately demanded an emergency session of the State Assembly in order to take up the issues raised by the Supreme Court's opinion, while others were reported to be urging a convention of the Speakers of all the State Assemblies and of the Lok Sabha, and prominent legislators from all over the country in order to "chalk out a common line of action since the rights and privileges of all the legislatures are equally affected by the Supreme Court's verdict." In New Delhi, the Lok Sabha discussed the Supreme Court's opinion on October 1st. One reporter described the discussion as "hectic";[143] another said of the hour-long discussion that "for some time the Lok Sabha was in the grip of strong emotion. Feelings ran so high that some members who attempted to speak in favour of the judiciary were shouted down."[144] The Law Minister, A. K. Sen, told the Parliament that the opinion of the Supreme Court would cause a "deep erosion" of the privileges of Parliament and the State legislatures.[145] Hukum Singh, the Speaker of the Lok Sabha, said he and other parliamentarians were "very much perturbed" by the opinion, and when a member of Parliament suggested that the Court may have reached the only decision it could have in view of the nature of the Indian Constitution, the Speaker drew cheers when he replied that "I repudiate the suggestion that we have submitted ourselves to the Supreme Court's jurisdiction. ...."[146] Hukum Singh argued that it was the intention of the framers of the Constitution to ensure that "whenever Parliament exercised the privilege to imprison anybody, the courts should not interfere,"[147] and that if the Supreme Court did not give effect to the "express wishes of the Constituent Assembly, it was for the Government to decide to amend the Constitution."[148]

One of the few voices of moderation was that of Prime Minister Lal Bahadur Shastri who, according to *The Statesman*, "urged the utmost restraint and caution in dealing with this 'delicate' matter."[149] Acting upon this suggestion of the Prime

---

[143] *The Hindu*, October 2, 1964, p. 1.

[144] *The Statesman*, October 2, 1964, p. 1.

[145] *The Statesman*, October 2, 1964, p. 1.

[146] *The Hindu*, October 2, 1964, p. 10.

[147] *The Statesman*, October 2, 1964, p. 1.

[148] *The Statesman*, October 2, 1964, p. 1; *The Hindu*, October 2, 1964, p. 10.

[149] October 2, 1964, p. 1. Although *The Hindu* in its headline story on October 2nd reports Shastri's reactions similarly, this paper elsewhere on page one carries a story which says that the Prime Minister is reported to have told a meeting of the Congress Parliamentary Party that "the Supreme Court functioned under certain limitations whereas Parliament had no limitations."

Minister, the executive committee of the Congress Party in Parliament set up a subcommittee to discuss the implications of the Supreme Court's opinion.[150]

This landmark opinion of the Supreme Court brings to the fore the most basic questions concerning the role of the Supreme Court and the nature of the Indian constitutional structure. Moreover, this opinion demonstrates better than any other opinion or decision the problems with which the Supreme Court must cope which have arisen out of the efforts of the framers of the 1950 Constitution to arrive at the best of all constitutional worlds by grafting together features of several very different constitutional systems. Article 194(3), in effect, embodies in the Indian Constitution a key feature of the institution of a sovereign legislature. Yet Articles 13 and 32 provide the Supreme Court with the power of judicial review and impose upon the Court the duty to see that fundamental rights are not abridged. It is clearly impossible to have both. Thus the Court was faced with the task of seeking to reconcile several features of the Constitution which are simply irreconcilable.

Upon careful examination of the questions raised in this advisory opinion, it is difficult to reach a conclusion contrary to the one reached by the Court. Indeed, in view of India's written constitution, which provides in the form of a bill of rights limitations on the exercise of executive or legislative powers, it is difficult to see how the Supreme Court could have held other than it did.[151]

[150] *The Times of India,* October 4, 1964, p. 1.

[151] Even so, it seems that this Supreme Court opinion comes very near to reversing an earlier decision. In the case of *Pandit M.S.M. Sharma* v. *Shri Sri Krishna Sinha and Others* [(1959) S.C.R. Supp. I 806], Sharma, who was the editor of The Searchlight, an English-language daily newspaper in Patna, argued that his fundamental right to freedom of speech and expression under Article 19(1)(a) had been infringed by an order of the Secretary of the Patna Legislative Assembly which directed him to show cause why action should not be taken against him for breach of privilege of the Speaker and the Assembly for publishing in its entirety a speech delivered in the Assembly, portions of which had been directed to be expunged by the Speaker. By a four to one majority, the Supreme Court held here that Article 194(3) is "as supreme as the provision of Part III [Fundamental Rights] ..., [and] in our judgement the principle of harmonious construction must be adopted and so construed, the provisions of Art. 19(1)(a), which are general, must yield to Article 194(1) and the latter part of its cl. (3) which are special" (p. 859, 860). Thus, in this 1959 decision, the majority held that Sharma's fundamental right of free speech was overridden by the legislative privilege. The dissenting judge, Subba Rao, the leading libertarian on the Indian Supreme Court, also purporting to be applying the principle of "harmonious construction," concluded that "the Legislature and its members have certainly a wide range of powers and privileges and the said privileges can be exercised without infringing the rights of a citizen, and particularly one who is not a member of the Legislature. When there is a conflict, the privilege should yield to the extent it

It will be interesting to see how the Union Government will attempt to resolve this crisis.

In countries where the executive is permitted to consult the judiciary, there is almost always some criticism of the practice, and some disagreement over the propriety and utility of permitting a court collectively or judges individually to serve as consultants to the executive. India is no exception. Though this is not the place to examine in detail the pros and cons of the Indian Supreme Court's[152] advisory jurisdiction, a few points are pertinent here.[153] Firstly, though an advisory opinion is not binding upon the referring authority, each opinion of the Supreme Court has been accepted by the executive.[154] Secondly, though an advisory opinion theoretically does not have the weight or binding

---

affects the fundamental right" (pp. 880–881).

As is quite clear from the discussion of the historic 1964 opinion, the majority in the recent opinion has adopted Justice Subba Rao's reasoning. Yet, according to the majority opinion in 1964, the *Searchlight* case should be understood as saying only that Article 194(3) is not subordinate to Article 19(1)(a), but that it must be regarded as subordinate to Article 21, which reads as follows: "No person shall be deprived of his life or personal liberty except according to procedure established by law." In other words, the crucial distinction between the *Searchlight* ruling and the present opinion, fine as it is, is that only free speech was at issue in the *Searchlight* case, whereas personal liberty, which, it is evident, the Supreme Court values more, is involved in the present advisory opinion. Thus the Supreme Court here distinguished between, rather than overruled, its earlier decision.

[152] Only the Supreme Court possesses an advisory jurisdiction; the State executives are not permitted to seek opinions from the High Courts. In the United States, on the contrary, the Supreme Court abstains from giving extra-judicial opinions, but some of the State constitutions make provision for advisory opinions.

[153] The two most useful analyses of the Supreme Court's advisory jurisdiction are William D. Popkin, "Advisory Opinions in India," *Journal of the Indian Law Institute*, IV (July–September, 1962), pp. 401–33, and Lily Isabel Thomas, "Advisory Jurisdiction of the Supreme Court of India," *Journal of the Indian Law Institute*, V (October–December, 1963), pp. 475–497. Cf. M. V. Pylee, *Constitutional Government in India* (New York: Asia Publishing House, 1960), pp. 436–439; T. K. Tope, "Power of President of India to Consult the Supreme Court of India: How Far is this Provision Desirable?," *Supreme Court Journal*, XIX (1956), pp. 118–22; William O. Douglas, *We The Judges: Studies in American and Indian Constitutional Law from Marshall to Mukherjea* (Garden City, New York: Doubleday and Company, Inc., 1956), pp. 46–54; and Mani Shankar, "Advisory Powers of the Indian Supreme Court," *Modern Review*, CVIII (August, 1960), pp. 113–114.

[154] The first exception may be the most recent one. At this writing, the Government had neither accepted nor rejected the opinion. This writer's guess is that whether or not the Government agrees with the recent opinion, it will accept it as binding. But if it disagrees, it will amend the Constitution.

effect of a regular judgment, there is no evidence that any of the lower courts have chosen to ignore any opinion of the Supreme Court. In other words, an advisory opinion seems to be as much a part of the "law of the land" as any judgment of the Court.[155] Thirdly, though one of the more weighty criticisms of advisory opinions is that they often are concerned with hypothetical questions based on premature controversies, the Supreme Court of India, following a practice initiated by the Federal Court,[156] has always sought to approximate in an advisory opinion the procedures employed in a usual adversary proceeding. Interested parties are invited to participate, the hearing is conducted in open court, a minimum of five judges must take part in the opinion,[157] and the opinion must be announced in open court,[158] thereby encouraging the care and deliberation which prevails when public scrutiny follows. Indeed, there is very little to distinguish an advisory opinion from a regular decision. The Supreme Court's consultative jurisdiction seems to serve as little more than a convenient avenue which the executive may utilize when it feels the need.

The strongest argument against the propriety of a consultative jurisdiction is that there is a risk that the executive might unwisely and, perhaps, needlessly, involve the Court in private or political controversy, which might have an adverse effect on the prestige of the judiciary. Certainly the *Berubari, Kerala* and *U. P. Contempt* references are examples of important political controversies into which the Court was drawn by the executive.[159]

However, though the Court has never chosen to do so, it does have the discretionary authority to refuse to render an opinion if it considered the questions raised too hypothetical or too embarrassing. In summary, so long as the integrity and independence of the judiciary are not undermined, the conclusion that advisory opinions serve useful purposes may not be unjustified.

---

[155] See, e.g., *State* v. *Tiwari*, A.I.R. 1956 Patna 188, 190, where the Patna High Court accepted the Delhi Laws Act opinion as binding precedent with full *stare decisis* effect.

[156] *In re Levy of Estate Duty*, (1944) F.C.R. 317.

[157] Constitution of India, Article 145(3).

[158] Constitution of India, Article 145(4).

[159] In the Kerala opinion, the Kerala Government not only opposed the intervention of the Union Government (i.e., by referring the education bill to the Supreme Court for an opinion), but accused the Union Government of discrimination in not referring other, similar measures to the Court, and of using the advisory jurisdiction for political ends. Although one cannot be certain of the Union Government's motives, it looks as though the ruling party at the Centre, having lost the political battle in the Kerala Legislature, sought to win the second round by dragging the Supreme Court into the whirlpool of political strife. Cf. Popkin, pp. 412–420.

5 The Supreme Court in the Indian System of Government

The extensiveness of the original, appellate and advisory jurisdiction discussed in the preceding chapter would seem to indicate that those who were instrumental in framing the Constitution of India sought to create a supreme judicial tribunal which would occupy a position of great importance in independent India. Thus it would seem that the members of the Constituent Assembly were enthusiastic supporters of a powerful judiciary, and that they had a great deal of faith and trust in the judicial process. To a certain extent, this is true. Courts in India had long enjoyed the esteem of the public. They had established an excellent reputation during the long period of British rule. Indeed, a strong case can be made for the statement that the greatest legacies of the British *raj* were an impartial and independent judiciary and a widespread belief in the rule of law. Given this valuable base, it seemed only natural to many members of the Constituent Assembly that the successor to the Federal Court should enjoy a position of prominence in the new India. Many regarded the Supreme Court of the United States as the model to emulate in India.

But there is another side to this story, which leads to a very different attitude toward the Supreme Court and judicial review. A prestigious Supreme Court was only one of a number of ends sought by the makers of the Indian Constitution. Leading figures in the Assembly were committed also to the parliamentary form of government, to far-reaching economic and social reforms, and to a bill of rights. Thus the questions arose very early in the constitution-making process as to just what role should the Supreme Court play. The United States Supreme Court enjoyed a vast amount of prestige and a position of central importance, if not pre-eminence, but could India emulate that institution and at the same time reconcile it with a parliamentary system of government according to the English model? The real issue, of course, was who would have the last word? Should it be Parliament or the Supreme Court? So it was a question of politicians versus judges. The Indian National Congress was committed also to extensive social and economic reform. How would a powerful Supreme Court, endowed with extensive review powers, react to legislation aimed at uplifting the status of hundreds of millions of Indians at the expense of the vested economic interests and traditional social practices? The membership of the Constituent Assembly included many of India's most distinguished lawyers, most of whom were very familiar with the way in which the Supreme Court of the United States had frustrated the will of the majority of Americans in the pre-1937 period. Would the high bench of India, if endowed with broad powers of judicial review, act similarly and declare unconstitutional legislation embodying policies of which most of the public approved?

Another long-standing Indian nationalist demand was a bill of rights or, as this is termed in India, a list of "fundamental rights." It being generally recognized in the Assembly that no rights can be guaranteed absolutely, the question arose as to who should determine ultimately whether restrictions on speech, press, association, movement, religion, property and personal liberty were reasonable or unreasonable? Should this judgment be reserved to the executive on the basis of yardsticks determined by Parliament, or should the Supreme Court make this decision?

All these questions, and others as well, concerned the relationship between Parliament and the Supreme Court. It was a question of judges versus politicians, and it was a consideration which was of central importance in the process of constitution-making. Endowing the Court with original, civil and criminal appellate, and advisory powers provoked practically no controversy, but when it came to the question of creating a Court with review powers so broad as to enable the Court to thwart the will of Parliament, a great deal of controversy was generated. It is easiest to understand how this question of judges versus politicians was resolved by summarizing the fate in the Constituent Assembly of the erstwhile "due process" clause, and by taking note of the debate in the Assembly over the question of the degree to which private property should receive constitutional protection. The decisions made by the Assembly on the questions of due process and property indicate quite clearly the role that the framers intended the Supreme Court to play. Following this discussion, some of the landmark post-1950 personal liberty and property decisions will be examined in order to determine how the Supreme Court has interpreted the Constitution and, in so doing, how it has defined its role.

The Debate over "Due Process"

On April 19, 1947, several months before the advent of national independence, an Advisory Committee of which Sardar Vallabhbhai Patel was chairman presented to the Constituent Assembly the *Interim Report on Fundamental Rights*.[1] Clause 9 of this report contains the provision that "no person shall be deprived of his life, or liberty, without due process of law, nor shall any person be denied the equal treatment of the laws within the territories of the Union." Without one word of discussion (other features of this report provoked comment), this clause was adopted by the Assembly on April 30, 1947. Though this marked only the acceptance of an interim recommendation, and not a final decision that the new constitution would have a due process clause, the complete absence of articulated dissent at this stage is an indication, evident elsewhere in the debates of this period, that the power of the judges was liberally conceded in the initial stages of constitution-making.

Once accepted by the Constituent Assembly, this and other committee reports were turned over to Sir Benegal N. Rau, a distinguished member of the Indian Civil Service and former Calcutta High Court judge, who had been appointed as Constitutional Adviser to the Constituent Assembly. On the basis of these reports, Rau prepared a first draft of what would later become the Draft Constitution, which would form the basis of discussion in the Constituent Assembly. Clause 15 of the draft produced by Rau contains the provision that "no person shall be deprived of his life or liberty without due process of law," i.e., a provision identical to that suggested earlier by the Patel Committee, with the exception that the "equal treatment of the laws" portion was deleted and placed in a separate clause elsewhere in Rau's draft.[2]

As noted earlier,[3] the Assembly also appointed in the summer of 1947 a Drafting Committee, with Dr. B. R. Ambedkar as its chairman. This Committee, working with Rau, was entrusted with the task of preparing the Draft Constitution for the Constituent Assembly's scrutiny and discussion.

---

[1] No. CA/24/COM/47. Printed in the *Constituent Assembly Debates*, III (1947), April 29, 1947, pp. 422–429.

[2] This writer has never seen a complete copy of Rau's draft. If printed, it must have had only a limited circulation. Substantial portions of Rau's draft are printed in Sir Benegal Rau, *India's Constitution in the Making*, Edited by B. Shiva Rao (second revised edition; Madras: Allied Publishers, 1963). However, the section on fundamental rights is one of the parts of the draft not found in this selective collection of Rau's papers. Clause 15, quoted before, is attributed to Rau by, among several others, Durga Das Basu, *Commentary on the Constitution of India*, II, 77.

[3] Chapter III, p. 85.

When the *Report of the Drafting Committee*[4] and the *Draft Constitution of India*[5] appeared in February of 1948, the due process clause was gone. In its place was Article 15 of the Draft Constitution, which provided that "[n]o person shall be deprived of his life or personal liberty except according to *procedure established by law.*"[6] At the bottom of this page of the Draft Constitution there is a footnote which, in words uncommonly succinct, notes that this new phraseology was substituted because it is "more specific." There is further understatement in the accompanying *Report*, which in paragraph 5 (designated "Fundamental Rights"), notes that "the Committee has attempted to make these rights and limitations to which they must necessarily be subject as definite as possible, since the courts may have to pronounce upon them."

Although the deliberations of the Drafting Committee were not recorded, there is sufficient evidence available to explain why the due process clause was dropped. By any measure the most interesting of the evidence is a report prepared by Sir Benegal Rau after he returned from a trip to the United States, Canada, Eire and Great Britain. He made this trip during the last three months of 1947 at the request of the President of the Constituent Assembly in order to discuss aspects of India's draft constitution with various constitutional experts. While in Washington, D. C., Rau met with, among others, Justice Felix Frankfurter who, according to Rau's account, "considered that the power of judicial review implied in the due process clause ... is not only undemocratic (because it gives a few judges the power of vetoing legislation enacted by the representatives of the nation) but also throws an unfair burden on the judiciary. ..."[7] Justice Learned Hand of the Circuit Court of Appeal in New York went even further. Rau writes that "Justice Hand considered that it would be better to have all fundamental rights as moral precepts than as legal fetters in the constitution."[8] Upon his return to India, Rau, "as the result of these discussions ...," proposed an amendment to his earlier draft, then under discussion

[4] Dated February 21, 1948 and printed in *Reports of Committees of the Constituent Assembly of India* (New Delhi: Manager, Government of India Press, 1950), pp. 172–177.

[5] New Delhi: Manager, Government of India Press, 1948.

[6] Emphasis supplied.

[7] "A Visit to U.S.A., Canada, Eire and Great Britain," *India's Constitution in the Making*, p. 329. Sir B. N. Rau apparently made a favorable impression on Justice Frankfurter, for Frankfurter is reported by Sir Girja Shankar Bajpai to have said later that "if the President of the U.S.A. were to ask me to recommend a judge for our Supreme Court on the strength of his knowledge of the history and working of the American Constitution, B. N. Rau would be the first on my list" (quoted in B. Shiva Rao's biographical sketch of B. N. Rau, *India's Constitution in the Making*, p. xxviii.)

[8] B. N. Rau, *India's Constitution in the Making*, p. 329.

by the Drafting Committee, "designed to secure that when a law made by the State in the discharge of one of the fundamental duties imposed upon it by the constitution happens to conflict with one of the fundamental rights guaranteed to the individual, the former should prevail over the latter: in other words, the general welfare should prevail over the individual right."[9] Though this statement by Rau admittedly is vague, it is evident that he is expressing the view that the "general welfare," as defined by the legislature, should be accorded higher value than the individual right, and that if the due process clause was retained, this might not always be carried out by the Supreme Court. Thus it is evident that Rau, apparently one of those who earlier had supported the idea of including a due process clause in India's Constitution, could not be counted as a proponent of due process by late 1947.

Moreover, it is apparent that the Drafting Committee itself was divided over the propriety of a due process clause. This became evident during the general debate in the Constituent Assembly when Alladi and Munshi, probably the two most important members of the Committee, argued different points of view, Alladi opposing, and Munshi favoring the inclusion of a due process clause. The substitution of the "procedure established by law" phraseology for the due process clause provoked one of the lengthiest and certainly one of the most important debates in the Constituent Assembly. Munshi, as leader of the pro-due process element, argued that it was an essential feature of the constitution if a balance between individual liberty and social control was to be achieved. He made it quite clear that he believed the courts to be better suited to perform this balancing function than the legislatures.[10] Similar was the position of Pandit Thakur Das Bhargava, who wanted

> two bulwarks for our liberties. One is the legislature and the other is the judiciary. But even if the legislature is carried away by party spirit and is sometimes panicky, the judiciary will save us from the tyranny of the legislature and the executive. Hence "due process of law" should be retained. I want the judiciary to be exalted to its right position of palladium of justice and the people to be secure in their rights and liberties under its protecting wings.[11]

Most articulate of the critics of due process was Alladi, whose most effective argument was that if there was a due process clause in the Indian Constitution, it might "serve as a great handicap for all social legislation."[12] Familiar with the United States Supreme Court's various interpretations of due process, he argued

[9] B. N. Rau, *India's Constitution in the Making*, p. 328.
[10] *Constituent Assembly Debates*, VII (1948), December 6, 1948, pp. 851–853.
[11] *Constituent Assembly Debates*, VII (1948), December 6, 1948, p. 848.
[12] *Constituent Assembly Debates*, VII (1948), December 6, 1948, p. 854.

that the expression has come to mean "what the Supreme Court says it means in any particular case."[13] He urged that it would be too risky to permit the Indian Supreme Court to pass upon the constitutionality of legislation by applying a test as vague as due process. He pointed out that the "procedure established by law" clause was "more definite," and that it would ensure against uncertainty in the interpretation and application of laws passed by Parliament.

Not without interest was the admission by Alladi and other members of the Drafting Committee that the "procedure established by Law" phraseology had been taken from the Japanese Constitution of 1946, Article 31 of which provides that "no person shall be deprived of life or liberty, nor shall any other criminal penalty be imposed, except according to procedure established by law." This is all the more interesting in that this Japanese Constitution, as is well known, was written in large part by Americans then in occupation in Japan.[14] While no member of the Indian Constituent Assembly said so explicitly, the implication is that if the Americans were delighted with the application and interpretation of the due process clause in the United States, they would have included one in the Japanese Constitution.

The debate over the due process clause extended over several days in the Constituent Assembly in December, 1948. The debate culminated on December 13th, when Dr. Ambedkar, in an important and lucid speech, summed up the arguments pro and con and called for a vote:

> The question of "due process" raises, in my judgment, the question of the relationship between the legislature and the judiciary. ... Every law in a federal constitution, whether made by the Parliament at the Centre or made by the legislature of a State, is always subject to examination by the judiciary from the point of view of the authority of the legislature making the law. The "due process" clause, in my judgment, would give the judiciary the power to question the law made by the legislature on another ground. That ground would be whether that law is in keeping with certain fundamental principles relating to the rights of the individual. In other words, the judiciary would be endowed with the authority to question the law not merely on the ground whether it was in excess of the authority of the legislature, but also on the ground whether the law was good law, apart from the question of the powers of the legislature making the law. ... The question now raised by the introduction of the phrase "due process" is whether the judiciary should be given the additional power to question the laws made by the State on the ground that they violate certain fundamental principles.

[13] *Constituent Assembly Debates*, VII (1948), December 6, 1948, p. 853.

[14] Robert E. Ward, "The Origins of the Present Japanese Constitution," *American Political Science Review*, L (1956), pp. 980–1010; Theodore McNelly, "The Japanese Constitution: Child of the Cold War," *Political Science Quarterly*, LXIV (1960), pp. 176–195.

There are two views on this point. One view is this: that the legislature may be trusted not to make any law which would abrogate the fundamental rights of man, so to say, the fundamental rights which apply to every individual, and consequently, there is no danger arising from the introduction of the phrase "due process." Another view is this: that it is not possible to trust the legislature; the legislature is likely to err, is likely to be led away by passion, by party prejudice, by party considerations, and the legislature may make a law which may abrogate what may be regarded as the fundamental principles which safeguard the individual rights of a citizen. We are therefore placed in two difficult positions. One is to give the judiciary the authority to sit in judgment over the will of the legislature and to question the law made by the legislature on the ground that it is not good law, in consonance with fundamental principles. Is that a desirable principle? The second position is that the legislature ought to be trusted not to make bad laws. It is very difficult to come to any definite conclusion. There are dangers on both sides. For myself I cannot altogether omit the possibility of a Legislature packed by party men making laws which may abrogate or violate what we regard as certain fundamental principles affecting the life and liberty of the individual. At the same time, I do not see how five or six gentlemen sitting in a Federal or Supreme Court examining laws made by the Legislature and by dint of their own individual conscience or their bias or their prejudices can be trusted to determine which law is good and which law is bad. It is rather a case where a man has to sail between Charybdis and Scilla and I, therefore, would not say anything. I would leave it to the House to determine in any way it likes.[15]

A voice vote followed and the "procedure established by law" phraseology was adopted.[16]

The convincing rhetoric of Alladi, a distinguished lawyer himself, seems to have been the single most important factor in determining the ultimate decision. He was able to persuade the Assembly that the legislatures as well as the judiciary could be trusted, or, at any rate, that it was better to trust the legislatures than run the risk of the judiciary becoming a third chamber which might thwart the will of the elected representatives of the people. So the question of due process or procedure established by law was one of judges versus politicians, and the politicians carried the day.

There were other reasons for the deletion of the due process clause from the original draft. Among these the most important was the genuine fear that the Supreme Court might interpret due process so liberally in favor of individual freedom that legislation designed to restrict personal liberty in the interests of the security of the state and public order might fail to pass the constitutionality test. When the Assembly convened first in 1946 there

---

[15] *Constituent Assembly Debates*, VII (1948), December 13, 1948, pp. 1000–1001.

[16] *Constituent Assembly Debates*, VII (1948), December 13, 1948, p. 1001.

was general agreement that if the constitution did little else, it should seek to protect the individual against both legislative and executive encroachments on his liberties. This, of course, was but a natural feeling in view of the critical periods through which India was passing, periods when thousands of Indians had been jailed without trial by the alien rulers. Thus Indian leaders were determined that once they could decide their own destinies, they would make certain that such infringements upon personal liberty would end. But with the advent of independence and the partition of the subcontinent in August, 1947, there came a tragic outbreak of bloodshed and communal violence. Hundreds of thousands of people died violently, and disorder was endemic in parts of the subcontinent. These dramatic developments resulted in a change of emphasis in the Constituent Assembly from guaranteeing liberally individual liberties to devising means for providing adequate security to the State against subversive and, as they are called in India, "anti-social" elements. Thus the Assembly had to consider the problem of how to provide some constitutional protection to individual rights and at the same time assure that the Government could deal effectively with those who would abuse their liberties.

Ironically, the excellent record established by the Federal Court in upholding individual rights and embarrassing the alien executive during World War II was probably one of the major reasons why the members of the Constituent Assembly feared that the Supreme Court might lean too much in favor of the individual, thereby making it difficult for the Government to maintain order. At any rate, the due process clause was one of the first casualties of this change of mood in the Constituent Assembly. By 1948 due process was regarded as something which would confer just too much discretion on the Supreme Court.

The "procedure established by law" clause which is found today in Article 21[17] of the Constitution of India thus represents a conscious effort of the framers to limit the scope of judicial review over legislation affecting life and personal liberty. This clause was understood by the framers to mean that the degree to which life and liberty would be protected would be determined by the legislatures, and not by the judiciary. In other words, Article 21 restricts only the *executive* from proceeding against the life or personal liberty of the individual, except under the authority, and in accordance with the procedure prescribed by a law passed by a legislature. Article 21 was not intended as any constitutional limitation upon the powers of the *legislature*. Or, in words familiar to the student of American

---

[17] The exact wording is "no person shall be deprived of his life or personal liberty except according to procedure established by law."

constitutional law, Article 21 embodies features of "procedural due process," but none of "substantive due process."[18]

There is one final aspect of the due process debate which merits some consideration here, for it demonstrates that those, both inside and outside of the Assembly, who fought but lost the battle for due process made up a sizeable segment of politically-significant public opinion in India. This became evident near the end of the constitution-making process when Dr. Ambedkar in September of 1949 introduced into the Constituent Assembly a new article designed to placate to some degree those who feared that the legislatures would treat individual liberties lightly. Introducing the new article, Ambedkar observed:

> I know that a large part of the House including myself were greatly dissatisfied with the wording of article 15 [present Article 21]. It will also be recalled that there is no part of our Draft Constitution which has been so violently criticized by the public outside as article 15 because all that article 15 does is this—it only prevents the executive from making an arrest. All that is necessary is to have a law and the law need not be subject to any conditions or limitations. In other words, it was felt that while this matter was being included in this Chapter dealing with Fundamental Rights, we are giving a *carte blanche* to Parliament to make and provide for the arrest of any person under any circumstances as Parliament may think fit. We are therefore now, by introducing article 15A [present Article 22], making, if I may say so, compensation for what was done then in passing article 15. In other words, we are providing for the substance of the law of "due process" by the introduction of article 15A.[19]

Ambedkar meant that this new article was designed to embody features of "procedural" due process in the section on Fundamental Rights, for it guarantees to an arrested person the rights to be informed of the grounds of his arrest, to consult and be defended by a lawyer of his choice, and to be produced before the nearest magistrate within a period of twenty-four hours of his arrest. But these procedural guarantees would not apply to either enemy aliens or to persons "arrested or detained under any law providing for preventive detention."[20] Such

---

[18] The fate of the due process clause in India's Constituent Assembly is quite in line with the experience elsewhere. In a recent book, Donald H. Bayley observes that "in the twentieth century there has been a general retreat from a broad application of 'due process' which included appeals to natural law. The phrase has become more restrictively interpreted and is now used only against the manner or procedure in which a law is administered. 'Substantive due process' has given ground to 'procedural due process.' In many of the developing nations great pains have been taken to prevent the judiciary from assuming as much as the American Supreme Court had" (*Public Liberties in the New States* (Chicago: Rand McNally & Company, 1964), p. 128).

[19] *Constituent Assembly Debates*, IX (1949), September 15, 1949, p. 1497.

[20] Constitution of India, Article 22(3)(b).

persons were guaranteed only the right to be informed of the grounds of their detention and access to an Advisory Board so that they might be able to make "a representation against the order ..." of detention. Whereas the procedural guarantees of this new article were welcomed by the proponents of due process, the denial of these guarantees to individuals under preventive detention provoked a stormy debate in the Constituent Assembly. Indeed, the very idea of mentioning preventive detention in the Constitution was repugnant to many. Arrest and detention without trial, first introduced in India in 1793,[21] came to be one of the most hated features of British rule. It symbolized to Indian nationalists the divergence between British rule in India and government in Great Britain, a distinction Indians claimed was based on contempt and utilized in order to coerce. The late Prime Minister Nehru, speaking at the annual meeting of the Indian National Congress in 1936, said of preventive detention:

> Of one thing I must say a few words, for to me it is one of the most vital things that I value. That is the tremendous deprivation of civil liberties in India. A government that has to rely on the Criminal Law Amendment Act and similar laws ... that keep people in prison without trial ... is a government that has ceased to have even a shadow of justification for its existence. I can never adjust myself to these conditions; I find them intolerable.[22]

However, by 1948 and 1949 those who were piloting the Draft Constitution through the Constituent Assembly had become supporters of legislation authorizing preventive detention, owing chiefly to the upsurge of violence and chaos which arose out of the partition of the subcontinent. Those now in power, most of whom had experienced detention without trial themselves,[23] were now convinced that the executive must continue to be armed with this weapon, and that the courts must not be permitted to make difficult the utilization of preventive detention. By September of 1949 the framers no longer needed to conjecture as to how the courts in independent India would regard preventive detention measures for, as was pointed out in Chapter II, the Federal Court in 1949 had declared invalid two post-independence preventive detention enactments, and in a third decision had examined the grounds of a detention order in an effort to determine whether the detention order was justified.[24] Thus the new article

---

[21] In the East India Company Act of that year.

[22] Jawaharlal Nehru, *Towards Freedom* (New York: The John Day Company, 1941), p. 392.

[23] Nehru spent over nine years in jail without trial. Yet this did not prevent Nehru from urging Parliament in 1952 to renew the Preventive Detention Act, and from telling Parliament that preventive detention is "not only right but is wholly democratic" (*Lok Sabha Debates*, IV (1952), August 2, 1952, col. 5200).

[24] See pp. 42–45.

introduced by Dr. Ambedkar had as its object not only to embody some of the features of procedural due process in the Indian Constitution, but also to provide a constitutional basis for preventive detention enactments.

Private Property and Land Reform

Before examining some of the decisions in which the Supreme Court since 1950 has interpreted and applied Articles 21 and 22, some attention should be devoted to the manner in which the framers dealt with property rights, and how they conceived of the Supreme Court's role in this important area. The discussion in the Constituent Assembly concerning property rights and the compulsory acquisition of land generated even more heated debate than did the due process clause. This is quite understandable in view of the fact that the decision as to the degree to which property rights would receive constitutional protection would have a great bearing on a whole host of other considerations, the most notable of which were land reform and improving the grim lot of the Indian peasantry. Thus the question had far-reaching social, economic, and political implications. While there was general agreement in the Assembly that the Government of the day should introduce land reforms and improve the economic and social status of the peasantry, many complex questions were raised and opinion in the Assembly was sharply divided, especially over the question of compensation for land acquired by the Government. The end result was Article 31, which represented a compromise formula which attempted to reconcile the competing claims of the right of the individual to property and the duty of the state to acquire private property for public purposes. In the account which follows, only the highlights of the debate can be touched upon; anything further would be beyond the scope of this chapter.[25]

The subjects of private property and land reform were first discussed in the Constituent Assembly on May 2, 1947, when the Assembly took up clause 19 of the Patel Committee's *Interim Report on Fundamental Rights*.[26] This clause

---

[25] For a more complete account, see the three excellent articles by H. C. L. Merillat: "Compensation for the Taking of Property: A Historical Footnote on Bela Banerjee's Case," *Journal of the Indian Law Institute*, I (1958–1959), pp. 375–397; "Chief Justice S. R. Das: A Decade of Decisions on Right to Property," *Journal of the Indian Law Institute*, II (1959–1960), pp. 183–213, and "The Indian Constitution: Property Rights and Social Reform," *Ohio State Law Journal*, XXI (1960), pp. 616–642. Cf. T. S. Rama Rao, "The Problem of Compensation and Its Justiciability in Indian Law," *Journal of the Indian Law Institute*, IV (1962), pp. 481–509, and Charles H. Alexandrowicz, *Constitutional Developments in India* (Bombay: Oxford University Press, 1957).

[26] *Constituent Assembly Debates*, III (1947), May 2, 1947, pp. 505–518.

provided that "no property, movable or immovable, of any person or corporation, including any interest in any commercial or industrial undertaking shall
be taken or acquired for public use unless the law provides for the payment of
compensation for the property taken or acquired and specified the principles
on which and the manner in which the compensation is to be determined."
Immediately the debate turned to the three most important issues raised by this
clause—the matter of zamindari abolition, the amount of compensation to be
paid when property is acquired by the State, and the degree to which the courts
should get involved in such matters.

The zamindars were landlords who had been created by the Moghul and
British rulers in order to simplify the collection of land revenue. In return for
the grant of permanent title to the land, the zamindar agreed to collect and turn
over to the Government an amount of land revenue that was fixed forever.[27]
These zamindars or "intermediaries" usually parcelled out the land, assigning
small plots to tenants who cultivated it and paid annual rent to the zamindar.
The zamindar kept the difference between the amount of revenue he collected
and the fixed amount he had agreed to pay to the Government, a difference
that increased enormously through the years. In the words of M. V. Pylee, the
zamindari system led to

> a double evil in the country. On the one hand, the tenant, feeling that the land was
> not his, never effected any permanent improvements on the land but was inter-
> ested only in his immediate gain. This contributed in large measure to the quali-
> tative deterioration of the land and the consequent diminishing returns. On the
> other hand, a new class of people emerged in India, a class that had lived almost
> entirely on the fruits of the labor of others. Thus, both on the economic and social
> level there was degeneration and the consequent lack of vitality among large sec-
> tions of Indian society.[28]

Long before the Constituent Assembly discussed land reform, Nehru and the
leadership of the Indian National Congress had agreed that the only solution to
the zamindari problem could be its abolition and the distribution of their land-
holdings among the tenant-farmers. Speaking in 1928 to the Annual Session of
the United Provinces Congress Committee, Nehru declared:

> We in this Province have to face the zamindar and Kisan [peasant-farmer] problem.
> To our misfortune we have zamindars everywhere, and like a blight they have pre-
> vented all healthy growth. ... We must, therefore, face this problem of landlordism,
> and if we face it what can we do but abolish it? There is no halfway house. It is a

---

[27] This is known as the "permanent settlement."

[28] *Constitutional Government in India*, p. 273.

feudal relic of the past utterly out of keeping with modern conditions. The abolition of landlordism must, therefore, occupy a prominent place in our programme.[29]

The debate in the Assembly, though brief, raised questions which were to loom large until 1949 when the final compromise was hammered out. Some argued that "just" compensation, i.e., full market value, should be paid to the expropriated zamindars;[30] others argued that when a "poor man's property" is to be taken by the State, he should be compensated for "the cost of the land and something more even,"[31] but that the zamindar if he was to be compensated at all, did not deserve compensation at full market value.[32] Others urged that enlightened zamindars who had treated their tenants well should be fully compensated, while others should be treated less favorably.[33] Ultimately, this brief debate resolved nothing—the *Interim Report on Fundamental Rights* was accepted, turned over to Sir B. N. Rau, and the questions were saved for another day.

It was not until September of 1949, in the final stages of constitution-making, that these questions were debated again in the Assembly, though these matters undoubtedly received much consideration in the interim, behind the scenes in Congress Party meetings. When the subject was brought up in 1949, the draft article destined to become Article 31 was introduced by no less a figure than Prime Minister Nehru. This underlines the importance of the complex and important issues raised, for, of the twenty-four articles in the section on Fundamental Rights, the influential Nehru introduced, and thus put his prestige behind, only this one. Moreover, by late 1949 enactments designed to bring about the abolition of the zamindari system were already pending in the important States of Bihar, Madras and the United Provinces. None of these enactments provided for compensation of the zamindars or other intermediaries at full market value—partial payment was provided on a downward graduated scale depending upon the value of the holding.[34]

Nehru's speech introducing the draft article is too lengthy to be reproduced in its entirety here, but so relevant are some portions of this speech to the debate

---

[29] Quoted in Frank J. Moore and Constance A. Freydig, *Land Tenure Legislation in Uttar Pradesh* (Berkeley: Modern India Project, Institute of East Asiatic Studies, University of California, 1955), p. 3.

[30] *Constituent Assembly Debates*, III (1947), May 2, 1947, p. 505.

[31] At this time the basic land acquisition enactment in India was the Land Acquisition Act, 1894, which provided that when the State took land it had to pay compensation at the rate of full market value plus a "solatium" of fifteen per cent.

[32] *Constituent Assembly Debates*, p. 507.

[33] *Constituent Assembly Debates*, p. 511.

[34] Merillat, "Compensation for the Taking of Property: A Historical Footnote on Bela Banerjee's Case," p. 386.

which has gone on in India since 1950 concerning the intent of the framers that these portions should be quoted. Nehru began by saying that

> let us be quite clear that there is no question of any expropriation without compensation so far as this Constitution is concerned. If property is required for public use it is a well-established law that it should be acquired by the State, by compulsion if necessary, and compensation is paid and the law has laid down methods of judging that compensation. Now, normally speaking in regard to such acquisition of small bits of property or even relatively large bits, if you like, for the improvement of a town, etc.—the law has been clearly laid down [i.e., the Land Acquisition Act, 1894]. But more and more today the community has to deal with large schemes of social reform, social engineering, etc., which can hardly be considered from the point of view of that individual acquisition of a small bit of land or structure. Difficulties arise—apart from every other difficulty, the question of time. Here is a piece of legislation that the community, as presented [sic] in its chosen representatives, considers quite essential for the progress and the safety of the state and it is a piece of legislation which affects millions of people. Obviously you cannot leave that piece of legislation to long, widespread and continuous litigation in the courts of law. Otherwise the future of millions of people may be affected; otherwise the whole structure of the State may be shaken to its foundations: so that we have to keep these things in view. If we have to take the property, if the State so wills, we have to see that fair and equitable compensation is given, because we proceed on the basis of fair and equitable compensation. But when we consider the equity of it, we have always to remember that the equity does not apply only to the individual but to the community. No individual can override ultimately the rights of the community at large.[35]

Nehru then directed his remarks to the role of the courts vis-à-vis Parliament in the matter of determining the proper balance between individual property rights and compulsory acquisition of land by the State:

> You may balance it to some extent by legal means, but ultimately the balancing authority can only be the sovereign legislature of the country, which can keep before it all the various factors—all the public, political and other factors—that come into the picture. ... The law should provide for the compensation for the property and should either fix the amount of compensation or specify the principles under which or the manner in which the compensation is to be determined. *The law should do it. Parliament should do it. There is no reference to any judiciary coming into the picture.* Much thought has been given to it and there has been much debate as to where the judiciary comes in. Eminent lawyers have told us that on a proper construction of this clause, normally speaking, the judiciary should not and does not come in. *Parliament either fixes the compensation itself or the principles*

---

[35] *Constituent Assembly Debates*, IX (1949), September 10, 1949, p. 1192.

governing that compensation and they should not be challenged except for one reason,
where it is thought that there has been a gross abuse of the law, where in fact there has
been a fraud on the Constitution. Naturally the judiciary comes in to see if there has
been a fraud on the Constitution or not. But normally speaking one presumes that
any Parliament representing the entire community of the nation will certainly not
commit a fraud on its own Constitution and will be very much concerned with
doing justice to the individual as well as the community.[36]

Nehru then, because "I am a little afraid that this House may be moved by
legal arguments of extreme subtlety and extreme cleverness, ignoring the human
aspect of the problem and the other aspects which are really changing the world
today," repeated the Congress Party's pledge to abolish the zamindari system, and
then made some strong comments on judicial review which probably have a wider
application than merely to judicial review of zamindari-abolition enactments:

We will honour our pledges. Within limits no judge and no Supreme Court can
make itself a third chamber. No Supreme Court and no judiciary can stand in
judgement over the sovereign will of Parliament representing the will of the entire
community. If we go wrong here and there it can point it out, but in the ultimate
analysis, where the future of the community is concerned, no judiciary can come in
the way. And if it comes in the way, ultimately the whole Constitution is a creature
of Parliament. ... *The fact remains that the legislature must be supreme and must not be*
interfered with by the courts of law in such matters of social reform.[37]

In short, Nehru's major points were that (i) a distinction must be made
between the compulsory acquisition of "small bits of land," and the acquisition of
large amounts of land such as zamindari-abolition, the purpose of this distinction
being that in cases of the former full compensation should be paid, and in cases of
the latter the amount of compensation should be determined by the legislature;
and (ii) that he took a very dim view of the courts interfering with any aspect of
land reform, unless the legislature committed a "fraud on the Constitution."

Following Nehru's speech there was a debate in the Assembly which lasted
for several days, a debate which reflected a number of points of view concerning
land reform, compensation, and the role of the courts. After carefully researching these debates, as well as contemporary newspaper accounts, H. C. L. Merillat
concluded that three main points of view were represented, with many shadings
of opinion within them.[38] One group would give the legislature authority to pay

[36] *Constituent Assembly Debates*, IX (1949), September 10, 1949, p. 1193. Emphasis
supplied.

[37] *Constituent Assembly Debates*, IX (1949), September 10, 1949, pp. 1195–1196. Emphasis
supplied.

[38] Merillat, "Compensation for the Taking of Property—A Historical Footnote to Bela
Banerjee's Case," p. 386.

or withhold compensation in all cases where the State took over property for public purposes. They would leave it to the legislature, or to the executive acting on the basis of legislated principles, to fix the amount of compensation, if any, and place its decision beyond the reach of the courts.[39]

A second group would require that full compensation was paid in all cases of compulsory acquisition, including zamindari-abolition, and would permit at least some degree of judicial review.[40]

The third group would exclude zamindaris and similar holdings from the requirement of full compensation, but keep that requirement for all other cases in which the State took private property, and would permit some degree of judicial review over non-zamindari-abolition and similar enactments.[41]

As it was ultimately passed by the Assembly, Article 31 reads as follows:

(1)   No person shall be deprived of his property save by authority of law.

(2)   No property, movable or immovable, including any interest in, or in any company owning, any commercial or industrial undertaking, shall be taken possession of or acquired for public purposes under any law authorising the taking of such possession or such acquisition, unless the law provides for compensation for the property taken possession of or acquired and either fixes the amount of compensation, or specifies the principles on which, and the manner in which, the compensation is to be determined and given.

(3)   No such law as is referred to in clause (2) made by the Legislature of a State shall have effect unless such law, having been reserved for the consideration of the President, has received his assent.

(4)   If any Bill pending at the commencement of this Constitution in the Legislature of a State has, after it has been passed by such Legislature, been reserved for the consideration of the President and has received his assent, then, notwithstanding anything in this Constitution, the law so assented to shall not be called in question in any court on the ground that it contravenes the provisions of clause (2).

(5)   Nothing in clause (2) shall affect—

    (a)   the provisions of any existing law other than a law to which the provisions of clause (6) apply, or

    (b)   the provisions of any law which the State may hereafter make—

        (i)   for the purpose of imposing or levying any tax or penalty, or

        (ii)   for the promotion of public health or the prevention of danger to life or property, or

---

[39] "Compensation for the Taking of Property—A Historical Footnote to Bela Banerjee's Case," p. 387. Cf. *Constituent Assembly Debates*, IX (1949), September 10, 1949, pp. 1199–1205, 1249–1250, and 1261–1262.

[40] Merillat, p. 387, and *Constituent Assembly Debates*, pp. 1233–1238 and 1257–1260.

[41] Merillat, p. 387, and *Constituent Assembly Debates*, pp. 1222–1224, 1243–1247, and 1248–1249.

> (iii) in pursuance of any agreement entered into between the
> Government of the Dominion of India and the Government of
> any other country, or otherwise, with respect to property declared
> by law to be evacuee property.
>
> (6)   Any law of the State enacted not more than eighteen months before the
> commencement of this Constitution may be within three months from
> such commencement be submitted to the President for his certification; and
> thereupon, if the President by public notification so certifies, it shall not
> be called in question in any court on the ground that it contravenes the
> provisions of clause (2) of this article or has contravened the provisions of
> sub-section (2) of Section 299 of the Government of India Act, 1935.

Merillat concludes, and this writer concurs, that Article 31 represents acceptance of the views of the third group so far as zamindari-abolition is concerned,
i.e., that clauses 4–6 were designed to exclude from the guarantees of clause 2
the zamindari-abolition enactments then pending implementation in several
Provinces and to be enacted in others, and to exclude any judicial review of
the quantum of compensation payable to zamindars fixed by these enactments.
Indeed, there is no question that the majority of the members of the Constituent
Assembly understood Article 31 to place such measures on a special footing.

But on the important and difficult questions of what should be the appropriate measure of compensation in other cases of State acquisition of property,
and who shall have the final voice in determining that measure, Merillat says
that Article 31 leaves so much doubt as to whether the framers intended that
full compensation be paid that there is "ample basis" for the courts believing
that the framers intended the *full* compensation be paid.[42] Further, he says
categorically that evident also in Article 31 is the Assembly's ultimate decision
"deliberately to retain judicial review of the compensation given in other cases
[non-zamindari-abolition] of property taken by the State."[43]

These latter conclusions of Merillat, it is submitted, are, in part at any rate,
in error. Although various members of the Assembly spoke of compensation
"equivalent in money value of the property on the date of the acquisition,"
of "fair and equitable compensation," of compensation that is an "equitable
recompense," and of "just" compensation, Article 31 in its final form provides
only that "compensation" should be paid, and that either the amount of the
compensation or the principles on which the compensation is to be determined
will be decided by law, i.e., by the legislature. The Constitution says nothing

---

[42] "Compensation for the Taking of Property—A Historical Footnote to Bela Banerjee's
Case," p. 396.

[43] "Compensation for the Taking of Property—A Historical Footnote to Bela Banerjee's
Case," p. 392.

about this compensation being "just" or a "fair equivalent" of the property taken. It is extremely significant that several amendments to the draft article aimed at requiring the State to pay full compensation were specifically rejected by a vote of the Assembly.[44] Moreover, equally significant is the fact that the Land Acquisition Act of 1894, which embodied the cardinal features of the law of eminent domain, required that compensation amount to "the market value of the land" plus "a sum of fifteen per centum of such market value, in consideration of the compulsory nature of the acquisition."[45] Had the framers intended that Article 31 embody the same provisions, they surely would have added the appropriate adjectives. But, as the debates show, the framers deliberately omitted the important adjective "just" or "full" before the term compensation.

Merillat, however, is partly correct in concluding that judicial review of non-zamindari-abolition and land acquisition legislation is not excluded by Article 31, but there is little evidence to support Merillat's statement that the scope of judicial review was intended to include the amount of compensation awarded by the legislatures. Surely, in view of the amount of heat generated by the debate over the justiciability of compensation, if the framers had intended the courts to be the final judge of the fairness of the compensation, they would have made this clear. Indeed, when one considers the nature of the debate in the Assembly over both due process and compulsory acquisition of land, the conclusion is all but totally inescapable that the role assigned the courts was minimal, confined to matters of procedure and not substance.

It has been the purpose of this discussion of due process and compulsory acquisition to provide some insight into the attitudes of the makers of the Indian Constitution toward the judiciary in general and toward the Supreme Court in particular, and thus set the stage for a discussion of some of the leading constitutional law cases decided since 1950. It is quite clear from the evidence adduced thus far that while the judiciary had its supporters in the Assembly, the majority looked upon the exercise of judicial review of legislation with a somewhat jaundiced eye. Though aware of the value of a Supreme Court which enjoyed the confidence and respect of the nation, the Congress Party leadership was unwilling to run the risk of creating so powerful a Supreme Court that its policies and actions might be thwarted or, in the least, delayed by time-consuming litigation. The attitude of the most influential of the framers, especially B. N. Rau, B. R. Ambedkar, Alladi Krishnaswami Aiyar, and Nehru, was that judicial review was fine so long

---

[44] *Constituent Assembly Debates*, IX (1949), September 12, 1949, pp. 1303–1311. In these pages, all the various proposals with regard to acquisition of property were put to a vote. On p. 1307, e.g., a version of Article 31 which would guarantee "fair and equitable compensation based on market value" was specifically rejected by the Assembly.

[45] Land Acquisition Act, 1894, Section 23(2).

as it was kept within limits and did not threaten the primacy of Parliament. As we have seen, by 1949 it was very clear that the new government had every intention of embarking on a path of economic and social reform, and that it was convinced that preventive detention must continue on into the constitutional period. If the framers had believed that the Supreme Court could be counted upon as a cooperative partner in implementing these plans, the Court probably would have been placed in a stronger position. But this was not the expectation of the framers—they clearly feared that the Supreme Court would not react favorably to all they had planned. Thus they attempted to assure, in striking a balance between the British system of an all-powerful Parliament and the American system of a powerful Supreme Court, that the scales were weighted in favor of Parliament.

At the same time, and in curious contrast to Articles 21 and 31 which reflect a certain distrust of the judiciary, the framers explicitly provided for judicial review in Article 13,[46] and in Article 32 conferred an extraordinarily wide remedial jurisdiction on the Supreme Court—so wide, in fact, as to grant to every person direct access to the Supreme Court for the enforcement of his fundamental rights. Surely it must have been anticipated that much legislation passed by an aspiring welfare state would be impugned by persons whose various rights were adversely affected by such legislation. Yet it was apparently believed that the fundamental rights were so phrased and judicial review so limited as to permit the Government to pursue its goals successfully.

At any rate, restricted though the Supreme Court's role seemed to be on January 26, 1950 when the Constitution came into operation, there is no doubt that the Court was catapulted into a position more powerful than its predecessor. The mere presence of a bill of rights and an authorization to declare unconstitutional any laws or actions of the executive in violation of these rights, both absent in the Government of India Act of 1935, assured the Supreme Court of a position of importance. How the Supreme Court has in practice interpreted its authority is discussed in the remaining pages of this chapter.

The Supreme Court and Personal Liberty

Those who wondered how the Supreme Court would interpret its role under Articles 21 and 22 had to wait but a few months after the inauguration of the Constitution, for the very first case to reach the Court concerning the

---

[46] The most important feature of Article 13 is clause 2, which provides that "the State shall not make any law which takes away or abridges the rights conferred by this Part [Fundamental Rights] and any law made in contravention of this clause shall, to the extent of the contravention, be void."

interpretation of the Constitution was one which required the Court to expound on the meaning of Articles 21 and 22. This was the historic case of *A. K. Gopalan* v. *State of Madras*,[47] and, in its decision spanning nearly two hundred and fifty pages in the *Supreme Court Reports*, the Court made a number of pronouncements of great interest to the student of Indian constitutional law.

The petitioner, a well-known Indian Communist Party leader, had been in jail without trial continuously since 1947 under various preventive detention enactments, the latest of which was the Preventive Detention Act of 1950, passed by the Union Parliament less than a month after the coming into effect of the 1950 Constitution.[48] As soon as the Constitution became operative, Gopalan took immediate advantage of Article 32 by petitioning for a writ of habeas corpus, and demanding his release from jail on the ground, among others, that the Preventive Detention Act contravened the provisions of Articles 21 and 22. The essence of his argument was that the word "law" in Article 21 meant "general law" or "principles of natural justice," and, therefore, that it should be assigned the same meaning as that of the word "law" in the due process clause of the Fifth and Fourteenth Amendments to the Constitution of the United States. In other words, notwithstanding that the Constituent Assembly had rejected the phrase, Gopalan contended that the expression "procedure established by law" corresponded to the phrase "due process of law," and must, accordingly, be understood in the same wide and flexible sense as comprising the fundamental principles of natural justice. He urged also that "*established*" by law did not mean the same thing as "*prescribed*" by law, for if these were equated there would be no protection for the individual against legislative tyranny.

---

[47] (1950) S.C.R. 88, dated May 19, 1950.

[48] This Act was introduced and passed on February 25th. It was introduced and guided through Parliament by Sardar Patel, the Home Minister, who said it was imperative that the Union Government pass such legislation because "certain [High Court] judicial pronouncements or decisions which have been made during the last couple of weeks, and certain litigation which is pending before the Courts have created a situation in which, I feel, having regard to the conditions prevailing today, that unless this House takes immediate action, a grave peril to the security of the State is involved. ... These judicial pronouncements have therefore created a situation in more than one State in which it would no longer be possible for us to keep under detention persons about whose dangerous and subversive activities the State Governments have no doubt" (*Parliamentary Debates*, II (Part II), 1950, p. 875). Patel made it quite clear that the legislation he was urging upon the House was regarded principally as an anti-communist measure when he said that "I shall not weary the House by telling it how exactly the communists in India, who have been by far the largest number of detenus, constitute a danger to the existence and security of the State ..." (*Parliamentary Debates*, II (Part II), 1950, p. 875).

All six members of the Supreme Court participated in the decision, and all six delivered separate judgments (there was no majority opinion), a factor which makes any summary of findings somewhat difficult. In brief, however, four[49] of the six judges held that the word "law" in Article 21 meant a State-made law, and not law in the abstract or transcendental sense of embodying the principles of natural justice. The view of the majority is represented best by this extract from the opinion of the Chief Justice:

> No intrinsic aid is needed to interpret the words of article 21, which in my opinion, are not ambiguous. Normally read, and without thinking of other Constitutions, the expression "procedure established by law" must mean procedure prescribed by the law of the State. If the Indian Constitution wanted to preserve to every person the protection given by the due process clause of the American Constitution there was nothing to prevent the Assembly from adopting the phrase or if they wanted to limit the same to procedure only, to adopt that expression with only the word "procedural" prefixed to "law." However, the correct question is what is the right given by Art. 21? The only right is that no person shall be deprived of his life or liberty except according to procedure established by law. One may like that right to cover a larger area, but to give such a right is not the function of the Court; it is the function of the Constitution, To read the word "law" as meaning rules of natural justice will land one in difficulties because the rules of natural justice, as regards procedure, are nowhere defined and in my opinion, the Constitution cannot be read as laying down a vague standard. ...
>
> The deliberate omission of the word "due" from article 21 lends strength to the contention that the justiciable aspect of "law," i.e., to consider whether it is reasonable or not by the Court, does not form part of the Indian Constitution. The omission of the word "due," the limitation imposed by the word "procedure" and the insertion of the word "established," thus brings out more clearly the idea of legislative prescription in the expression used in article 21. By adopting the phrase "procedure established by law" the Constitution gave the legislature the final word to determine the law.[50]

Similar were the views of Justice Mukherjea, who observed that

> it is quite clear that the framers of the Indian Constitution did not desire to introduce into our system the elements of uncertainty, vagueness and changeability that have grown round the "due process" doctrine in America. They wanted to make the provision clear, definite and precise and deliberately chose the words "procedure established by law," as in their opinion no doubts would ordinarily arise about

---

[49] Chief Justice Harilal J. Kania, Justices Mehr Chand Mahajan, Bijan Kumar Mukherjea, and Sudhi Ranjan Das. The views of the latter three are all the more important in that all three served eventually as Chief Justice.

[50] *A. K. Gopalan v. State of Madras* (1950) S.C.R. 88, 111–113.

the meaning of this expression. The indefiniteness in the application of the "due process" doctrine in America has nothing to do with the distinction between substantive and procedural law. The uncertainty and elasticity are in the doctrine itself which is a sort of hidden mine, the contents of which nobody knows and is merely revealed from time to time to the judicial conscience of the Judges. This theory, the Indian Constitution deliberately discarded and that is why they substituted a different form in its place which, according to them, was more specific.[51]

In short, it was the view of the majority that Article 21 did not permit the judiciary to raise the question of whether the procedure established by the legislature was proper and just, for this provision guaranteed only that whatever procedure was established by law must be observed by the executive when life or personal liberty is taken away.

Justices Fazl Ali and Sastri, while agreeing with the majority that Article 21 signified a rejection by the framers of due process as that is understood in the United States, were unwilling to agree that *any* procedure established by the legislature would meet the requirements of Article 21. Sastri said that "procedure established by law" implied that the legislature should incorporate into legislation "the ordinary and well-established criminal procedure."[52] Fazl Ali went further and held that to meet the requirements of Article 21 a law authorizing the deprivation of one's life or personal liberty must incorporate "certain fundamental principles of justice which inhere in every civilized system of law."[53] In his view these included notice, opportunity to be heard, an impartial tribunal, and orderly procedure.[54] In other words, both he and Sastri were of the opinion that Article 21, though clothing the legislature with far-reaching authority to restrict personal liberty, did not give the legislatures carte blanche authority to disregard the general procedural safeguards which were a part of Western law.

The majority, having decided that "law" in Article 21 means not jus, i.e., not law in the abstract in the sense of principles of natural justice, but lex, i.e., statute law, went on to examine the Preventive Detention Act with the only criteria at their disposal—the procedural safeguards guaranteed by Article 22. After doing this, the majority upheld the validity of this enactment with the exception of Section 14, which was unanimously declared invalid. This provision forbade any court from permitting the disclosure before it of the substance of any communication of the grounds of detention made by the Government to a person

---

[51] *A. K. Gopalan* v. *State of Madras* (1950) S.C.R. 88, 275–276.

[52] *A. K. Gopalan* v. *State of Madras* (1950) S.C.R. 88, 205.

[53] *A. K. Gopalan* v. *State of Madras* (1950) S.C.R. 88, 162–163.

[54] *A. K. Gopalan* v. *State of Madras* (1950) S.C.R. 88, 163, 169. In the course of his opinion, Fazl Ali drew extensively upon his knowledge of American constitutional law, especially of the development of procedural due process in the United States.

detained, or of the representation made by the person to the Government. The Supreme Court regarded this provision as an appalling illustration of the Government carrying confidentiality to the extreme, for it prevented the courts from examining the relevancy, as distinguished from the sufficiency, of the grounds of detention.[55] The unanimous Court held that this section violated Article 22(5) of the Constitution, which guarantees a detenu the right of "making a representation" against the detention order. In the words of Justice Mukherjea, if this section was allowed to stand, it would be impossible for the Court in a habeas corpus proceeding to come to any decision, for "the entire proceedings are rendered ineffective and altogether illusory."[56] Though declaring this section *ultra vires*, the Court said this particular provision was severable and, accordingly, the invalidity of Section 14 did not affect the validity of the Act as a whole.

While the validity of the remainder of the Act was upheld, the members of the Court made it quite clear that they did so only because they believed that Article 21 so limited their role that they could do nothing else. Every single justice denounced preventive detention and deplored the fact that provision for such an undemocratic invasion of personal liberty was found in free India's Constitution. Justice Sastri described preventive detention as a "sinister-looking feature, so strangely out of place in a democratic constitution";[57] Justice Mahajan said that "preventive detention laws are repugnant to democratic constitutions and they cannot be found to exist in any of the democratic countries of the world";[58] and Justice Mukherjea observed that preventive detention "cannot but be regarded as a most unwholesome encroachment upon the liberties of the people."[59] But the Court said that in view of Article 21 it was helpless to do anything, that even if Parliament provided for the taking of life by "boiling in oil," it could not prevent this.[60]

Not only did the Court uphold the validity of the Preventive Detention Act, it also held that it had no authority to enquire into the sufficiency of the grounds of detention. Section 3 of the Act conferred power on the executive to issue

---

[55] Due to Section 14, Gopalan was prohibited from disclosing the grounds for his detention, which meant that the whole argument had to be directed against the constitutionality of the various provisions of the Act *in abstracto*. Cf. Pradyumna K. Tripathi, "Preventive Detention: The Indian Experience," *American Journal of Comparative Law*, IX (Spring, 1960), pp. 219–248.

[56] A. K. Gopalan v. State of Madras (1950) S.C.R. 88, 284.

[57] A. K. Gopalan v. State of Madras (1950) S.C.R. 88, p. 208.

[58] A. K. Gopalan v. State of Madras (1950) S.C.R. 88, p. 220.

[59] A. K. Gopalan v. State of Madras (1950) S.C.R. 88, p. 250.

[60] A. K. Gopalan v. State of Madras (1950) S.C.R. 88, p. 320.

detention orders if the executive was "satisfied" that such action "is necessary." Gopalan argued that the Court should make an independent determination as to whether the grounds communicated to him were sufficient to justify the detention order. All except Fazl Ali, however, rejected this argument and held that the Court could not question the subjective satisfaction of the executive since, given the nature of preventive detention, no objective standards could be established. The view of the Court on this question is summed up well by Justice Sastri, who observed that

> for the purposes of preventive detention it would be difficult, if not impossible to lay down objective rules of conduct, failure to conform to which should lead to such detention. As the very term implies, the detention in such cases is effected with a view to prevent the person concerned from acting prejudicially to certain objects which the legislation providing for such detention has in view. Nor would it be practicable to indicate or enumerate in advance what acts or classes of acts would be regarded as prejudicial. The responsibility of the State and the maintenance of public order etc. having been laid on the executive Government, it must naturally be left to that Government to exercise the power of preventive detention whenever they think the occasion demands it.[61]

The Court's judgment makes it very clear that in taking this position the Court relied heavily on two decisions of the House of Lords handed down during the world wars. During these emergency periods the executive in Great Britain was authorized to detain a person without trial for reasons of national security. The House of Lords ruled that no court could examine the sufficiency of the grounds of detention because, according to Lord Finlay, "a Court is the least appropriate tribunal to investigate the question whether circumstances of suspicion exist warranting the restraint of a person."[62] The Indian Supreme Court applied these precedents and concluded that any judicial review of the sufficiency of grounds of detention was precluded; a detention order was a matter simply of executive discretion.

Another feature of the *Gopalan* decision which is of importance is that in the course of their separate opinions, several of the justices commented on the position of the Supreme Court vis-à-vis Parliament under the new Constitution. The most articulate was Justice S. R. Das who, at the very outset of his opinion, observed that

> it is necessary to bear in mind the scope and ambit of the powers of the Court under the Constitution. The powers of the Court are not the same under all

[61] *A. K. Gopalan v. State of Madras* (1950) S.C.R. 88, 212.

[62] *The King v. Halliday*, 1917 Appeal Cases 260, 269. This ruling was reaffirmed in *Liversidge v. Anderson*, 1942 Appeal Cases 206.

Constitutions. In England Parliament is supreme and there is no limitation upon its legislative powers. Therefore, a law duly made by Parliament cannot be challenged in any Court. The English Courts have to interpret and apply the law; they have no authority to declare such a law illegal or unconstitutional. By the American Constitution the legislative power of the Union is vested in the Congress and in a sense the Congress is the supreme legislative power. But the written Constitution of the United States is supreme above all the three limbs of Government and, therefore, the law made by the Congress, in order to be valid, must be in conformity with the provisions of the Constitution. If it is not, the Supreme Court will intervene and declare that law to be unconstitutional and void. ... [T]he Supreme Court of the United States, under the leadership of Chief Justice Marshall, assumed the power to declare any law unconstitutional ..., [and] it is thus that the Supreme Court established its own supremacy over the executive and the Congress. In India the position of the Judiciary is somewhere in between the Courts in England and the United States. While in the main leaving our Parliament and Legislatures supreme in their respective legislative fields, our Constitution has, by some of the articles, put upon the Legislatures certain specified limitations. ... The point to be noted, however, is that in so far as there is any limitation on the legislative powers, the Court must, on a complaint being made to it, scrutinise and ascertain whether such limitation has been transgressed and if there has been any transgression the Court will courageously declare the law unconstitutional, for the Court is bound by its oath to uphold the Constitution. But outside the limitations imposed on the legislative powers our Parliament and the State Legislatures are supreme in their respective legislative fields and the Court has no authority to question the wisdom or policy of the law duly made by the appropriate legislature. Our Constitution, unlike the English Constitution, recognises the Court's supremacy over the legislative authority, but such supremacy is a very limited one, for it is confined to the field where the legislative power is circumscribed by limitations put upon it by the Constitution itself. Within this restricted field the Court may, on a scrutiny of the law made by the Legislature, declare it void if it is found to have transgressed the constitutional limitations. But our Constitution, unlike the American Constitution, does not recognize the absolute supremacy of the Court over the legislative authority in all respects, for outside the restricted field of constitutional limitations our Parliament and the State Legislatures are supreme in their respective legislative fields and in that field there is no scope for the Court in India to play the role of the Supreme Court of the United States. It is well for us constantly to remember this basic limitation on our own powers.[63]

Essentially the same views were expressed by Chief Justice Kania:

There is considerable authority for the statement that the Courts are not at liberty to declare an Act void because in their opinion it is opposed to a spirit supposed

---

[63] *A. K. Gopalan v. State of Madras*, (1950) S.C.R. 88, 286–287.

to pervade the Constitution but not expressed in words. Where the fundamental law has not limited, either in terms or by necessary implication, the general powers conferred upon the Legislature we cannot declare a limitation under the notion of having discovered something in the spirit of the Constitution which is not even mentioned in the instrument. It is difficult upon any general principles to limit the omnipotence of the sovereign legislative powers by judicial interposition, except so far as the expressed words of a written Constitution give that authority. It is also stated, if the words be positive and without ambiguity, there is no authority for a Court to vacate or repeal a Statute on that ground alone. But it is only in express constitutional provisions limiting legislative power and controlling the temporary will of a majority by a permanent and paramount law settled by the deliberate wisdom of the nation that one can find a safe and solid ground for the authority of Courts of justice to declare void any legislative enactment. Any assumption of authority beyond this would be to place in the hands of the judiciary powers too great and too indefinite either for its own security or the protection of private rights.[64]

In view of the background material presented earlier concerning the debate over due process in the Constituent Assembly, it is evident that the Supreme Court in the *Gopalan* case understood Article 21 to mean just what the framers had intended. Indeed, that this decision was welcomed by the Government may be inferred from the absence of any criticism of it.[65] The Court acknowledged that the phraseology of Article 21 was intended to limit drastically the scope of judicial review in cases involving deprivation of life and personal liberty. It refused also to question the subjective judgment of the executive in passing out detention orders. Moreover, the latter quotations concerning the scope of judicial review in general under the new constitutional system would seem to be quite in keeping with the intention of the framers. In short, from the perspective of the framers,[66] this must have been regarded as a very prudent decision.[67]

[64] *A. K. Gopalan v. State of Madras*, (1950) S.C.R. 88, 120–121.

[65] As will be seen in the chapter, when the Government is not pleased with a decision of the Supreme Court, it makes this quite evident.

[66] It is important to note that pending national elections, which were not held until late 1951 and early 1952, the Constituent Assembly had transformed itself into a unicameral Union Parliament. So the constitution-makers were now the national legislators.

[67] Yet few Indian and foreign commentators have regarded the *Gopalan* decision as a wise or prudent one. Much has been written about this decision, and the majority of the writers feel that the Indian Supreme Court unduly limited its role and conceived too narrowly the scope of its powers. See e.g., M. M. Ismail, "The Doctrine of Judicial Supremacy and the Indian Constitution," *Year Book of Legal Studies*, II (1958), pp. 84–106; Bernard Schwartz, "A Comparative View of the Gopalan Case," *Indian Law Review*, IV (1950), pp. 276–99; Pradyumna K. Tripathi, "Preventive Detention: The Indian Experience," *American Journal of Comparative Law*, IX (1960), pp. 219–248; Charles H. Alexandrowicz,

The only aspect of the *Gopalan* decision which might have distressed the Government was the Court's unanimous finding that Section 14 of the Preventive Detention Act was unconstitutional. But apparently the Government must have agreed that this was an absurd provision, for, following the *Gopalan* ruling, Parliament quickly amended the Act so as to delete that provision.[68]

There is one final feature of the *Gopalan* decision to which attention should be called, and this is the fact that all members of the Court made at least a passing reference to the *Constituent Assembly Debates*. The general practice of British and Indian courts, unlike the American and French attitude, is that materials such as legislative proceedings, committee reports and preparatory debates are not admissible in courts as aids in construing the intended meaning of a statute or the constitution.[69] In the *Gopalan* decision, however, the Court, while saying that the real meaning of the Constitution must be ascertained from its "plain words," did refer to the fact that the due process clause had been dropped deliberately from the first draft by the framers. Chief Justice Kania, e.g., observed that

> our attention was drawn to the debates and report of the drafting committee of the Constituent Assembly in respect of the wording of this clause. The report may not be read to control the meaning of the article, but *may be seen in case of ambiguity.*
> ... [While] it is not proper to take into consideration the individual opinions of

---

"The Indian Constitution," *The Year Book of World Affairs*, VII (1953), pp. 258–282, and Edward McWhinney, *Judicial Review in the English-Speaking World* (Toronto: University of Toronto Press, 1956), pp. 126–140.

Though none of these writers goes so far as to say that Article 21 incorporates the due process clause as that is understood in the United States, they do believe that the Court should have asserted the authority to enquire into the sufficiency of the grounds for a detention order. Alexandrowicz argues that the Indian Supreme Court made a grievous error in relying on the *Halliday* and *Liversidge* decisions of the House of Lords. He points out that those decisions were handed down during periods of great crisis, and asserts that "it is clear beyond doubt that such a limitation of personal liberty cannot extend to peacetime conditions ..." in Great Britain (p. 263) Thus, since the Indian Preventive Detention Act is a non-wartime measure, Alexandrowicz says that the British decisions are not applicable as precedents, and that the Indian Supreme Court should have established an objective test for determining the validity of each detention order.

While there is certainly some force to this criticism of the *Gopalan* decision, there is room for arguing that while India was not at war in 1950, internal security and public order were endangered by a variety of political and religious movements. Cf. Donald H. Bayley, "The Indian Experience with Preventive Detention," *Pacific Affairs*, XXXV (Summer, 1962), 99–115. In this excellent essay Bayley offers more persuasive justifications for preventive detention that the Government of India has been able to produce.

[68] The Preventive Detention (Amendment) Act, 1950.

[69] Cf. Sheldon D. Elliot, "Statutory Interpretation and the Welfare State," *Journal of the Indian Law Institute*, II (1960), pp. 257–272.

Members of Parliament or Convention to construe the meaning of the particular clause, *when a question is raised whether a certain phrase or expression was up for consideration at all or not, a reference to the debates may be permitted.* In the present case the debates were referred to to show that the expression "due process of law" was known to exist in the American Constitution and after a discussion was not adopted by the Constituent Assembly in our Constitution.[70]

The fact that the Supreme Court referred to these debates in the *Gopalan* case seemed of little significance in 1950, but became important later when the Supreme Court refused ever again to consult the debates. In the decisions on compulsory acquisition of property, to be discussed as follows, which involved an interpretation of Article 31, an article not drafted with any outstanding clarity or elegance, the Supreme Court steadfastly refused to use the debates as an aid in ascertaining correctly the intent of the framers. As will be seen, this refusal to use the debates has been, in part at least, a factor in several decisions which so upset the Government that it responded with constitutional amendments designed to limit the scope of judicial review.

For the purpose of this study, it is unnecessary to examine later decisions concerning Articles 21 and 22, for the Court has continued to give a literal interpretation to these articles. The Preventive Detention Act is still in effect and, although there have been many decisions involving preventive detention in the past fifteen years, the *Gopalan* decision is *stare decisis* and the Supreme Court has never asserted that it could do any more for the detenu than make certain that the procedural safeguards guaranteed in Article 22 are observed by the executive. However, it should be noted that in insisting on strict compliance with these procedural safeguards the Court has moved somewhat in the direction of a greater degree of protection for personal liberty. Thus, e.g., it is now well established that if the grounds communicated to the detenu are so "vague" as to prevent him from making an effective representation against the detention order, the Court will order his release. The Court made this ruling in the case of *Dr. Ram Krishnan Bhardwai v. The State of Delhi and Others*,[71] and observed that "preventive detention is a serious invasion of personal liberty and such meagre safeguards as the Constitution has provided against the improper exercise of this power must be jealously watched and enforced by the Court."[72] Similarly, if any one of the grounds that led to the issuance of the detention order is found to be irrelevant to the object of the legislation, the detention would be held invalid even if there are other relevant grounds, for the Court has said that it

[70] *A. K. Gopalan* v. *State of Madras* (1950) S.C.R. 88, 110–111. Emphasis supplied.

[71] *Dr. Ram Krishnan Bhardwai* v. *The State of Delhi and Others* (1953) S.C.R. 708. Cf. *The State of Bombay* v. *Atma Ram Sridhar Vaidya*, (1951) S.C.R. 167.

[72] *Dr. Ram Krishnan Bhardwai* v. *The State of Delhi and Others* (1953) S.C.R. 708, 713.

cannot be certain to what extent the irrelevant reasons affected the executive's thinking, or whether the detention order would have been made at all if the irrelevant ground had not been considered.[73] On the other hand, the Court has acknowledged that the executive authority need not disclose the specific *facts* which provoked the detention order, if, in his discretion, he deems it to be against the public interest to make such a disclosure.[74] He need disclose only the *grounds* (e.g., that the detention without trial of an individual is necessary in the interest of "public order").

Though the Court has been able to secure the release of some *detenus* after disclosing procedural irregularities, the Court has stuck to an interpretation of Article 21 which leaves little room for judicial scrutiny. Once the Court determines that a statute enacted under Article 21 is within the competence of the legislature, it is powerless to question its "justness" or propriety, or in any way to modify its effect on the ground that it seeks unduly to restrict personal liberty. While the personal liberty decisions have distressed the civil libertarians, if the intention of the framers is to be the criterion, it is evident that the Supreme Court has only accepted the role chartered for it by the constitution-makers.

The Supreme Court and Property Rights

In the discussion earlier it was pointed out that a major feature of the compromise formula finally hammered out by the Constituent Assembly concerning the compulsory acquisition of land was that legislation providing for the abolition of zamindars and other intermediaries was placed on a special footing so as to exclude any judicial review of the amount of compensation determined by the legislatures. By late 1950 much of this legislation had been enacted by the State Legislatures, had received the assent of the President of India, and the implementation process began. Although there was no uniform pattern to these land-reform enactments, the usual formula established by the legislatures for determining the amount of compensation was to fix the rate of compensation as a multiple of the net income or net assets of the zamindar's estate. The Bihar Land Reforms Act of 1950, e.g., established a sliding scale of payment ranging from twenty times the net income where such income did not exceed 500 rupees to three times the net income when it exceeded 100,000 rupees. In other words, small zamindars or intermediaries were generally allowed a higher multiple than the larger ones. None of this legislation provided for the

---

[73] *Shamasao V. Parulekar* v. *The District Magistrate, Thana, Bombay and Two Others*, (1952) S.C.R. 683. Cf. *Sodhi Shamsher Singh* v. *The State of Punjab*, A.I.R. 1954 S.C. 276.

[74] *The State of Bombay* v. *Atma Ram Sridhar Vaidya*, (1951) S.C.R. 167.

payment of compensation at full market value of the property taken, but none provided for no compensation at all.

No sooner had the President given his assent to this legislation when the High Courts in several states were literally inundated with applications for writ petitions from zamindars who challenged the constitutionality of these enactments. In the State of Uttar Pradesh alone, "about 7000" petitions had been filed by February, 1951.[75] The immediate effect of these petitions was to delay implementation of the legislation until the judiciary could determine its validity.

Of the several cases which were begun in the High Courts at approximately the same time, the most important decision to emerge was that of the Patna High Court in *Kameshwar Singh* v. *State of Bihar*,[76] for the Court ruled unanimously that the Bihar Land Reforms Act was unconstitutional in that it discriminated between rich and poor zamindars by adopting different rates of compensation for estates of different sizes. This, said the Court, was an unreasonably discriminatory classification, and was in violation of Article 14 of the Constitution, which provides that "the State shall not deny to any person equality before the law or the equal protection of the laws within the territory of India." The Court pointed out, quite accurately, that Article 31(4), which, it will be recalled, removes from the scrutiny of the courts legislation pending at the commencement of the Constitution provided it had received the assent of the President, merely saved legislation from judicial challenge on the ground of contravention of Article 31(2), and not on the ground of contravention of any other of the fundamental rights.

At about the same time, the High Courts at Allahabad and Nagpur *upheld* the validity of similar zamindari-abolition statutes of the Uttar Pradesh and Madhya Pradesh legislatures,[77] but appeals from these decisions were lodged immediately in the Supreme Court by the dispossessed zamindars. At this point, without waiting for the Supreme Court's ruling in the appeal of the *Kameshwar Singh* decision (it, also, had been appealed by the State of Bihar), the Union Government, in order to speed up the process of land reform, introduced in Parliament a bill to amend the Constitution. It was Prime Minister Nehru who introduced the Constitution (First Amendment) Bill in the Parliament, and he

[75] *National Herald* (Lucknow), February 7, 1951.

[76] A.I.R. 1951 Patna 91. Kameshwar Singh, a wealthy Bihar zamindar, was a member of the Constituent Assembly, who, not surprisingly, was a leading critic of Article 31 in the Assembly.

[77] *Raja Suryapalsingh* v. *The Uttar Pradesh Government*, A.I.R. 1951 Allahabad 674, and *Visweshwar Rao* v. *The State of Madhya Pradesh*. This latter case is not reported in the All India Reporter, but was reviewed by the Supreme Court in an appeal bearing the same name, (1952) S.C.R. 1020.

recalled that it had been the intention of the framers "to take away the question of zamindari and land reform from the purview of the courts."[78] Nehru made it quite clear that he was upset by the Patna decision and by the litigation which was delaying the implementation of the various land-reform measures. He was especially scornful of the "highly legalistic" approach of the Court to land reform, and of the fact that the Patna High Court had invoked Article 14 to strike down the Bihar Act for, he asserted, "this business of the equality of law may very well mean, as it has come to mean often enough, the making of existing inequalities rigid by law."[79]

Given the popularity among members of Parliament of zamindari-abolition, and the ease with which the Constitution may be amended,[80] by June 18, 1951, the amendment had received the approval of Parliament and the President's assent, and was in force.

The First Amendment affected land-reform legislation in two respects. Firstly, by the insertion of a new article into the Constitution—Article 31A the provision was added that "notwithstanding anything in the foregoing provisions of this Part, no law providing for the acquisition by the State of any estate or of any rights therein or for the extinguishment or modification of any such rights shall be deemed to be void on the ground that it is inconsistent with, or takes away or abridges any of the rights conferred by, any provisions of this Part. ..." In short, this new article granted such legislation a blanket immunity from attack in any court on the basis of infringement of *any* fundamental right; interference by the judiciary was sought to be removed once and for all. Moreover, this new article was accorded retrospective effect, for the Amendment Act provides that this article "shall be deemed always to have been inserted. ..."[81]

Secondly, by the insertion of another new article—31B—thirteen State land-reform measures were listed in the Ninth Schedule of the Constitution, and, concerning these, Article 31B provides that none of them

> shall be deemed to be void, or ever to have become void, on the ground that such
> Act, Regulation or provision is inconsistent with, or takes away or abridges any
> of the rights conferred by, any provisions of this Part, and notwithstanding any

[78] *Parliamentary Debates*, XII (1951), May 18, 1951, col. 9083.

[79] *Parliamentary Debates*, XII (1951), May 18, 1951, col. 9083.

[80] In most respects, an amendment may be effected by only a special majority of the Parliament—a majority of the total membership in each House and of not less than two-thirds of the members present and voting (Article 368). Since the Congress Party has had an overwhelming majority in Parliament since 1950, it is evident that this amending process poses no obstacle to the Government when it seeks an amendment.

[81] The Constitution (First Amendment) Act, 1951, Section 4. Articles 31, 31A, and 31B.

judgment, decree or order of any court or tribunal to the contrary, each of the said Acts and Regulations shall, subject to the power of any competent Legislature to repeal or amend it, continue in force.

Thus, this article also was given retrospective effect. It is no surprise that one of the thirteen enactments revived by Article 31B is the same Bihar Land Reforms Act of 1950 which was declared *ultra vires* by the Patna High Court in *Kameshwar Singh* v. *State of Bihar*.

It can be assumed safely that the Government expected that the First Amendment would bring an end to the litigation involving legislation aimed at the abolition of zamindaris and other intermediaries, and would pave the way for speedy implementation of this aspect of agrarian reform. But the zamindars were not to be subdued so easily and, indeed, this Amendment merely provided their lawyers with other opportunities to exercise their ingenuity. The Amendment had no sooner been added to the Constitution than the zamindars approached the Supreme Court with the argument that the entire Amendment Act was unconstitutional. Their argument was based chiefly on the fact that the Act had been passed by a Parliament which had only one House,[82] whereas the amendment procedure prescribed in the Constitution spoke of two houses of Parliament. Therefore, argued the zamindars, no amendment could be passed until after the national elections. This argument failed, however, and the Supreme Court unanimously upheld the competence of the Provisional Parliament to amend the Constitution.[83]

Though the position of the zamindars looked quite hopeless at this juncture, the Supreme Court had not yet heard the series of appeals which had been filed by zamindars prior to the passing of the First Amendment. It was not until May 5, 1952, nearly a year after the enactment of the First Amendment, that the Supreme Court handed down its judgment in the case of *The State of Bihar* v. *Maharajadhiraja Sir Kameshwar Singh of Darbhanga and Others*.[84] Further, in spite of the First Amendment, the Supreme Court, by a three to two majority, declared unconstitutional two provisions of the Bihar Land Reforms Act. The Supreme Court took the position that whereas the First Amendment meant that the Bihar Act could not be challenged on the ground of violation of any fundamental right, there was nothing to prevent the Court from declaring that some of the provisions of the Act amounted to a "colourable exercise of legislative power" and a "fraud on the Constitution."[85] One of the provisions held to the ultra

---

[82] Recall that pending the 1951–1952 national elections, the old Constituent Assembly was functioning as the Provisional (one House) Parliament.

[83] *Sri Sankari Prasad Singh Deo* v. *Union of India and State of Bihar*, (1952) S.C.R. 89.

[84] *Sri Sankari Prasad Singh Deo* v. *Union of India and State of Bihar*, (1952) S.C.R. 89, 889.

[85] *Sri Sankari Prasad Singh Deo* v. *Union of India and State of Bihar*, (1952) S.C.R. 89, 890, 951.

vires had authorized the State to take over fifty per cent of the arrears of rent due to the zamindar on the date of the compulsory acquisition of his property. The majority held that this provision "has no connection with land reform ...," and that its object was only to raise revenue to pay compensation to the zamindars for the acquisition of their estates.[86] In the words of Justice Mukherjea, "taking of the whole and returning a half means nothing more or less than taking half without any return and this is naked confiscation, no matter in whatever specious form it may be clothed or disguised."[87]

The other provision declared unconstitutional was one stating that the income figure to be used as the base for computing compensation should be reduced by four to twelve and one-half per cent on account of costs of works to benefit the tenants. According to the majority,

> this is an obvious device to reduce the gross assets and to bring it down to as low a level as possible. The Act does not say that this charge represents the expenditure on works of benefit or improvements which the *zamindars* and proprietors were under any legal obligation to carry out and which they failed to discharge. Nor are we told anything about the future destination of this deducted sum. It is an arbitrary figure which the legislature has said must be deducted from the gross assets. The deduction is a mere contrivance to reduce the compensation and it is a colourable device or fraudulent exercise of legislative power to subtract a fanciful sum from the calculation of gross assets.[88]

Thus, notwithstanding the efforts made by the Provisional Parliament to ensure the validity of the Bihar and other land-reform enactments, the Supreme Court was able to declare void portions of the Bihar Land Reforms Act. While no member of the Court in this case made any reference to the debates in the Constituent Assembly, it may be inferred that the arguments of "fraud" and "colourable legislation" were based on the statements made by Nehru and Alladi in the Constituent Assembly to the effect that only if the legislatures committed a "fraud on the constitution" could the courts question the validity of land-reform legislation.[89] If this doctrine of fraud or colourable legislation is a vague and uncertain criterion, the Court might well respond that the doctrine was devised by two leading members of the Constituent Assembly. At any rate, the Government was curiously silent after the Supreme Court announced its decision in the *Kameshwar Singh* appeal. The reason for the Government's reticence is probably that in two other appeals decided the same day, the Supreme Court

---

[86] *Sri Sankari Prasad Singh Deo* v. *Union of India and State of Bihar*, (1952) S.C.R. 89, 944.

[87] *Sri Sankari Prasad Singh Deo* v. *Union of India and State of Bihar*, (1952) S.C.R. 89, 962.

[88] *Sri Sankari Prasad Singh Deo* v. *Union of India and State of Bihar*, (1952) S.C.R. 89, 1018.

[89] See pp. 161–162.

upheld the validity of the Madhya Pradesh[90] and Uttar Pradesh[91] zamindari-abolition enactments. Neither of these enactments contained provisions similar to those which were found to be unconstitutional in the *Kameshwar Singh* case. Apparently the Government, too, agreed that the Bihar Act's provisions for determining the amount of compensation were merely a cloak or guise for confiscatory legislation.

Although the *Kameshwar Singh* decision did not provoke another constitutional amendment, the battle between the courts and the Government over property rights and land acquisition did not abate in 1952. Indeed, in less than three years Nehru was again standing before Parliament and introducing another amendment designed to clarify further "the intent of the framers" with regard to Article 31. During this period the controversy shifted from agrarian reform measures to statutes making provision for acquisition of property or restrictions on property rights which fell outside of the land-reform program. The matters of zamindari-abolition and related agrarian reforms having been removed from the judicial arena by the First Amendment, it remained to determine precisely the meaning of the general clause concerning compulsory acquisition, namely Article 31(2). A number of questions arose relating to the real meaning of Article 31(2) during the 1952–54 period, but there were four landmark Supreme Court decisions handed down within a span of less than a year (December 1953–October 1954) which provoked the Government to amend again Article 31. The significant features of these decisions were the Supreme Court's interpretation of the term "compensation," and its answer to the question of what sort of a "taking" or "deprivation" of property rights requires the payment of compensation.

The first of these decisions came on December 11, 1953 in the case of *The State of West Bengal v. Mrs. Bela Banerjee and Others*.[92] This case involved a State acquisition of land under the authority of the West Bengal Land Development and Planning Act of 1948, one provision of which limited compensation to the market value of the property as of December 31, 1946. According to the Government of West Bengal, this date had been selected in order to prevent land speculators from benefiting from the sharp rise in land values that followed independence, the partition of the subcontinent, and the influx of refugees from Pakistan. Thus, the questions raised for the consideration of the Court were (i) how much compensation was due to a person when the State acquired his property for a public purpose, and (ii) who has the final word as to the appropriateness of the compensation.

---

[90] *Visweshwar Rao v. The State of Madhya Pradesh,* (1952) S.C.R. 1020.
[91] *Raja Suriya Pal Singh v. The State of U.P. and Another,* (1952) S.C.R. 1056.
[92] (1954) S.C.R. 558.

In a very brief ruling, which belied its momentous consequences, the Court ruled unreservedly and unanimously that compensation for expropriated property must be "a *just equivalent* of what the owner has been deprived of."[93] The judgment of the Court was delivered by Chief Justice Patanjali Sastri, who said that

> while it is true that the legislature is given the discretionary power of laying down the principles which should govern the determination of the amount to be given to the owner for the property appropriated, such principles must ensure that what is determined as payable must be compensation, that is, a just equivalent of what the owner has been deprived of. Within the limits of this basic requirement of *full indemnification* of the expropriated owner, the Constitution allows free play to the legislative judgment as to what principles should guide the determination of the amount payable. Whether such principles take into account all the elements which make up the true value of the property appropriated and exclude matters which are to be neglected, *is a justiciable issue to be adjudicated by the Court.*[94]

In short, notwithstanding the fact that the framers had omitted any requirement in Article 31(2) that compensation be "just" or "full," the Supreme Court read these qualifying adjectives into the Constitution. Moreover, the Court refused to interpret Article 31(2) in such a way as to give the legislature a free hand to fix any standards or principles upon which the amount of compensation would be determined. The Court said simply that all such legislation was subject to judicial scrutiny, and that it would be declared unconstitutional unless it provided for compensation in the amount of full market value of the property at the time of acquisition. Apparently the Court saw nothing ambiguous about Article 31(2), for in its seven page ruling not a reference is made to the debates of the Constituent Assembly.

Less than a week later, in the case of *The State of West Bengal* v. *Subodh Gopal Bose and Others,*[95] the Supreme Court made its first pronouncement on the difficult question of when does a *restriction* on property rights become so great as to amount to a *deprivation* of property rights, and thus call for compensation. Bose, a West Bengal landlord, had purchased a large tract of property in 1942. According to the Bengal Land Revenue Sales Act of 1859, he had the right to evict all tenants living on this property. When, however, several years later Bose gave notice of eviction to certain tenants, the legislature of West Bengal moved

---

[93] *The State of West Bengal* v. *Mrs. Bela Banerjee and Others*, (1954) S.C.R. 563. Emphasis supplied.

[94] *The State of West Bengal* v. *Mrs. Bela Banerjee and Others*, (1954) S.C.R. 563–564. Emphasis supplied.

[95] (1954) S.C.R. 563, 587.

quickly to amend the 1859 enactment in order to prevent "unwarranted large-scale eviction."[96] The amended Act deprived Bose of the right to evict tenants, but at the same time authorized certain increases in rent.

The major question to be answered by the Supreme Court was whether this limitation on the respondent's property rights amounted to a "deprivation" or "taking" of property within the meaning of Article 31(2), or whether it was an abridgment short of deprivation which would not be compensable under that provision of the Constitution. The majority ruled that

> no cut and dried test can be formulated as to whether in a given case the owner is "deprived" of his property within the meaning of Art. 31; each case must be decided as it arises on its own facts. Broadly speaking, it may be said that an abridgement would be so substantial as to amount to a deprivation within the meaning of Art. 31 if, in effect, it withheld the property from the possession and enjoyment of the owner, or seriously impaired its use and enjoyment by him, or materially reduced its value.[97]

After applying this test to the facts in the instant case, the majority concluded that although Bose's property rights were curtailed to some degree without any provision for compensation, the fact that he was permitted to raise rents off-set this interference and meant that the impairment of the owner's property rights was not so serious as to call into play the requirement of compensation. Hence, the main significance of this case lies not in the fact that the Bengal Land Revenue Sales (West Bengal Amendment) Act of 1950 was upheld, but in the general test formulated by the Court in order to distinguish between cases where governmental interference with property rights would require compensation and cases where it would not.

Moreover, that the Supreme Court attached much more importance to property rights than did the Government was brought out very clearly when the Chief Justice, speaking for the majority, quoted with approval Blackstone's statement that "the public good is in nothing more essentially interested than in the protection of every individual's private rights as modelled by the municipal law."[98] There is probably no better illustration of the wide divergence in views toward private property between the judges and the politicians than this refer-ence by the Court to Blackstone.

If the Government had any doubts about the importance of the deprivation test formulated by the Chief Justice, it had to wait only a few hours for its worst expectations to be confirmed by the decision in *Dwarkadas Shrinivas of Bombay* v.

---

[96] *The State of West Bengal* v. *Subodh Gopal Bose and Others*, (1954) S.C.R. 594.

[97] *The State of West Bengal* v. *Subodh Gopal Bose and Others*, (1954) S.C.R. 594, 618.

[98] *The State of West Bengal* v. *Subodh Gopal Bose and Others*, (1954) S.C.R. 594, 613.

The Sholapur Spinning and Weaving Co. Ltd., and Others[99] handed down the following day. The facts of this dispute may be stated briefly. The Sholapur textile mill, which had been one of India's largest and most successful textile producers, encountered both financial difficulties and serious disputes with its employees. By 1949 the management had concluded that it was uneconomical to continue operations and, accordingly, they closed the mill. This action caused serious unemployment in the area, for the Sholapur mill employed over thirteen thousand workers. Reacting quickly to this situation, the Government appointed an investigatory committee, which later reported that the shutdown was caused by mismanagement by the company officials. Upon the basis of these findings, the Government promulgated the Sholapur Spinning and Weaving Company (Emergency Provisions) Ordinance of 1950 (later replaced by a Parliamentary enactment) which provided that the Government would take over the management of the mill. The Ordinance enabled the Union Government (i) to appoint new directors and remove the former directors; (ii) to suspend the right of the shareholders to appoint directors; (iii) to ignore any shareholder resolutions, and (iv) to prevent any liquidation of the company's assets.

Soon thereafter, one of the preferred stockholders of the company, who had been served with a notice by the Government-appointed directors making a call of 50 rupees on each of the preferred shares, filed a suit challenging the validity of the Ordinance and questioning the right of the directors to make such a call. When his case failed in the Bombay High Court, he brought it to the Supreme Court on appeal. The main question to be decided by the Supreme Court was what, in substance, was the loss or injury suffered by the shareholder. In other words, was the Ordinance merely regulatory in character, or was the abridgement of the petitioner's property rights "so substantial as to amount to a deprivation within the meaning of Article 31?"

In delivering the majority opinion, Justice Mahajan observed that

> it is one thing to superintend the affairs of a concern and it is quite another thing to take over its affairs and then proceed to carry on its trade through agents appointed by the State itself. It seems to me that under the guise of superintendence the state is carrying on the business or trade for which the company was incorporated with the capital of the company but through its own agents who take orders from it and are appointed by it and in the appointment and dismissal of whom the shareholders have absolutely no voice. ... The Company is debarred from carrying on its business in the manner and according to the terms of its charter. Its old complexion stands changed by the terms of the Ordinance. The Ordinance overrides the directors, deprives the shareholders of their legal rights and privileges and puts an end to the contract of the managing agents. Without there being any vacancy

---

[99] (1954) S.C.R. 594, 674.

in the number of directors, new directors step in and old directors and managing agents stand dismissed. Exercise of any power by them under the articles is subject to heavy penalties. In this situation it is not possible to subscribe to the contention of the learned Attorney-General that the effect of the Ordinance is that the Central Government has taken over the superintendence of the affairs of the company and that the impugned legislation is merely regulative in character. In the present case, practically all incidents of ownership have been taken over by the State and all that has been left with the company is mere paper ownership.[100]

Since this amounted to a deprivation of property without payment of any compensation, the Ordinance was held unconstitutional as a violation of Article 31(2).

In ruling that to constitute a "taking" of property the owner need not be dispossessed of the *totality* of the rights which the ownership of the object connotes, the Indian Supreme Court was adopting the reasoning of the United States Supreme Court that the difference between regulation and "taking possession of" is one of degree. In fact, the opinion of Justice Holmes to this effect in *Pennsylvania Coal Company* v. *Mahon*[101] is cited several times by the Indian Supreme Court in this decision.[102]

To summarize, the Supreme Court informed the Government in this decision that if a restriction or deprivation was so substantial as to amount to a real impairment of property rights, the requirement of compensation would be attracted, even though the State had not formally acquired, or taken possession of the property. The consequence of this decision was that the Government could not take over the management of a mill or other property, however imperative the public interest involved, unless compensation, and full compensation at that, had been paid.

The fourth and final Supreme Court decision which was a contributing factor in the further amendment of Article 31 was that of *Saghir Ahmad* v. *The State of U.P. and Others*.[103] At issue in this case was the constitutional validity of the Uttar Pradesh Road Transport Act of 1951, which empowered the State to operate road transport services as a government monopoly. Existing permits belonging to private bus operators were revoked and the private operators were prohibited from running their vehicles on the routes taken over by the State. The result, of course, was that the buses of the private owners were rendered practically useless.

The petitioners (106 private bus owners) contended that they had been deprived of their property within the meaning of Article 31(2) and, since they

---

[100] *Dwarkadas Shrinivas of Bombay* v. *The Sholapur Spinning and Weaving Co. Ltd., and Others*, (1954) S.C.R 689–90.

[101] 260 U.S. 393 (1922).

[102] *Dwarkadas Shrinivas of Bombay* v. *The Sholapur Spinning and Weaving Co. Ltd., and Others*, (1954) S.C.R. 674, 728

[103] (1955) S.C.R. 707. Announced on October 13, 1954.

had received no compensation, argued that the Act should be declared unconstitutional. The Supreme Court, applying the doctrines of the *Bose* and *Sholapur* cases, held that even though the State had not acquired any tangible property belonging to the bus owners, it had nonetheless deprived them of valuable property, i.e., their right to use the public highways for paid transportation services. Accordingly, the unanimous Supreme Court held that the Act offended Article 31(2) in that no provision was made for compensation.[104]

As might be expected, the Government was not happy with any of these decisions. The attitude of the Nehru Government was that it would not be possible to carry out the great schemes of "social engineering" if compensation in the amount of full market value had to be paid, and if the State's power of eminent domain was not distinguished from the operation of merely regulatory legislation. It was Nehru who introduced and guided through Parliament what was to become the Fourth Amendment. In urging the adoption of the Amendment, Nehru claimed at the outset that "there is no question of challenging, modifying, limiting or minimizing the authority of the judiciary in this country."[105] He said his Government "accepted" these decisions but, having found the decisions "not in consonance with the social and economic policy that we think the country should pursue ...,"[106] it was necessary to amend the Constitution so as to clarify the intent of the framers.[107] A few weeks later, just before the Fourth Amendment Bill won the overwhelming[108] approval of both Houses of Parliament, Nehru chose to express his personal views on private property in words which, when contrasted with Chief Justice Sastri's quotation from Blackstone in the *Bose* decision,[109] bring out very clearly the vast divergence between the approaches of the chief judicial officer and the topmost political leader to private property:

> Mind you, I have no respect for property. I have no respect for property at all except perhaps some small belongings. I respect the other person's respect for property

---

[104] *Saghir Ahmad* v. *The State of U.P. and Others,* (1955) S.C.R. 730.

[105] *Lok Sabha Debates,* II (1955), March 14, 1955, col. 1947.

[106] *Lok Sabha Debates,* II (1955), March 14, 1955, col. 1948.

[107] Several weeks later in Parliament Nehru said of the Fourth Amendment Bill: "All I can say is that the Constitution was not worded as precisely as the framers of the Constitution intended. What the framers of the Constitution intended is there for anyone to see. All that has been done now is to make that wording more precise and more in accordance with what the framers of the Constitution at that time meant and openly said. That is the only thing" (*Lok Sabha Debates,* III (1955), April 11, 1955, col. 4834).

[108] 299 to 5 in the Lok Sabha, and 139 to 0 in the Rajya Sabha.

[109] *The State of West Bengal* v. *Subodh Gopal Bose and Others,* (1954) S.C.R. 613

occasionally; that is a different matter. But I am speaking—the House will forgive me—in a personal sense. It seems a burden to me to carry the property; it is a nuisance. In life's journey one should be lightly laden; one cannot be tied down to a patch of land or building or something else.[110]

From the perspective of the courts, the major change introduced by the Fourth Amendment is that henceforth no law providing for compulsory acquisition of property "shall be called into question on the ground that the compensation provided by law is not adequate."[111] Thus, after April 27, 1955, when this amendment went into operation, the adequacy of compensation ceased to be a justiciable issue in India; the legislatures determine the amount of compensation at their discretion, and the courts are prohibited from questioning the reasonableness or justness of the legislative determination. That this feature of the Fourth Amendment was aimed directly at the Supreme Court's judgment in the *Banerjee* case is a matter of common knowledge.

A second important change affected by the Fourth Amendment was the addition of clause 2A to Article 31:

> Where a law does not provide for the transfer of the ownership or right to possession of any property to the State or to a corporation owned or controlled by the State, it shall not be deemed to provide for the compulsory acquisition or requisition of property, notwithstanding that it deprives any person of his property.

Clearly, the object of this new clause was to restrict the wide meaning given by the Supreme Court to the terms "deprivation" and "acquisition" in the *Bose*, *Sholapur* and *Saghir Ahmad* cases, for the Court had included in its definition of those terms any substantial abridgement of the right of the owner to use his property. Clause 2A was designed so as to exclude the possibility of the courts again applying such a definition, for it provides that the obligation to pay compensation will not arise unless the ownership or the right to possession of any property is *transferred* to the State or to a corporation owned or controlled by the State. Hence, this new clause brings out the distinction between compulsory acquisition and requisition of property for public purposes on the one hand, and deprivation of property or property rights by the operation of regulatory laws on the other hand. In short, the only cases where compensation is now required under Article 31 are those where property is physically and constructively transferred to the State or to a corporation owned or controlled by the State. If, for instance, the State undertakes to carry on any business to the

---

[110] *Lok Sabha Debates*, III (1955), April 11, 1955, col. 4840.
[111] This change was affected by substituting a new clause (2) for the original Article 31(2).

exclusion of private traders, no question of compensation would arise either on account of the fact that the private traders had lost their right to carry on the business, or that the stock-in-trade of such business had been rendered useless by reason of their ouster by the State.

Thirdly, the Amendment substituted for Article 31A, which had been added to the Constitution by the First Amendment, an entirely new article. Whereas the original Article 31A was designed to remove only zamindari-abolition and similar agrarian reform measures from the requirement that legislation must not infringe any of the Fundamental Rights, the new article exempts four additional categories of laws from any judicial determination of compatibility with the Fundamental Rights. These new categories exempt laws providing for (i) taking over the management of any property by the State for a limited period; (ii) amalgamation of two or more corporations; (iii) extinguishment or modification of rights accruing under any agreement, lease or license relating to minerals, and (iv) extinguishment or modification of rights of persons interested in corporations. Any law having any of these objects is not subject to judicial review on the ground of contravention of any of the Fundamental Rights. It is clear that the exclusion from judicial review of the aforementioned categories (i) and (iv) was aimed at counteracting the effects of the Supreme Court ruling in the *Sholapur* case.

Finally, the Constitution (Fourth Amendment) Act added seven new entries to the Ninth Schedule.[112] By bringing these seven additional enactments within the purview of Article 31B and the Ninth Schedule, the judicial decisions which declared these enactments to be void were superceded and their validity was ensured with retrospective effect. All of the additional entries in the Ninth Schedule were laws which had been declared void either because the compensation provided was something less than full market value, or because they had provided for taking over the management of private property without making provision for payment of compensation.

As a result of the Fourth Amendment, the scope of judicial review over legislation affecting private property was so diminished as to be hardly worthy of mention. Following this Amendment nearly every law journal in India contained one or more essays decrying the burial of judicial review and expressing dismay over the erosion of property rights. For the next several years the Supreme Court entered into what T. S. Rama Rao has called "the period of retreat,"[113] for the boldness it had demonstrated earlier was superceded by

---

[112] The Ninth Schedule, it will be recalled, listed thirteen State land-reform enactments which were specifically exempted from judicial scrutiny.

[113] "Judicial Review in India: A Retrospect," p. 142.

admissions in a series of decisions that it was unable to offer much protection to individual property owners.[114]

But then, on December 6, 1961, the Supreme Court discovered a loophole in the Fourth Amendment Act which enabled it to declare the Kerala Agrarian Relations Act of 1961 unconstitutional,[115] and thus the third major battle between the courts and the Government over property rights commenced. The key to the Court's decision was its discovery that whereas Article 31A excluded from judicial scrutiny legislation providing for the acquisition by the State of any "estate," the definition of the term "estate" in Article 31A(2)(a) and (b) did not embrace *ryotwari* lands. Therefore, the Kerala Act, which imposed ceilings on *ryotwari* land holdings, and authorized the acquisition of lands in excess of the ceiling limit, was not immune from judicial challenge. Having made this determination, the Court proceeded to examine the provisions of the Act and, finding that the method of computing compensation for acquired land discriminated between rich and poor property-owners, the Court unanimously declared that Article 14 (equal protection of the laws) was violated. Speaking for the Court, Justice Wanchoo said "there is no reason why when two persons are deprived of their property, one richer than the other, they should be paid at different rates when the property of which they are deprived is of the same kind and differs only in extent."[116]

The decision of the Supreme Court, of course, was binding upon the High Courts, and the result was that several of the High Courts began declaring unconstitutional other State land-reform enactments for similar reasons. Seeing its land-reform program again threatened by judicial decisions, the Government introduced in Parliament another constitutional amendment designed to settle, once and for all, questions about the validity of these measures. In urging the adoption of the Constitution (Seventeenth Amendment) Bill, Law Minister A. K. Sen asserted that "we are determined to cast away all impediments, technical and legal, in our way in order to achieve this noble purpose of ensuring a minimum amount of land to everyone."[117] He said the amendment had not been introduced "out of any disrespect to the judiciary,"[118] but "to remove the fetters in the way of introducing land

---

[114] See, e.g., *Sri Ram Narain Medhi* v. *The State of Bombay*, (1959) S.C.R. Supp. I 489, where the validity of the Bombay Tenancy and Agricultural Lands (Amendment) Act, 1956, was upheld, and *Attar Singh and Others* v. *The State of U.P.*, (1959) S.C.R. Supp, I 928, where the Uttar Pradesh Consolidation of Holdings Act, 1954, was upheld.

[115] *Karimbul Kunhikoman* v. *State of Kerala*, (1962) S.C.R. Supp. I 829.

[116] *Karimbul Kunhikoman* v. *State of Kerala*, (1962) S.C.R. Supp. I 829, 866–867.

[117] *The Hindu*, June 2, 1964, p. 7.

[118] *The Hindustan Times*, June 2, 1964, p. 6.

reforms."[119] This Amendment Bill received the overwhelming approval of the Lok Sabha (381 to 27) on June 2nd, and of the Rajya Sabha (177 to 9) on June 5th, and became a part of the fundamental law of the land upon receiving the assent of the President on June 20, 1964.[120]

The main effect of the Seventeenth Amendment is to amend the definition of "estate" in Article 31A so as to include *ryotwari* lands "and also other lands in respect of which provisions are normally made in land-reform enactments."[121] A second major feature of this amendment, and indicative of the Government's growing impatience with the judiciary, is the fact that the amendment adds not less than forty-four more land-reform enactments to the Ninth Schedule, thus bringing the total of enactments accorded a blanket immunity from judicial review to sixty-four. Moreover, of course, one of these forty-four is the Kerala Land Reforms Act. Never very tolerant of judicial review of land-reform measures, the Government's patience evidently is wearing very thin.

Significantly, however, this amendment does add to Article 31A the proviso that when the State acquires any land which is within the ceiling limit[122] and under the personal cultivation of the property owner, then the law must provide for payment of compensation "at a rate which shall not be less than the market value thereof."[123] Thus the Constitution finally acknowledges clearly the distinction, made years before by Nehru and others, between the large landlords and the "small people," the former to receive whatever compensation the legislatures deem appropriate, and the latter to receive full compensation. However, it is unclear at present whether the courts have any jurisdiction to make certain that these small property-owners receive full compensation, for this new proviso is a part of Article 31A, which imposes severe limitations on the scope of judicial review.

---

[119] *The Hindustan Times*, June 3, 1964, p. 12.

[120] This Amendment Bill actually was moved in Parliament on April 28, 1964 but, to the embarrassment of the Congress Party, so few members were present in Parliament on that day that the Bill failed to receive a sufficient number of votes. The vote was 206 to 19 when a simple majority of 510 was needed. Thus a special session of Parliament had to be called to reconsider the Bill.

[121] "Statement of Objects and Reasons," Bill No. 46 of 1964, *The Gazette of India Extraordinary*, Part II, Section 2, p. 410, dated May 27, 1964.

[122] Land ceilings differ from State to State, taking into account such factors as the traditional land system, degree of arability of land, and size of families. The Kerala Land Reforms Act sets the ceiling at 15 acres for a family of not more than five persons, and 7½ acres for an unmarried adult.

[123] New proviso to Article 31A(1).

6 Judicial Review in a Modern Democratic Welfare State

In the preceding chapters an effort has been made to present a general and balanced picture of the paramount judiciary in India over the past several decades. Within this chapter attention will be drawn to a consideration of the role of the Supreme Court of India and the exercise of judicial review in the context of a modern democratic welfare state. These are especially important matters of concern because the most serious clashes which have taken place since 1950 between the Government and the Supreme Court have arisen out of the manner in which the Supreme Court has approached its tasks and exercised its powers of judicial review.

It was seen in the last chapter that the framers of the Indian Constitution sought to arrive at a compromise between a virtually sovereign Parliament of the British variety and a virtually paramount Supreme Court of the American variety. The Supreme Court was constituted with powers of review over legislation, which limits the sovereignty of Parliament, but these review powers were sought to be limited in such a way as to prevent the Court from occupying too powerful a position. Such a delicate balance between legislative and judicial power is difficult to articulate clearly in any constitution and even more difficult to maintain in practice. The altercations between the Government and the Supreme Court arising out of Article 31 illustrate very well these difficulties. But the constitutional crises which have arisen out of Article 31 are really only illustrative. As will be seen presently, there have been other decisions of the Supreme Court which have provoked other amendments to the Constitution. These clashes between the Government and the Supreme Court have had several effects. Firstly, they have provoked a considerable amount of criticism of the Supreme Court, and of the judicial process in general, by important political leaders. The gist of this criticism is that the Court has so emphasized individual rights as to sacrifice the larger community interest, that the Court is so preoccupied with narrow legalisms as to miss completely the purposes behind the Constitution and many enactments. It is accused of delaying sorely needed reforms by the time-consuming process of litigation. Criticism of this nature reached a climax in 1957 when Prime Minister Nehru, addressing a conference of State Law Ministers in New Delhi, observed sarcastically that the function of judges "is not merely to sit in wig and gown for a number of hours a day and look very learned," and accused the judges of "living in an ivory tower, unconnected with the world, unconnected with social developments, social forces, and everything that is happening, and thereby getting isolated from what is happening, from the facts of life."[1] Others have taken up this refrain, with the result that one frequently hears the charges made that the Supreme Court is an inconvenience, if not a real obstruction to the creation of a modern democratic welfare state, and that judicial review is a serious impediment to social and economic legislation.

Secondly, these clashes and the resultant criticism have had the effect of diminishing the prestige of the Supreme Court and, indeed, of the entire judiciary and legal profession. The Law Commission took note of this fallen prestige in 1958 when it reported that

in the opening years of the Republic views were expressed by important persons which led to an impression in the public mind that judges, law courts and lawyers were superfluous institutions which hindered the progress of the social welfare State, which is the ideal of our Constitution. ... Thus, instead of appreciating the more important role which law and those administering it must play in a democratic social welfare State the public came to look down upon law, lawyers and those holding judicial office and to regard them as obstacles to the progress of the nation. Indeed, not infrequently, judicial pronouncements were treated with scant respect and commented upon in assemblies and public platforms.[2]

The Law Commission also quoted a judge of the Supreme Court as saying that

the first (namely, decreasing respect in Government circles) is purely psychological but is important. When men are looked up to and respected, they rise to the occasion and live up to the expectations required of them. But, if they are constantly sneered at and pushed aside while some worthless self-serving demagogue with nothing like their erudition and learning is fulsomely worshipped (until he is set

[1] *Proceedings of the Conference of Law Ministers* (mimeographed, New Delhi: Library of Parliament, dated September 18, 1957), p. c-1.

[2] Law Commission's *Fourteenth Report*, I, 78. Note that the Law Commission regarded mere comment upon decisions by politicians as irreverent and disrespectful.

aside by another), a feeling of disgust for high office is naturally engendered and many find it difficult to put forth their finest effort under these conditions.[3]

A third effect of these clashes and criticisms is, as was brought out in the preceding chapter, a piecemeal abolition of judicial review. Although there has not yet been any major effort to abolish judicial review in toto, every amendment to the Constitution precipitated by a decision of the Supreme Court has imposed further limitations on the scope of judicial review. In this sense, in every dispute between the Government and the Supreme Court, the Government has emerged the victor. The powers of the Court have been progressively minimized, with the result, of course, that the powers of Parliament have been increased. In justifying this trend toward a less powerful judiciary the critics of the judiciary say, in effect, that there is no reason why Parliament is less to be trusted than the courts.

Finally, and this is a point almost too obvious to require mention, the amendments to the Constitution make it patently clear that the Parliament is in a far more powerful position than the Supreme Court, notwithstanding the protestations of the Supreme Court that the Constitution as ultimately interpreted by the Court is supreme. The amendment procedure is hardly an obstacle to the Parliament when it seeks to override a decision of the Supreme Court and accord retrospective validity to legislation declared invalid by the judiciary. Ultimately, the Constitution means what the Congress Party says it means, and not what the Court wills. Judicial review has certainly not meant judicial supremacy in India.

In view of this conflict between the Supreme Court and the Government since 1950, it is important to seek an understanding of the basis of the conflict, as well as to attempt to ascertain why the Supreme Court has proceeded as it has.

One might begin with an examination of the Constitution itself, for, in a number of respects, it contains the seeds of the conflict which has persisted between the Government and the Supreme Court since 1950. This Constitution, easily the lengthiest fundamental law in the world,[4] probably ranks also as one of the most eclectic ever produced. India's constitution-makers sought neither innovation nor originality, but frankly and earnestly sought the best of all constitutional worlds by borrowing what they regarded as the best of the ideas and institutions tested and found successful by other nations. The Constitution makes provision for a parliamentary system adapted from the British model, a federation patterned after the Government of India Act of 1935 and the Canadian Constitution, a set of emergency powers similar to those set forth

---

[3] Law Commission's *Fourteenth Report*. Cf. II, 671–675.

[4] Initially 395 articles and covering 254 pages in the official edition, and growing at the rate of more than one amendment per year.

in the Weimar Constitution, a lengthy list of fundamental rights adapted from the American experience with a Bill of Rights, a Supreme Court endowed with express powers of judicial review for which the American Supreme Court served as the model, and list of "Directive Principles of State Policy" patterned after the Constitution of Eire.

In describing this unique document, Indian writers are given to such exuberances as "our Constitution is thus a happy amalgam of the best features of the leading constitutions of the world,"[5] or that "the *Indian* Constitution wonderfully adopts the via media between the American system of Judicial Supremacy and the English principle of Parliamentary Supremacy."[6] But another view is that eclecticism and emulation is carried so far in the Constitution that the questions arise as to whether these alien institutions, doctrines and ideas are really transferable to India's social and political setting, and whether it is possible to reconcile the copious and not always discriminate borrowings. This latter point is nowhere brought out any better than in the recent advisory opinion where the Supreme Court attempted to reconcile unbridled legislative privilege with guarantees of individual liberties.

One who reads the 1950 Constitution would find it very difficult to attach one of the more familiar labels to it, for no single philosophy permeates the document. Nowhere in the Constitution are the words "individualism" or "socialism" found, but both are reflected in sections of the Constitution. Some degree of attachment to individual rights is certainly evident in the section on fundamental rights, and an attachment to socialism is certainly evident in the section entitled "Directive Principles of State Policy." These directives lay down the lines on which the Government should work and establish goals which the Government should pursue. Two of the most important of these directives are Articles 38 and 39:

(38) The State shall strive to promote the welfare of the people by securing and protecting as effectively as it may a social order in which justice, social, economic and political, shall inform all the institutions of the national life.

(39) The State shall, in particular, direct its policy toward securing—

    (a) that the citizens, men and women equally, have the right to an adequate means of livelihood;

    (b) that the ownership and control of the material resources of the community are so distributed as best to subserve the common good;

---

[5] R. Rangiah, "Certain Salient Features of Judicial Review," *Indian Advocate*, II (1962), p. 51.

[6] Basu, *Commentary on the Constitution of India*, I, 22.

(c) that the operation of the economic system does not result in the concentration of wealth and means of production to the common detriment;

(d) that there is equal pay for equal work for both men and women;

(e) that the health and strength of workers, men and women, and the tender age of children are not abused and that citizens are not forced by economic necessity to enter avocations unsuited to their age or strength;

(f) that childhood and youth are protected against exploitation and against moral and material abandonment.

It would be beyond the scope of this study to attempt to assign a precise meaning to such phrases as "social justice" or "economic justice." Suffice to say that the directive principles have provided the constitutional basis and justification for the Government's efforts to establish a welfare state, or, to use the designation preferred by Indian leaders, a "socialist pattern of society." Although these directive principles read very much like an election manifesto, they were never intended to be pious declarations, for Article 37 provides that the directive principles are *"fundamental in the governance of the country and it shall be the duty of the State to apply these principles in making laws."*[7] But, and this has been of the utmost importance from the perspective of the Supreme Court, Article 37 states also that these directive principles *"shall not be enforceable by any court."*[8] Thus the sanction behind the directives is political and not juridical. The Supreme Court cannot compel the Government of the day to implement them, nor can it declare any legislation invalid on the ground that it does not conform to these directives.

Thus the Constitution contains a list of fundamental rights which guarantee certain freedoms and rights to the individual. These are not only justiciable, but Article 13 provides that any law which takes away or abridges these rights shall be declared void, and Article 32 provides the Supreme Court with an extensive writ jurisdiction designed to enable the Court to enforce effectively these rights. On the other hand, the directive principles are a set of instructions to the Government of the day to legislate into being a welfare state, which means, of course, an emphasis on the social and economic uplift of the community at large and a corresponding subtraction from individual rights. It is the duty of the Government to apply these principles in making laws. In short, the Constitution confers upon the Supreme Court the task of making the fundamental rights meaningful against possible infringements by the legislatures and executives,

[7] Emphasis supplied.
[8] Emphasis supplied.

and makes it obligatory for the Government to bring about changes in the social and economic life of the nation, changes which were bound to affect adversely some private rights.

It is conceivable, at least, that both the Supreme Court and the Government could have pursued their respective tasks without conflict, but this did not happen. The legislatures, purporting to be doing no more than carrying out the duties prescribed in the directive principles, enacted legislation which the Supreme Court found to be in conflict with some of the fundamental rights. This happened first in the landmark case of *The State of Madras* v. *Srimathi Champakam Dorairajan*,[9] a decision which marks a parting of the ways between the Government and the Court. Briefly, the facts of this case were as follows. The State of Madras was maintaining four medical colleges to which a total of three hundred and thirty new students were admitted each year. Finding that the number of applicants far exceeded the number which could be admitted, and realizing that unrestricted competition would have the effect of disqualifying those sections of the community which were educationally backward and economically underprivileged, the Government of Madras apportioned the three hundred and thirty places on the basis of the relative educational backwardness and communal composition of the different groups in the State. For every fourteen places to be filled, candidates were selected on the following basis: non-Brahmin Hindus (6), backward Hindus (2), Brahmins (2), Harijans (2), Anglo-Indians and Indian Christians (1), and Muslims (1).[10]

As a consequence, overall or general competition was expressly eliminated; candidates competed for admission within the single category into which they fitted. Miss Dorairajan was a Brahmin candidate who, though scoring higher than some of those who gained admission under the non-Brahmin Hindu category, was denied admission because the Brahmin quota had been filled by more meritorious Brahmin applicants. She therefore approached the courts, arguing that her fundamental right under Article 29(2) was abridged by the selection procedure. Article 29(2) provides that "no citizen shall be denied admission into any educational institution maintained by the State or receiving aid out of State funds on grounds only of religion, race, caste, language or any of them."

But the State of Madras, through its Advocate-General, argued that Article 29(2) must be read along with Article 46, one of the directive principles which makes it incumbent on the State to "promote with special care the educational and economic interests of the weaker sections of the people, and, in particular,

---

[9] (1951) S.C.R. 525.

[10] *The State of Madras* v. *Srimathi Champakam Dorairajan*, (1951) S.C.R. 527.

of the Scheduled Castes and the Scheduled Tribes, and [to] protect them from social injustice and all forms of exploitation." The Advocate-General argued that in fixing the scheme for apportioning seats among different communities the Government was only carrying out one of its constitutionally-prescribed duties. Thus the Supreme Court was faced with a dispute in which the Brahmin applicant had a very strong claim based on one of the fundamental rights, and the Government claimed to be in an equally tenable position because of Article 46. It would seem that the Supreme Court faced a real dilemma.

The Supreme Court, however, saw no dilemma at all. The seven-member Court, without making any effort to harmonize Articles 29 and 46, was unanimous in ruling in favor of Miss Dorairajan. Speaking through Justice S. R. Das, the Court held that

> the directive principles of State policy, which by article 37 are expressly made unenforceable by a Court, cannot override the provisions found in Part III which, notwithstanding other provisions, are expressly made enforceable by appropriate Writs, Orders or directions under article 32. *The chapter of Fundamental Rights is sacrosanct* and not liable to be abridged by any Legislative or Executive Act or order, except to the extent provided in the appropriate article in Part III. *The directive principles of State policy have to conform to and run as subsidiary to the Chapter of Fundamental Rights.*[11]

It would have been impossible for the Court to have taken a stronger stand on behalf of the fundamental rights, for sacrosanct means sacred. This unanimous decision absolutely proclaims the superiority of individual rights over the subsidiary and inferior directive principles.

Neither the Madras Government nor the Union Government was happy with this decision, for it was understood as making it impossible for the State to give special consideration and protection to the "backward classes." The Union Government was convinced that an amendment to the Constitution was imperative if its social policy of protective discrimination was to be implemented. Prime Minister Nehru introduced the amendment in Parliament, and his remarks on this occasion deserve quotation at some length because he spelled out very succinctly and forcefully the Government's attitude toward both the fundamental rights and the directive principles of State policy.

> The real difficulty which has come up before us is this. The Constitution lays down certain Directive Principles of State Policy. We agreed to them after a long discussion and they point out the way we must travel. The Constitution

---

[11] *The State of Madras v. Srimathi Champakam Dorairajan,* (1951) S.C.R. 527, 531. Emphasis supplied.

also lays down certain Fundamental Rights. Both are important. *The Directive Principles of State Policy represent a dynamic move towards a certain objective. The Fundamental Rights represent something static;* their object is to preserve certain rights which already exist. Both again are right. But sometimes it might so happen that the dynamic movement and the static concept do not quite fit in with each other.

A dynamic movement toward a certain objective necessarily means certain changes: that is the essence of the movement. Now, it may be that, in the process of movement, certain existing relationships are altered, varied or affected. In fact, it is meant to affect those settled relationships and yet if you come back to the Fundamental Rights they are meant to preserve, though not always directly, certain settled relationships. There is a certain conflict between the two approaches but I am sure it is not an inherent one. However, there is some difficulty and, naturally, when the courts of the land have to consider these matters, they have to lay stress more on the Fundamental Rights than on the Directive Principles of State Policy. The result is that the whole purpose behind the Constitution, which was meant to be a dynamic constitution, leading to a certain goal step by step, is hampered and hindered by the static element which has been emphasized a little more than the dynamic element; and we have to find a way out of the difficulty.

The essential difficulty lies in the fact that the whole conception of fundamental rights is for the protection of individual liberty and freedom. This is a basic conception and to know where it was derived from you have to go back to European history in the latter days of the eighteenth century, roughly speaking, from the days of the French Revolution on to the nineteenth century. That might be said to be the dominating idea of the nineteenth century and it has continued to be a matter of fundamental importance. Nevertheless, as the nineteenth century marched into the twentieth and as the twentieth century wore on, other additional ideas came into the field which are represented by our Directive Principles of State Policy. In the process of protecting individual liberty, if you also protect individual or group inequality, then you have come into conflict with that directive principle. If, therefore, an appeal to individual liberty and freedom is construed as an appeal for the continuation of the existing inequality, then you come up against difficulties. You become static and unprogressive and cannot change; you cannot realize the ideal of an egalitarian society. ...[12]

There are few better illustrations of the Government's approach to the fundamental rights and directive principles than this speech by the late Prime

---

[12] *Parliamentary Debate,* XII (1951), May 16, 1951, cols. 8820–8823. Emphasis supplied. This speech is reprinted in volume two of *Jawaharlal Nehru's Speeches, 1949–53* (New Delhi: Ministry of Information and Broadcasting, The Publications Division, 1954), pp. 486–501.

Minister. In describing the fundamental rights as representative of eighteenth and nineteenth century thinking, as something "static" and "unprogressive" in contrast with the twentieth century and "dynamic" ideas represented in the directive principles, Nehru left no doubt as to which he considered more important. Thus the Supreme Court described the fundamental rights as "sacrosanct" and Nehru considered them static and unprogressive; the Supreme Court passed off the directive principles as "subsidiary" to the fundamental rights and Nehru saw them as establishing the dynamic goals and providing the beacons for the social and economic policies his Government was committed and anxious to pursue.

Shortly after Nehru's speech the Constitution (First Amendment) Act, 1951, was passed.[13] In order to get around the *Dorairajan* ruling, clause (4) was added to Article 15 (one of five articles guaranteeing the "right to equality"). This new clause provides that "nothing in this article or in clause (2) of Article 29 shall prevent the State from making any special provision for the advancement of any socially and educationally backward classes of citizens or for the Scheduled Castes and the Scheduled Tribes."

Although the *Dorairajan* decision and First Amendment occurred in 1951, the attitudes of the Government and the Supreme Court toward the fundamental rights and the directive principles have remained essentially the same. The Court has continued to regard itself as the protector of individual rights, and the Government remains dedicated to pursuing the goals set forth in the directive principles. Whenever legislation is found by the Court to be in conflict with one of the fundamental rights, the Court has always enforced the fundamental right. Indeed, there have been recent decisions such as *Mohd. Hanif Quareshi & Others* v. *The State of Bihar*[14] where the Court has unanimously quoted with approval the view taken in the *Dorairajan* case that "the directive principles of State policy have to conform to and run as subsidiary to the Chapter of Fundamental Rights." In short, the Supreme Court maintains still that whatever is enforceable in a court of law is by definition superior to that which is unenforceable. However, as will be seen, in recent years the Supreme Court has acknowledged that the Government must be guided in its actions by the directive principles, and in a few cases judges of the Supreme Court have even endorsed the directive principles as worthy goals.

---

[13] It will be recalled that the First Amendment also effected changes in Article 31 arising out of certain zamindari-abolition decisions. The First Amendment was really an omnibus amendment, for it effected changes in ten articles of the Constitution, and added two new articles and the ninth schedule to the Constitution.

[14] (1959) S.C.R. 629, 648.

Before considering further the implications of the Court's position on the directive principles, it will be useful to examine the general approach to which the Court subscribes in interpreting the Constitution and legislative enactments. This is a subject related closely to the Court's approach to the directive principles, but is different in that whereas the Court can point to provisions of the Constitution (Articles 13 and 32) which compel it to enforce the fundamental rights, its general rules of constitutional and statutory interpretation are not set forth in the Constitution, meaning, of course, that the Court has some discretion in selecting these rules.[15]

The basic approach of the Supreme Court to constitutional and statutory interpretation has been to interpret words and provisions as *literally* as possible. The Court has seldom made any distinction between constitutional and statutory interpretation. To say that the Supreme Court's general approach has been one of literal interpretation means that the Court usually adheres rigidly to the letter of the law as written, that it seeks to discover the meaning of a particular word or phrase by examining the "plain words" of the Constitution or statute, that it usually refuses to take note of social and policy considerations in seeking to arrive at the meaning of a phrase or provision, that it eschews any consideration of the "spirit of the Constitution," and that it is usually unwilling to utilize extrinsic aids such as Constituent Assembly debates, Parliamentary debates, committee reports and the like in order to understand as accurately as possible the intended aim of a provision or enactment. In short, the Court's general approach has been rather narrow, technical and mechanical; interpretation of the Constitution and statutes is approached essentially as an exercise in grammar.[16]

---

[15] There is an exception which should be noted. Article 367(1) of the Constitution provides that "the General Clauses Act, 1897, shall ... apply for the interpretation of this Constitution as it applies for the interpretation of an Act of the Legislature of the Dominion of India." But the General Clauses Act seems to be used chiefly in order to determine the meaning of such terms as "magistrate," "month," "oath," "repeal," "financial year," and the like. Further, see Basu, *Commentary on the Constitution of India*, I, 43.

[16] Others, in varying degrees, have made essentially the same points. See, e.g., M. P. Jain, *Indian Constitutional Law* (Bombay: N. M. Tripathi Private Ltd., 1962), pp. 607–608, 610–612; Alexandrowicz, *Constitutional Developments in India*, pp. 226–230; Sheldon D. Elliott, "Statutory Interpretation and the Welfare State," *Journal of the Indian Law Institute*, II (January–June, 1960), pp. 257–272. Elliott, a professor of law at New York University, was a visiting consultant to the Indian Law Institute in 1960. Edward McWhinney, *Judicial Review in the English-Speaking World* (Toronto: University of Toronto Press, 1956), examines in cursory fashion a few early decisions of the Indian Supreme Court and concludes that the Court has followed "a baldly positivist approach" (p. 130).

Since this description of the dominant approach of the Supreme Court to constitutional and statutory interpretation may be regarded as a rather serious indictment of the judicial process, and would seem to have little to commend it as an aid to carrying forward the developmental policies of an aspiring welfare state, evidence must be adduced in support of this description of the Court's general approach.

Whenever the allegation is made that the Indian Supreme Court interprets the Constitution literally, the illustration most frequently cited[17] is the *Gopalan* decision, where the majority concluded that the "procedure established by law" phraseology in Article 21 meant that the degree to which life and personal liberty would receive protection was entirely a matter for the legislature to decide, and that any procedure established by a legislature, including boiling in oil, would be upheld by the Supreme Court.[18] In response to the argument presented by Gopalan's counsel that such an interpretation was opposed to the "spirit of the Constitution," i.e., the Constitution was a modern, democratic one which should be interpreted liberally in favor of personal liberty, the Chief Justice said simply that the Court could not consider the "spirit of the Constitution" in determining the meaning or validity of a particular enactment or provision of the Constitution.[19] As a result of this strict interpretation, Article 21 is rendered meaningless as any protection of life and personal liberty against legislative encroachments. However, as was pointed out earlier, this literal interpretation of Article 21 brought the Court to a conclusion which reflected accurately the intention of the framers, with the result that the *Gopalan* decision was implicitly acclaimed by the Union Government.

But when, less than one week after the *Gopalan* decision was handed down, the Court gave a literal interpretation to the free speech guarantee in Article 19, its ruling precipitated an amendment to the Constitution. The original Article 19(1)(a) and (2) provided that "all citizens shall have the right to freedom of speech and expression ...," but that the State would be permitted to restrict speech which "undermines the security of, or tends to overthrow, the State." When the Madras Government imposed a ban on the entry and circulation of the *Crossroads*, a weekly publication of the Communist Party of

---

[17] Alexandrowicz, *Constitutional Developments in India*, p. 226; McWhinney, *Judicial Review in the English-Speaking World*, pp. 130–140; and Rama Rao, "Judicial Review in India: A Retrospect," p. 124ff.

[18] *A. K. Gopalan v. The State of Madras*, (1950) S.C.R. 88. See pp. 167–175. It was Justice S. R. Das who said the Court was powerless if the legislature sanctioned the taking of life by boiling in oil (*A. K. Gopalan v. The State of Madras* (1950) S.C.R. 88, 289).

[19] See pp. 172–173.

India, it acted under the authority of the Madras Maintenance of Public Order Act of 1949, which authorized the State Government to impose such restrictions "for the purpose of securing the public safety and the maintenance of public order. ..."[20] Similarly, when the Chief Commissioner of Delhi imposed restrictions on the distribution of the weekly journal *Organizer*, which had been carrying anti-Muslim and anti-Pakistan editorials, he relied on the East Punjab Public Safety Act of 1949, which authorized such action "for the purpose of combating any activity prejudicial to the public safety or maintenance of public order. ..."[21]

In these two cases the Supreme Court was quick to point out that whereas these two enactments authorized restrictions on speech in the interests of maintaining "public order" and "public safety," Article 19 permitted restrictions on freedom of speech only if it "undermines the security of, or tends to overthrow, the State." By a six to one majority, the Court held that "unless a law restricting freedom of speech and expression is directed *solely* against the undermining of the State or the overthrow of it ...,"[22] it would have to be declared unconstitutional, which is just what the Court did in each of these cases.[23] The Court's position was simply that in the absence of the words "public order" and "public safety" in Article 19(2), they could not be read into the Constitution by the Court.

As a result of these two rulings and of similar High Court decisions,[24] the Union Parliament amended Article 19 with the result that "public order," "friendly relations with foreign States," and "incitement to an offence" were added to Article 19(2) as additional bases for restrictions on freedom of speech and expression.[25]

In summary, whereas a literal interpretation of Article 21 led to a very restrictive interpretation of the life and personal liberty guarantee, a literal interpretation of Article 19 led, according to the Government at any rate, to a too-liberal judicial rendering of the free speech guarantee, which necessitated an amendment to the Constitution.

[20] *Romesh Thappar* v. *The State of Madras*, (1950) S.C.R. 594, 597.

[21] *Brij Bhushan and Another* v. *The State of Delhi*, (1950) S.C.R. 605, 608.

[22] *Romesh Thappar* v. *The State of Madras*, (1950) S.C.R. 594, 602.

[23] *Romesh Thappar* v. *The State of Madras*, (1950) S.C.R. 594, 603, and *Brij Bhushan and Another* v. *The State of Delhi*, (1950) S.C.R. 605, 608.

[24] *Srinivasa Bhat* v. *State of Madras*, A.I.R. 1951 Madras 70; *Tara Singh Gopi Chand* v. *The State*, A.I.R. 1951 Punjab 27, and *Amar Nath Bali* v. *The State*, A.I.R. 1951 Punjab 18. See also G. N. Joshi and W. H. Mann, "Comparative Constitutional Problems of Freedom of Speech, Press, and Assembly," in Lawrence F. Ebb (ed.), *Public Law Problems in India* (Stanford: School of Law, Stanford University, 1957), pp. 95–98.

[25] Constitution (First Amendment) Act, 1951.

Another illustration of a strictly literal interpretation of the Constitution is the decision of the Court in *Keshavan Madhava Menon* v. *The State of Bombay*.[26] This decision also brings out very clearly how the Supreme Court interprets the Constitution just as an ordinary law. The main question for the consideration of Court was whether a person could be punished after the commencement of the Constitution (January 26, 1950) for an offense committed in 1949, under the provisions of the Indian Press (Emergency Powers) Act of 1931, an enactment which contained provisions which were inconsistent with the free speech provision in Article 19. In other words, could Menon's lower court conviction be upheld on the basis of a statute which could no longer pass the constitutional test?

By a majority of five to two, the Supreme Court answered affirmatively. The Court acknowledged that Article 13(1) of the Constitution provided that "all laws in force in the territory of India immediately before the commencement of this Constitution, in so far as they are inconsistent with the provisions of this Part, shall, to the extent of such inconsistency, be void." But the Court then held that "every Statute is *prima facie* prospective unless it is expressly or by necessary implications made to have retrospective operation. There is no reason why this rule of interpretation should not be applied for the purpose of interpreting the Constitution."[27] Accordingly, continued the majority, Article 13(1)

> has no retrospective effect and if, therefore, an act was done before the commence-
> ment of the Constitution in contravention of the provisions of any law which,
> after the Constitution, becomes void with respect to the exercise of any of the
> fundamental rights, the inconsistent law is not wiped out so far as the past act is
> concerned for, to say that it is, will be to give the law retrospective effect. There is
> no fundamental right that a person shall not be prosecuted and punished for an
> offense committed before the Constitution came into force. So far as the past acts
> are concerned the law exists, notwithstanding that it does not exist with respect to
> the future exercise of fundamental rights.[28]

The incongruous result of this narrow interpretation of the Constitution was that Menon's conviction under a law adjudged to be unconstitutional was upheld. It is interesting to note that Menon's counsel argued that the Indian Press (Emergency Powers) Act of 1931 "was one of the many repressive laws enacted by an alien Government with a view to stifle the liberty of the Indian subjects and particularly of the Indian Press ...," and that "it was against the spirit of the Constitution ... that a free citizen of India should still continue to

---

[26] (1951) S.C.R. 228.

[27] *Keshavan Madhava Menon* v. *The State of Bombay*, (1951) S.C.R. 233.

[28] *Keshavan Madhava Menon* v. *The State of Bombay*, (1951) S.C.R. 233, 235–236.

be persecuted under such a retrograde law. ..."[29] But the Court was not at all impressed with this argument, and replied that

> an argument founded on what is claimed to be the spirit of the Constitution is always attractive, for it has a powerful appeal to sentiment and emotion; but a court of law has to gather the spirit of the Constitution from the language of the Constitution. What one may believe or think to be the spirit of the Constitution cannot prevail if the language of the Constitution does not support that view.[30]

It is difficult to imagine a more narrow interpretation of the Constitution. The Supreme Court in this decision has treated the Constitution of India in the same light as an ordinary statute, to be construed restrictively without any regard to the policies that the instrument is intended to embody.

One final example of the customary narrow approach taken by the Court in constitutional adjudication is the decision of the unanimous Court in *The State of Punjab* v. *Ajaib Singh and Another*.[31] Here the counsel for the respondent argued that the Constitution "should be construed liberally so that the fundamental rights conferred by it may be of the widest amplitude."[32] The Court's answer to this was that "if the language of the article is plain and unambiguous and admits of only one meaning then the duty of the court is to adopt that meaning irrespective of the inconvenience that such a construction may produce."[33]

What will the Court do if the language of the Constitution is not "plain and unambiguous"? This question may be answered by indicating the Court's attitude toward the use of extrinsic aids, and toward social and economic policy considerations in construing the Constitution and statutes. In the preceding chapter, it was pointed out in the discussion of the *Gopalan* decision that all members of the Supreme Court referred to the *Constituent Assembly Debates* in an effort to ascertain correctly the intent of the framers with regard to Article 21.[34] It will be recalled that the Court's attitude then was that normally such extrinsic evidence was inadmissible, but that it "may be seen in case of ambiguity."[35] Since the *Gopalan* decision in 1950, however, the Supreme Court has never again referred to these debates when confronted with problems of constitutional interpretation. Instead, it seeks to ascertain the meaning of the provisions of the Constitution from the very words employed in the Constitution. As was pointed

---

[29] *Keshavan Madhava Menon* v. *The State of Bombay*, (1951) S.C.R. 231, 232.

[30] *Keshavan Madhava Menon* v. *The State of Bombay*, (1951) S.C.R. 231, 232.

[31] (1953) S.C.R. 254.

[32] *The State of Punjab* v. *Ajaib Singh and Another*, (1953) S.C.R. 263.

[33] *The State of Punjab* v. *Ajaib Singh and Another*, (1953) S.C.R. 263, 264.

[34] See pp. 174–175.

[35] *A. K. Gopalan* v. *State of Madras*, (1950) S.C.R. 88, 110.

out earlier in the discussion of the *Banerjee* case, the Court ignored completely the *Constituent Assembly Debates* in interpreting Article 31(2), and concluded that "compensation" meant implicitly "just" or "full" compensation.[36] Had the Supreme Court consulted the debates it would have seen that all efforts made in the Constituent Assembly to add the adjective "just" or "full" before the term compensation were deliberately rejected by a vote of the Assembly. In the least, one may criticize the Court for not employing consistent principles of interpretation, for it is difficult to understand how Article 31 could possibly be regarded as less ambiguous than Article 21.

The Court's attitude toward statutory interpretation is essentially the same. It generally refuses to seek guidance from the debates of Parliament and reports of investigatory committees and commissions, preferring instead to ascertain the meaning of a provision from the very words employed.[37] Moreover, the Court will generally not refer to the "statement of objects and reasons"[38] as an aid in construing an enactment. Chief Justice Kania once explained why the Court would not use statements of objects and reasons:

> As regards the propriety of the reference to the statement of objects and reasons, it must be remembered that it seeks only to explain what reasons induced the mover to introduce the Bill in the House and what objects he sought to achieve. But those objects and reasons may or may not correspond to the objective which the majority of members had in view when they passed it into law. The Bill may have undergone radical changes during its passage through the House or Houses, and there is no guarantee that the reasons which led to its introduction and the objects thereby sought to be achieved have remained the same throughout till the Bill emerges from the House as an Act of the Legislature, for they do not form part of the Bill and are not voted upon by the members. We, therefore, consider that the statements of objects and reasons appended to the Bill should be ruled out as an aid to the construction of a statute.[39]

The attitude of the Supreme Court toward having recourse to policy considerations is equally narrow. Whereas the Government, since 1950, has introduced many programs of far-reaching social and economic reform in an effort to achieve the goals of social justice, economic justice, and the socialist pattern of society, the Court has seldom even acknowledged what is going on outside of its chambers. Much of the legislation passed in furtherance of these goals has been

---

[36] See p. 182

[37] *Aswini Kumar Ghosh and Another v. Arabinda Bose and Another*, (1953) S.C.R. 1, 27–29.

[38] When the Government introduces a Bill, it prepares a brief "statement of objects and reasons" which explains the purposes sought to be served by the Bill.

[39] *Aswini Kumar Ghosh and Another v. Arabinda Bose and Another*, (1953) S.C.R. 1, 28.

subjected to judicial review, but one seldom finds the phrases "social justice" or "economic justice" employed by judges of the Supreme Court. The Court's usual posture is to avoid mention of matters of social and economic policy by adhering to a strict and literal interpretation of the Constitution and Laws, Thus, e.g., in the two hundred and forty-six page *Gopalan* decision there is not a single reference to the fact that Gopalan is a leading figure in the Communist Party of India, and in the vast majority of the property and land acquisition decisions the Court has not mentioned or acknowledged the purposes of agrarian reform enactments.

Although the Court's usual posture is to ignore the social and economic policy considerations implicit or explicit in an enactment or in the Constitution, there is at least one decision in which a unanimous four-judge division bench took what seems to be an explicitly disapproving, if not scornful attitude toward considering the matter of "social justice" in industrial adjudication. The Labour Appellate Tribunal, in reaching a decision in a dispute between workers and management over what constitutes a "fair bonus," had commented in its decision that "considerations of social justice cannot be disregarded altogether, in relations between capital and labour."[40] When this dispute reached the Supreme Court, the unanimous Court, in the process of reversing the ruling of the Labour Appellate Tribunal, hastened to point out that

> the considerations of social justice imported by the Labour Appellate Tribunal in arriving at the decision in favour of the respondent were *not only irrelevant but untenable*. Social justice is a very vague and indeterminate expression and no clear-cut definition can be laid down which will cover all the situations.[41]

Admittedly, "social justice" is a phrase which carries no fixed meaning and which means various things to different people. Yet to ignore completely such considerations can only mean an evasion of real issues in industrial disputes, leaving the Court open to the charges that it fails to perceive and appreciate real issues present in the disputes it seeks to settle, and that, as the Law Commission has pointed out, the Court is deciding ultimately industrial disputes without "the means or materials for adequately informing itself about the different aspects of the questions which arise in these appeals and therefore finds it difficult to do adequate justice."[42] It was pointed out in Chapter IV that the Indian Supreme Court has accepted many hundreds of appeals from labor tribunals, and that the Court "had become the supreme rule-maker of

---

[40] *Muir Mills Co., Ltd.* v. *Suti Mills Mazdoor Union, Kanpur*, (1955) S.C.R. I 991, 1000.

[41] *Muir Mills Co., Ltd.* v. *Suti Mills Mazdoor Union, Kanpur*, (1955) S.C.R. I 991, 1001. Emphasis supplied.

[42] Law Commission's *Fourteenth Report*, I, 50–51.

the nation's industrial relations system ...,"[43] notwithstanding efforts made by Parliament to exclude tribunal awards from judicial scrutiny. The Supreme Court's unwillingness to consider the social, economic and political implications of its role, and its unwillingness to consider external aids in order to educate itself to the facts of industrial reality and conditions of labor, raise serious questions about the appropriateness of the Supreme Court having anything to do with such matters.[44]

Although the predominant approach to constitutional and statutory interpretation has been set forth in the preceding pages, there have been occasions on which the Supreme Court has utilized extra-legal materials, and even some remarkable endorsements of the welfare state. Justice S. R. Das, e.g., who described the fundamental rights as sacrosanct and the directive principles as subsidiary in 1951, just a year later wrote a dissenting opinion in the historic *Kameshwar Singh* (zamindari-abolition) decision in which he observed that

> with the onward march of civilization our notions as to the scope of the general interest of the community are fast changing and widening with the result that our old and narrower notions as to the sanctity of the private interest of the individual can no longer stem the forward flowing tide of time and must necessarily give way to the broader notions of the general interest of the community. The emphasis is unmistakably shifting from the individual to the community. This modern trend in the social and political philosophy is well reflected and given expression to in our Constitution.[45]

Then, in words which would be less surprising if not spoken by the same Justice S. R. Das who had earlier talked about sacrosanct fundamental rights and subsidiary directive principles, he noted with apparent enthusiasm that

> what were regarded only yesterday, so to say, as fantastic formulae have now been accepted as directive principles of State policy prominently set out in Part IV of the Constitution. The ideal we have set before us in article 38 is to evolve a State which must constantly strive to promote the welfare of the people by securing and

---

[43] Robinson, in "The Supreme Court and Section 33 of the Industrial Disputes Act, 1947-Part II," pp. 183–184. See pp. 126–131.

[44] Surprisingly little research has been done on the subjects of industrial relations and labor-management dispute adjudication in India. The best study this writer has seen is that by Solomon E. Robinson, in "The Supreme Court and Section 33 of the Industrial Disputes Act, 1947-Part II". Robinson is a former Fulbright Scholar who spent 1960–61 at the Tata Institute of Social Sciences, Bombay.

[45] *The State of Bihar* v. *Maharajadhiraja Sir Kameshwar*, (1952) S.C.R. 889, 996.

making as effectively as it may be a social order in which social, economic and political justice shall inform all the institutions of national life.[46]

Finally, after describing zamindari-abolition as something which would "subserve the common good,"[47] he concluded with the comment that "we must not read a measure implementing our mid-twentieth century Constitution through spectacles tinted with early nineteenth century notions as to the sanctity or inviolability of individual rights."[48]

But this dissenting opinion does not mean that Justice Das had departed from his earlier position, for, in 1959, just before he reached retirement age, the then Chief Justice Das, speaking for a unanimous five-judge division bench, reiterated his earlier statement that "the directive principles of State policy have to conform and run subsidiary to the Chapter of Fundamental Rights."[49] Significantly, he did add at this time that "a harmonious interpretation has to be placed upon the Constitution and so interpreted it means that the State should certainly implement the directive principles but it must do so in such a way that its laws do not take away or abridge the fundamental rights. ..."[50]

Probably the area in which the Supreme Court in recent years has moved farthest in the direction of taking into consideration welfare state objectives is that of industrial dispute adjudication. Whereas in 1955 the division bench which heard the *Muir Mills* case was unanimous in describing considerations of social justice as "not only irrelevant but untenable,"[51] a unanimous three-judge division bench in 1958 commented that

with the emergence of the concept of a welfare state, collective bargaining between trade unions and capital has come into its own and has received statutory recognition; the state is no longer content to play the part of a passive onlooker in an industrial dispute. The old principle of the absolute freedom of contract and the doctrine of laissez faire have yielded place to new principles of social welfare and common good. ... There can be no doubt that in fixing wage structures in different industries, industrial adjudication attempts, gradually and by stages though it may be, *to obtain the principle objective of a welfare state, to secure "to all citizens justice, social and economic."* To the attainment of this ideal the Indian Constitution has given a *place of pride* and that is the basis of the new guiding principles of social welfare and common good to which we have just referred.[52]

[46] *The State of Bihar* v. *Maharajadhiraja Sir Kameshwar*, (1952) S.C.R. 889, 997.

[47] *The State of Bihar* v. *Maharajadhiraja Sir Kameshwar*, (1952) S.C.R. 889, 998.

[48] *The State of Bihar* v. *Maharajadhiraja Sir Kameshwar*, (1952) S.C.R. 889, 999.

[49] *Mohd. Hanif Quareshi & Others* v. *The State of Bihar*, (1959) S.C.R. 629, 648.

[50] *Mohd. Hanif Quareshi & Others* v. *The State of Bihar*, (1959) S.C.R. 629, 648.

[51] (1955) S.C.R. I 991, 1001.

[52] *Messrs. Crown Aluminum Works* v. *Their Workmen*, (1958) S.C.R. 651, 660. Emphasis supplied.

A year later, in a dispute involving an Act of Parliament[53] aimed at improving the working conditions and salaries of journalists, the Constitution bench[54] discussed at considerable length the concepts of a "living wage," a "fair wage" and a "minimum wage."[55]

A final illustration of a recent decision in which the Court has explicitly taken note of social and economic policy considerations is that of *Jyoti Pershad* v. *The Administrator for the Union Territory of Delhi.*[56] In this ruling the Constitution bench was unanimous in upholding the validity of the Slum Areas (Improvement and Clearance) Act of 1956 against the arguments of certain landlords that their property rights were unreasonably restricted by this enactment. In the course of its decision, the Court made it quite clear that it was not only aware of evils sought to be removed, but that it supported the efforts of the Union Parliament:

> If law failed to take account of unusual situations of pressing urgency arising in the country, and of the social urges generated by the patterns of thought-evolution and of social consciousness which we witness in the second half of this century, it would have to be written down as having failed in the very purpose of its existence. Where the legislature fulfils its purpose and enacts laws, which in its wisdom, is [*sic*] considered necessary for the solution of what is after all a very human problem, the tests of "reasonableness" have to be viewed in the context of the issues which faced the legislature. In the construction of such laws and particularly in judging of their validity the Courts have necessarily to approach it from the point of view of furthering the social interest which it is the purpose of the legislation to promote, for the Courts are not, in these matters, functioning as it were in vacuo, but as parts of a society which is trying, by enacted law, to solve its problems and achieve a social concord and peaceful adjustment and thus furthering the moral and material progress of the community as a whole.[57]

In recent years the Supreme Court has also moved somewhat away from its earlier position that extrinsic aids are inadmissible in Court. In the *Express Newspapers* case,[58] in order to become educated as to wage levels and working conditions in other industries, the Court quoted liberally from the Report of the Press Commission and the Report of the Committee on Fair Wages. Further,

---

[53] Working Journalists (Conditions of Service) and Miscellaneous Provisions Act, 1955.

[54] *Express Newspapers (Private) Ltd., and Another* v. *The Union of India and Others*, (1959) S.C.R. 12, 13.

[55] *Express Newspapers (Private) Ltd., and Another* v. *The Union of India and Others*, (1959) S.C.R. 12, 79–103.

[56] (1962) S.C.R. II 125.

[57] *Jyoti Pershad* v. *The Administrator for the Union Territory of Delhi*, (1962) S.C.R. II, 148.

[58] (1959) S.C.R. 12.

in the *Quareshi* case, where the Court had to deal with the sensitive matter of cow slaughter, the Court discussed considerations of a religious, nutritive, agricultural and economic nature, and relied heavily on various reports on cow slaughter and cattle preservation, and even discussed the views on the Planning Commission on these subjects.[59]

The Court has also modified its earlier stand on the admissibility of statements of objects and reasons. As was seen earlier, in 1953 the Court said the statement of objects and reasons appended to Bills "should be ruled out as an aid to the construction of a statute."[60] But in 1955, in a minority opinion in the *Subodh Gopal Bose* decision, Justice S. R. Das said that such statements may be referred to "for the limited purpose of ascertaining the conditions prevailing at the time which actuated the sponsor of the Bill to introduce the same and the extent and urgency of the evil which he sought to remedy."[61] Then in 1958 the majority accepted this view of limited reference to statements of objects and reasons.[62]

In summary, though the usual approach of the Supreme Court has been to interpret the Constitution literally without any regard for social and economic policy considerations and without any reference to external aids, there have been exceptions to the general practice. Moreover, most of the exceptions have occurred in recent years, which just may indicate that the Court is coming around to a position of recognizing that many questions which reach the Supreme Court in a modern democratic welfare state are less legal than social, economic or political. It is still too early, however, to speak in terms of any new trend, for the decisions just discussed have been exceptional, and none of the earlier decisions were specifically overruled.[63]

---

[59] (1959) S.C.R. 629, 687ff.

[60] *Aswini Kumar Ghosh and Another* v. *Arabinda Bose and Another*, (1953) S.C.R. 28.

[61] (1954) S.C.R. 587, 628.

[62] *The Commissioner of Income-Tax, Madhya Pradesh and Bhopal* v. *Sodra Devi*, (1958) S.C.R. 1, 17.

[63] While most reluctant to overrule earlier decisions, the Indian Supreme Court does not adhere blindly to the doctrine of *stare decisis*. Thus, in 1955, in the case of *The Bengal Immunity Company Limited* v. *The State of Bihar and Others*, (1955) S.C.R. II 603, the Court by a four to three majority overruled its earlier decision in *The State of Bombay and Another* v. *The United Motors (India) Ltd. and Others*, (1953) S.C.R. 1069. At issue in these cases was the power of the States to impose a tax on the sale or purchase of goods in inter-state commerce. In view of the uncertainty resulting from the Supreme Court decisions, Parliament passed the Constitution (Sixth Amendment) Act, 1956, which amended Article 286 of the Constitution so as to make clear that the legislative power to tax sales taking place in the course of inter-state trade was vested exclusively in the Union Parliament.

Much attention has been given in this and the preceding chapter to the manner in which the Supreme Court has interpreted the Constitution and construed various enactments. In commenting upon the various judicial pronouncements, great stress has been put on the rules of interpretation to which the Court subscribes. But one need not be so naïve as to believe that the judicial decision-making process is a purely mechanical one, and that the values of the judges have no bearing on the outcome of a dispute decided by the Court. Indeed, the Roberts' "slot-machine" simplistic explanation of judicial review[64] is no more credible concerning Indian judges than American.

However, having said this much, it is difficult to say more, for no research has yet been done on such matters as the social and economic values subscribed to by Indian Supreme Court judges, or on the social and political backgrounds of these judges.[65] Indeed, merely to raise such questions in India is regarded as disrespectful and irreverent, for the Supreme Court judges are alleged to be above allowing their personal values to affect their decisions. The myth is propagated that they are aloof from policy considerations, and that if they do subscribe to certain views these would never have any bearing in a dispute before them.

In the absence of data, it is difficult to attach labels such as liberal and conservative to Indian judges. Yet there are at present two members of the Court who, on the basis of both, the opinions they have written and the speeches they have made, can be regarded as having made quite clear their own personal positions on questions of great public importance. One of these is Justice K. Subba Rao, who was elevated to the Supreme Court in 1958 from his earlier post of Chief Justice of the Andhra Pradesh High Court. Subba Rao is well known as a civil libertarian, as the most ardent and outspoken

---

[64] In the important New Deal case of *United States* v. *Butler*, 297 U.S. 1 (1936), Justice Roberts said that "when an act of Congress is appropriately challenged in the courts as not conforming to the constitutional mandate the judicial branch of the Government has only one duty—to lay the article of the Constitution which is invoked beside the statute which is challenged and to decide whether the latter squares with the former. All the court does, or can do, is to announce its considered judgment upon the question. The only power it has, if such it may be called, is the power of judgment. This court neither approves nor condemns any legislative policy. Its delicate and difficult office is to ascertain and declare whether the legislation is in accordance with, or in contravention of, the provisions of the Constitution; and having done that, its duty ends ..." (pp. 62–63).

[65] Further, only recently did the first autobiography of a Supreme Court justice appear: Mehr Chand Mahajan, *Looking Back* (Bombay: Asia Publishing House, 1963). No biographies have appeared.

advocate of individual rights ever to sit on the supreme bench.[66] The other is P. B. Gajendragadkar, who became Chief Justice in February of 1964 upon the retirement of B. P. Sinha. Chief Justice Gajendragadkar, who was once described by former Chief Justice S. R. Das as one whose "heart is literally bleeding for the underdogs,"[67] has on many occasions endorsed the welfare state objectives of the Government, objectives which he finds also embodied in the Constitution. For example, speaking in 1961 he stated that "do not let us also forget that the sooner we attain the ideal of the welfare State the better for democracy in this country."[68]

Although little is known at present about the individual views of Supreme Court judges, it is certain that few, if any, active members of the Congress Party have been appointed to the Supreme Court. Indeed, there is no evidence that any justice of the Supreme Court has ever been a member of the Congress Party. Certainly no active politician has ever been appointed. As was seen earlier in Chapter III, the selection process is designed to reduce to the barest minimum the possibility of political considerations entering into the selection of Supreme Court judges. All who have served on the Supreme Court have been promoted from one of the fifteen High Courts. Moreover, according to former Chief Justice Sinha, it is the Chief Justice of India who really determines who is promoted from a High Court to the Supreme Court.[69] Thus there is, indeed, little room for political considerations to enter in, and if such considerations are of real

[66] Speaking in 1958, Subba Rao, pointing out the ease with which Parliament may set aside inconvenient Supreme Court judgments by amending the Constitution, declared that "it is therefore clear that the Constitution itself contains the seeds of its destruction; for there may be a despot in the womb of the future—we hope that he will be stillborn–who may, by controlling Parliament, seek to repeal the fundamental rights Chapter, and thus by using the same Constitution which brought him into power bring into existence an authoritarian State of Government" (*Proceedings of the Mysore State Lawyers' Conference, 1958* (no publisher or place of publication given), p. 5). In the course of a convocation address at Madras University in 1962, Subba Rao said that "there was now practically no fundamental right of liberty of person and life" (*Hindustan Times,* September 25, 1962).

[67] Taken from a speech by Das on the eve of his retirement. This speech is printed in (1959) S.C.R., pp. xii–xvi; the quotation is from p. xvi.

[68] "Fundamental Obligations of Democracy," *All India Reporter Journal,* XLVIII (1961), p. 22. See also his 1963 speech to the Advocates Association of Western India, "Law, Lawyers and Judges," *Supreme Court Journal,* XXIX (1963), pp. 14–27, and the report in *The Statesman,* April 1, 1964, of a speech in which he said that the judiciary "had a positive role to play in helping changes that tend to promote public good."

[69] Interview with Chief Justice B. P. Sinha, New Delhi, February 14, 1963.

significance at any stage, it would have to be at the time when prospective Supreme Court was first appointed to the High Court.[70]

Irrespective of the political, social and economic backgrounds of Supreme Court judges, that clashes have taken place since 1950 between the Government leaders and the judges is hardly surprising in view of the apparent different approach they have taken to their respective tasks. Free India's leaders, having been frustrated for so long by the presence of a colonial ruler, brought a burning zeal and enthusiasm to the discharge of their new responsibilities. Flushed with the pride of victory after decades of opposition to the British, they were extremely eager to get on with the tasks of legislating social and economic justice, and of eliminating quickly all obstacles to the creation of the welfare state. Though dedicated to democratic methods, the aspirations of the new leaders were nothing short of revolutionary. The State, which under the British had been a static thing functioning largely in order to maintain law and order, was transformed after independence into a dynamic organization which undertook vast responsibilities.

The judges, on the other hand, bred in the old tradition of the judiciary, maintained a posture of aloofness from what went on about them. Whereas the leaders of the Government were anxious to usher into being the welfare state, the judges seemed to have approached their task in a rather leisurely manner. Moreover, as Sri Ram Sharma has written, the judges "could be naturally expected to look askance on persons in high places. ... They do not possess the civil servants compelling virtue of faithfulness to the powers that be. They did not need the self-effacement which a civil servant was expected to practise."[71]

In view of the fact that the Supreme Court's powers have been diminished since 1950 by a piecemeal abolition of judicial review and by the restoration with retrospective effect of many enactments declared void by the Court, and in view of its fallen prestige, the two most important questions to consider in the final pages of this chapter are (i) what is the most important function which the Supreme Court of India should perform in an aspiring modern welfare state, and (ii) how can the Court perform this function most effectively, while at the same time maintaining, if not increasing, its role in the political system?

The single most important and most difficult function for the Supreme Court of India to perform in the foreseeable future is that of reconciling freedom and justice for the individual with the needs of a modern government charged with the promotion of far-reaching social and economic reforms, and which exercises

---

[70] The Law Commission in its *Fourteenth Report* did allege that "executive influence" was a key factor in some appointments to the High Courts. I, 69.

[71] "The Supreme Court in the Indian Constitution," *Public Law* (1958) p. 121.

a high degree of control over the individual. The framers of the Constitution having included in the Constitution a list of fundamental rights as well as having set forth the goals of a welfare state, the Supreme Court's major function and responsibility is to seek to establish the most proper and most equitable balance between the legitimate rights of the individual and the needs of the Government.

There is, of course, no more difficult task for any court to perform in any modern state than that of reconciling individual rights with the public interest, as defined by the legislatures and executives. Under any circumstances it calls for judicial statesmanship of the highest order. In India, however, this function is all the more important in view of the fact that at the Union level, and in most of the States, opposition to the Congress Party has been negligible since 1950. At the Union level, the Congress Party has never held fewer than seventy-two per cent of the seats in Parliament. Thus the Congress Party is able to legislate into beings its programs without having to contend with much opposition. In the absence of meaningful political opposition which could ordinarily be expected to serve as a curb on legislative and executive arbitrariness, the Supreme Court's position increases in importance because it is really the only forum which can provide redress against legislation and actions of the executive which are unmindful of constitutional limitations and guarantees of individual rights. The Indian press, although probably the freest in Asia, is not able to be an effective check upon an occasionally over-zealous Government. The inadequacy of the press is in part due to the distressingly low literacy rate; it is difficult to alert the public to important matters if they cannot read. Thus it is not possible to speak of a vigilant public opinion on many issues in India. Moreover, the largely illiterate Indian masses are lacking not only the democratic tradition, but also the more basic tradition of standing up to battle for their rights against the remote authorities who have for centuries pushed them around. If those who control the Government are poor defenders of individual rights and unwilling to operate within the constitutional framework, the masses, the theoretical bulwark of democracy, can hardly be counted upon in India to rise to the defense of unfamiliar rights and institutions. In short, if there is to be any effective arbiter between the Government and the individual, the judiciary, particularly the Supreme Court, will have to perform this function.

Even if the Supreme Court would wish to avoid this responsibility, it is unable to escape it because the Constitution provides explicitly for judicial review, and confers upon the Court the duty of making certain that the fundamental rights are not infringed. The Indian Supreme Court has never had to assume the power of judicial review; this power has been literally thrust upon it. Moreover, given the extensiveness of the remedies available to an aggrieved individual under

Article 32, and the fact that much welfare state legislation is bound to be seen by some as affecting adversely their private rights, the Court is called upon very frequently to perform a very difficult and delicate balancing function.

This is a function which the Federal Court seldom performed. Between 1937 and 1950, in the absence of a Bill of Rights, and in view of the fact that the colonial government was usually content to maintain the status quo, the Federal Court faced few situations in which it had to harmonize individual rights and social control. To be sure, several of the most prominent Federal Court decisions concerned personal liberty, but these few were exceptional. The typical case before the Federal Court was one which called for a judicial delimitation of the subject-matter areas in which a legislature could operate. Since 1950, however, a major portion of the cases decided by the Supreme Court have involved disputes between the State and an individual. Indeed, it appears that the largest single litigant before the Supreme Court has been the State. Each time the Court decides one of these disputes it is compelled to choose between the competing demands of the individual and the State.

There can be no doubt, then, that with the advent of the new Constitution the Supreme Court was placed in a very strategic position, and endowed with powers far greater than those exercised by its predecessor. Notwithstanding the fact that the framers sought to impose certain limitations on the scope of judicial review, it is evident that the power to declare unconstitutional an enactment which the Court finds in violation of one of the fundamental rights represents a subtraction from unlimited majority rule, and the conferment of important responsibilities on the Supreme Court.

The Court's major function having been established as that of reconciling freedom and justice for the individual with the needs of a modern government, remaining to be considered is the question of how can the Supreme Court be most effective in performing this task. Firstly, the Supreme Court might well acknowledge that the power of judicial review requires the Court to exercise functions which are essentially political in character. Any tribunal which is empowered to declare unconstitutional, and thus void and inoperative, a law passed by elected representatives of the people, is performing a function which is in a very real sense political—not necessarily in the sense of partisanship, but in the sense of policy-making. It is very clear that most of the important political issues of the day eventually reach the Supreme Court of India in the form of litigation. What David B. Truman said of the United States Supreme Court applies with equal force to the Indian Supreme Court: "To assert that such decisions are not policy choices but rather the largely automatic result of technical legal procedures and constitutional knowledge is to perpetuate a myth that is highly inaccurate, however useful it may be in inducing acceptance to the

Court's views."[72] In short, the Court should acknowledge that in addition to interpreting the Constitution and laws, it is capable also of making law.

Similarly, it should acknowledge that in interpreting the Constitution and enactments it must grapple with the stresses and strains of a changing society, and that it must make choices between conflicting values. In the words of Cardozo, "the great tides and currents which engulf the rest of men, do not turn aside in their course, and pass the judges by."[73] In short, it should be recognized that a great deal of discretion is present in constitutional and statutory interpretation, that the Court can restrict or expand a provision, and that its task is much more than a purely technical one.

It must also take note of the aims and aspirations embodied by the framers in the Constitution and by the legislators in statutes, and seek, by a liberal interpretation of these, to further these aims and aspirations. It must demonstrate in its decisions an awareness of the social and economic policies of the Government which reflect shifts in public opinion, must acknowledge that the concept of a social welfare state has been accepted by the majority of Indians, and must be reluctant to declare invalid legislation passed by the elected representatives of the people. The Indian Supreme Court simply cannot afford to ignore the dominant values of the society, or what Holmes termed the "felt necessities of the times."[74] Indeed, in order to maintain its institutional importance, much less maximize its own values, it must be attuned to the values of the majority, and seek to exercise its functions in harmony with these accepted values.

In order to ascertain accurately the aims and purposes of the Constitution and statutes, and the political, social and economic policy considerations which may not be explicit in them, the Supreme Court might be wise to reconsider the utility of the traditional rules of interpretation which forbid the use of extrinsic aids such as the debates of the Constituent Assembly and Parliament, important committee reports, and the like. The Indian Supreme Court's customary refusal to utilize extrinsic aids and its insistence on a rigid adherence to the letter of the law is based on traditional British rules of statutory interpretation; in refusing to consult such aids the Court has cited English decisions and authoritative treatises such as *Maxwell on the Interpretation of Statutes* and *Craies on Statute Law*.[75] In an aspiring welfare state, however, a more prudent approach to constitutional

---

[72] *The Governmental Process: Political Interests and Public Opinion* (New York: Alfred A. Knopf, 1951), p. 481.

[73] Benjamin N. Cardozo, *The Nature off the Judicial Process* (New Haven: Yale University Press, 1921), p. 168.

[74] Oliver Wendell Holmes, *The Common Law* (Boston: Little, Brown and Co., 1881), p. 1.

[75] *A. K. Gopalan v. The State of Madras*, (1950) S.C.R. 88, 111.

and statutory interpretation might be that of the late Justice Felix Frankfurter, who once wrote that "if the purpose of construction is the ascertainment of meaning, nothing that is logically relevant should be excluded."[76] Indeed, if judicial review is an inherently political function, and if the Court must attempt to maintain a balance between liberty and authority, it seems clear that self-imposed traditional techniques of interpretation, which may prevent the Court from understanding fully the intent of the framers and legislators, should be reappraised, modified, and adapted to the new responsibilities the Supreme Court must shoulder.[77]

Finally, and very important, the Court must distinguish between constitutional and statutory interpretation, and give the Constitution a markedly more imaginative and liberal interpretation. An eminently political document, it should hardly be interpreted in a narrow, mechanical and literal fashion. If the Indian Constitution is to prevail as a norm for the political, social and economic life of the nation, it must be interpreted in such a way as to enable it to serve the expanding needs of the society it is supposed to govern. Powers contained in a constitution ought to be construed liberally in favor of the public good; the Court must be reluctant to play the role of a seeker of loopholes, and must seek to assist, rather than frustrate, the implementation of the developmental programs. The rule of law and narrow legalisms must not be confused.[78]

---

[76] Frankfurter, Felix, "Some Reflections on the Reading of Statutes," *Columbia Law Review*, XLVII (1947), p. 541.

[77] Professor Sheldon D. Elliott, who, as noted earlier, served as a visiting consultant to the Indian Law Institute in 1960, has written in regard to the Indian Supreme Court's refusal to consult extrinsic aids that "artificial myopia should not blur the court's vision in reviewing all possible sources of enlightenment as to the true legislative meaning, intent and purpose." "Statutory Interpretation and the Welfare State" (p. 268).

[78] Somewhat similar observations were made recently by Professor Arthur T. von Mehren, who served recently as a visiting professor at the Indian Law Institute and consultant on legal education for the Ford Foundation in New Delhi. Although writing in very general and often euphemistic terms (e.g., "The Indian judicial process is in an interesting, though not satisfactory position."), he was quite forthright in his criticisms of legal education in India: "Nor does Indian legal education today produce, by and large, the men and the minds that a truly creative judicial process requires. India has some outstanding jurists but it is perhaps fair to say that they are outstanding in spite of—not because of—the legal education they received in India. Instruction proceeds by the lecture method. These lectures, so far as my observations go, are almost exclusively devoted to a presentation of the formal structure of legal rule and doctrine. Little attention is paid either to the policies that underlie and inform the legal principles discussed or to the processes of growth and development through which the legal system adapts existing rules

It is not submitted that these suggestions as to how the Supreme Court might best proceed are universally applicable, or even that these are prudent suggestions for courts in other developing states. But given the realities of the Indian situation, especially the overwhelming power of the Congress Party and the ease with which the Constitution may be amended to override decisions of the Supreme Court, these do seem to be prudent suggestions for the Supreme Court of India to consider. If the Court is concerned with its institutional preservation, which one must assume it is, it can ill afford the tension which has developed between it and the national leadership. Hopefully, the recent judgments in which the Supreme Court has moved away from its earlier, rather mechanical and unimaginative approach to constitutional and statutory interpretation are indications of a new trend.

---

or announces new ones" ("The Judicial Process with Particular Reference to the United States and to India," *Journal of the Indian Law Institute*, V (April–June, 1963), p. 279).

7 Summary and Conclusions

In summarizing the evolvement of the paramount judiciary in India between 1921 and 1964, one can single out at least ten events which are of special importance. In listing these chronologically, the first would be Sir Hari Singh Gour's resolution, introduced during the first session of the Central Legislative Assembly in 1921, in which he urged the establishment of an indigenous appellate tribunal. Gour's resolution marked the beginning of efforts made to persuade the colonial authorities, and Indian nationalist leaders as well, that there was real need and justification for the creation of a central judicial institution on Indian soil. The purposes Gour sought to achieve were really quite modest. He sought the establishment in India of a court which would be empowered to decide civil and criminal appeals from the High Courts of British India, and a reduction in the number of such appeals which for decades had gone directly from the High Courts to the Judicial Committee of the Privy Council in London. Although Gour and others could offer many substantial arguments in support of their proposals, their efforts met with failure for several years, chiefly because key Indian leaders were not convinced that India's interests would be served best by decreasing the role of the Privy Council, which over the years had earned a reputation for impartiality and integrity which placed it in a category apart from all other colonial institutions.

The next development of significance took place in 1930 at the opening session of the Indian Round Table Conference in London. At this conference, spokesmen for the Indian States indicated a willingness to participate in a federation with the Provinces of British India, and the leaders of each side agreed that should a federation emerge, a Federal Court would be essential to interpret the constitution and settle disputes which might arise between the federated units.

This general agreement, however, concerned the creation of a central tribunal which would exercise only a purely federal jurisdiction. Considerable controversy was evident on the question of conferring a general appellate, not merely federal, jurisdiction on the proposed court. The result was a compromise, for the Government of India Act of 1935 made provision for a Federal Court without a general appellate jurisdiction, but which might at some future date take over the appellate jurisdiction of the Privy Council.

A third milestone was the inauguration of the Federal Court in 1937. Although this event marked the establishment of India's first central judicial institution, this beginning was quite unspectacular. Composed of only two puisne judges and a Chief Justice, the Federal Court was smaller than any of the Provincial High Courts and looked little like an important institution. Its jurisdiction was very limited, the subcontinent-wide federation for which it was to serve as the demarcator of spheres of authority had failed to materialize, and its decisions were subject to review by the Privy Council.

For a few years, the existence of the Federal Court was almost unnoticed, for it handed down only twenty-seven decisions and two advisory opinions over the first four and one-half years. But in April of 1942 the Federal Court handed down the first of a series of decisions in which it either boldly struck down provisions of the infamous sedition, preventive detention and special criminal court ordinances and legislation, or declared that the executive had not acted within the limits of its authority. All but one of these decisions were unanimous, with the British Chief Justice joining his Indian colleagues in restraining the alien executive from interfering arbitrarily with individual liberties. These decisions were proof of the resoluteness, impartiality and independence of the Federal Court, and they served to inspire a high degree of confidence in the Court. Thus these World War II decisions must be regarded as a fourth milestone in the evolution of the paramount judiciary in India.

The achievement of national independence had hardly an effect on the functioning of the Federal Court. But just over two years later a very significant step was taken by the Constituent Assembly when it passed the Abolition of Privy Council Jurisdiction Act. The fact that judicial autonomy was delayed until over two years after the achievement of national independence indicates that considerable thought was given to desirability of severing all ties with the Privy Council. In terms of the evolvement of the Indian judiciary, the effect of severing ties with the Privy Council was largely psychological, for as long as India maintained these ties the Federal Court was looked upon by many as an intermediate appellate tribunal, notwithstanding the fact that the Privy Council reversed Federal Court decisions only five times.

A sixth event of great significance was the replacement of the Federal Court by the Supreme Court in 1950 when the Constitution of India became operative.

Although continuity was apparent in that judges of the Federal Court continued to serve on the Supreme Court, the jurisdiction and powers of the Supreme Court bear little resemblance to those of its predecessor. Sitting at the summit of a pyramidal and unified judicial system, endowed with an extraordinarily wide jurisdiction, and explicitly authorized to exercise the power of judicial review, the Supreme Court was placed in a position of central importance.

Seventh in this listing must be the decision of the Supreme Court in the case of *A. K. Gopalan v. The State of Madras*. This was the first case in which the Supreme Court was called upon to interpret the new Constitution, the first to involve the fundamental rights, the first to involve the controversial Preventive Detention Act, the first in which an individual bypassed all lower courts and took his grievance directly to the Supreme Court, and the first in which the Supreme Court, in the exercise of its new powers, declared unconstitutional a portion of a Parliamentary enactment. Understandably, the *Gopalan* decision has been more commented upon by foreign writers than any other decision of the Court. In one important respect, however, the *Gopalan* ruling is atypical, for in this decision the Court was modest in defining its own powers and role vis-à-vis Parliament. While it is true that the Court started off on a modest and self-distrustful note regarding its powers of review in this case, this certainly has not been the general approach of the Supreme Court in cases involving other fundamental rights. Indeed, in many of the cases involving property rights the Court has been adamant in insisting that property rights may not be restricted unless the enactment in question has satisfied one or more of the tests applied by the Court.

The next important development took place in 1951 when the Supreme Court handed down its ruling in the *Dorairajan* case. This decision must be regarded as one of the most important ever rendered by the Supreme Court, for it was the first to involve both the fundamental rights and the directive principles, and the Court in its decision not only enforced the fundamental right over the directive principle, but went so far as to describe the fundamental rights as "sacrosanct" and the directive principles as "subsidiary." Whereas the Government made it quite clear that it would be guided by the directive principles, the Court made no effort to harmonize these with the fundamental rights guaranteed by the Constitution. This decision, and the late Prime Minister Nehru's comments upon it in Parliament, illustrate very well the divergence which prevailed at least until the late 1950s between the approaches of the Supreme Court and the Government toward their respective roles and responsibilities.

Ninth in this listing, and the single most important constitutional development since 1950, is the enactment of the Constitution (Fourth Amendment) Act in 1955. Precipitated by several Supreme Court decisions concerning the degree to which property rights were protected by the Constitution, the Fourth

Amendment had the effect of limiting the Court's review powers in cases involving restriction and acquisition of property rights. If proof was necessary that the Government intended to proceed with its various programs affecting property rights irrespective of decisions of the Supreme Court, or that judicial review in India does not mean judicial supremacy, the Fourth Amendment provides the relevant evidence.

A tenth and final development of significance is the Supreme Court's shift toward a more liberal interpretation of the Constitution, which has become perceptible since the late 1950s. In a few recent decisions, the Court has discussed rather freely the social and economic policy considerations which are either explicit or implicit in the Constitution and various enactments, and has even endorsed the directive principles as worthy goals. While such decisions have been too few to justify speaking in terms of a new trend, they may indicate that the Court is attempting earnestly to accommodate both itself and the Constitution with the welfare state aims of the Government. Important in this regard is the fact that the present Chief Justice is himself an advocate of a modern democratic welfare state.

Although the Supreme Court has been treated here as the lineal descendant of the Federal Court, the differences between the two institutions are much more notable than the similarities. Small in size, limited in jurisdiction, and functioning during the tumultuous twilight of the British *raj* and the difficult period which followed national independence and the partition of the subcontinent, the Federal Court was an institution of peripheral importance. Few important questions were submitted to the Federal Court for its adjudication; indeed, the major questions which stirred the subcontinent between 1937 and 1950 were hardly justiciable.

The real importance of the Federal Court lies in the fact that it was a stable and respected institution which functioned according to the terms of its charter during the most critical period in the history of modern India, and that in spite of the severe handicaps under which it operated, it was independent of the executive. Indeed, it demonstrated all the qualities—independence, impartiality, integrity, and dignity—which Indians associated with the Privy Council, and which they wished to have emulated by the judiciary in India. The Federal Court earned the respect and confidence of the Indian public, and when the Supreme Court replaced the Federal Court in 1950, it inherited this invaluable legacy.

In contrast with the Federal Court, the present Supreme Court of India occupies a position of central importance. Its jurisdiction is so extraordinarily extensive that there are very few questions or disputes which can escape the scrutiny of the Court. Indeed, literally thousands of decisions have been handed down by the Supreme Court since 1950. Provision for judicial review of Union and State legislation is made explicit in the new Constitution, and the Supreme Court is empowered to declare unconstitutional legislation and actions of the executive which it finds beyond the scope of the division of powers set forth in the Constitution, or which it finds in violation of one or more of the fundamental rights guaranteed by the Constitution. The Federal Court exercised the former type of judicial review, but not the latter variety, for the 1935 Act did not contain a list of protected fundamental rights.

The Supreme Court has passed upon such a wide variety of disputes and has handed down such a large number of decisions that one has to be somewhat arbitrary in talking about one function of the Court which seems to be of the most importance. However, the decisions of the Supreme Court which have earned the most notoriety since 1950 have been those in which the Court has sought to enforce the fundamental rights against what it has regarded as encroachments upon these rights by the Union and State legislatures and executives. Important though the Court's role may be as the supreme civil and criminal appellate tribunal, there can be little doubt that the most important function performed by the Supreme Court in the Indian polity is that of seeking to reconcile freedom and justice for the individual with the needs of a modern government charged with the promotion of far-reaching social and economic reforms. The Court has found this task to be a difficult one, for a number of its decisions have provoked amendments to the Constitution which have had the effect of limiting its review powers, of reviving legislation earlier declared unconstitutional by the Court, and of restricting the scope of the fundamental rights. Whereas decisions of the Federal Court which embarrassed the British won the acclaim of the Indian nationalist leaders and served to increase the prestige of the Federal Court, decisions of the Supreme Court which have thwarted the Government of the Republic of India have produced the opposite effect. The ease with which the Indian Constitution may be amended in order to overcome the effect of a Supreme Court decision indicates that while the Court's jurisdiction is extraordinarily wide, its ultimate power is limited. Ultimately, the Constitution means what the Congress Party says it means, and not what the Court wills. Judicial review has certainly not meant judicial supremacy in India.

Selected Bibliography

I. Cases Cited

Aher Raja Khima v. *The State of Saurashtra*, (1955) S.C.R. II 1285.

A. K. Gopalan v. *State of Madras*, (1950) S.C.R. 88.

Albert West Meads v. *The King*, (1948) F.C.R. 67.

A. L. S. P. P. L. Subrahmanyan Chettiar v. *Muttaswami Goundan*, (1941) F.C.R. 4.

A. L. S. P. P. L. Subrahmanyan Chettiar v. *Muttuswami Goundan, Advocate-General of Madras*, (1940) F.C.R. 188.

Ambard v. *Attorney-General for Trinidad and Tobago*, (1936) A.C. 335.

Arnold v. *The King Emperor*, (1914) A.C. 644.

Asiatic Steam Navigation Co., Ltd. v. *Sub-Lt. Arabinda Chakravarti*, (1959) S.C.R. Supp. I 979.

Aswini Kumar Ghose and Another v. *Arabinda Bose and Another*, (1953) S.C.R. 1.

Attar Singh and Others v. *The State of U.P.*, (1959) S.C.R. Supp. I 928.

Baladin and Others v. *The State of Uttar Pradesh*, A.I.R. 1956 S.C. 181.

Bank of Commerce, Limited, Khulna v. *Amulya Krishna Basu Roy Chowdhury and Others*, (1947) F.C.R. 54 P.C.

Bank of Commerce Ltd, v. *Amulya Krisha Basu Roy Chovdhury; Bank of Commerce Ltd.* v. *Brojo Mal Mitra*, (1944) F.C.R. 126.

Bank of Commerce, Ltd. v. *Kunja Behari Kar and Upendra Chandra Kar*, (1944) F.C.R. 370.

Basantra Chandra Ghose v. *The King Emperor*, (1944) F.C.R. 295; 1945 F.C.R. 81.

Bechan Chero v. *The King Emperor and Jubba Mallah and Ramphal Dhanuk* v. *The King Emperor*, (1944) F.C.R. 178.

Bengal Chemical and Pharmaceutical Works Ltd. v. *Their Employees*, A.I.R. 1959 S.C. 633.

Bengal Immunity Company Limited v. *The State of Bihar and Others*, (1955) S.C.R. II 603.

Bhagwan Das v. *The State of Rajasthan*, (1957) S.C.R. 854.

Bharat Bank Ltd., Delhi v. *Employees of the Bharat Bank Ltd., Delhi*, (1950) S.C.R. 459.

Bhola Prasad v. *The King-Emperor*, (1942) F.C.R. 17.

Brahma Prakash Sharma and Others v. *The State of Uttar Pradesh*, (1953) S.C.R. 1169.

Brij Bhushan and Another v. *The State of Delhi*, (1950) S.C.R. 605.

Chiranjit Lal Chowdhuri v. *The Union of India and Others*, (1950) S.C.R. 869.

Clerks Depot and Cashiers of the Calcutta Tramway Co., Ltd. v. *Calcutta Tramway Co.*, A.I.R. 1957 S.C. 78.

Commissioner of Income-Tax, Madhya Pradesh and Bhopal v. *Sodra Devi*, (1958) S.C.R. 1.

Darshan Singh v. *State of Punjab*, (1953) S.C.R. 319.

Daryao and Others v. *The State of U. P. and Others*, (1962) S.C.R. I 574.

Deep Chand v. *The State of Rajasthan*, (1962) S.C.R. I 622.

Devkishindas v. *The King Emperor*, (1944) F.C.R. 165.

Dhakeswari Cotton Mills Ltd. v. *Commissioner of Income Tax, West Bengal*, (1955) S.C.R. I 941.

Dr. Ram Krishnan Bhardwaj v. *The State of Delhi and Others*, (1953) S.C.R. 708.

Durga Shankar Mehta v. *Thakur Raghuraj Singh and Others*, (1955) S.C.R. I 267.

Dwarkadas Shrinivas of Bombay v. *The Sholapur Spinning and Weaving Co. Ltd., and Others*, (1954) S.C.R. 674.

Election Commission, India v. *Saka Venkata Subba Rao*, (1953) S.C.R. 1144.

Errol MacKay and Others v. *Oswald Forbes*, A.I.R. 1940 P.C. 16.

Express Newspapers (Private) Ltd., and Another v. *The Union of India and Others*, (1959) S.C.R. 12.

Gill and Another v. *The King*, (1948) F.C.R. 19 P.C.

Governor-General in *Council* v. *Province of Madras*, (1943) F.C.R. 1; (1945) F.C.R. 179 P.C.

Greene v. *Secretary of State for Home Affairs*, (1942) A.C. 284.

Hanumant v. *The State of Madhya Pradesh and Raojibhai* v. *The State of Madhya Pradesh*, (1952) S.C.R. 1091.

Hanskumar Kishanchand v. *The Union of India*, (1959) S.C.R. 1177.

Haripada Dey v. *The State of West Bengal and Another*, (1956) S.C.R. 639.

Hem Raj v. *State of Aimer*, (1954) S.C.R. 1133.

H. H. B. Gill v. *The King Emperor and Anil Lahiri* v. *The King Emperor*, (1946) F.C.R. 123.

High Commissioner for India and High Commissioner for Pakistan v. *I. M. Lall*, (1948) F.C.R. 44 P.C.

Hori Ram Singh v. *The Crown*, (1939) F.C.R. 159.

Hori Ram Singh v. *The King-Emperor*, (1940) F.C.R. 15 P.C.

Hulas Narain Singh and Others v. *Deen Mohammad Mian and Others*, A.I.R. 1943 F.C. 9.

Hulas Narain Singh and Others v. *The Province of Bihar*, (1942) F.C.R. 1.

Hulas Narain Singh v. *Deen Mohammad Mian and Others*, A.I.R. 1944 F.C. 24.

India General Navigation and Railway Co., Ltd. v. *Their Workmen*, (1960) S.C.R. II 1.

In re Abraham Mallory Dillet, (1887) 12 A.C. 459.

In re Hira Lal Dixit and Two Others, (1955) S.C.R. I 677.

In re the Allocation of Lands and Buildings in a Chief Commissioner's Province, (1943) F.C.R. 20.

In re the Berubari Union and Exchange of Enclaves, (1960) S.C.R. III 250.

In re the Central Provinces and Berar Sales of Motor Spirit and Lubricants Taxation Act, 1938, (1939) F.C.R. 18.

In re the Delhi Laws Act, 1912, (1951) S.C.R. 747.

In re the Editor, Printer and Publisher of "The Times of India," (1953) S.C.R. 215.

In re the Hindu Women's Rights to Property Act, 1937, and the Hindu Women's Rights to Property (Amendment) Act, 1938, (1941) F.C.R. 12.

In re the Kerala Education Bill, 1957, (1959) S.C.R. 995.

In re the Power of the Federal Legislature to Provide for the Levy of an Estate Duty in Respect of Property Other Than Agricultural Land, Passing Upon the Death of Any Person, (1944) F.C.R. 317.

Jaigobind Singh and Others v. Lachmi Narain Ram and Others, (1940) F.C.R. 61.

Jammu and Kashmir and Others v. Thakur Ganga Singh and Another, (1960) S.C.R. II 346.

Jatindra Nath Gupta v. The Province of Bihar, (1949) F.C.R. 595.

J. K. Gas Plant Manufacturing Co., (Rampur) Ltd. and Others v. The King Emperor, (1947) F.C.R. 141.

Jyoti Pershad v. The Administrator for the Union Territory of Delhi, (1962) S.C.R. II 125.

Kailash Nath v. State of U. P., A.I.R. 1957 S.C. 790.

Kalawati and Another v. The State of Himachal Pradesh, (1953) S.C.R. 546.

Kameshwar Singh v. State of Bihar, A.I.R. 1951 Patna 91.

Kapildeo Singh v. The King, (1949–50) F.C.R. 834.

Karimbul Kunhikoman v. State of Kerala, (1962) S.C.R. Supp. I 829.

Karnani Properties Ltd. v. Augustin, (1957) S.C.R. 20.

Kathi Raning Rawat v. The State of Saurashtra, (1952) S.C.R. 435.

Kavalappara Kottarathil Kochunni Moopil Nayar v. The State of Madras and Others, (1955) S.C.R. Supp. II 316.

Keshavlal Lallubhai Patel and Others v. Lalbhai Trikumlal Mills Ltd., (1959) S.C.R. 213.

Keshavan Madhava Menon v. The State of Bombay, (1951) S.C.R. 228.

Keshav Talpade v. The King Emperor, (1943) F.C.R. 49.

Khushal Rao v. The State of Bombay, (1958) S.C.R. 552.

King-Emperor v. Benoari Lall Sarma, (1945) F.C.R. 161 P.C.

King Emperor v. Benoari Lall Sarma and Others, (1943) F.C.R. 96.

King v. Halliday, 1917 A.C. 260.

King Emperor v. Keshav Talpade, (1944) F.C.R, 59.

King Emperor v. Sibnath Banerjee, (1944) F.C.R. 1.

King-Emperor v. Sibnath Banerji, (1945) F.C.R. 195 P.C.

Kishori Lal v. Governor in Council, Punjab, (1940) F.C.R. 12.

K. L. Gauba v. The Hon'ble The Chief Justice and Judges of the High Court of Judicature at Lahore and Another, (1941) F.C.R. 54.

Lakhi Narayan Das v. The Province of Bihar, (1949) F.C.R. 693.

Lakhpat Ram v. Behari Lal Misir and Others, (1939) F.C.R. 121.

Lieutenant Hector Thomas Huntley v. The King Emperor, (1944) F.C.R. 262.

Liversidge v. Anderson, 1942 A.C. 206.

Machindar Shivaji Mahar v. The King, (1949–50) F.C.R. 827.

Manikkasundara Bhattar and Others v. R. S. Nayudu and Others, (1946) F.C.R. 67.

McCulloch v. Maryland, 4 Wheat. 316 (1819).

Megh Raj and Another v. Allah Rakhia and Others, (1942) F.C.R. 109; (1947) F.C.R. 77 P.C.

Messrs. Crown Aluminum Works v. Their Workmen, (1958) S.C.R. 651.

Mill Manager, Model Mills v. *Dharam Das,* A.I.R. 1958 S.C. 311.

Mohammed Amin Brothers Ltd. and Others v. *Dominion of India and Others,* (1949–50) F.C.R. 842.

Mohd. Hanif Quareshi & Others v. *The State of Bihar,* (1959) S.C.R. 629.

Muir Mills Co., Ltd. v. *Suti Mills Mazdoor Union, Kanpur,* (1955) S.C.R. I 991.

Mukunda Murari Chakravarti and Others v. *Pabitramoy Ghosh and Others,* (1944) F.C.R. 351.

Mst. Atiga Begum and Others v. *The United Provinces and Others,* (1941) F.C.R. 7.

Nar Singh and Another v. *The State of Uttar Pradesh,* (1955) S.C.R. I 238.

Niharendu Datt Majamdar v. *The King Emperor,* (1942) F.C.R. 38.

Nirmal Bose v. *Union of India,* A.I.R. 1959 Calcutta 506.

North-West Frontier Province v. *Suraj Narain Anand,* (1942) F.C.R. 66; (1948) F.C.R. 103 P.C.

N. S. Krishnaswami Ayyangar and Others v. *Perimal Goundan (since deceased) and Others,* A.I.R. 1950 P.C. 105.

Pandit M. S. M. Sharma v. *Shri Sri Krishna Sinha and Others,* (1959) S.C.R. Supp. I 806.

Pashupati Bharti v. *The Secretary of State for India in Council and Another,* (1939) F.C.R. 13.

Pennsylvania Coal Company v. *Mahon,* 260 U. S. 393 (1922).

Piare Dusadh and Others v. *The King Emperor,* (1944) F.C.R. 61.

Prafulla Kumar Mukherjee and Others v. *Bank of Commerce, Limited, Khulna,* (1947) F.C.R. 28 P.C.

Pritam Singh v. *The State,* (1950) S.C.R. 453.

Province of Madras v. *Boddu Paidanna & Sons,* (1942) F.C.R. 90.

Punjab Province v. *Daulat Singh and Others,* (1942) F.C.R. 67; (1946) F.C.R. 1 P.C.

Raigarh Jute Mills v. *Eastern Railway,* A.I.R. 1958 S.C. 525.

Rai Sahib Ram Javaya Kapur and Others v. *The State of Punjab,* (1955) S.C.R. II 225.

Raja Suriya Pal Singh v. *The State of U. P. and Another,* (1952) S.C.R. 1056.

Raja Suryapalsingh v. *The Uttar Pradesh Government,* A.I.R. 1951 Allahabad 674.

Raj Krushna Bose v. *Binod Kanungo and Others,* (1954) S.C.R. 913.

Raleigh Investment Company, Limited v. *Governor-General in Council,* (1947) F.C.R. 59 P.C.

Ramgarh State v. *The Province of Bihar,* (1948) F.C.R. 79.

Ramkrishna Dalmia v. *Shri Justice S. R. Tendolkar,* (1959) S.C.R. 279.

Rao Bahadur Kunwar Lal Singh v. *The Central Provinces and Berar,* (1944) F.C.R. 284.

Rashid Ahmed v. *Municipal Board, Kairana,* (1950) S.C.R. 566.

Reference by the President of India under Article 143(1) of the Constitution, 1964 S.C.J. 51.

Rex v. *Abdul Majid,* (1949) F.C.R. 29.

Rex v. *Basudev,* (1949) F.C.R. 657.

Rm. Ar. Ar. Rm. Ar. Ar. Umayal Achi v. *Lakshmi Achi and Others,* (1944) F.C.R. 1.

R. Muthammal (Died) and Paramesvari Thayammal v. *Sri Subramaniaswami Devasthanan, Tiruchendur,* (1960) S.C.R. II 729.

Rohtas Industries Ltd. v. *Brijinandan Pandey and Others,* A.I.R. 1957 S.C. 1.

Romesh Thappar v. *The State of Madras,* (1950) S.C.R. 594.

R. Subbarayan and Others v. *The King Emperor,* (1944) F.C.R. 161.

Saghir Ahmad v. *The State of U. P. and Others,* (1955) S.C.R. 707.

Sangram Singh v. *Election Tribunal, Kotah, Bhurey Lal Baya,* (1955) S.C.R. II 1.

Santosh Kumar v. *Bhai Mool Singh,* (1958) S.C.R. 1211.

Sanwat Singh and Others v. *State of Rajasthan,* (1961) S.C.R. III 120.

Sardar Syedna Taher Saifuddin Saheb v. *The State of Bombay,* (1958) S.C.R. 1007.

Sarwan Singh v. *The State of Punjab,* (1957) S.C.R. 953.

Shamasao V. Parulekar v. *The District Magistrate, Thana, Bombay and Two Others,* (1952) S.C.R. 683.

Shrimati Vidya Verma, Through Next Friend R. V. S. Mani v. *Dr. Shiv Narain Verma,* (1955) S.C.R. II 983.

Shyamakant Lal v. *Rambhajan Singh and Others,* (1939) F.C.R. 193.

Sidheswar Ganguly v. *The State of West Bengal,* (1958) S.C.R. 749.

Sir Igbal Ahmad v. *Allahabad Bench of the Allahabad High Court,* (1949–1950) F.C.R. 813.

S. Kuppuswami Rao v. *The King,* (1947) F.C.R. 180.

Smt. Ujjam Bai v. *State of Uttar Pradesh,* (1963) S.C.R. I 778.

Sodhi Shamser Singh v. *The State of Punjab,* A.I.R. 1954 S.C. 276.

Sree Meenakshi Mills, Ltd. v. *Their Workmen,* (1958) S.C.R. 878.

Srinivasa Bhat v. *State of Madras,* A.I.R. 1951 Madras 70.

Srinivas Ram Kumar v. *Mahabir Prasad and Others,* (1951) S.C.R. 277.

Sri Ram Ram Narain Medhi v. *The State of Bombay,* (1959) S.C.R. Supp. I 489.

Sri Sankari Prasad Singh Deo v. *Union of India and State of Bihar,* (1952) S.C.R. 89.

State of Bihar v. *Maharajadhiraja Sir Kameshwar Singh of Darbhanga and Others,* (1952) S.C.R. 889.

State of Bombay and Another v. *The United Motors (India) Ltd. and Others,* (1953) S.C.R. 1069.

State of Bombay v. *Atma Ram Sridhar Vaidya,* (1951) S.C.R. 167.

State of Madras v. *Srimathi Champakam Dorairajan,* (1951) S.C.R. 525.

State of Punjab v. *Ajaib Singh and Another,* (1953) S.C.R. 254.

State of Seraikella and Others v. *Union of India and Another,* (1951) S.C.R. 474.

State v. *Tiwari,* A.I.R. 1956 Patna 188.

State of West Bengal v. *Mrs. Bela Banerjee and Others,* (1954) S.C.R. 558.

State of West Bengal v. *Subodh Gopal Bose and Others,* (1954) S.C.R. 587.

State of West Bengal v. *Union of India,* A.I.R. 1963 S.C. 1241.

Subhanand Chowdhary & Another v. *Apurba Krishna Mitra and Another,* (1940) F.C.R. 31.

Sudhir Kumar Dutt v. *The King,* (1948) F.C.R. 86.

Surendra Prasad Narain Singh v. *Sri Gajadhar Prasad Sahu Trust Estate and Others,* (1940) F.C.R. 39.

Tara Singh Gopi Chand v. *The State,* A.I.R. 1951 Punjab 27.

Thakur Jagannath Baksh Singh v. *United Provinces,* (1944) F.C.R. 51; (1946) F.C.R. 111 P.C.

Trojan & Co., Ltd. v. *Rm. N. N. Nagappa Chettiar,* (1953) S.C.R. 789.

United Provinces v. *Mst. Atiqa Begum and Others,* (1940) F.C.R. 110.

United Provinces v. *The Governor-General in Council,* (1939) F.C.R. 124.

United States v. *Butler,* 279 U.S. 1(1936).

Virendra Singh and Others v. *The State of Uttar Pradesh,* (1955) S.C.R. I 415.

Visweshwar Rao v. *The State of Madhya Pradesh,* (1952) S.C.R. 1020.

Wallace Brothers and Company, Limited v. *Commissioner of Income Tax, Bombay City and Bombay Suburban District,* (1948) F.C.R. 1 P.C.

II. Official Documents

A. India

Abolition of Privy Council Jurisdiction Act, 1949.

Comments on the Provisions Contained in the Draft Constitution of India. New Delhi: Government of India Press, 1948.

Constituent Assembly Debates, 1947–1950. Twelve volumes.

Constitutional Proposals of the Sapru Committee. Bombay: Padma Publications, Ltd., 1945.

Constitution of India (as modified up to March 1, 1963). Delhi: Manager of Publications, 1963.

Constitution (Seventeenth Amendment) Act, 1964.

Council of State Debates, 1921–1946.

Draft Constitution of India. New Delhi: Government of India Press, 1948.

Federal Court (Enlargement of Jurisdiction) Act, 1947.

Federal Court Order, 1947.

Federal Court Reports, 1939–1950.

Fourteenth Report of the Law Commission of India: Reform of Judicial Administration. Two volumes. Delhi: Manager of Publications, 1958.

India (Provisional Constitution) Order, 1947.

Legislative Assembly Debates, 1921–1946.

Lok Sabha Debates, 1952–1964.

Parliamentary Debates, 1950–1952.

Proceedings of the Conference of Law Ministers. Mimeographed. New Delhi: Library of Parliament, 1957.

Reports of Committees of the Constituent Assembly. New Delhi: Government of India Press, 1948.

Report of the Committee appointed by the Conference to determine the principles of the Constitution for India. Allahabad: All India Congress Committee, 1928.

Supreme Court Judges (Conditions of Service) Act, 1958.

Supreme Court (Number of Judges) Act, 1956.

Supreme Court (Number of Judges) Amendment Act, 1960.

Supreme Court Reports, 1950–1964.

B. Great Britain

Third Report of the Federal Structure Committee, 1932. Cmd. 3997.

Government of India Act, 1935. 25 & 26 Geo. V.

Indian Independence Act, 1947. 10 & 11 Geo. VI.

Proposals for Indian Constitutional Reform, 1933. Cmd. 4268.

Report of the Indian Central Committee, 1928–1929. Cmd. 3451.

Report of the Indian Statutory Commission, 1930, Cmd. 3568.

Report of the Joint Committee on Indian Constitutional Reform, 1934.

III. Books and Articles

Achariar, S. K. "Extension of Jurisdiction of the Federal Court," *All India Reporter Journal,* XXXII (1945), 13.

Aiyar, A. N. *Constitutional Laws of India and Pakistan.* Madras: Company Law Institute of India Ltd., 1947.

Aiyar, Thaikad Subramania. "Property Rights and Constitutional Amendments to Article 31," *All India Reporter Journal,* XLII (1955), 51–55.

Alexandrowicz, Charles Henry. *Constitutional Developments in India.* Bombay: Oxford University Press, 1957.

——. The Indian Constitution," *The Year Book of World Affairs,* VII (1953), 258–282.

"Amending the Constitution: The Amendment Bill," *Calcutta Weekly Notes,* LIX (1955), 26.

Anand, C. L. *The Government of India Act, 1935.* Second edition. Lahore: The University Book Agency, 1944.

"An Unseemly Wrangle," *The Eastern Economist,* XXXII (1959), 642–643.

"Appeals to the Privy Council," *Calcutta Weekly Notes,* LII (1948), 27–28.

Banerjee, Debendra Nath. "Some Aspects of the Indian Judiciary: I. A General Discussion," *Modern Review,* CVIII (1960), 269–277.

Banerji, B. "Federal Court and Privy Council," *All India Reporter Journal,* XXVIII (1941), 1–2.

——. "India, The Dominions and the Privy Council," *The All India Reporter,* XXVIII (1941), 27.

Basu, Durga Das. *Commentary on the Constitution of India.* Four volumes, fourth revised edition. Calcutta: S. C. Sarkar and Sons (Private) Ltd., 1961–1963.

Bayley, Donald H. *Public Liberties in the New States.* Chicago: Rand McNally & Company, 1964.

——. "The Indian Experience with Preventive Detention," *Pacific Affairs,* XXXV (1962), 99–115.

Behari, Gopal. "Enlargement of Federal Court's Jurisdiction," *The Allahabad Law Journal,* XLII (1944), 17–18.

Beotra, B. R. "The Federal Court in India," *All India Reporter Journal,* XXVIII (1941), 36–39.

Bindra, Narotam Singh. *Law and Practice of the Federal Court of India.* Allahabad: Law Book Company, 1949.

Cardozo, Benjamin N. *The Nature of the Judicial Process.* New Haven: Yale University Press, 1921.

Chagla, M. C. "Some Aspects of the Constitution of India," *Modern Review,* CVII (1960), 269–274.

Chatterjee, N. C. "Presidential Address to the All India Civil Liberties Conference," *All India Reporter Journal,* XLV (1958), 55, 57–61.

"Chief Justice of India Meets Bar Council," *The Allahabad Law Journal,* XLI (1943), 44–45.

"Concept and Content of Social Justice: A Syndicate Study," Supplement to the *Journal of the National Academy of Administration,* VII (July, 1962), 1–118.

"Constitutional Law: India Follows the U. S.," *Time,* LXXXIV (October 23, 1964) 54, 56.

Diwan, Paras. "Nationalisation under the Indian Constitution," *The Supreme Court Journal*, XVI (1953), 21–50.

Dixit, Y. V. "The Judiciary and Political Appointments," *All India Reporter Journal*, XXXIII (1959), 2–3.

Douglas, William O. *We the Judges: Studies in American and Indian Constitutional Law from Marshall to Mukherjea*. Garden City: Doubleday and Company, Inc., 1956.

Ebb, Lawrence F. *Public Law Problems in. India*. Stanford: School of Law, Stanford University, 1957.

Eddy, J. P. "India and the Privy Council: The Last Appeal," *The Law Quarterly Review*, LXVI (1950), 206–215.

Elliott, Sheldon D. "Statutory Interpretation and the Welfare State," *Journal of the Indian Law Institute*, II (1959–60), 257–272.

"Expansion of the Federal Court's Jurisdiction," *The Madras Law Journal*, II (1943), 33–35.

"Enlargement of the Jurisdiction of the Federal Court," *Federal Law Journal*, III (1939–1940), 25–38.

"Enlargement of the Jurisdiction of the Federal Court," *Federal Law Journal*, VI (1943), 8–20.

"Enlargement of the Jurisdiction of the Federal Court," *Indian Cases*, CLXXXVII (1940), 39–40.

Evans, Evan A. "Political Influences in the Selection of Federal Judges," *Wisconsin Law Review* (1948), 330–351.

"Federal Court: A Problem," *Calcutta Weekly Notes*, XLV (1940–1941), 49–50.

"Federal Court and Its Expansion," *The Allahabad Law Journal*, XLII (1944), 31–32.

"Federal Court and Its Expansion-II," *The Allahabad Law Journal*, XLII (1944), 37–39.

"Federal Court as Ultimate Court for Indian Appeals," *The Law Weekly*, LII (1941), 21–22.

"Federal Court—Can It Be Made a Court of Criminal Appeal for India," *Madras Weekly Notes* (November 22, 1943), xxv–xxvi.

"Federal Court," *Calcutta Weekly Notes*, XLII (1938), 73–74.

"Federal Court, Conversion of, into a Supreme Court," *Calcutta Weekly Notes*, XLIV (1939–1940), 62–64.

"Federal Court, Leave to Appeal from," *Calcutta Weekly Notes*, XLVII (1943), 45–46.

"Federal Court, Proposed Enlargement of Jurisdiction of," *Calcutta Weekly Notes*, XLIX (1945), 23–24.

"Federal Court: Proposed Extension of Jurisdiction of," *Calcutta Weekly Notes*, XLVII (1944), 15–18.

Frankfurter, Felix. "Some Reflections on the Reading of Statutes," *Columbia Law Review*, XLVII (1947), 527–546.

Freeman, Harrop A. "An Introduction to Hindu Jurisprudence," *The American Journal of Comparative Law*, VIII (1959), 29–43.

———. "Needed: A Jurisprudential Theory for Liberal Democracy," *Journal of the Indian Law Institute*, II (1959), 49–70.

Gajendragadkar, P. B. "Fundamental Obligations of Democracy," *All India Reporter Journal*, XLVIII (1961), 21–22.

———. "Law, Lawyers and Judges," *The Supreme Court Journal*, XXIX (1963), 14–27.

Galanter, Marc. "'Protective Discrimination' for Backward Classes in India," *Journal of the Indian Law Institute*, III (1961), 39–69.

Gledhill, Alan. "Life and Liberty in the First Ten Years of Republican India," *Journal of the Indian Law Institute*, II (1960), 241–256.

Gour, Sir Hari Singh. "Abolish Privy Council," *Allahabad Weekly Notes*, XVI (1946), 5.

———. "The Privy Council—And After," *All India Reporter Journal*, XV (1928), 3–34.

"Government's Proposals for Expansion of the Federal Court's Jurisdiction," *Federal Law Journal*, VIII (1945), 1–2.

Haksar, K. N. and K. M. Panikkar. *Federal India*. London: Martin Hopkinson Ltd., 1930.

Holmes, Oliver Wendell. *The Common Law*. Boston: Little, Brown and Co., 1881.

"Indian Branch of the Privy Council?," *Calcutta Weekly Notes*, L (1946), 94–95.

Indian Law Institute, New Delhi. *Judicial Review through Writ Petitions*. Bombay: N. M. Tripathi Private Ltd., 1962.

Ismail, M. M. "The Doctrine of Judicial Supremacy and the Indian Constitution," *Year Book of Legal Studies*, II (1958), 83–106.

Jagota, S. P. "Social Justice under the Constitution," *Journal of the National Academy of Administration*, VII (1962), 61–65.

Jain, D. C. "Concept of Property and the Supreme Court," *All India Reporter Journal*, LI (1964), 6–11.

Jain, M. P. *Indian Constitutional Law*. Bombay: N. M. Tripathi Private Ltd., 1962.

———. *Outlines of Indian Legal History*. Delhi: Delhi University Press, 1952.

"Judges versus Politicians," *The Economist*, October 17, 1964, 249–50.

Kania, Harilal J. "Speech Delivered at Inauguration of High Court of Assam," *All India Reporter Journal*, XXXV (1948), 13–16.

Keith, Arthur Berriedale. A *Constitutional History of India: 1600–1935*. Second edition. London: Methuen & Co., Ltd., 1936.

———. *Responsible Government in the Dominions*. Two volumes, second edition. London: Oxford University Press, 1927.

Khan, Sir Shafa'at Ahmad. *The Indian Federation*. London: MacMillan and Co., Ltd., 1937.

Kulshreshtha, Visheshwar Dayal. *Landmarks in Indian Legal History*. Lucknow: Eastern Book Company, 1959.

Kumar, Y. "Supreme Court and Socialist Pattern, "*Mainstream*, I (October 6, 1962), 9–12.

LaPalombara, Joseph (ed.). *Bureaucracy and Political Development*. Princeton: Princeton University Press, 1963.

"Law Commission's Report," *The Eastern Economist*, XXXII (1959), 598–599.

Mahajan, Mehr Chand. *Looking Back*. Bombay: Asia Publishing House, 1963.

Markose, A. T. "The First Decade of the Indian Constitution," *Journal of the Indian Law Institute*, II (1960), 157–160, xxxii.

Mathur, Ramesh Narain. "Interpretation of the Constitution," *The Supreme Court Journal*, XXI (1958), 35–47.

———. "Role of Federal Judiciary in Modern Federations," *The Supreme Court Journal*, XXI (1958), 227–49.

McNelly, Theodore. "The Japanese Constitution: Child of the Cold War," *Political Science Quarterly*, LXIV (1959), 176–95.

McWhinney, Edward. *Judicial Review in the English-Speaking World*. Toronto: University of Toronto Press, 1956.

Merillat, H. C. L. "Chief Justice S. R. Das: A Decade of Decisions on Right to Property," *Journal of the Indian Law Institute*, II (1959–1960), 183–213.

———. "Compensation for the Taking of Property: A Historical Footnote on Bela Banerjee's Case," *Journal of the Indian Law Institute*, I (1958–59), 375–397.

———. "The Indian Constitution: Property Rights and Social Reform," *Ohio State Law Journal*, XXI (1960), 616–642.

Moore, Frank J. and Constance A. Freydig. *Land Tenure Legislation in Uttar Pradesh*. Berkeley: Modern India Project, Institute of East Asiatic Studies, University of California, 1955.

"Motion to Enlarge the Jurisdiction of the Federal Court," *Federal Law Journal*, I (1937–1938), 67–68.

"Mr. Nehru's Indefensible Remarks," *The Eastern Economist*, XXXII (1959), 1117.

Nambiyar, M. K. "Constitutional Amendment to Judicial Review," *All India Reporter Journal*, XLII (1955), 36–39.

———. "Seventeenth Amendment of the Constitution," *The Supreme Court Journal*, XXIX (1963), 1–8.

Nathanson, Nathaniel L. "Indian Constitutional Law in American Perspective," *Northwestern University Law Review*, LVI (1961), 190–204.

Nehru, Jawaharlal. *Toward Freedom*. New York: The John Day Company, 1941.

"Notes: The Law Commission and Pandit Pant," *Modern Review*, CV (1959), 187–188.

"Our Supreme Court," *Calcutta Weekly Notes*, LI (1947), 173–174.

"Outgoing and Incoming Chief Justices of the Supreme Court," *The Madras Law Journal*, XXII (1959), 33–34.

Padmanabhan, K. V. *Federal Court: Practice and Procedure*. Delhi: Metropolitan Book Co., 1948.

Pathak, A. M. "A Note on Social Justice Relating to Property and Judicial Interpretation," *Journal of the National Academy of Administration*, VII (1962), 45–53.

Peltason, Jack W. *Federal Courts in the Political Process*. Garden City: Doubleday and Company, Inc., 1955.

"Pending Privy Council Appeals," *Calcutta Weekly Notes*, LIII (1949), 155–156.

Popkin, William D. "Advisory Opinions in India," *Journal of the Indian Law Institute*, IV (1962), 401–433.

"Privy Council Appeals and the Federal Court," *Calcutta Weekly Notes*, XLIV (1939–40), 137–139.

"Privy Council's Future," *Calcutta Weekly Notes*, LI (1947), 115–116.

Pylee, M. V. *Constitutional Government in India*. New York: Asia Publishing House, 1960.

———. "Judicial Review," *The Supreme Court Journal*, XVI (1953), 67–86.

Ramachandran, V. G. "The Judicial Power in Protection of Fundamental Rights," *The Indian Advocate*, I (1961), 6–16.

———. "The Significance of the Directive Principles of State Policy in the Indian Constitution," *The Supreme Court Journal*, XVIII (1955), 233–242.

Ramalingam, T. "The Supreme Court of India and the Doctrine of *Stare Decisis*," *The Supreme Court Journal*, XIX (1956), 9–13.

Rangachari, K. "Relations between States and Centre," *The Statesman*, January 26, 1964.

Rangiah, R. "Certain Salient Features of Judicial Review," *The Indian Advocate*, II (1962), 51–58.

Rao, K. Narayana. "The Indian Directive Principles—A Case for a New Interpretation," *The Indian Year Book of International Affairs*, VIII (1959), 110–28.

Rao, K. Someshwara. "Judiciary under the Constitution Act," *All India Reporter Journal*, XXVII (1940), 53–60.

———. "The Privy Council," *All India Reporter Journal*, XXVII (1940), 61–67.

Rao, K. V. *Parliamentary Democracy of India*. Calcutta: The World Press Private Ltd., 1961.

Rao, K. Venkoba. *The Indian Constitution*. Madras: The Madras Publishing House Limited, 1948.

Rao, P. Kodanda. "Appointment of Judges in India," *Hindustan Standard*, April 16, 1962.

———. "Politicians and Judges," *The Eastern Economist*, XXXVII (1961), 688.

Rao, T. S. Rama. "Judicial Review in India: A Retrospect," *Year Book of Legal Studies*, I (1957), 121–145.

———. "The Problem of Compensation and Its Justiciability in Indian Law," *Journal of the Indian Law Institute*, IV (1962), 481–509.

Rau, Benegal N. *India's Constitution in the Making*. Edited by B. Shiva Rao. Second revised edition. Madras: Allied Publishers, 1963.

Robinson, Solomon E. "The Supreme Court and Section 33 of the Industrial Disputes Act, 1947," *Journal of the, Indian Law Institute*, III (1961), 15–38; 161–204.

Roy, Naresh Chandra. *The Constitutional System of India*. Calcutta: Calcutta University Press, 1937.

Sapru, P. N. *The Relation of the Individual to the State under the Indian Constitution*. Calcutta: University of Calcutta Press, 1959.

Sapru, Sir Tej Bahadur. *The Indian Constitution*. Madras: The National Secretary's Office, 1926.

Sastri, Patanjali. "Presidential Address to the Ninth Madras State Lawyers' Conference," *All India Reporter Journal*, XLII (1955), 25–30.

Schwartz, Bernard. "A Comparative View of the Gopalan Case," *Indian Law Review*, IV (1950), 276–99.

Setalvad, M. C. *War and Civil Liberties*. New Delhi: Indian Council of World Affairs, Oxford University Press, 1946.

Shankar, Mani. "Advisory Powers of the Supreme Court," *Modern Review*, CVIII (1960), 113–114.

Sharma, Sri Ram. *The Supreme Court and Judicial Review in India*. Sholapur: Institute of Public Administration, 1953.

———. *The Supreme Court in the Indian Constitution*. Delhi: Rajpal and Sons, 1959.

———. "The Supreme Court in the Indian Constitution," *Public Law* (1958), 119–134.

Sinha, Balbir Sahai. *Legal History of India*. Lucknow: Eastern Book Company, 1953.

Spens, Sir Patrick. "The Judiciary in India and Pakistan under the New Conditions," *The Asiatic Review*, XLV (1949), 449–468.

Srinivasacharya, R. S. "Recruitment to the Judiciary," *The Madras Law Journal*, XVIII (1955), 45–48.

Subbarao, G. C. Venkata. "Missed Constitutional Opportunities," *Year Book of Legal Studies*, II (1958), 10–24.

Subramanian, N. A. "The Judiciary in India," *The Indian Year Book of International Affairs*, IV (1955), 275–288.

Thomas, Lily Isabel. "Advisory Jurisdiction of the Supreme Court of India," *Journal of the Indian Law Institute*, V (1963), 475–497.

Tope, T. K. "Natural Law Theory, Positivism and Indian Legal Thought," *The Supreme Court Journal*, XXVII (1962), 47–56.

———. "Power of President of India to Consult the Supreme Court of India: How far is this Provision Desirable?," *The Supreme Court Journal*, XIX (1956), 118–122.

———. *The Constitution of India*. Bombay: Popular Book Depot, 1960.

———. "The Supreme Court of India and the Right of Property," *The Bombay Law Reporter*, LVII (1955), 67–72.

Tripathi, Pradyumna K. "Directive Principles of State Policy," *The Supreme Court Journal*, XVII (1954), 7–36.

———. "Free Speech in the Indian Constitution: Background and Prospect," *Yale Law Journal*, LXVII (1958), 384–400.

———. "India's Experiment in Freedom of Speech: The First Amendment and Thereafter," *The Supreme Court Journal*, XVIII (1955), 106–138.

———. "Preventive Detention: The Indian Experience," *The American Journal of Comparative Law*, IX (1960), 219–248.

Truman, David B. *The Governmental Process: Political Interests and Public Opinion*. New York: Alfred A. Knopf, 1951.

Umamaheswaran, K. "Role of Judiciary under the Constitution," *All India Reporter Journal*, XLVII (1960), 5–8.

Varma, J. N. and M. M. Gharekhan. *The Constitutional Law of India and England*. Fifth revised edition. Bombay: The Popular Book Depot, 1937.

Venkataramanan, S. "Judicial Review and Guaranteed Rights," *The Supreme Court Journal*, XVII (1954), 37–46.

———. "Some Reflections on the Fourteenth Report of the Law Commission," *The Supreme Court Journal*, XXII (1959), 121–132.

Venkataraman, T. S. "Directive Principles of State Policy in the New Constitution—Their Value," *Federal Law Journal*, XI (1948), 67–74.

"Vivian Bose Enquiry Board," *Calcutta Weekly Notes*, LXII (1959), 99–100.

von Mehren, Arthur T. "The Judicial Process with Particular Reference to the United States and to India," *Journal of the Indian Law Institute*, V (1963), 271–80.

Ward, Robert E. "The Origins of the Present Japanese Constitution," *American Political Science Review*, L (1956), 980–1010.

IV. Unpublished Material

Pylee, M. V. "The Federal Court of India," Unpublished D. Litt. thesis, Patna University, 1961.

Index

About the Author and the Editors

Author

George H. Gadbois, Jr was born in Boston, Massachusetts, USA in 1936. After serving in the US Army for three years, he received his BA degree in Political Science and History from Marietta College in Ohio, graduating with high honours. He received his PhD in political science from Duke University in North Carolina, in 1965. He was a graduate student when he spent the year 1962–1963 in India. Supported by fellowships from the American Institute of Indian Studies, he continued his research in India during 1969–1970, 1982–1983, and 1988–1989. A close observer of the Indian Supreme Court for more than a half century, he taught political science at the University of Kentucky. He passed away in February 2017.

Editors

Vikram Raghavan is a private scholar of Indian constitutional law and history. About a decade ago, he created and occasionally contributes to *Law and Other Things*, a widely read blog about public law in India. He is the author of *Communications Law in India* and the co-editor of *Comparative Constitutionalism in South Asia* (Oxford University Press 2013). He is presently working on a book about India's founding as a republic in 1950. He lectures frequently on that subject and more broadly about international law, history, and the art of British India.

Vasujith Ram graduated from the West Bengal National University of Juridical Sciences, India, where he was chief editor of the *Journal of Indian Law and Society*. He is presently pursuing a master's degree at Harvard Law School. He has worked with a senior advocate at India's Supreme Court. He is also a research assistant to Marc Galanter, Professor of Law Emeritus at the University of Wisconsin Law School. A regular contributor to *Law and Other Things*, Vasujith's interests include public law and interdisciplinary approaches to law.